Adverbial Clauses in Mandarin Chinese

European University Studies
Europäische Hochschulschriften
Publications Universitaires Européennes

Series XXI
Linguistics

Reihe XXI Série XXI
Linguistik
Linguistique

Vol./Band 374

PETER LANG
Bern · Berlin · Bruxelles · Frankfurt am Main · New York · Oxford · Wien

May L-Y Wong

Adverbial Clauses in Mandarin Chinese

A Corpus-based Study

PETER LANG
Bern · Berlin · Bruxelles · Frankfurt am Main · New York · Oxford · Wien

Bibliographic information published by die Deutsche Nationalbibliothek
Die Deutsche Nationalbibliothek lists this publication in the Deutsche Nationalbibliografie; detailed bibliographic data is available on the Internet at ‹http://dnb.d-nb.de›.

British Library Cataloguing-in-Publication Data: A catalogue record for this book is available from The British Library, Great Britain

Library of Congress Cataloging-in-Publication Data

Wong, May Lai-Yin,
Adverbial clauses in Mandarin Chinese : a corpus-based study / May Lai-Yin Wong.
pages cm. – (Europäische Hochschulschriften. Reihe XXI, Linguistik, ISSN 0531-7320 ; Bd. 734 = Publications universitaires européennes. Série XXI, Linguistique v. 374 = European university studies. Series XXI, Linguistics v. 374)
Includes bibliographical references.
ISBN 978-3-0343-1120-5
1. Chinese language–Adverbial. 2. Chinese language–Clauses. I. Title.
PL1233.W66 2013
495.1'576–dc23
2012049416

ISSN 0721-3352
ISBN 978-3-0343-1120-5 pb. ISBN 978-3-0351-0497-4 eBook

Hochfeldstrasse 32, CH-3012 Bern, Switzerland
info@peterlang.com, www.peterlang.com

Printed in Switzerland

Contents

Chapter Five
A Typology of Adverbial Clauses in Written Chinese 127

Chapter Six
Non-overt Subjects of Chinese Adverbial Clauses:
A Government and Binding Approach 191

Chapter Nine
Conclusion

Acknowledgements

The main input for this book arouse out of research done at both the University of Hong Kong and Lancaster University. In the course of carrying out my research, I have been fortunate to have had the opportunity of interacting with a number of leading researchers (either in terms of having studied with them or correspondence via electronic mail) on the subject of adverbial clauses and Chinese grammar, of whom the following merit special mention: Professor Tony McEnery, Professor Luke Kang-kwong, Dr Owen Nancarrow, Professor Geoffrey Sampson, Dr Willem Hollmann, Dr Richard Xiao, Dr Scott Piao, Mrs Catherine Nancarrow, and Dr Ya-ling Chang.

The data and corpora cited in this book have been taken from various sources. The PFR People's Daily POS Tagged Chinese Corpus was produced by the joint effort of the Peking University, the People's Daily newspaper and the Fujitsu Research and Development Centre. I wish to thank the Institute of Computational Linguistics at Peking University for permission to draw from the PFR corpus in the book. I am grateful to Professor Tony McEnery and Dr Richard Xiao for permission to use the data drawn from the Lancasater Corpus of Mandarin Chinese (LCMC) created by them and their research team at Lancaster University, and I hasten to add that whatever factual errors made in reporting on the LCMC corpus are mine alone. Parts of Chapter Seven and Eight appeared in my journal article published in Corpora; thanks are due to the editors for allowing me to incorporate the essay in this book.

I wish to record my many thanks to Martina Räber and her colleagues at Peter Lang Publishing for their guidance, patience and excellent copy editing.

Finally, I am indebted to my family, friends, colleagues and students for providing me with their moral support and various types of assistance.

Abbreviations

ADVL	Adverbial marker (地 *de*)
BA	*Ba* construction (把 *ba*, 将 *jiang*)
BI	Comparative construction (比 *bi*)
C	Coordinating conjunction
CAC	Chinese adverbial clause
CL	Classifier (e.g. 個 *ge*, 件 *jian*)
COMP	Complementiser (得 *de*, 到 *dao*)
DE	*De* construction (的 *de*)
EAGLES	Expert Advisory Group for Language Engineering Standards
EXP	Experiential aspect marker (过 *guo*)
GB	Government and Binding Theory
GEN	Genitive marker (的 *de*)
LCMC	Lancaster Corpus of Mandarin Chinese
LDC	Linguistic Data Consortium
MLCT	Multilingual Corpus Toolkit
NLP	Natural language processing
NP	Noun phrase
PART	Particle (e.g. 了 *le*, 的 *de*, 嘛 *ma*, 呀 *a*, 呢 *le*, 啊 *a*, 哈 *ha*, 啦 *le*, 吧 *ba*)
PASSIVE	Passive marker (被 *bei*)
PERF	Perfective aspect marker (了 *le*)
PL	Plural marker (们 *men*)
POS	Part of speech
PRO	Non-overt (or null) subject in a Chinese adverbial clause
PROG	Progressive aspect marker (在 *zai*, 着 *zhe*, 正 *zheng*, 正在 *zhengzai*)
S	Subordinating conjunction
SGML	Standard Generalised Markup Language
TEI	Text Encoding Initiative
UCREL	University Centre for Computer Corpus Research on Language
VP	Verb phrase
XML	Extensible Markup Language

Chinese Adverbial Subordinators

甭管 *bengguan* "no matter what"
不单 *budan* "in addition to"
不管 *buguan* "no matter what"
不论 *bulun* "whether or, whatever"
不论是 *bulunshi* "whether or, whatever"
不说 *bushuo* "let alone …"
除非 *chufei* "unless"
从而 *conger* "in order that; as a result"
而是 *ershi* "rather"
故 *gu* "so that"
果真 *guozhen* "supposing that"
何况 *hekuang* "not to mention …"
假如 *jiaru* "supposing that"
假若 *jiaruo* "supposing that"
即便 *jibian* "even if"
尽管 *jinguan* "even though"
既然 *jiran* "since, as"
即使 *jishi* "even if"
就是 *jiushi* "even if"
哪怕 *napa* "even if"
且不说 *qiebushuo* "let alone …"
任 *ren* "no matter what"
如 *ru* "If"
如果 *ruguo* "if"
若 *ruo* "if"
若果 *ruoguo* "if"
若是 *ruoshi* "if"
如若 *ruruo* "if"
尚且 *shangqie* "even"
虽 *sui* "though"
虽然 *suiran* "although"
虽说 *suishuo* "while admitting that …"
随着 *suizhe* "as soon as"
倘 *tang* "supposing that"
倘若 *tangruo* "supposing that"
万一 *wanyi* "in case"
无论 *wulun* "whether or, whatever"
无论是 *wulunshi* "whether or, whatever"
要 *yao* "assuming that"
要不是 *yaobushi* "if not, otherwise"
要是 *yaoshi* "assuming that"
以 *yi* "in order that"
以便 *yibian* "in order that"
以免 *yimian* "in order that… not…"
因 *yin* "because"
因为 *yinwei* "because"
以致 *yizhi* "as a result"
以至于 *yizhiyu* "consequently"
由于 *youyu* "owing to the fact that"
与其 *yuqi* "rather than"
与其说 *yuqishuo* "rather than say that"
只是 *zhishi* "except that"
之所以 *zhisuoyi* "why there is a consequence of"
只要 *zhiyao* "provided that"
只有 *zhiyou* "only if"
纵 *zong* "even if"
纵使 *zongshi* "even if"

Chapter One

Introduction

1.1 Corpus-based approach to studying adverbial clauses

This book is motivated by the fact that none of the previous analyses of adverbial clauses in Chinese have based their illustrative examples and exposition on extensive corpus evidence. Rather, researchers have typically relied on their own intuitions about language (e.g. Liu et al., 1996; Chu and Chi, 1999), sometimes supplemented by adapting example sentences from influential novels (e.g. Ding et al., 1979).

Recent work by Wang (1995, 1998, 1999 and 2002) breaks fresh ground in studying adverbial clauses by adopting a corpus-based approach. She quantitatively analyses the distribution and information structure of four main types of adverbial clause (viz temporal, conditional, concessive and causal clauses) in spoken Chinese on the basis of a corpus of six hours worth of naturally occurring face-to-face, two party, and multi-party conversations and call-in broadcasts on local radio and television in Taiwan. However, her studies focus solely on a limited range of adverbial clauses and are largely based on the spoken register of Chinese. Also her spoken corpus is rather small and yields just some 700 adverbial clauses in total. Hence, the novelty of a corpus-based study on adverbial clauses in written Chinese as well as an in-depth analysis on the typology of adverbial clauses in Chinese argue for a more thorough quantitative and qualitative account of them in order to discover new insights into their use in written data. Furthermore, as far as adverbial clauses are concerned, theoretically informed corpus-based research is rare (cf. Quintero, 2002). More work can therefore be done on marrying corpus linguistics with linguistic theory in this area. This book aims to achieve such a marriage.

To investigate the use and structure of a grammatical construction, most researchers have found it profitable to investigate constructions that occur relatively frequently, since if a construction occurs too infrequently, it is often hard to make strong generalisations about its form and usage (Meyer, 1991). For this reason, to study infrequent linguistic constructions, it is often necessary to study reasonably large corpora, like the two corpora of written Chinese used in this book, both of which contain one million words, namely the PFR Chinese Corpus and the Lancaster Corpus of Mandarin Chinese (henceforth LCMC).

1.2 Research objectives and the organisation of the book

Given the need for a corpus-based approach to linguistic theory and the need for a more extensive corpus-based account of a wider spectrum of adverbial clauses in written Chinese, this book uses a skeleton treebank (i.e. a corpus annotated with basic level syntactic constituents) to explore the syntactic structure of the Chinese language in order to shed light on the following research questions.

(1) How does the sample skeleton treebank help in the identification of adverbial clauses and revealing the peculiarities of Chinese syntactic properties?
(2) What are the adverbial subordinators in Chinese that are responsible for overtly marking adverbial clauses?
(3) Which semantic roles do these adverbial clauses play in relation to the main clause they modify?
(4) Does the PRO theorem in the Government and Binding (GB) Theory apply in written Chinese?
(5) How do the semantic types of adverbial clauses vary across genres/text types in written Chinese?
(6) How does the distribution of PROs vary across both semantic domains and text types in written Chinese?
(7) Do research findings based on written Chinese hold for spoken Chinese?

In the course of exploring the adverbial subordinators in the PFR corpus, a critique will be provided of the catch-all term 连词 *lianci* "conjunction" as it has been used in Chinese grammars to refer to both a coordinating conjunction and a subordinating conjunction (Lu and Ma, 1990; Hou, 1998). As will be demonstrated in Chapter Six (section 6.1), Chinese is a pro-drop language (Huang, 1989) i.e. a language which allows the omission of a subject in a clause. While there is an immense literature on null subjects in Chinese (see, for example, Huang, 1987 and Chen, 1990), the focus of the previous literature was on pro-drop in complement clauses and not on pro-drop in adverbial clauses. Hence, my book contributes by investigating null subjects in Chinese adverbial clauses in order to fill the gap in the literature of the pro-drop phenomenon. In particular, this book focusses upon the distribution of non-overt subjects across various semantic types of adverbial clauses because certain of these adverbial clause types (e.g. purpose and contrast clauses) may show a stronger tendency for dropping the subject than other types. By *a priori* reasoning, if a person performs an action (as described in the main clause), s/he must intend to do it for a particular purpose (as described in the adverbial clause of purpose). Thus the subject of the purpose clause is likely to be omitted, which is always the same as the subject of the associated main clause. Clauses of contrast make a contrast between two situations described in the main clause and the adverbial clause. The two situations are closely related to each other as they are in fact two contrasting descriptions regarding the same subject; the situation of the main clause is taken to be wrong and the situation of the adverbial contrastive clause is what is right about the subject of the main clause. It is therefore hardly surprising that the subject of the contrastive clause, which is co-referential with the subject of the main clause, can be dropped. Yet all of these predictions stem purely from intuitions about the behaviour of adverbial clauses. To test these introspective assumptions, a corpus-based analysis is conducted in this book into how null subjects distribute across adverbial semantic classes.

In pursuing these research objectives, my book is organised into three major parts. The first part, Chapter Two, deals primarily with issues relating to the PFR Chinese Corpus, including a brief history of the construction of this corpus and the annotation of sentence boundary markers in the part-of-speech (POS) tagged corpus; the LCMC corpus will also be briefly described. Though it is a corpus-based study, my book is not atheoretical. In my book, a corpus-based approach to theory is advocated. The approach taken to the investigating of my research questions is as follows: rather than set out to use corpus data to testify the validity of theoretical assumptions, I start my research by examining my corpus data closely, looking for any systematic patterns in the behaviour of the adverbial clause; those patterns or properties of adverbial clauses are then explained in a theoretical framework that lends itself well to the analysis of similar phenomena. In other words, my work does not presuppose the use of nor the rejection of a particular theoretical framework; rather, when it becomes relevant to my discussion of the corpus data, a theory is selected on its merits and adopted to explain my findings. Hence in the second part of my book (Chapters Three to Five), as a prelude to the theory based approach of the third part, initial results are presented in relatively theory-neutral terms, to make the emerging patterns of adverbial clauses in Chinese as accessible to linguists as possible. In the third part (Chapters Six to Eight), the same data are analysed within the Government and Binding Theory Framework in order to understand the description of the adverbial clause developed in this book within a theoretical framework in which a theorem (PRO theorem) is important to the explanation of the occurrence of non-overt subjects in the adverbial clause. The findings concerning the distribution of non-overt subjects are then put to the test in the LCMC corpus which, unlike the PFR corpus, is a balanced corpus with fifteen text types of written Chinese and can therefore provide a sound basis for making reliable generalisations of the properties of adverbial clauses in written Chinese across a range of genres. A contrastive study of the distribution of non-overt subjects in the adverbial clauses in spoken and written Chinese is also conducted on the basis of the CALLHOME Mandarin Chinese Transcripts Corpus, which is a spoken Chinese corpus developed in 1996.

1.2.1 Brief chapter summaries

Chapter One, the present chapter, expressly states the rationale and research objectives of this book.

Chapter Two will present a brief review of the development of written Chinese corpora and their use in linguistics and beyond. The two written corpora used in this book, the PFR Chinese Corpus and the LCMC corpus, will also be described. A literature review of previous studies of Chinese adverbial clauses will be presented, most of which is concerned with the discourse functions of adverbial clauses in different positions in a sentence – either they are placed clause-initially (i.e. before all obligatory elements) or clause-finally (i.e. after all obligatory elements) – and this positioning influences the discourse functions the clause takes. Following from this, I will justify why a comprehensive analysis of the interclausal semantic roles of adverbial clauses is worth undertaking.

Chapter Three will describe at length how to produce a skeleton treebank by using a sample text of approximately 100,000 word tokens (amounting to about 2,500 Chinese sentences) to build up a body of examples of adverbial clauses. A clearly-defined parsing scheme will be given, which comprises 17 constituent labels and 11 textual markers, followed by a detailed treatment of the bracketing system and parsing guidelines. A discussion of the difficulties that I encountered during the manual parsing process will be included and the sample skeleton treebank will be evaluated against some quality-control criteria.

Chapter Four is devoted to the identification of adverbial subordinators that occur in the PFR Chinese Corpus. I will offer a critique of the vague grammatical category *lianci* that was traditionally employed in Chinese grammars to refer to both a coordinating conjunction and a subordinating conjunction. I will develop a more fine-grained approach to classifying different types of conjunctions in Chinese. A working definition of an adverbial subordinator and a list of subordinators used in my corpus will also be given. Some observations about the use of these adverbial subordinators will also be made.

Chapter Five will concentrate on a detailed and systematic typology of the adverbial clauses found in my corpus. I adopt a problem-oriented tagging approach in identifying the adverbial clauses together with their associated main clauses, and propose eleven interclausal semantic domains of adverbial clauses. Adverbial subordinators which are used to mark these semantic relations will be given and illustrated with examples drawn from the corpus. It will be shown that some semantic classes of adverbial clauses are linked so that they even share the same introductory adverbial subordinator: both clauses of purpose and result can be introduced by the adverbial subordinator 从而 *conger* "in order to; consequently". The syntactic and semantic characteristics of two interesting subordinators, 因为 *yinwei* "because" and 而是 *ershi* "rather", will be discussed. Finally, a table of the frequency of occurrence of each adverbial clause type will be provided.

Chapter Six will focus on non-overt NPs, represented as PRO in Government and Binding Theory, which occur as the subject of the Chinese adverbial clause. I will first justify the postulation of such an empty category and then examine its features, distribution and interpretation. More specifically, the feature composition of PRO will be argued to be anaphoric and pronominal, and the interpretation of PRO will be shown to be regulated by control theory in different forms of control such as obligatory control and subject control. PRO will be proved to occur only in ungoverned positions, and its distribution among different semantic types of adverbial clauses will also be discussed.

Chapter Seven will discuss the occurrence of the eleven semantic classes of adverbial clauses in the fifteen genres of the LCMC corpus as well as the distribution of non-overt subjects across both semantic domains of adverbial clauses and genres of written Chinese. The semantic types of adverbial clauses will be shown to occur more frequently in certain text types. The results obtained in Chapter Six will also be compared with those obtained in this chapter. The hypothesis that the effect of adverbial semantic domain on the use of PRO depends on text type will be tested, and the influence of text type on the type of control of PRO will be considered.

Chapter Eight will present the differences between spoken and written Chinese in the use of adverbial clauses. Previous accounts of differences between spoken and written registers will be addressed when they become relevant to my discussion of the behaviour of the adverbial clause in these two modes. The results obtained from the two written Chinese corpora (i.e. the PFR and LCMC corpora) will also be compared with those obtained from the CALLHOME corpus. In this chapter, I will investigate whether or not the distribution pattern of adverbial clauses in narrative texts of written Chinese can be found in spoken Chinese, and discuss the differences between spoken and written Chinese in the contrast of the type of control of PRO and the distribution of subjects across adverbial semantic domains between the LCMC and CALLHOME.

Chapter Nine will conclude the book by summarising my research findings. The potential limitations of this book will also be discussed. Finally, future research on the exploitation of Chinese corpora in language studies will also be suggested.

Chapter Two

General Review

In this chapter, a definition of the term corpus (section 2.1) and a brief survey of Chinese corpora (section 2.2) will be given. A detailed description of the PFR Chinese Corpus used in this book will also be provided. Section 2.3 of this chapter is concerned with my object of study, adverbial clauses. This section provides a review of the literature on corpus-based accounts of adverbial clauses with a discussion of features such as the characterisation of adverbial clauses and their syntactic/semantic and discourse properties. This review of previous work on adverbial clauses will provide a justification of the focus of this book on the adverbial clause.

2.1 Defining corpus

Modern corpora are typically large, finite, collections of language data in machine readable form. Yet a corpus is more than a simple collection of data; rather it is "a large and principled collection of natural texts" (Biber, Conrad and Reppen, 1998: 12). A principled collection is distinct from a haphazard collection of materials; it attempts to represent language in such a way as to control for a range of variables. These variables may be wide ranging, e.g. genre, speaker's age or context/situation of utterances. In attempting to control such variables, most corpus builders appeal to the concepts of *sampling* and *representativeness*. Sampling involves the process of determining how many text samples are required for valid generalisations to be made about the variety of language under examination and what range of language users need to be selected for a valid representation of the population supplying the text samples (Meyer, 2002: 40). A corpus is representative of the language variety being examined if it accurately reflects the tendencies of that variety (Biber, 1990; 1993a; 1993b). Hence, a refined definition of a corpus is that a corpus is a collection of machine-readable texts which are of finite size and carefully sampled in order to be maximally representative of a language variety being studied (Leech, 1992; Kirk, 1994; McEnery and Wilson, 2001: 32; McEnery, 2003: 449–450).

It is important to note, as other corpus linguists do (see, for example, Chafe, 1992: 88; Biber, Conrad and Reppen, 1998: 9; Kennedy, 1998: 7; McEnery and Wilson, 2001: 25), in advance of reviewing corpus-based studies, that corpus-based analysis should not be treated as being in competition with linguists' intuitions and other theories of language; rather it is complementary to these approaches. Corpus linguistics is a methodology that can easily be combined with other forms of linguistics (Leech, 1992). My book is contributing to corpus linguistics in this spirit, by combining corpus and theoretical linguistics. In the following subsections, a brief history of Chinese corpora and their uses in various fields will be considered.

2.2 Chinese corpora and their application

With the creation of English corpora, Chinese corpora began to come into being. While the earliest machine readable corpora in English are the Brown corpus (Francis and Kučera, 1964) and the LOB corpus (Johansson et al., 1978), both of which sample the American/British English language used in 1961[1], the earliest machine readable Chinese corpus is the Modern Chinese Word Frequency Corpus (Beijing Yuyan Xueyuan Yuyan Jiaoxue Yanjiusuo, 1986), which commenced constructing in 1979 and was completed in 1983, as reviewed in Feng (2002) and Sun et al. (2002). As my book is mainly based on data taken from

1 The Frown (Freiburg-Brown) corpus (Hundt et al., 1999) and the FLOB (Freiburg-Lancaster-Oslo-Bergen) corpus (Hundt et al., 1998), both of which sample the American/British English language used in 1991, are modern equivalents of the Brown and LOB corpora respectively.

written Chinese corpora, it is important in this chapter to give a survey of the Chinese written corpora.[2]

2.2.1 A survey of corpora of written Chinese

One of the most well-known written Chinese corpora is the Mandarin Chinese PH (*People's Republic of China Xin Hua*) Corpus (Guo, 1993).[3] It comprises news texts taken from the Xinhua News Agency which were written between January 1990 and March 1991. After the publication of the PH corpus, many Chinese corpora came into being such as the Mandarin Chinese News Text[4], the PFR People's Daily Chinese Corpus (Yu, 1999), the Chinese Penn Treebank (Xia et al., 2000; Chiou et al., 2001; Xue et al., 2002) and the Lancaster Corpus of Mandarin Chinese or LCMC (McEnery et al., 2003)[5]. These corpora, with the exception of the LCMC corpus, are not balanced: instead of containing a range of genres of written Chinese, they consist of a homogeneous collection of journalistic texts[6] taken roughly from the period 1994 to 1998. It is inevitable that the texts that they contain are rather restricted and not particularly representative of written Chinese. In contrast, the Lancaster Corpus of Mandarin Chinese is a balanced and representa-

2 The information about the Chinese corpora that are described below is provided by the following websites:
(1) Linguistic Data Consortium (LDC): <http://www.ldc.upenn.edu/Catalog/> (accessed 15 May 2012);
(2) Oxford Text Archive (OTA): <http://ota.ahds.ac.uk/> (accessed 15 May 2012);
(3) David Lee's web page: <http://www.uow.edu.au/~dlee/CBLLinks.htm> (accessed 15 May 2012);
(4) Barbara Manuel's web page: <http://www.bmanuel.org/> (accessed 15 May 2012).

3 The corpus is in GB code and its cleaned-up (with punctuations and clearly recognised proper names) segmented version can be freely downloaded by FTP as a single file. URL: <ftp://ftp.cogsci.ed.ac.uk/pub/chinese/> (accessed 15 May 2012).

4 See LDC's web page at <http://www.ldc.upenn.edu/> (accessed 15 May 2012) for description.

5 See LCMC's web page at <http://www.lancs.ac.uk/fass/projects/corpus/LCMC/> (accessed 15 May 2012).

6 While most Chinese corpora are part-of-speech tagged, the Chinese Penn Treebank is annotated with syntactic bracketing.

tive corpus, divided into 2000-word samples representing varying text types/genres of written Chinese, including press reportage, editorials, government documents, technical writing and fiction. The corpus was built as a match, in terms of sampling frame, for the FLOB corpus (Hundt et al., 1998).

In this book, I use the PFR corpus as the training corpus to explore as many features of the adverbial clause as possible. I use the LCMC corpus as the test corpus to obtain a more comprehensive analysis of the use of adverbial clauses in written Chinese. While the LCMC corpus will be described in more detail in Chapter Seven, the PFR corpus is discussed in the following subsections as it will be used in Chapters Three, Four, Five and Six.[7]

2.2.2 The PFR Chinese Corpus

The PFR (*Peita-Fujitsu-Renmin Ribao*) People's Daily POS Tagged Chinese Corpus (abbreviated to PFR Chinese Corpus hereafter) Release 1.0 was produced by the joint effort of the Institute of Computational Linguistics of the Peking University, the People's Daily Newspaper and the Fujitsu Research and Development (R&D) Centre Limited. With the permission of the People's Daily News and Information Centre, this corpus was based on extracts taken from one of the most popular Chinese newspapers, the People's Daily, from January to June in 1998. The corpus was composed of about 27 million Chinese characters, which were properly segmented into some 10 million words. These words were then annotated with part-of-speech tags.[8] In April 2001, the three corpus builders agreed to provide the public with free access to part of their research output, which contains the set of newspaper extracts assembled in January 1998, totalling some 3,000,000 characters, corresponding to about 1 million Chinese words. This subcorpus, on which part of my book is based, is freely available to the research community to use. Yet the PFR Chinese Corpus consists of texts more re-

7 The reason why I used the PFR corpus rather than the LCMC for the bulk of this research is that the latter was not ready early enough (until my second year of study).

8 As a by-product of the corpus construction, the institute has recently launched in its web page an online tool for word segmentation and POS tagging for short or medium-sized Chinese texts.

stricted than most researchers would ideally like as it covers only one publisher, one genre and a very narrow time span.[9] However, its value should not be ignored as it is one of the largest part-of-speech tagged Chinese corpora freely available at the time of writing.

2.2.2.1 The PFR tagset

Texts in the PFR corpus are arranged in ascending order according to date, page number and paragraph number. Moreover, every word of the texts is POS tagged. The tagset[10] comprises 26 basic word classes, including noun (*n*), time word (*t*), space word (*s*), directional locality (*f*), numeral (*m*), classifier (*q*), non-predicate adjective (*b*), pronoun (*r*), verb (*v*), adjective (*a*), descriptive[11] (*z*), adverb (*d*), preposition (*p*), conjunction (*c*), auxiliary (*u*), modal particle (*y*), interjection (*e*), onomatopoeia (*o*), idiom[12] (*i*), fixed expression (*l*), abbreviation (*j*), prefix[13] (*h*), suffix[14] (*k*), morpheme[15] (*g*), unclassified item[16] (*x*), and punctuation (*w*). Apart from this basic set of 26 POS markers, proper nouns were divided into personal names (*nr*), place names (*ns*), organisation names (*nt*) and other proper nouns (*nz*). Furthermore, another 20 markers which

9 As the subset of PFR was not chosen by me but was made freely available online by corpus compilers, I would assume that the question of how to "balance" the selections is an issue beyond the scope of this book.

10 The tagset that was used in the PFR Chinese Corpus was actually extended from the one proposed in Yu et al. (1998).

11 Descriptives are typically formed by reduplication or compounding, for example, 实实在在 *shishizaizai* "indeed, really, honestly", 绿茵茵 *lüyinyin* "green", 久远 *jiuyuan* "far back, ages ago, remote", 烂漫 *lanman* "bright-coloured; unaffected".

12 In Chinese, idoms, or 成语 *chengyu*, are expressions with a frozen internal structure. Their constituents and structure cannot be described in terms of morphological categories. They have to be treated as single morphological units. They should be distinguished from the fixed expressions, or 习用语 *xiyongyu*, the internal structure of which can be broken down into meaningful morphological units.

13 Examples include 非 *fei* "not", 超 *chao* "super", 无 *wu* "not", 过 *guo* "too", etc.

14 Examples include 儿 *er* "little", 们 *men* "expressing plurality", 型 *xing* "model, type" , 式 *shi* "type, style", etc.

15 Examples are 桌 *zhuo* "table", 身 *shen* "body", 鸭 *ya* "duck", etc.

16 Unlike morphemes, unclassified items do not carry any meaning at all. They must be combined with another unclassified item to give a meaningful word. Examples are 鹌 *an* (-鹑 *-chun*) "quail", 蟑 *zhang* (-螂 *-lang*) "cockroach", 蛤 *ge* (-蚧 *-jie*) "clam", etc.

address the peculiarities of Chinese linguistics were used, allowing for linguistic investigations specific to Chinese. The following table gives a description of the abbreviations used in this PFR tagset.

No.	*Tagset*	*POS (in Chinese)*	*POS (in English)*
1	Ag	形语素	Adjective Morpheme[17]
2	a	形容词	Adjective
3	ad	副形词	Adjective as Adverbial[18]
4	an	名形词	Adjective with Nominal Function[19]
5	Bg	区别语素	Non-predicate Adjective Morpheme
6	b	区别词	Non-predicate Adjective
7	c	连词	Conjunction
8	Dg	副语素	Adverb Morpheme
9	d	副词	Adverb
10	e	叹词	Interjection
11	f	方位词	Directional Locality
12	g	语素	Morpheme
13	h	前接成分	Prefix
14	i	成语	Idiom
15	j	简略语	Abbreviation
16	k	后接成分	Suffix
17	l	习用语	Fixed Expression
18	Mg	数语素	Numeric Morpheme
19	m	数词	Numeral
20	Ng	名语素	Noun Morpheme
21	n	名词	Common Noun
22	nr	人名	Personal Name
23	ns	地名	Place Name
24	nt	机构团体	Organisation Name
25	nx	外文字符	Nominal Character String
26	nz	其它专名	Other Proper Noun

17 The definition of morpheme was clearly stated in the institute's corpus annotation manual which states that a morpheme refers to the smallest meaningful unit which cannot be used independently. In Chinese, many characters may have their own meaning but they cannot stand alone (Norman, 1988: 154–156). They have to be combined with another character or word in the word formation process. Therefore, an adjective morpheme, resembling a common adjective semantically, is a morpheme signifying an attributive meaning to the word to which it is attached.

18 It refers to those adjectives functioning as adverbial without any modification to their morphological or phonological form.

19 It refers to those adjectives which can fulfil nominal functions in a clause.

No.	*Tagset*	*POS (in Chinese)*	*POS (in English)*
27	o	拟声词	Onomatopoeia
28	p	介词	Preposition
29	Qg	量语素	Classifier Morpheme
30	q	量词	Classifier
31	Rg	代语素	Pronoun Morpheme
32	r	代词	Pronoun
33	s	处所词	Space Word
34	Tg	时间语素	Time Word Morpheme
35	t	时间词	Time Word
36	Ug	助语素	Auxiliary Morpheme
37	u	助词	Auxiliary
38	Vg	动语素	Verb Morpheme
39	v	动词	Verb
40	vd	副动词	Verb as Adverbial[20]
41	vn	名动词	Verb with Nominal Function[21]
42	w	标点符号	Punctuation
43	x	非语素字	Unclassified Item
44	Yg	语气语素	Modal Particle Morpheme
45	y	语气词	Modal Particle
46	z	状态词	Descriptive

Table 1: The 46 PFR tagset.

2.2.2.2 The format of the PFR corpus

The PFR Chinese Corpus was saved in a plain text with the file extension "txt". In this corpus, every single line represents a paragraph or headline in the original newspaper scripts. At the beginning of each line, a string of numbers provide detailed information on the date (YYYYMMDD), page number, article number and paragraph number of each line. These are separated from one another by a hyphen –. For instance, as illustrated below, the numerical string "19980101-01-001-001" indicates that the piece of text under examination is the first paragraph of the first article appearing on the first page of the newspaper dated 1st January 1998. This crude metadata was simply tagged as a number in the corpus.

20 It refers to those verbs functioning as adverbial without any change to their form, both morphologically and phonologically.

21 It refers to those verbs that have acquired some nominal functions in a clause.

19980101-	01-	001-	001
Date (YYYYMMDD)	**Page**	**Article**	**Paragraph**

```
19980101-01-001-001/m  迈向/v  充满/v  希望/n  的/u  新/a  世纪/n  ——/w  一九九八年/t  新年/t  讲话/n  （/w  附/v  图片/n  １/m  张/q  ）/w
……
```

Figure 1: An excerpt of PFR text (1).

While there was no blank line between paragraphs of the same article, one blank line was used to mark the boundary between two different articles. For each single line, words were carefully and consistently segmented and tagged in the form of "word/POS tag". These words were then separated by two whitespaces and the last word of each paragraph (with no following word) was also followed by two spaces to ensure consistency.

Furthermore, square brackets are used to group together single words belonging to the same proper noun. For instance, in the text string, "通过/p [中央/n 人民/n 广播/vn 电台/n]nt 、/w *tongguo*/p [*Zhongyang*/n *Renmin*/n *Guangbo*/vn *Diantai*/n]nt 、/w 'Through the Zhongyang Renmin Broadcasting Station,'", the pair of square brackets [ ] marks the beginning and the end of a proper noun, which refers to a broadcasting organisation, the whole unit being tagged "/nt". Each single word inside the square brackets still carries its own POS tag.

```
19980101-01-001-006/m  在/p  １９９８年/t  来临/v  之际/f  ，/w  我/r  十分/m  高兴/a  地/u  通过/p  [中央/n  人民/n  广播/vn  电台/n]nt  、/w  [中国/ns  国际/n  广播/vn  电台/n]nt  和/c  [中央/n  电视台/n]nt  ，/w  向/p  全国/n  各族/r  人民/n  ，/w  向/p  [香港/ns  特别/a  行政区/n]ns  同胞/n  、/w  澳门/ns  和/c  台湾/ns  同胞/n  、/w  海外/s  侨胞/n  ，/w  向/p  世界/n  各国/r  的/u  朋友/n  们/k  ，/w  致以/v  诚挚/a  的/u  问候/vn  和/c  良好/a  的/u  祝愿/vn  ！/w
```

Figure 2: An excerpt of PFR text (2).

2.2.2.3 Modifications to the PFR Chinese Corpus: The use of "underscore" and the breakdown into subcorpora

Almost all of the features that appear in the original PFR Chinese Corpus were used without modification in my book. However, for the purposes of my research, two minor modifications were made. Firstly, an "underscore" was used to replace the original "slash" placed between a word and its tag so as to make the corpus more compatible with standard corpora, for example, the British National Corpus (Aston and Burnard, 1998). Secondly, the corpus was broken down into several smaller subcorpora by date for easy retrieval of the language data by corpus tools such as the Multilingual Corpus Toolkit or MLCT (Piao, 2002; Piao et al., 2002). This process broke the corpus into 278 separate files.

2.2.2.4 The annotation of the sentence boundaries

As noted earlier (section 2.2.2.1), every word in the PFR corpus is part-of-speech tagged. These part-of-speech tags are useful in those studies in which words of a particular word class are closely examined. However, the part-of-speech information may be of fairly limited use in the study of those grammatical constructions which operate over a phrase and/or clause/sentence boundary; an adverbial clause, for instance, is linked to the main clause preceding or following it and is thus studied at the clausal/sentential level rather than at the word level. The PFR Chinese Corpus as published does not mark any of these boundaries, so I decided to insert sentence boundary markers in my corpus to ease my investigation of the adverbial clause. The Multilingual Corpus Toolkit or MLCT (Piao, 2002; Piao et al., 2002) uses the tool "Sentence/Paragraph Splitter" to annotate sentence and paragraph boundaries. It works well with raw data i.e. data that are not marked with any form of annotation. However, it cannot mark sentence boundaries correctly in POS tagged text. As MLCT does not work properly with POS tagged texts and there is no available corpus tool that can be used to properly mark out the sentence boundaries in my corpus, I decided to write my own computer program in Java for the annotation of the sentence boundaries. One of the key features of the Java programming language that makes it particularly suitable for processing corpus data of different languages is that it is capable of dealing with non-Latin writing systems (Mason, 2000: 5). While most computer languages are restricted for use in basic Latin alphabet (cf. Butler, 1985a) Java supports the full Unicode character set (Graham, 2000; Unicode Consortium, 2000), enabling it to process corpus data in a wide range of writing systems. Readers who are interested in the Java program used in this book are advised to write to the author for a copy.[22] For illustrative purposes, I selected a text of rather short length (i.e. 34 sentences) from the corpus and used the program to annotate the sentence boundaries in the input text, as shown in the following output.

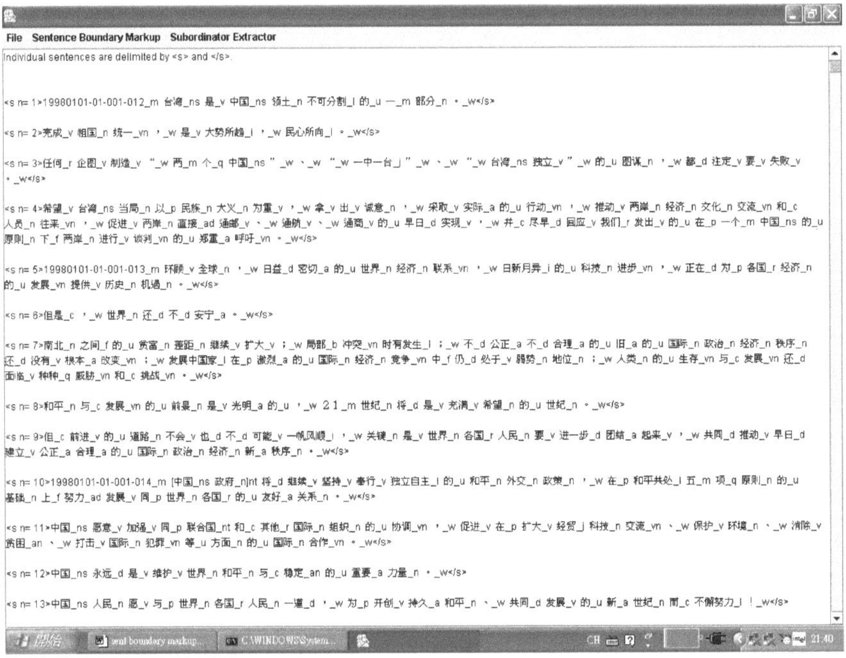

Figure 3: An output of the SentenceMarkup Java program.

22 As the concepts of Java programming are beyond the scope of this book, interested readers can consult some introductory books on how to make a program in Java (see, for example, Farrell, 1999; Cadenhead, 2001; Russell, 2001; Shelly et al., 2001; Deitel and Deitel, 2002).

2.2.3 The use of Chinese corpora

Like English corpora, Chinese corpora have been used in various fields of linguistics such as lexicography (Jin and Chen, 1995; Chen and Lee, 1996), pragmatics (Yeung, 1997), grammar (Li et al., 1995), etc. Apart from language studies, there are numerous corpus-driven NLP analyses on such topics as improving Chinese text retrieval systems (Liang et al., 1996) as well as on building corpus tools such as Chinese taggers (Liu et al., 1995; Zhang and Sheng, 1997) and Chinese word segmentation tools (Wong and Chan, 1996; Zhang and Sheng, 1996; Sun et al., 1998 and 2000; Yuan and Kim, 1998). Furthermore, corpora can be used by NLP researchers in evaluating the computer processing of Chinese characters (CPCC) such as Wu and White (1990), and developing speech recognition systems (Li et al., 1999).

When reviewing the use of Chinese corpora, it is not surprising to find that Chinese corpora have not been exploited to their full potential in analyses of grammatical phenomena, given the short history and limited number of Chinese corpora available. This in part motivates my research. However, why I decided to focus on adverbial clauses specifically can only be answered by reviewing current research on adverbial clauses.

2.3 An overview of adverbial clauses

2.3.1 Characterisation of adverbial clauses

There are at least three conflicting characterisations of adverbial clauses in the literature. Firstly, Thompson and Longacre (1985: 172) and Häcker (1999: 23) consider adverbial clauses to be one of the three types of subordinate clause (together with relative clauses and complement clauses),[23] and define these adverbial subordinate clauses as ones which

23 For a description of different types of subordinate clauses, see for example Winter (1982), Beaman (1984), Thompson (1984 and 1987), Lehmann (1988), Matthiessen and Thompson (1988), Greenbaum and Nelson (1995).

modify a verb phrase or a sentence. Secondly, Ford (1993: 23) explicitly states three requirements for a grammatical unit to be regarded as an adverbial clause, which were not clearly specified in Häcker's account: (1) the grammatical unit must have a subject and a verb, i.e. be a clause/sentence; (2) it must be introduced by an adverbial conjunction; and (3) it cannot be functioning as a subject or object of the main clause verb. Thirdly, within the theory of the Functional Grammar, Quintero (2002: 16–17) takes an adverbial clause as one which can be removed without affecting the grammaticality of the main clause; unlike the second analysis, the adverbial clause can occur with or without an introductory subordinator, and it can begin with or without a subject.

In my view, a clause is considered subordinate if it depends for its occurrence on another clause. As it is dependent for its occurrence on a main clause and is thus a subordinate clause, an adverbial clause is taken to be structurally optional in that it can be omitted without affecting the grammaticality of the main clause. Whether we decide that it is introduced by a subordinator and whether it has a subject relies chiefly on the extent of adverbial clauses that a particular study intends to cover.

2.3.1.1 Distinguishing adverbial clauses from complement clauses and relative clauses

Apart from adverbial clauses, there are two other common types of subordinate clause: complement clauses and relative clauses. Complement clauses function as core arguments of a predicate (Noonan, 1985) and thus they are obligatory constituents of the main clause and cannot be omitted. Adverbial clauses, however, are adjuncts functioning as an adverbial (Thompson and Longacre, 1985: 171) and thus they are not obligatory and can be omitted. Like adverbial clauses, (non-defining) relative clauses are adjuncts that can be omitted. However, the two kinds of subordinate clause can be distinguished from each other. Relative clauses have always been a major focus of debate in Chinese linguistics and some scholars (e.g. Chao, 1968; Paul, 2005) claim that they do not exist in Chinese (see Chapter Three, section 3.4.1). Even if relative clauses do exist in Chinese, they are modifiers of a noun phrase (Keenan, 1985), while adverbial clauses modify an associated main clause or a verb phrase (Diessel, 2001: 435ff.).

Hence, the defining characteristics of dependency and structural optionality are sufficient to separate adverbial clauses from other types of subordinate clauses. On the basis of these previous studies, I will propose in Chapter Three (section 3.5.1.1) an operational definition of the adverbial clause as used in this book for the construction of a skeleton treebank. For now, I will proceed on the basis of the definition of the adverbial clause adopted here.

2.3.2 Corpus-based approaches to adverbial clauses

Non corpus-based studies of such complex grammatical constructions as adverbials often depend upon invented, atypical, examples. As Mair (1987: 546) notes, more often than not, the grammaticality of examples used in such cases is questionable. A corpus-based study, which provides an account of a feature based on attested language use, can provide a more reliable evidence base and hence account (see, for example, Chafe, 1986; Biber and Finegan, 1988 and 1989; Kortmann, 1995; Wang, 1995). It is unsurprising, therefore, that there has recently been considerable interest in using corpus-based approaches to investigating adverbial clauses. In the following, various kinds of corpus-based studies of adverbial clauses are briefly reviewed and those analyses are presented with respect to two different perspectives i.e. syntax/semantics and discourse.

2.3.2.1 Syntactic/semantic analyses of adverbial clauses

Adverbial clauses can be expressed in many different ways across the languages of the world, as Hengeveld (1998), who examined a sample of 45 languages, observed. In English, for instance, a distinction can be established between adverbial clauses expressed through two different verb forms, namely independent forms (finite indicative and subjunctive) and dependent forms (infinitive, *-ing* and past participle forms). These expression formats may be systematically related to the semantic types of adverbial clauses. Greenbaum's (1973) study, for example, was concerned with the correlation between syntactic behaviour and the semantic classes of adverbial clauses. Setting out to test a generally-held belief that in English an adverbial non-finite clause would be related transformationally to a finite clause, he comes to the conclusion that the non-finitisation transformation is allowed with some semantic classes of adverbial clauses (viz temporal clauses, concessive clauses and causal clauses) but is blocked with others. This view was confirmed later by Ljung's (1997) genre-based study in which twenty-two genres of English were examined: it was found that the tendency to use non-finite and verbless adverbial clauses is stronger in temporal clauses than in adverbial clauses expressing other meanings.

As another good illustration of the syntax/semantics interface, Quintero (2002) persuasively demonstrates that while clauses of concession are expressed exclusively through independent verb forms that are introduced by e.g. *although*, *even though*, and *whilst*, clauses of purpose are more likely to be expressed through dependent forms introduced by e.g. *in order to*. In contrast to most traditional classifications (see, for example, Thompson and Longacre, 1985), the criterion used for the semantic classification of adverbial clauses in Quintero's study is not simply the basic meaning of the conjunction introducing the subordinate clause. Instead, her classification is based on a systematic and consistent application of four semantic parameters: Entity Type, Time Dependency, Factuality and Presupposition. The relevance of the application of these parameters is not only that they allow for the establishment of a complete and exhaustive typology of adverbial clauses, but they also form the basis for four implicational hierarchies that determine the distribution of expression formats along the different semantic types of adverbial clauses, as illustrated with concession clauses and purpose clauses above.

Though the facts thrown up in these studies appear to form a good basis for the re-evaluation using Chinese language data, it is not possible to study the correlation between verb forms (finite and infinitive clauses) and semantic types of adverbial clauses in Chinese. Chinese verbs do not mark such a finite/non-finite distinction (Rai-Chu, 1982: 78ff.; Norman, 1988: 163; Hu et al., 2001), consequently I did not follow these approaches in my book.

2.3.2.2 Discourse analyses of adverbial clauses

It does not come as a surprise that many previous accounts of adverbial clauses are discourse-based analyses as adverbial clauses seem to tie back to the previous discourse in several different ways by specifying time, condition, purpose, etc. As Thompson and Longacre (1985: 232–

233) point out, "adverbial clauses may be of relevance to a stretch greater than the sentence in which they find themselves" in that "they may provide cohesion for an entire discourse, or they may provide cohesion for some paragraph within it". In particular, the focus of these studies is concerned with the discourse factors which influence the choice of position for various kinds of adverbial clauses.

In contrast to some previous accounts (see, for example, Tai, 1973, 1975, and 1985) which attribute the differences in adverbial placement to iconic motivation (that is, the temporal clause, for instance, must precede the main clause if the event described in the temporal clause takes place earlier than the one in the main clause), the discourse analyses described in the following adopt a rather disparate approach.[24] A case in point is Ford's (1993) study on the distribution and discourse functions of *temporal, conditional* and *causal adverbial clauses* in American English conversations. In her findings, discourse-structuring functions are realised through initial adverbial clauses, while final adverbial clauses tend to work more locally in narrowing main clause meaning without forging links or shifting points in relation to the prior discourse. As illustrated in example (1), *if*-clauses tend to occur initially in order to create temporary discourse realities, introducing and forming the background for the main clause whereas causal clauses are more likely to appear postverbally to give an explanation of the events or states that have been mentioned in the preceding main clause. Temporal clauses are used predominantly in postverbal position to ground the situation described in the main clause in time as in example (2). When they are placed initially, they set the time frame for the whole discourse of sequenced events as in example (3). A similar observation, that the position of an adverbial clause varies with its discourse functions, is made in Diessel's (2001) typological account of a representative sample of 40 languages: conditional clauses precede the main clause more often than temporal clauses, which in turn are more often preposed

24 It should be noted that Greenbaum and Nelson (1996) examine some of the factors (other than cognitive and discourse factors) e.g. clause length that may influence the positional choice of the adverbial clause and conclude that the semantic types of adverbial clauses, rather than clause length, determine the position of the adverbial clause in a sentence. See also Horová (1976) and Hasselgård (1992) for a similar view on the description of spatial and temporal adverbials.

than causal, result and purpose clauses. The distributional patterns are motivated by discourse-pragmatic factors.

(1) ***If*** you wanna leave about eleven, I'll walk down with you ***cause*** I have to go to school. (Ford, 1993: 48)
(2) So then .hh I was there, I was there. I heard it, doctor knew what he was talking about, made my dad feel comfortable, said that he was talking about, made my dad feel comfortable, said that he's gonna have this same operation, ***when*** he's – in about twenty years, cause he had bad knees from football, n-in highschool. (Ford, 1993: 71–72)
(3) No I know. I'd be pretty sure it was ***when***- I went to this thing, When a pe(r)- when a old man reaches seventy seven, they have this big ceremony, (i wu)s like this rebirth or, something. An' they do wha- they carry him on his back, n' put him in a chariot, n' carry him around all the kids drag him around through the village, an' stuff (they do all this) the(n'they have these big jars full of this mm- it's like fermententED wi(n) or-fermented rice, It's like they y'know rice- (Ford, 1993: 29)

Apart from investigating various adverbial clauses in a single study, some studies focus on a specific type of adverbial clause; the discourse functions of *conditional clauses* have recently become a prime concern, for example. While traditional accounts of conditional clauses are primarily based on introspective judgements (see, for example, Haiman, 1978; Comrie, 1986; Bhatt and Pancheva, 2001) and are thus unable to provide a discourse analysis, corpus-based studies (Ford and Thompson, 1986; Ramsay, 1987; Wang, 1998) are well-suited to offering a clear understanding of the behaviour of the conditional clause in discourse. These studies have come to more or less the same conclusion that can be attested in such languages as English and Chinese: the positioning of the conditional clause i.e. before or after the main clause is determined by the organisation of discourse: while initial conditional clauses have a clear discourse function by creating backgrounds for subsequent propositions as in example (4), final conditional clauses qualify or elaborate the previous clause without displaying an explicit connection with preceding or subsequent discourse as in example (5).

(4) ***If*** things are allowed to drift, [...] there will be an atomic war. In such a war, even if the worst consequences are avoided, Western

Europe, including Great Britain, will be virtually exterminated. If America and the U.S.S.R. survive as organized states, they will presently fight again. (Ford and Thompson, 1986: 358)

(5) Our confused and difficult world needs various things ***if*** it is to escape disaster, and among these one of the most necessary is that, in the nations which still uphold Liberal beliefs, these beliefs should be whole-hearted and profound, not apologetic towards dogmatisms [...]. (Ford and Thompson, 1986: 360)

Besides conditional clauses, the theme that preposed adverbial clauses perform a different job in discourse than do postposed ones holds across other adverbial clause types. Thompson's (1985) paper on the distribution of *purpose clauses* in English texts is another attempt at defining the distribution of adverbial clauses in discourse. She identifies the discourse factors that determine whether a purpose clause will be placed before or after its main clause and concludes that initial and final clauses are performing different functions in discourse. Initial purpose clauses in English guide the attention of the reader in a very specific way, by stating a problem which arises from expectations created by the text or inferences from it, to which the following material of more clauses provides a solution, as shown in example (6). Final purpose clauses do not have the same function but a very localised one: they only serve to state the purpose for which the action named in the main clause is performed, as shown in example (7). Furthermore, Thompson (1983) scrutinises the discourse function of *adverbial -ing clauses* (both in the initial and final positions) in English and shows that these clauses serve as a local grounding device: they are background specifically for the associated main clause in that either they provide material that further elaborates what is in the main clause or they represent an event co-occurring simultaneously with or providing a comment on or motivation for the event described in the main clause.

(6) *Brendan* was rushing madly farther and farther out to sea. ***To slow her down*** we streamed a heavy rope in a loop from the stern and let it trail in the water behind us to act as a brake, and, hopefully, to smooth the worst of the wave crests. From the stern also dangled a metal bucket; only twenty-four hours earlier we had been using it to cook an excellent meal of Irish crabs. Now it clanked mournfully every time a wave broke against it. (Thompson, 1985: 62)

(7) George had always been my first choice for crew. Twenty-six years old, he had served in the army and later gone to the Middle East ***to train soldiers for an oil-rich sheik***. With the money saved from this venture, he had decided to take a couple of years looking around the world and pleasing himself. (Thompson, 1985: 68)

Abraham (1991), Kirkpatrick (1993) and Wang (1999 and 2002) characterise Chinese *causal clauses* with reference to their patterns of occurrence in discourse. While both Abraham and Kirkpatrick argue for "because-therefore" sequence as the preferred pattern for expressing causal relations in Chinese, Wang forcefully demonstrates, on the basis of a spoken corpus, that causal clauses in spoken Chinese occur overwhelmingly after their modified main clause in order to provide a further account or clarification of the prior utterance made by the speaker, thereby providing more information to promote better mutual understanding in communication. A similar pattern has been found in English causal relations as well (Newsome, 1958; Altenberg, 1984; Schiffrin, 1985). As Altenberg's study has shown, in both the London-Lund Corpus of Spoken English (LLC) and the Lancaster-Oslo/Bergen Corpus of British English, RC (or result-cause) order is preferred to CR (or cause-result) order; what determines this causal sequence is the contextual or pragmatic adjustment which facilitates the progression of discourse topic and interaction among participants in discourse.

These studies of adverbial clauses, by and large, concentrate on the discourse functions of just a few semantic classes of the adverbial clause (e.g. conditional, temporal and causal adverbial clauses) and rely on spoken corpora. The discourse functions of adverbial clauses have been examined rather thoroughly, studies of which converge on the conclusion that initial adverbial clauses are used to set a frame for the following clauses whereas final adverbial clauses are used to modify the preceding main clause only. As Wang (1998, 1999 and 2002) has taken those claims in the literature and re-evaluated and corroborated them in the light of Chinese data, there seems to be no point in carrying out a further investigation of this matter as it is unlikely that new, significant, insights would be offered. More research, however, is needed to give an in-depth analysis of all of the potential semantic types of adverbial clauses in Chinese as previous work has mainly focussed on a subset of the semantic domains. This analysis will be conducted using a large amount of written and spoken corpus data in this book. Furthermore, I will adopt a theoretically informed corpus-based approach in my book as previous studies of adverbial clauses taking this approach are rather limited in the sense that rather than combine theoretical and corpus linguistics (e.g. Quintero, 2002), these studies are based on corpus evidence without using a theoretical framework (e.g. Greenbaum, 1973; Thompson and Longacre, 1985) or they are based on a theory formed by introspections at the expense of a wealth of language data that can be obtained from a corpus (e.g. Comrie, 1986; Givón, 1993: 287–313 and 2001: 330–351; Bhatt and Pancheva, 2001). This book therefore aims to achieve a corpus-based, wide ranging, theoretically informed study of all semantic types of adverbial clauses in Chinese.

2.4 Chapter summary

Previous accounts of adverbial clauses examine their syntactic/semantic properties and discourse functions. The distribution of different verb forms that are used in adverbial clauses tends to be systematically related to their semantic roles; for instance, there is a strong tendency for temporal and purpose adverbial clauses to be expressed by non-finite rather than finite verb forms. The discourse function of adverbial clauses has been a major focus of recent research. It has been convincingly demonstrated that the positioning of an adverbial clause, before or after the main clause, is largely determined by the organisation of discourse. Initial adverbial clauses appear to set a frame or create a background for subsequent clauses and thus they have a clear discourse function, whereas final adverbial clauses play a more localised role in that they qualify or elaborate the main clause with which they are associated without having any clear connection to the preceding or following discourse.

Yet previous analyses focus only on a limited range of adverbial clauses in Chinese and those analyses are mainly based on spoken data. In the light of this, my research contributes by providing a comprehensive, corpus-based, theoretically informed analysis of all of the potential semantic types of adverbial clauses in Chinese on the basis of both spoken and written data.

Chapter Three

Treebanking: The Compilation of a Sample PFR Corpus of Skeleton-parsed Sentences

3.1 Introduction

The PFR Chinese Corpus used in this book is part-of-speech (POS) tagged. For the purposes of this book, however, I decided to add a further level of annotation to the corpus – constituent structure or syntactic annotation. As its name suggests, syntactic annotation makes explicit the constituent structure of sentences, usually in the form of labelled brackets. In the following sections, I will discuss the methods and issues relevant to the syntactic annotation of the PFR Chinese Corpus by building a sample treebank. The goal in undertaking this annotation is to ease the identification of adverbial clauses in Chinese, which is the prime object of my book.

Treebanks are simply corpora in which syntactic constituent structure is made explicit by a process of corpus annotation (Leech and Garside, 1991: 15; Abeillé, 2003: xiv). My major concern here is not with software to achieve this annotation automatically (as at the time of writing, there are no effective available parsers designed for the Chinese language), but with the establishment of a parsing scheme and its manual application to written Chinese corpus data. More specifically, the approach taken here is inspired by the *skeleton parsing* approach (Eyes and Leech, 1993; Garside, 1993; Black et al., 1996; Leech and Eyes, 1997). Skeleton parsing seeks to produce simplified constituent-structure annotations. I do not intend to go into a deep or logical annotation which would apply functional labels for constituents (e.g. subject, object, etc.) as traditional reference grammar books do (Quirk et al., 1985). Rather, I will focus on categorial labels such as noun phrase, prepositional phrase, adverb phrase, etc.

The reason why I use categorial labels rather than functional labels is that the former suffice for the identification of my object of study. Adverbial clauses function only as adjuncts in the sentences in my corpus. However, not all adjuncts are adverbial clauses: apart from the adverbial clause, an adjunct can take various syntactic forms such as noun phrase, prepositional phrase, adverb phrase, etc., which are all grammatical categories. As will be shown in the description of my parsing scheme (section 3.4), a separate label is set up for a grammatical category to function as an adjunct (e.g. adverbial noun phrase, adverbial prepositional phrase, etc.). As the only grammatical function that is relevant here is adjunct, which can be adequately identified by the use of categorial labels, other grammatical functions such as subject, object, etc. that are not directly related to the goal of this book can in principle be put aside for the sake of simplicity in skeleton parsing. I will return, however, in the conclusion of my book to the possible advantages of future research considering functional labelling.

3.2 An overview of past parsing projects

Both Bateman et al. (1997) and Leech and Eyes (1997) provide a detailed survey of a variety of approaches taken to syntactic annotation by different projects, namely the Lancaster/IBM Treebank (Barnett et al., 1996), the SUSANNE Corpus (Sampson, 1995), the Nijmegen Treebanks comprising both the Nijmegen Corpus (Keulen, 1986) and the TOSCA Corpus (Oostdijk, 1991), the Constraint Grammar parser of the Helsinki group (Karlsson et al., 1995) and the Penn Treebank (Marcus et al., 1993; Marcus et al., 1994). These parsing projects were chiefly concerned with the syntactic annotation of the English language.[1] Recently, however, syntactic annotation has been extended to languages other than English. The Penn Chinese Treebank Project[2] (Xia et al.,

1 Though, the Constraint Grammar system is currently being developed for Finnish (Karlsson, 1990; Koskenniemi, 1990), Swedish (Voutilainen, 2001), Danish (Bilgram and Keson, 1998), German (Nießen and Ney, 2001), Basque (Aduriz et al., 1997) and French (Chanod and Tapanainen, 1995).

2 The first version of the treebank was released via LDC in December 2000. See the project's web page: <http://www.cis.upenn.edu/~chinese/> (accessed 15 May 2012).

2000; Chiou et al., 2001; Xue et al., 2002) is a case in point. While this Chinese treebank initially seemed to be a promising corpus on which to carry out my research, it proved to be unsuitable for my purpose as well, as will be outlined shortly.

The TOSCA and Constraint Grammar based work was also unsuitable; the Nijmegen Treebanks are produced by a semi-automatic parser which provides an interactive environment allowing human intervention to complete and correct the parsing. The Penn Treebank[3] and the Bank of English Corpus were annotated by the Constraint Grammar (CG) parser[4], a fully automatic parser. The TOSCA and CG parsers have one thing in common: they adopt a considerable number of syntactic tags. The CG Framework marks 29 syntactic functions, while the TOSCA annotation scheme contains 16 categorial labels, over 90 functional labels and over 100 attribute labels (e.g. active/passive voice, raised direct object, etc.). My work entails manual parsing and it is difficult for a sole human analyst to annotate consistently and accurately with such complex annotation systems. Hence I rejected the use of the CG and TOSCA schemes and I will not go into details of these automatic/semi-automatic parsing models further in this book. Nevertheless, this is not to ignore the annotation schemes totally. The categorial labels were carefully reviewed in working out my final parsing scheme.

Of the parsing schemes under consideration, only the Lancaster/IBM Treebank, SUSANNE Corpus and Penn Chinese Treebank were manually parsed. At the level of surface grammar, which identifies constituents in a clause and assigns labels to these constituents, the annotation schemes used in both the SUSANNE Corpus and Penn Chinese Treebank are very similar to that of the Lancaster Treebank, although more detail is included in both the SUSANNE and Penn corpora. The SUSANNE Corpus and Penn Chinese Treebank give detailed analyses of elements of syntactic functions and deep structure like traces, syntactic ambiguities, semantic roles, etc. that are of no use to this study.

3 The Penn Treebank has undergone an extensive manual post-editing and proved that correcting the parser's output is significantly faster than manually parsing a corpus (Marcus et al. 1993: 317).

4 The Constraint Grammar formalism is notable for incorporating a dependency grammar framework, in contrast to the phrase structure grammar models employed for most other treebanks.

A further major drawback, for my book, of the Penn Chinese Treebank is that it is not theory neutral. The influence of Government and Binding Theory (GB)[5] is clear in the corpus. Though it is claimed that only those assumptions of GB that are least controversial are adopted in the annotation scheme (Xue et al., 2000: 4–5), this inevitably called for a number of abstract covert phrasal categories such as IP[6], CP[7], etc. Those phrasal categories may be well-motivated within the theory but their significance cannot be maintained across other theoretical frameworks. Hence, the treebank is far from theory neutral. Since a primary goal of corpus annotation is to provide empirical data for linguistic investigations, it is desirable to annotate categories/features that are the most commonly shared among theories, so that others can use the treebank for their own purposes, without being encumbered with unwanted theoretical assumptions; the minimal basic level syntactic categories are the ones that are shared by all theories. Thus I rejected the use of the Penn Chinese Treebank in part because it jeopardised my goal of theory neutrality.

A final, crucial, point that led to me not using the Penn Chinese Treebank is that its parsing scheme does not contain a separate label for the adverbial clause and thus no attempt was made to give a definition of adverbial clause in this scheme. Rather, it tends to subsume the adverbial clause under the entry of subordinate clause (including relative clause and appositive clause) and VP adjunct. If I were to use the Penn Chinese Treebank, I would have had to restart the annotation from scratch: first, I would have had to introduce a clear definition of what an adverbial clause should be; second, with this clear working definition, I would have to have taken pains to screen all of the subordinate clauses and VP adjuncts, labelling and sorting out only those adverbial clauses of interest to me, on the basis of the assumption that the subor-

5 For details of the Government and Binding Theory, see Haegeman (1994).

6 IP refers to both finite and infinitival clauses, depending on the content of the node INFL, which is a terminal node signifying the inflectional morphology of the verb, affixes and infinitival *to* (Haegeman, 1994: 114 ff.).

7 Complementisers, represented as C, such as *whether*, *if*, *that* and *for* in English introduce a sentence (IP): C selects an IP-complement. The choice of the type of IP depends on the choice of C. The complementisers *that* and *if* select a finite clause as their complement; *for* selects an infinitival clause and *whether* selects either type of clause. Thus CP refers to either a finite or non-finite clause introduced by a complementiser. See Haegeman (1994: 116 ff.).

dinate clauses and VP adjuncts include all of the adverbial clauses I want. In other words, there is not much difference between using the data produced by the Penn Chinese Treebank and conducting my own manual parsing. I therefore decided to start afresh and conduct my own annotation. Having decided not to use the Penn treebank annotation, I considered whether to use the raw corpus texts. I decided not to use the raw corpus data from the Penn Chinese Treebank firstly because the newspaper articles available in the treebank were taken from the Xinhua newswire between 1994 and 1998, which were comparatively less recent than other data I had available to me (Yu, 1999: 20); secondly, the Penn Chinese Treebank contains about 100K words, which is ten times smaller in size than the data available to me, which amounted to approximately 1 million Chinese words.

Having decided that I needed to develop a theory neutral annotation of Chinese, and having also rejected schemes such as CG, TOSCA and SUSANNE as they were too complex and in some cases required partial automation, I decided to follow the approach to syntactic annotation used in the Lancaster/IBM Treebank. With reference to skeleton parsing, the Lancaster/IBM Treebank (compiled between 1987 and 1991), consisting of approximately 3 million words, is the largest of all of the manually annotated treebanks. It was produced by Leech and Garside (1991), in collaboration with IBM. The Lancaster/IBM treebank built upon the work carried out on its precursors, the Lancaster-Leeds Treebank (Lang, 1989; Edwards, 1993: 298) and the LOB Corpus Treebank (Sampson, 1987: 83–84). One of the major innovations of the Lancaster/IBM treebank was the skeleton parsing approach (see Garside and McEnery, 1993). The simplicity of skeleton parsing not only expedites the process of treebank compilation, it also reduces the intellectual complexity of the task of parsing for human analysts, thereby minimising inconsistencies and inaccuracies in treebanking practice. This makes it an attractive approach for the lone scholar. Given that I had no suitable treebanked Chinese corpus available, I proceeded to construct my own using the skeleton parsing approach.

In the remainder of this chapter, I will discuss at length the treebanking method I have developed for Chinese. In doing so, I will analyse in detail the processing of a sample text. I discuss first, in section 3.3, the selection of the text sample. In section 3.4, I describe the key components of a standard parsing scheme as exemplified by the

UCREL skeleton parsing tagset and then give a detailed description of my own parsing scheme. In section 3.5, I explain the elaborate guidelines developed for the purposes of consistency and accuracy in my annotation. I then explain the process of assigning labelled brackets to the part-of-speech-tagged sentences and the difficulties encountered in the application of the annotation practices proposed (section 3.6). Following from this, the parses of adverbials and, most importantly, adverbial clauses will be examined (section 3.7). The conclusion will give an evaluation of the success of my manual skeleton parsing (section 3.8).

3.3 PFR Sample Skeleton Treebank: Text selection

From the PFR Chinese Corpus, a sample text of some 100,000 word tokens, yielding approximately 2,500 sentences, was chosen for the production of my treebank. I contend that a standard block of about one hundred thousand words is a unit of about the right size for skeleton parsing and handling by a human treebanker. Furthermore, my choice of text was governed by the need to produce a parsed sample corpus of reasonable length which could not only be manageable for hand-parsing but also represent a typical chuck of the data that would eventually be treebanked by me.

3.4 PFR Sample Skeleton Treebank: Parsing scheme

As Sampson (1995: 2ff.) puts it, the process of parsing refers to the ability to extract from a linear sequence of words the underlying hierarchical grammatical structure, and thus a *parsing scheme* "is a set of categories and notational conventions allowing the grammatical properties of a text to be made explicit". In other words, it is a guideline document which helps the human analyst parse sentences (Leech and Garside, 1991: 15–16). A clearly defined parsing scheme is essential for the production of a satisfactorily parsed text.

3.4.1 UCREL skeleton parsing annotation scheme

As most of the existing treebanks are primarily based upon English texts, it does not come as a surprise that the annotation schemes used on those treebanks chiefly reflect the syntactic categories which are directly relevant to English grammar. A case in point is the UCREL skeleton parsing scheme, as illustrated in the following table.[8]

UCREL	*Skeleton Parsing Annotation Scheme*
Fa	Adverbial Clause
Fc	Comparative Clause
Fn	Noun Clause
Fr	Relative Clause
G	Genitive
J	Adjective Phrase (predicative)
N	Noun Phrase
Nr	Adverbial Noun Phrase (temporal)
Nv	Adverbial Noun Phrase (non-temporal) (not in AP or SEC corpora)
P	Prepositional Phrase
S	Sentence (used eg in quoted speech, also with + and & as co-ordinates)
Tg	-ing Clause
Ti	Infinitive Clause
Tn	Past Participle Clause
V	Verb Phrase
(null)	Unlabelled Constituent

Table 2: The UCREL skeleton parsing annotation scheme.

As stated, some of the syntactic constituent labels in the UCREL skeleton parsing scheme are specially designed to suit English grammar. When I attempted to adopt this scheme wholesale for my own research, I found that some modifications were needed to accommodate the syntactic properties of the Chinese language.

First of all, since there is no conclusive morphological evidence that motivates the postulation of infinitival clauses in Chinese (Xue et al., 2000: 32), the non-finite clauses, including the *-ing* clause (Tg),

8 The table was adapted from UCREL (University Centre for Computer Corpus Research on Language)'s website <http://ucrel.lancs.ac.uk/skeletontags.html> (accessed 15 May 2012).

infinitive clause (Ti) and past participle clause (Tn) were not taken over from the UCREL parsing scheme to my parsing scheme. Similarly, I did not include the noun clause (Fn) or the relative clause (Fr) as they are also not compatible with Chinese syntax. Relative clauses have long been a source of controversy in Chinese linguistics. Some scholars (e.g. Li and Thompson, 1989: 579ff.; Aoun and Li, 1993; Chiu, 1993; Wu, 2000) believe that a nominalisation (whereby a verb, verb phrase, or sentence, followed by the particle *de*, functions as a noun phrase) can be called a relative clause in Chinese if the head noun that it modifies refers to an unspecified element involved in the situation described by the nominalisation. For instance, in such a noun phrase as "卖报纸的老人 *mai baozhi de laoren* 'the old man who sells newspapers'", the relative clause refers to the verb phrase marked by the following particle *de*, i.e. 卖报纸的 *maibaozhi de* "sell newspapers". In this relative clause, the subject, namely the person who sells newspapers, is missing. Accordingly, the head noun 老人 *laoren* refers to this missing subject. The particle *de* is functionally equivalent to the English relative pronoun *who* which indicates a gap or trace that is co-referential with the head noun.

On the other hand, Chao (1968), among others, does not adopt the notion of relative clause in his descriptive grammar of Chinese.[9] Relative clauses may not exist in Chinese for at least two reasons. First, rather than a relativiser, the particle 的 *de*, as Chao (1968: 285) points out, is a marker of explicit modification. It is inserted after the premodifier of a noun phrase to make explicit the modifier-modified structure. Zhu (1982 and 2000) also notes that this particle is "multi-functional" in that it can be a genitive marker (e.g. 他的书 *ta de shu* "his book"), a marker of nominalisation (e.g. 买书的是个学生 *mai shu de shi ge xuesheng* "The person who bought the book is a student"), and an adjectival marker (e.g. 勤劳的学生 *qinlao de xuesheng* "a hardworking student"). It is therefore not a proper "counterpart" of the English relative pronoun which is "unifunctional" (except *that*).[10] The second rea-

9 He does not use the term relative clause; rather, he refers to those constructions marked by *de* as *adjectival clauses* which can modify any nominal expression (Chao, 1968: 111).

10 The function word, *that*, is a relative pronoun, a demonstrative pronoun and a conjunction (Quirk et al., 1985).

son is that some relative clauses do not actually include a gap that the head noun can co-refer to. So far scholars have been considering relative clauses to be clauses in which either the subject or object is missing, thereby producing a gap that co-refers to the head noun the relative clauses modify. Such gaps are used as evidence to prove the existence of relative clauses in Chinese. However, such a gap does not always exist as in 我写信的房子 *wo xie xin de fangzi* "the room in which I write letters". In this case the so-called relative clause marked by the particle *de* (i.e. 我写信的 *wo xie xin de* "I write letters") is a well-formed clause without any missing subject or object. In cases such as this, two conflicting explanations were proposed. Chu and Chi (1999: 226) claim that the construction is no longer a relative clause but an appositive clause on the grounds that no gap can be identified in the noun phrase and they use this as a definitive test for distinguishing a relative clause from an appositive clause. Yet, Xue et al. (2000: 80ff.) and Li and Thompson (1989: 582ff.) still perceive it as a relative clause though with an PP trace rather than an NP trace; it differs from the relative clause with an NP trace in that the gap is an adjunct position. Since this is a highly controversial and unresolved issue, I chose not to use this grammatical category in my parsing scheme. Instead, constructions marked by the particle *de* were left unspecified by using unlabelled brackets (see section 3.5.2.1).

Nominal clauses are also difficult in Chinese linguistics. The notion of the nominal clause may be useful in English as the clauses used as sentential subject or object are formally distinctive from those used independently: they are typically introduced by the conjunction *that* as in "That John stole my book was totally incredible" (Quirk and Greenbaum, 1973: 316–322). Chinese clauses or sentences, however, do not vary morphosyntactically when they are used as subject or direct object (Liu et al., 1996: 245, 253). Hence, there is no justification for adopting this grammatical category in a parsing scheme designed for the Chinese language. The lack of previous accounts of nominal clauses in Chinese tends to serve as counterevidence to the notion that nominal clauses exist in Chinese.

Furthermore, owing to the fact that different languages tend to employ different strategies in signalling the same grammatical relation, the parsing label of comparative clause (Fc) was also not adopted in my parsing scheme. While English makes use of a clause to give comparisons, the comparative constructions in Chinese are expressed by means of a prepositional phrase. The comparative marker 比 *bi* "than" and the phrase that immediately follows it form a prepositional phrase which serves as a preverbal adjunct (Zhao, 1989; Liu, 1999: 204ff.). Compare the following contrived sentences from English and Chinese respectively, both of which express the same meaning:

(1a) He does the assignment **[Fc** better than I do **Fc]**.

(1b)	他	做	的	功课	做	得	**[P** 比	我 **P]**	好。
	ta	*zuo*	*de*	*gongke*	*zuo*	*de*	**[P** *bi*	*wo***P]**	*hao*
	he	do	DE	assignment	do	COMP	BI	I	well

"He does the assignment better than I do."

Lastly, I did not take the genitive (G) as one of the constituent labels in my parsing scheme so as to avoid terminological controversy. The genitive constructions in English *roughly* correspond to those constructions marked by the particle 的 *de* in Chinese. However, this apparent correspondence is complicated by two issues. Firstly, possessive constructions in Chinese do not necessarily take the particle 的 *de* (Li and Thompson, 1989: 115) as in 他爸爸 *ta baba* and 他的爸爸 *ta de baba* which both indicate the same meaning "his father". Secondly, apart from marking possessions, the particle 的 *de* can be an adjectival marker and a marker of nominalisation and explicit modification, as mentioned earlier. Since the term "genitive" is confusing as far as Chinese linguistics is concerned, I decided to exclude this constituent from my parsing scheme.

In view of the differences between the English and Chinese grammatical systems, new constituent labels that are not used in the UCREL skeleton parsing scheme had to be invented for the purposes of this research. These are: adverb phrase, correlative clause, adverbial idiom/set phrase, adverbial adjective phrase, adverbial prepositional phrase, adverbial verb phrase and verbal object, which are to be discussed below.

3.4.2 PFR skeleton parsing labels

As Leech and Eyes (1997: 37) note, Sampson's (1995) annotation scheme demonstrates three key components of a clearly specified parsing scheme:

(a) A list of symbols used in the annotation: non-terminals, terminals, and other symbols;
(b) A basic definition of the symbols: e.g. N = noun phrase;
(c) A description, which is as detailed as possible, of how the symbols are actually applied to text sentences. For example, how do annotators recognise a noun phrase when they see one, and how do they distinguish noun phrase tokens from words or word sequences which are not noun phrases?

With respect to the first and second points, in keeping with Sampson, I intend to provide these 3 sets of data for my treebank: (a) the non-terminal labels and (b) their definitions with illustrative examples[35] are given for the PFR treebank in Table 3.

Nonterminal category	**Symbol**	**Example**
Adverbial Clause	Fa	**<Fa>**只要_c <N>我们_r</N> <R>进一步_d</R> <解放思想_i ，_w 实事求是_i> ，_w <V>抓住_v <N>机遇_n</N></V> ，_w <开拓进取_l>**</Fa>** ，_w **<Fa>***zhiyao*_c <N>*women*_r</N> <R>*jinyibu*_d</R> <*jiefangsixiang*_i ，_w *shishiqiushi*_i> ，_w <V>*zhuazhu*_v <N>*jiyu*_n</N></V> ，_w <*kaituojinqu*_l>**</Fa>** ，_w "If we become more open-minded and realistic and make every effort to explore new possibilities,"

35 All of the examples in this book are given in the Chinese characters, followed by *pinyin* romanisations, glosses and English translations.

Nonterminal category	Symbol	Example
Correlative Clause	Fc	**<Fc>**越_d 走_v 越_d 宽广_a**</Fc>** **<Fc>***yue*_d *zou*_v *yue*_d *kuanguang*_a**</Fc>** "the more we walk, the broader (the road) will be"
Main Clause (to which the adverbial clause is subordinated)	Fm	**<Fm>**<Fa>只要_c <N>我们_r</N> <R>进一步_d</R> <解放思想_i ，_w 实事求是_i> ，_w <V>抓住_v <N>机遇_n</N></V> ，_w <开拓进取_l></Fa> ，_w <N><V>建设_v <V>有_v <N>中国_ns 特色_n 社会主义_n</N></V></V> 的_u 道路_n</N> 就_c <V>会_v <Fc>越_d 走_v 越_d 宽广_a</Fc></V> 。_w**</Fm>** **<Fm>**<Fa>*zhiyao*_c <N>*women*_r</N> <R>*jinyibu*_d</R> <*jiefangsixiang*_i ，_w *shishiqiushi*_i> ，_w <V>*zhuazhu*_v <N>*jiyu*_n</N></V> ，_w <*kaituojinqu*_l></Fa> ，_w <N><V>*jianshe*_v <V>*you*_v <N>*Zhongguo*_ns *tese*_n *shehuizhuyi*_n</N></V></V> *de*_u *daolu*_n</N> *jiu*_c <V>*hui*_v <Fc>*yue*_d *zou*_v *yue*_d *kuanguang*_a</Fc></V> 。_w**</Fm>** "If we become more open-minded and realistic and make every effort to explore new possibilities, we are in a better position to set up an ideology which can fully represent Chinese values."
Adverbial Idiom/Set Phrase	Ia	**<Ia>**坚定不移_i 地_u**</Ia>** **<Ia>***jiandingbuyi* _i *de*_u**</Ia>** "persistently"

Nonterminal category	Symbol	Example
		<Ia>满怀信心_l 地_u**</Ia>** **<Ia>***manhuaixinxin*_l *de*_u**</Ia>** "confidently"
Adjective Phrase	J	**<J>**非常_d 重要_a 的_u**</J>** **<J>**很_d 不_d 平凡_a 的_u**</J>** 一_m 年_q **<J>***feichang*_d *zhongyao*_a *de*_u**</J>** **<J>***hen*_d *bu*_d *pingfan*_a *de*_u**</J>** *yi*_m *nian*_q "a very important and extraordinary year"
Adverbial Adjective Phrase	Ja	**<Ja>**成功_a 地_u**</Ja>** <V>召开_v 了_u <N>第十五_m 次_q 全国_n 代表大会_n</N></V> **<Ja>***chenggong*_a *de*_u**</Ja>** <V>*zhaokai*_v *le*_u <N>*dishiwu*_m *ci*_q *Quanguo*_n *Daibiaodahui*_n</N></V> "successfully held the 15th National People's Congress"
Noun Phrase	N	**<N>**百年_m 历史_n**</N>** **<N>***bainian*_m *lishi*_n**</N>** "a hundred years' history"
Adverbial Noun Phrase	Na	**<Na>**今天_t 上午_t**</Na>** **<Na>***jintian*_t *shangwu*_t**</Na>** "this morning" **<Na>**现在_t**</Na>** **<Na>***xianzai*_t**</Na>** "at present"
Prepositional Phrase	P	<S&><N>[中国_ns 政府_n]nt</N> <Ja>顺利_ad</Ja> <V>恢复_v **<P>**对_p <N>香港_ns</N>**</P>** <Vo>行使_v <N>主权_n</N></Vo></V></S&> <S&><N>[*Zhongguo*_ns *Zhengfu*_n]nt</N> <Ja>*shunli*_ad</Ja>

Nonterminal category	Symbol	Example
		<V>*huifu*_v **<P>***dui*_p <N>*Xianggang*_ns</N>**</P>** <Vo>*xingshi*_v <N>*zhuquan*_n</N></Vo></V></S&> "The Chinese government has succeeded in resuming its sovereignty over Hong Kong"
Adverbial Prepositional Phrase	Pa	<S N="7">**<Pa>**在_p <N>这_r 一_m 年_q 中_f</N>**</Pa>** ，_w <N>中国_ns 的_u <N><N&>改革_vn 开放_vn</N&> 和_c <N+>现代化_vn 建设_vn</N+></N></N> <V>继续_v <Vo>向前_v <Vo>迈进_v</Vo></Vo></V> 。_w</S> <S N="7">**<Pa>***zai*_p <N>*zhe*_r *yi*_m *nian*_q *zhong*_f</N>**</Pa>** ，_w <N>*Zhongguo*_ns *de*_u <N><N&>*gaige*_vn *kaifong*_vn</N&> *he*_c <N+>*xiandaihua*_vn *jianshe*_vn</N+></N></N> <V>*jixu*_v <Vo>*xiangqian*_v <Vo>*maijin*_v</Vo></Vo></V> 。_w</S> "In this year, our nation is progressing in our reform and modernisation."
Adverb Phrase	R	**<R>**还_d 不_d**</R>** **<R>***hai*_d *bu*_d**</R>** "not…though"
Sentence (including direct speech quotation, also with & and + as co-ordinates)	S	**<S N="1">**<Pa>在_p <N>这_r 一_m 年_q 中</N>_f</Pa> ，_w <N>中国_ns 的_u 外交_n 工作_vn</N> <V>取得_v 了_u <N>重要_a 成果_n</N></V> 。_w**</S>** **<S N="1">**<Pa>*zai*_p <N>*zhe*_r *yi*_m *nian*_q *zhong*</N>_f</Pa> ，_w <N>*Zhongguo*_ns *de*_u *waijiao*_n

Nonterminal category	Symbol	Example
		*gongzuo*_vn</N> <V>*qude*_v *le*_u <N>*zhongyao*_a *chengguo*_n</N></V> 。_w**</S>** "In this year, the Chinese government has gained great success in its diplomacy."
Verb Phrase	V	**<V>**展望_v <N>新_a 的_u 世纪_n</N>**</V>** **<V>***zhanwang*_v <N>*xin*_a *de*_u *sheji*_n</N>**</V>** "have hope in the new era"
Adverbial Verb Phrase	Va	**<Va>**迈向_v <N><充满_v 希望_n 的_u> １９９８年_t 之际_f</N>**</Va>** **<Va>***maixiang*_v <N><*chongman*_v *xiwang*_n *de*_u> １９９８*nian*_t *zhiji*_f</N>**</Va>** "at the moment we are looking forward to the prosperous year of 1998" **<Va>**退休_v 前_f**</Va>** **<Va>***tuixiu*_v *qian*_f**</Va>** "before retirement"
Verbal Object	Vo	<V>希望_v **<Vo>**依靠_v <N>大家_r</N>**</Vo>**</V> <V>*xiwang*_v **<Vo>***yikao*_v <N>*dajia*_r</N>**</Vo>**</V> "wish to rely on you"
Initial Conjunct	&	**<N&>**中国_ns 改革_v**</N&>** 和_c **<N&>***Zhongguo*_ns *gaige* v**</N&>** *he*_c "China's revolution"
Non-initial Conjunct	+	和_c **<N+>**发展_v 的_u 全局_n**</N+>** *he*_c **<N+>***fazhan*_v *de*_u *quanju*_n**</N+>** "and the entire development"

Table 3: The list of constituent labels for the PFR Sample Skeleton Treebank parsing scheme.

Before dealing with point three (see section 3.5), I would first like to discuss some issues relating to the use of this labelling scheme in my treebank.

3.4.2.1 Selection and coding of parsing labels

The hand-parsing task was simplified as much as possible by the use of a simple bracketing notation. This was used to annotate 17 nonterminal categories which were considered to be "canonical", as Leech and Garside (1991: 22) put it, i.e. likely to be uncontroversial, and to remain unaffected by differences of theory. The following table demonstrates the importance of adopting canonical nonterminal categories, by comparing seven different syntactic theories with respect to their phrasal categories, namely Transformational Grammar or TG (Radford, 1988), Government and Binding Theory or GB (Haegeman, 1994), Generalised Phrase Structure Grammar or GPSG (Gazdar et al., 1985), Head-driven Phrase Structure Grammar or HPSG (Pollard and Sag, 1994), Functional Grammar or FG (Dik, 1978, 1989 and 1997), Lexical-Functional Grammar or LFG (Bresnan, 2001), and Relational Grammar or RG (Blake, 1990). It shows that S, NP, VP, AP, PP and ADVP are the six core phrasal categories that exist among these theories. Additionally, the representation of conjuncts is different across theories: some theories (e.g. TG, GB, LFG, etc.) do not overtly mark the relationship of coordination between phrases, while others (i.e. GPSG and HPSG) represent the conjuncts using different abstract categorial labels. In the light of these differences across theories, in my bracketing system, the six core syntactic categories which are common to almost all of the syntactic theories above were adopted, and simple symbols (i.e. "&" and "+") were used to indicate a coordinate relationship between two or more phrases.

	S	NP	VP	AP	PP	ADVP	DP	IP	CP	X[CONJ NIL], X[CONJ *and*]	RP	[SUBCAT <N>]
TG	+	+	+	+	+	+	+	+	+	–	–	–
GB	+	+	+	+	+	+	+	+	+	–	–	–
GPSG	+	+	+	+	+	+	–	–	–	+	–	–
HPSG	+	+	+	+	+	+	+	–	–	–	+	+
FG	–	+	–	–	+	–	–	–	–	–	–	–
LFG	+	+	+	+	+	+	+	+	+	–	–	–
RG	+	+	+	–	+	–	–	–	–	–	–	–

Table 4: A comparison of phrasal categories in seven syntactic theories.[12]

Apart from these eight canonical nonterminal categories (i.e. six core syntactic categories plus two symbols for initial and non-initial conjuncts), I added six other parsing labels which focussed on the adverbial, i.e. *Fa* (adverbial clause), *Ia* (adverbial idiom/set phrase), *Ja* (adverbial adjective phrase), *Na* (adverbial noun phrase), *Pa* (adverbial prepositional phrase), and *Va* (adverbial verb phrase), because I was particularly interested in adverbials in this book in which adverbial clauses were investigated. To explicitly indicate the clause(s) to which the adverbial clause is subordinated, the constituent label *Fm* which stands for the main clause, was also included in the bracketing system. The last two parsing labels I added were correlative clause, *Fc*, and verbal object, *Vo*, which are specific to the Chinese language (see section 3.5.1.2 and 3.5.1.15).

Like the parsing symbols used for the Lancaster/IMB Treebank, the distinction between constituent tags and word tags is reflected in their coding: nonterminal categories (or syntactic constituents) consist of one upper case letter, optionally followed by one lower case letter

12 "+" indicates that the syntactic theory has the phrasal category, while "–" indicates that it does not. S stands for sentence; NP stands for noun phrase; VP stands for verb phrase; AP stands for adjective phrase; PP stands for prepositional phrase; ADVP stands for adverb phrase; DP stands for determiner phrase; IP stands for a clause with inflection (INFL) as its head; CP stands for a clause with complementiser (C) as its head; X[CONJ NIL] stands for an initial conjunct of any phrasal category (X), while X[CONJ and] stands for a final conjunct of any phrasal category (X); RP stands for any phrase projected from a relativiser; [SUBCAT <N>] stands for both the initial and final conjuncts which belong to the same phrasal category and thus must be marked with the same number N.

(representing feature values), e.g. "N" stands for noun phrase, "Na" refers to adverbial noun phrase, etc.; and terminal categories (or word classes), on the other hand, include just one or two lower case letters or one captial letter followed by one lower case letter, e.g. "n" for noun, "ns" for place name, "Ng" for "nominal morpheme".[13]

As we have seen, upper case letters were used to represent the constituent labels. However, the reverse happens in the annotation standard established by the Text Encoding Initiative (TEI): parsing labels are represented by lower case letters (rather than upper case ones as I used here), and POS tags are denoted by upper case letters. Since the compilers of the PFR Chinese Corpus used small letters to represent POS tags (Yu, 1999), in order to distinguish from the originally marked POS annotation, I use capital letters for the parsing labels, though I am aware that this goes against the TEI guidelines. It does, however, improve the readability of my treebank.

3.4.2.2 Set of annotation devices used

It is important to note that in my annotation scheme, the labels used to mark the grammatical structure of a sentence are not enclosed in a pair of square brackets as in the UCREL format (Leech and Garside, 1991); rather they are circumscribed by angled brackets as I wished to provide my treebank in a TEI-conformant interchange format, i.e. the syntactic information is enclosed using XML tags delimited by <…> and </…>. The reason for adopting this TEI-conformant style rather than the UCREL labelled-bracketing format is that the resulting skeleton parsed sample corpus can then be more readily re-used by many different users developing or testing natural language processing (NLP) software of varied kinds, for example, then would be possible using a "bespoke" format.

13 As we have seen, both the adverbials (e.g. adverbial noun phrase (*Na*)) and morphemes (e.g. nominal morpheme (*Ng*)) have the same coding format i.e. a capital letter followed by a lower case letter. However, as the latter is rare, syntactic tags (my annotation) and word tags (original annotation) are contrasting visually in most parts of my treebank.

3.4.2.3 Insertion of textual annotations

As the original PFR Chinese Corpus does not provide any textual markup such as the title of a text, this information was inserted in my sample treebank using TEI markup elements.[14] The following gives the various kinds of information added:

(a) <CAPTION> </CAPTION> contains the text of a caption of an illustration or a photograph printed in the original newspaper
(b) <DATE> </DATE> gives the date of an event described in the body of a text
(c) <ILLUSTRATION> </ILLUSTRATION> indicates an illustration or a photograph in the original text
(d) <JOURNALIST> </JOURNALIST> encloses a journalist's name
(e) <NAME> </NAME> indicates a proper noun referring to a person, a place or an organisation mentioned in the header
(f) <ORIGINALMP> </ORIGINALMP> encloses the original markup of the PFR Chinese Corpus, which includes the date, page no., article no. and paragraph no. of the newspaper text
(g) <SOURCEDESC> </SOURCEDESC> identifies the source of a text
(h) <SUBTITLE> </SUBTITLE> denotes a subtitle in a text
(i) <TITLE> </TITLE> encloses the title or headline of a text
(j) <UNCERTAIN> </UNCERTAIN> indicates an unknown unit in the text
(k) N="..." provides a sentence number

3.4.2.4 Layers of annotation undertaken

The EAGLES documentation (Kahrel et al., 1997: 237ff.) specifies a number of different layers of annotation, the first and second of which were adopted in my skeleton parsing scheme. The first layer, bracketing of segments, involves the delimitation of sentence segments which have a "syntactic integrity" (e.g. sentences, clauses, phrases, words) by nested pairs of angled brackets. The second layer, labelling of segments, indi-

14 These textual markers are based on the elements proposed in the guidelines of the Text Encoding Initiative (Sperberg-McQueen and Burnard (Eds.), 2001), except <ILLUSTRATION>, <JOURNALIST>, <ORIGINALMP> and <SUBTITLE> which have been invented for the purposes of this research.

cates the formal category of the non-terminal syntactic constituents identified by bracketing, such as noun phrase, verb phrase, adverbial clause, etc.

The other six layers, due to the complexity of analysis which they entail, were ignored for the purposes of this research. For the record, these unannotated layers would show: the relation of a head to its dependent(s) in a phrase or clause, syntactic function labels (e.g. subject, object, adjunct, etc.), subcategorisation or feature values of sentences (e.g. declarative, imperative, interrogative) and phrases (e.g. marking noun phrase as singular), deep/logical relations (e.g. co-referentiality, ellipsis, traces, etc.), ranking of syntactic categories (e.g. phrases being of lower rank than clauses, clauses being of lower rank than sentences), non-fluency phenomena (e.g. false starts, reiterations, etc.).

3.5. Guidelines of skeleton parsing

Having reviewed my annotation scheme in some depth, I can now present my guidelines for annotation, in keeping with my desire to match the advantages of Sampson's SUSANNE scheme (see section 3.4.2). The parsing scheme matches features (a) and (b) of a clear and explicit parsing scheme (Leech and Eyes, 1997: 37). Nonetheless, an annotation scheme is more than (a) and (b) above. Feature (c), a set of *parsing guidelines* should also be provided in order to explain how the parsing symbols are actually applied to text sentences to avoid undesirable inconsistency. Ideally, complete guidelines should be available to the annotators before annotation begins. However, linguistic problems posed by corpora are much more diverse and complicated than those discussed in theoretical linguistics or grammar books, and new problems arise as more data is annotated. Hence, the guidelines must be revised, updated and enriched incrementally as the annotation process progresses. Such guidelines are likened to case law as it represents a continuously refined system which changes as new cases occur, rather than a set of unchanging hard and fast rules.

During the course of annotation, as more data was analysed, the guidelines took shape and were recorded and updated. Hence, after I finished the task of parsing a sample text taken from the PFR Chinese

Corpus, I had a set of guidelines ready to be consolidated into a document to be available to users of the treebank and to future annotators who might want to adopt the same scheme. It is advisable, as Kahrel et al. (1997: 241 ff.) note, to document explicitly all of the decisions taken in the development of an annotation scheme, as well as its application so that future users can apply the scheme in a manner consistent with that of the originators of the scheme.

In section 3.5.1, I will give a clear account of the 17 non-terminal constituents that are defined and instantiated in my texts, with illustrative examples taken from the parsed sample treebank as well as an explanation of problem cases. Apart from a detailed treatment of parsing symbols[15], my documented parsing guidelines include practical issues related to map any parses on to sentences in the application of the parsing scheme, which will be discussed in section 3.5.2.

3.5.1 Detailed description of parsing symbols

3.5.1.1 Adverbial clause (Fa)

An adverbial clause functions as an adjunct. The occurrence of an adverbial clause, which is a type of subordinate clause, is dependent on that of a main clause which it modifies. However, omission of the adverbial clause does not affect the grammaticality of the main clause (Hengeveld, 1998; Quintero, 2002).

(2) <Fm>**<Fa>**只有_c <解放思想_i 、_w 实事求是_i>**</Fa>** ，_w 才_c <V>能_v 冲破_v <N>各种_r <<不_d 切合_v 实际_n 的_u 或者_c 过时_a 的_u> 观念_n 的_u> 束缚_vn</N></V> ，_w <R>真正_d</R> <V>做到_v <V><尊重_v 、_w 认识_v 和_c 掌握_v> <N>客观_a 规律_n</N></V></V> ，_w <R>勇于_d</R> <V>突破_v</V> ，_w <R>勇于_d</R> <V>创新_v</V> ，_w <R>不断_d</R> <V>开创_v <N><社会主义_n 现代化_vn 建设_vn 的_u> 新_a 局面_n</N></V></Fm>

15 When writing this detailed description, I was informed by the EAGLES Recommendations for the Syntactic Annotation of Corpora, Version of 11th March 1996. See Leech, Barnett and Kahrel (1996) available at EAGLES's web page: <http://www.ilc.cnr.it/EAGLES96/segsasg1/segsasg1.html> (accessed 15 May 2012).

<Fm>**<Fa>***zhiyou*_c <*jiefangsixiang*_i 、_w *shishiqiushi*_i>**</Fa>** ，_w
only.if be.open-minded realistic
*cai*_c <V>*neng*_v *chongpo*_v <N>*gezhong*_r <<*bu*_d *qiehe*_v
then can get.rid.of different.kinds.of not in.line.with
*shiji*_n *de*_u> *huozhe*_c <*guoshi*_a *de*_u *guannian*_n
pragmatism DE or obsolete DE values
*de*_u>> *shufu*_vn</N></V> ，_w <R>*zhenzheng*_d</R> <V>*zuodao*_v
DE restriction really realise
<V><*zhuanzhong*_v 、_w *renshi*_v *he*_c *zhangwo*_v> <N>*keguan*_a
respect understand and master practical
*guilü*_n</N></V></V> ，_w <R>*yongyu*_d</R> <V>*tupo*_v</V> ，_w
principles have.the.guts.to breakthrough
<R>*yongyu*_d</R> <V>*chuangxin*_v</V> ，_w <R>*buduan*_d</R>
have.the.guts.to break.fresh.ground continuously
<V>*kaichuang*_v <N><*shehuizhuyi*_n *xiandaihua*_vn *jianshe*_vn *de*_u>
create social.ideology modern construction DE
*xin*_a *jiumian*_n</N></V></Fm>
new situation
"Only if we become more open-minded and realistic, can we overcome the restrictions imposed by outdated practices, and know how to respect, understand and take advantage of what we learn in everyday life, thereby breaking through and continuously building an efficient modern society."

(3) <S N="21"><Fm>**<Fa>**只要_c <N>我们_r</N> <R>进一步_d</R> <解放思想_i ，_w 实事求是_i> ，_w <V>抓住_v <N>机遇_n</N></V> ，_w <开拓进取_l>**</Fa>** ，_w <N><建设_v 有_v 中国_ns 特色_n 社会主义_n 的_u> 道路_n</N> 就_c <V>会_v <Fc>越_d 走_v 越_d 宽广_a</Fc></V> 。_w</Fm></S>
<S N="21"><Fm>**<Fa>***zhiyao* _c <N>*women*_r</N> <R>*jinyibu*_d</R>
provided.that we further
<*jiefangsixiang*_i ，_w *shishiqiushi*_i> ，_w <V>*zhuazhu*_v
be.open-minded realistic grasp
<N>*jiyu*_n</N></V> ，_w <*kaituojinqu*_l>**</Fa>** ，_w <N><*jianshe*_v
opportunity work.hard.and.explore establish
*you*_v *Zhongguo*_ns *tese*_n *shehuizhuyi*_n *de*_u>
have China characteristics social.ideology DE

*daolu*_n</N> *jiu*_c <V>*hui*_v <Fc>*yue*_d *zou*_v *yue*_d
road then will the.more walk the.more
*kuanguang*_a</Fc></V> 。_w</Fm></S>
broad
"If we become more open-minded and realistic, and grasp every chance to explore new possibilities, we can come closer to building a society fully representing our national characteristics."

The first clauses of the following two sentences and sentences like them, however, were not accepted by me as adverbial clauses proper, though some scholars may accept them as such (e.g. Rai-Chu, 1982: 21–30; Liu et al., 1996: 505–513; Chu and Chi, 1999: 248f.). I did not consider them as adverbial clauses because these clauses do not show any explicit sign of their dependence on a main clause, i.e. the following clause. Chao (1968: 104–106) treats such kind of sentences as coordinate sentences or even separate sentences. As will be discussed in the next chapter (Chapter Four, section 4.1), English adverbial clauses, if not overtly marked by a subordinating conjunction to be subordinate clauses, are always non-finite clauses. Chinese adverbial clauses or clauses in general, however, do not have this finite/non-finite distinction (Norman, 1988: 163). Since it is not clear whether the first clauses of the following examples are subordinate clauses, they were not taken as adverbial clauses in my treebank.

(4) <S N="57"><R>进一步_d</R> <Ja>认真_ad</Ja> <V><学习_v 和_c 掌握_v> <N>十五大_j 精神_n</N></V> ，_w <解放思想_i 、_w 实事求是_i> ，_w <N>我们_r 的_u 各项_r 事业_n</N> <R>就_d</R> <V>能_v 结_v 出_v <N><更加_d 丰硕_a 的_u> 成果_n</N></V> 。_w</S>
<S N="57"><R>*jinyibu*_d</R> <Ja>*renzhen*_ad</Ja> <V><*xuexi*_v *he*_c
further seriously learn and
*zhangwo*_v> <N>*shiwuda*_j *jingshen*_n</N></V> ，_w
master 15.primary principles
<*jiefangsixiang*_i 、_w *shishiqiushi*_i> ，_w <N>*women*_r *de*_u
be.open.minded realistic our GEN
*gexiang*_r *shiye*_n</N> <R>*jiu*_d</R> <V>*neng*_v *jie*_v *chu*_v
various.kinds.of undertaking then can result.in out

<N><*gengjia*_d *fengshuo*_a *de*_u> *chengguo*_n</N></V> 。_w</S>
even.more promising result

"If we can better understand and master the Communist Party's 15 principles and become more open-minded and realistic, we can gain greater success in every venture we make."

(5) <S N="114"><Na>现在_t</Na> <N>条件_n</N> <J>好_a 了_y</J> ，_w 但_c <N><艰苦奋斗_i 、_w 无私奉献_i 的_u> 精神_n</N> <R>可_d</R> <V>不能_v 丢_v</V> 。_w ”_w</S>

<S N="114"><Na>*xianzai*_t</Na> <N>*tiaojian*_n</N> <J>*hao*_a
at.present condition better

*le*_y</J> ，_w *dan*_c <N><*jiankufengdou*_i 、_w
PERF but work.hard

*wusifengxian*_i *de*_u> *jingshen*_n</N> <R>*ke*_d</R>
contribute.unconditionally DE spirit yet

<V>*buneng*_v *diao*_v</V> 。_w ”_w</S>
cannot lose

"Although the situation is improved, we must continue to strive hard and contribute to our society unconditionally."

3.5.1.2 Correlative clause (Fc)

The term "correlative clause" is proposed by Chao (1968: 121 ff.) to refer to two coordinated clauses which are in parallel, in contrast, or in some other close relation, making a pair of dependent clauses typically marked by the correlative adverbs 越 *yue* … 越 *yue* "the more…, the more…" and repeated interrogative indefinite pronouns. The last two examples below are taken from Chao's analysis (1968: 121–122) as no examples of this sort can be found in my sample treebank.

(6) <S N="21"><Fm><Fa>只要_c <N>我们_r</N> <R>进一步_d</R> <解放思想_i ，_w 实事求是_i> ，_w <V>抓住_v <N>机遇_n</N></V> ，_w <开拓进取_l></Fa> ，_w <N><建设_v 有_v 中国_ns 特色_n 社会主义_n 的_u> 道路_n</N> 就_c <V>会_v **<Fc>**越_d 走_v 越_d 宽广_a**</Fc>**</V> 。_w</Fm></S>

<S N="21"><Fm><Fa>*zhiyao* _c <N>*women*_r</N> <R>*jinyibu*_d</R>
provided.that we further

<*jiefangsixiang*_i ，_w *shishiqiushi*_i> ，_w <V>*zhuazhu*_v
be.open-minded realistic grasp
<N>*jiyu*_n</N></V> ，_w <*kaituojinqu*_l></Fa> ，_w <N><*jianshe*_v
opportunity work.hard.and.explore establish
*you*_v *Zhongguo*_ns *tese*_n *shehuizhuyi*_n *de*_u> *daolu*_n</N>
have China characteristics social.ideology DE road
*jiu*_c <V>*hui*_v **<Fc>***yue*_d *zou*_v *yue*_d *kuanguang*_a**</Fc>**</V> 。
then will the.more walk the.more broad
_w</Fm></S>
"If we become more open-minded and realistic, and grasp every chance to explore new possibilities, we can come closer to building a society fully representing our national characteristics."

(7) **<Fc>**谁 先 来 谁 先 吃。**</Fc>**
<Fc>*Shui* *xian* *lai* *shui* *xian* *chi***</Fc>**
who early come who early eat
"Whoever comes first eats first."

(8) **<Fc>**哪儿 舒服 哪儿 睡。**</Fc>**
<Fc>*Naer* *shufu* *naer* *shui***</Fc>**
wherever comfortable wherever sleep
"Sleep wherever it is comfortable."

3.5.1.3 Main clause (Fm)

A main clause is the clause(s) which the adverbial clause is subordinated to and modifies.[16]

(9) <S N="20">**<Fm>**<Fa>尽管_c <N>我们_r</N> <P>在_p <N>经济_n 社会_n 发展_v 中_f</N></P> <R>还_d</R> <V>面临_v <N>不少_m 困难_an</N></V></Fa> ，_w 但_c <N>我们_r</N> <V>有_v <N>邓小

16 Although in examples (3) and (9) the main clause is the same as the sentence, this does not necessarily happen as in example (2), where the main clause is part of the whole sentence only. I distinguished main clause from sentence because in some cases like example (2), some clauses of the sentence (i.e. those clauses which are not included in the main clause) are hardly semantically relevant to the meaning of the adverbial clause.

平理论_n 的_u 指引_vn</N></V> ，_w <V>有_v <N><改革_v 开放
_v 近_a ２０_m 年_q 来_f> <N><N&>取得_v 的_u 伟大_a 成就
_n</N&> 和_c <N+>积累_v 的_u 丰富_a 经验
_n</N+></N></N></V> ，_w <R>还_d</R> <V>有_v <N>其他_r 的_u
各种_r 有利_a 条件_n</N></V> ，_w <N>我们_r</N> <R>一定_d</R>
<V>能够_v 克服_v <N>这些_r 困难_an</N></V> ，_w <V>继续_v <
稳步前进_l></V> 。_w**</Fm>**</S>
<S N="20">**<Fm>**<Fa>*jinguan*_c <N>*women*_r</N> <P>*zai*_p
even.though we in
<N>*jingji*_n *shehui*_n *fazhan*_v *zhong*_f</N></P> <R>*hai*_d</R>
economic society development within still
<V>*mianlin*_v <N>*bushao*_m *kunnan*_an</N></V></Fa> ，_w
face quite.a.number.of difficulties
*dan*_c <N>*women*_r</N> <V>*you*_v <N>*Dengxiaopinglilun*_n
but we have the.principles.of.Deng.Xiaoping
*de*_u *zhiyin*_vn</N></V> ，_w <V>*you*_v <N><*gaige*_v *kaifang*_v
DE instruction have reform open-up
*jin*_a ２０_m *nian*_q *lai*_f> <N><N&>*qude*_v *de*_u *weida*_a
near 20 years so.far obtain DE great
*chengjiu*_n</N&> *he*_c <N+>*jilei*_v *de*_u *fengfu*_a
achievements and accumulate DE rich
*jingyan*_n</N+></N></N></V> ，_w <R>*hai*_d</R> <V>*you*_v
experience additionally have
<N>*qita*_r *de*_u *gezhong*_r *youli*_a *tiaojian*_n</N></V> ，
other DE various.kinds.of advantageous conditions
_w <N>*women*_r</N> <R>*yiding*_d</R> <V>*nenggou*_v *kefu*_v
we certainly can overcome
<N>*zhexie*_r *kunnan*_an</N></V> ，_w <V>*jixu*_v
these difficulties continue
<*wenbuqianjin*_l></V> 。_w**</Fm>**</S>
proceed.steadily
"Although we are still encountering enormous difficulties in developing our economy, we can seek help from the set of principles established by our former president Deng Xiaoping, and benefit from the success of reform and open policy throughout the past 20 years, our own rich experience and many other advantageous factors, we must definitely get over all these difficulties and proceed ahead steadily."

3.5.1.4 Adverbial idiom/set phrase (Ia)

An adverbial idiom or set phrase functions as a modifier of a verb phrase.

(10) <S N="19"><Na>１９９８年_t</Na> ，_w <N>中国_ns 人民_n</N> <R>将_d</R> **<Ia>**满怀信心_l 地_u**</Ia>** <V>开创_v <N>新_a 的_u 业绩_n</N></V> 。_w</S>

<S N="19"><Na>１９９８*nian*_t</Na> ，_w <N>*Zhongguo*_ns
year.of.1998 China
*renmin*_n</N> <R>*jiang*_d</R> **<Ia>***manhuaixinxin*_l *de*_u**</Ia>**
citizens soon confidently ADVL
<V>*kaichuang*_v <N>*xin*_a *de*_u *yeji*_n</N></V> 。_w</S>
create new DE accomplishment
"In 1998, the Chinese people will have confidence in achieving great success."

(11) <S N="42"><Pa>在_p <N>这_r 一_m 年_q</N></Pa> ，_w <P>以_p <N>江_nr 泽民_nr 同志_n</N></P> <V>为_v <N>核心_n 的_u 党中央_nt</N></V> ，_w <V>继承_v <N><邓_nr 小平_nr 同志_n 的_u> 遗志_n</N></V> ，_w <V>高举_v <N>邓小平理论_n 的_u 伟大_a 旗帜_n</N></V> ，_w <V><V&>领导_v <N><N&>全党_n</N&> 和_c <N+>全国_n 各族_r 人民_n</N+></N></V&> <V+>**<Ia>**坚定不移_i 地_u**</Ia>** <P>沿着_p <N><V>建设_v <N><有_v 中国_ns 特色_n> 社会主义_n</N></V> 道路_n</N></P> <R>阔步_d</R> 前进_v</V+></V> ，_w <V>写_v 下_v 了_u <N><改革_v 开放_v 和_c 社会主义_n 现代化_vn 建设_vn 的_u> 辉煌_a 篇章_n</N></V> 。_w</S>

<S N="42"><Pa>*zai*_p <N>*zhe*_r *yi*_m *nian*_q</N></Pa> ，_w
in this one year
<P>*yi*_p <N>*Jiang*_nr *Zemin*_nr *tongzhi*_n</N></P> <V>*wei*_v
with Jiang Zemin comrade to.be
<N>*hexin*_n *de*_u *dangzhongyang*_nt</N></V> ，_w <V>*jicheng*_v
core DE central.government take.over
<N><*Deng*_nr *Xiaoping*_nr *tongzhi*_n *de*_u> *yizhe*_n</N></V> ，_w
Deng Xiaoping comrade's GEN wish
<V>*gaoju*_v <N>*Dengxiaopinglilun*_n *de*_u *weida*_a
hold the.principles.of.Deng.Xiaoping DE great

*qizhi*_n</N></V> ，_w <V><V&>*lingdao*_v
flag lead
<N><N&>*quandang*_n</N&> *he*_c <N+>*quanguo*_n
the.whole.party and across.the.country
*gezu*_r *renmin*_n</N+></N></V&>
various.ethnic.communities citizens
<V+>**<Ia>***jiandingbuyi*_i *de*_u**</Ia>** <P>*yuanzhe*_p <N><V>*jianshe*_v
persistently ADVL along build
<N><*you*_v *Zhongguo*_ns *tese*_n> *shehuizhuyi*_n</N></V>
have China characteristics social.ideology
*daolu*_n</N></P> <R>*kuobu*_d</R> *qianjin*_v</V+></V> ，_w
road take.a.big.step proceed
<V>*xie*_v *xia*_v *le*_u <N><*gaige*_v *kaifang*_v *he*_c *shehuizhuyi*_n
write down PERF reform open-up and social.ideology
*xiandaihua*_vn *jianshe*_vn *de*_u> *huihuang*_a *pianzhang*_n</N></V> 。
modern construction DE magnificent page
_w</S>

"In this year, led by our President Jiang Zemin, the Communist Party followed the principles established by our former president Deng Xiaoping, persistently leading its members and our people towards a better society and thus erecting a milestone of reform and modernisation."

3.5.1.5 Adjective phrase (J)

An adjective phrase consists of an adjective, optionally followed by the adjectival marker 的 *de* (Zhu, 2000), or a group of words (including adverbs) in which an adjective is the head of the phrase.

(12) <S N="31"><N><和平_n 与_c 发展_vn 的_u> 前景_n</N> <V>是_v
<J>光明_a 的_u**</J>**</V> ，_w <N>２１_m 世纪_n</N> <R>将_d</R>
<V>是_v <N><充满_v 希望_n 的_u> 世纪_n</N></V> 。_w</S>
<S N="31"><N><*heping*_n *yu*_c *fazhan*_vn *de*_u> *qianjing*_n</N>
peace and development DE prospects
<V>*shi*_v **<J>***guangming*_a *de*_u**</J>**</V> ，_w <N>２１_m
be bright PART 21

*shiji*_n</N> <R>*jiang*_d</R> <V>*shi*_v <N><*chongman*_v *xiwang*_n
century soon be full.of hope
*de*_u> *shiji*_n</N></V> 。_w</S>
DE century
"The prospects of maintaining peace and development are encouraging, making the 21st century a promising era."

(13) <S N="32">但_c <N>前进_v 的_u 道路_n</N> <V><V><V&>不会_v</V&> <R>也_d</R> <V+><R>不_d</R> 可能_v</V+></V> <一帆风顺_i></V> ，_w <N>关键_n</N> <V>是_v <S><N>世界_n 各国_r 人民_n</N> <V>要_v **<J>**进一步_d 团结_a 起来_v**</J>**</V></S></V> ，_w <V><V><V&><R>共同_d</R> 推动_v</V&> <V+><R>早日_d</R> 建立_v</V+></V> <N><公正_a 合理_a 的_u> 国际_n 政治_n 经济_n 新_a 秩序_n</N></V> 。_w</S>
<S N="32">*dan*_c <N>*qianjin*_v *de*_u *daolu*_n</N>
however proceed DE road
<V><V><V&>*buhui*_v</V&> <R>*ye*_d</R> <V+><R>*bu*_d</R>
will.not as.well.as not
*keneng*_v</V+></V> <*yifanfengshun*_i></V> ，_w <N>*guanjian*_n</N>
can smooth the.key.to.success
<V>*shi*_v <S><N>*shijie*_n *geguo*_r *renmin*_n</N> <V>*yao*_v
be world nations people have.to
<J>*jinyibu*_d *tuanjie*_a *qilai*_v**</J>**</V></S></V> ，_w
further unite stand.up
<V><V><V&><R>*gongtong*_d</R> *tuidong*_v</V&>
together uphold
<V+><R>*zaori*_d</R> *jianli*_v</V+></V> <N><*gongzheng*_a
as.soon.as.possible build just
*heli*_a *de*_u> *guoji*_n *zhengzhi*_n *jingji*_n *xin*_a
reasonable DE international political economic new
*zhixu*_n</N></V> 。_w</S>
order
"Yet progress will not come easily without people from all over the world combining efforts in building a fair and just global political and economic climate."

(14) <S N="71"><N>这_r</N> <V>是_v **<J>**非常_d 重要_a 的
_u**</J>**</V> 。_w</S>
<S N="71"><N>*zhe*_r</N> <V>*shi*_v **<J>***feichang*_d *zhongyao*_a
this be extremely important
*de*_u**</J>**</V> 。_w</S>
PART
"This is very important indeed."

3.5.1.6 Adverbial adjective phrase (Ja)

An adverbial adjective phrase functions as a modifier of a verb phrase, and may optionally be followed by the particle 地 *de* which is the adverbial marker in Chinese (Zhu, 1982).

(15) <S N="6"><N>[中国_ns 共产党_n]nt</N> **<Ja>**成功_a 地_u**</Ja>** <V>
召开_v 了_u <N>第十五_m 次_q 全国_n 代表大会_n</N></V> ，_w
<V>高举_v <N>邓小平理论_n 伟大_a 旗帜_n</N></V> ，_w <V>总结
_v <N>百年_m 历史_n</N></V> ，_w <V>展望_v <N>新_a 的_u
世纪_n</N></V> ，_w <V>制定_v 了_u <N><中国_ns 跨_v 世纪_n
发展_v 的_u> 行动_vn 纲领_n</N></V> 。_w</S>
<S N="6"><N>[*Zhongguo*_ns *Gongchandang*_n]nt</N> **<Ja>***chenggong*_a
China the.Communist.Party successfully
*de*_u**</Ja>** <V>*zhaokai*_v *le*_u <N>*dishiwu*_m *ci*_q *quanguo*_n
ADVL hold PERF the.15th CL national
*daibiaodahui*_n</N></V> ，_w <V>*gaoju*_v
congress hold
<N>*Dengxiaopinglilun*_n *weida*_a *qizhi*_n</N></V> ，_w
the.principles.of.Deng.Xiaoping great flag
<V>*zongjie*_v <N>*bainian*_m *lishi*_n</N></V> ，_w <V>*zhanwang*_v
conclude hundred.years history look.forward.to
<N>*xin*_a *de*_u *shiji*_n</N></V> ，_w <V>*zhiding*_v *le*_u
new DE century stipulate PERF
<N><*Zhongguo*_ns *kua*_v *shiji*_n *fazhan*_v *de*_u> *xingdong*_vn
China beyond century develop DE action
*gangling*_n</N></V> 。_w</S>
scheme

"The Communist Party of the People's Republic of China successfully held the 15th Annual General Meeting, reiterating the principles established by our former president Deng Xiaoping, summarising its success in the past hundred years, igniting hope in the new era, and laying down plans for future development of the country."

(16) <S N="17"><N>中国_ns</N> **<Ja>**积极_ad**</Ja>** <V>参与_v <N>[亚_j 太_j 经合_j 组织_n]nt 的_u 活动_vn</N></V> ，_w <V>参加_v 了_u <N><N><N&>东盟_ns —_w 中_j 日_j 韩_j </N&>和_c <N+>中国_ns —_w 东盟_ns 首脑_n</N+></N> 非正式_b 会晤_vn</N></V> 。_w</S>

<S N="17"><N>*Zhongguo*_ns</N> **<Ja>***jiji*_ad**</Ja>** <V>*canyu*_v
China actively take.part.in
<N>[*Ya*_j *Tai*_j *Jinghe*_j *Zuzhi*_n]nt *de*_u
Asia Pacific Economic.Co-operation organisation DE
*huodong*_vn</N></V> ，_w <V>*canjia*_v *le*_u
activity take.part.in PERF
<N><N><N&>*Dongmeng*_ns —_w *Zhong*_j *Ri*_j *Han*_j </N&>*he*_c
eastern.coalition China Japan Korea and
<N+>*Zhongguo*_ns —_w *Dongmeng*_ns *shounao*_n</N+></N>
China eastern.coalition leading.role
*feizhengshi*_b *huiwu*_vn</N></V> 。_w</S>
informal dialogue
"China took an active role in the activities organised by the Asia Pacific Economic Co-operation (APEC) and participated in the informal meeting with leaders of Japan and Korea."

(17) <S N="53"><N>我们_r</N> <V>要_v **<Ja>**更_d 好_a 地_u**</Ja>** <V>坚持_v <N><解放思想 i 、_w 实事求是_i 的_u> 思想_n 路线_n</N></V></V> 。_w</S>

<S N="53"><N>*women*_r</N> <V>*yao*_v **<Ja>***geng*_d *hao*_a
we have.to more good
*de*_u**</Ja>** <V>*jianchi*_v <N><*jiefangsixiang*_i 、_w *shishiqiushi*_i
ADVL insist.on be.open-minded realistic
*de*_u> *sixiang*_n *luxian*_n</N></V></V> 。_w</S>
DE ideology route
"We must closely follow the ideology of opening our mind and being more realistic."

3.5.1.7 Noun phrase (N)

A noun phrase generally has a noun or a pronoun as its head which may be preceded by determinative elements and/or premodifiers typically marked by the particle 的 *de*.

(18) <S N="29">但是_c ，_w **<N>**世界_n**</N>** <R>还_d 不_d</R> <J>安宁_a</J> 。_w</S>

<S N="29">*danshi*_c ，_w **<N>***shijie*_n**</N>** <R>*hai*_d *bu*_d</R>
however world still not
<J>*anning*_a</J> 。_w</S>
tranquil
"Nevertheless, the world is not in peace."

(19) <S N="53">**<N>**我们_r**</N>** <V>要_v <Ja>更_d 好_a 地_u</Ja> <V>坚持_v <N><解放思想_i 、_w 实事求是_i 的_u> 思想_n 路线_n</N></V></V> 。_w</S>

<S N="53">**<N>***women*_r**</N>** <V>*yao*_v <Ja>*geng*_d *hao*_a *de*_u</Ja>
we have.to more good ADVL
<V>*jianchi*_v <N><*jiefangsixiang*_i 、_w *shishiqiushi*_i *de*_u>
insist.on be.open-minded realistic DE
*sixiang*_n *luxian*_n</N></V></V> 。_w</S>
ideology route
"We must closely follow the ideology of opening our mind and being more realistic."

(20) <S N="22">**<N>**<实现_v 祖国_n 的_u> 完全_a 统一_vn**</N>** ，_w <V>是_v **<N>**<海内外_s 全体_n 中国_ns 人_n 的_u> 共同_b 心愿_n**</N>**</V> 。_w</S>

<S N="22">**<N>**<*shixian*_v *zuguo*_n *de*_u> *wanquan*_a
realise motherland DE complete
*tongyi*_vn**</N>** ，_w <V>*shi*_v **<N>**<*haineiwai*_s *quanti*_n
unification be local.and.overseas the.whole.group
*Zhongguo*_ns *ren*_n *de*_u> *gongtong*_b *xinyuan*_n**</N>**</V> 。_w</S>
China people DE shared wish
"Uniting the country entirely has long been the goal of both local and overseas Chinese people."

3.5.1.8 Adverbial noun phrase (Na)

An adverbial noun phrase functions as an adjunct in a sentence.

(21) <S N="19">**<Na>**１９９８年_t**</Na>** ，_w <N>中国_ns 人民_n</N>
<R>将_d</R> <Ia>满怀信心_l 地_u</Ia> <V>开创_v <N>新_a 的_u
业绩_n</N></V> 。_w</S>
<S N="19">**<Na>**１９９８*nian*_t**</Na>** ，_w <N>*Zhongguo*_ns
year.of.1998 China
*renmin*_n</N> <R>*jiang*_d</R> <Ia>*manhuaixinxin*_l *de*_u</Ia>
citizens soon confidently ADVL
<V>*kaichuang*_v <N>*xin*_a *de*_u *yeji*_n</N></V> 。_w</S>
create new DE success
"In 1998, the Chinese people will have confidence in achieving great success."

(22) <S N="104">**<Na>**现在_t**</Na>** ，_w <N>我们_r 的_u 首都_n</N>
<R>已经_d</R> <V>结束_v 了_u <N><拉_v 闸_n 限_v 电_n 的
_u> 历史_n</N></V> ，_w <V>希望_v <Vo>依靠_v <N>大家
_r</N></Vo></V> ，_w <V>使_v <N><拉_v 闸_n 限_v 电_n 的_u>
历史_n</N> <V><R>永远_d 不再_d</R> 重演_v</V></V> 。_w </S>
<S N="104">**<Na>***xianzai*_t**</Na>** ，_w <N>*women*_r *de*_u
at.present our GEN
*shoudu*_n</N> <R>*yijing*_d</R> <V>*jieshu*_v *le*_u <N><*la*_v *zha*_n
capital already end PERF pull barrier
*xian*_v *dian*_n *de*_u> *lishi*_n</N></V> ，_w <V>*xiwang*_v
limit electricity DE history hope
<Vo>*yikao*_v <N>*dajia*_r</N></Vo></V> ，_w <V>*shi*_v <N><*la*_v
count.on you make pull
*zha*_n *xian*_v *dian*_n *de*_u> *lishi*_n</N> <V><R>*yongyuan*_d
barrier limit electricity DE history forever
*buzai*_d</R> *chongyan*_v</V></V> 。_w </S>
never repeat
"Nowadays, a limited supply of electricity no longer occurs. However, I hope everybody can do their best to avoid a repetition of this event."

3.5.1.9 Prepositional phrase (P)

A prepositional phrase is made up of a preposition and its complement. The complement of a preposition is usually a noun phrase, but it can also be a verb phrase or a clause.

(23) <S N="39"><N>我们_r </N> <R>即将_d</R> **<P>**以_p <N>丰收_vn 的_u 喜悦_an</N>**</P>** <V>送_v 走_v <N>牛年_t</N></V> ，_w **<P>**以_p <N>昂扬_a 的_u 斗志_n</N>**</P>** <V>迎来_v <N>虎年_t</N></V> 。_w</S>

<S N="39"><N>*women*_r </N> <R>*jijiang*_d</R> **<P>***yi*_p
we imminently with
<N>*fengshou*_vn *de*_u *xiyue*_an</N>**</P>** <V>*song*_v *zou*_v
fruitful DE joy farewell walk
<N>*Niunian*_t</N></V> ，_w **<P>***yi*_p <N>*angyang*_a *de*_u
Year.of.Ox in high DE
*douzhi*_n</N>**</P>** <V>*yinglai*_v <N>*Hunian*_t</N></V> 。_w</S>
spirits welcome Year.of.Tiger

"We are going to bid farewell to the Year of Ox joyfully and welcome the arrival of the Year of Tiger in high spirits."

(24) <S N="18"><N>这些_r 外交_n 活动_vn</N> ，_w <V>符合_v <N><和平_n 与_c 发展_v 的_u> 时代_n 主题_n</N></V> ，_w <V>顺应_v <N><世界_n 走向_v 多极化_v 的_u> 趋势_n</N></V> ，_w **<P>**对于_p <V>促进_v <N><N&>国际_n 社会_n 的_u 友好_a 合作_vn</N&> 和_c <N+>共同_b 发展_vn</N+></N></V>**</P>** <V>作出_v 了_u <N>积极_a 的_u 贡献_n</N></V> 。_w</S>

<S N="18"><N>*zhexie*_r *waijiao*_n *huodong*_vn</N> ，_w <V>*fuhe*_v
these diplomatic activities be.in.line.with
<N><*heping*_n *yu*_c *fazhan*_v *de*_u> *shidai*_n *zhuti*_n</N></V> ，_w
peace and develop DE era theme
<V>*shunying*_v <N><*shijie*_n *zouxiang*_v *duojihua*_v *de*_u>
follow peace walk.towards diversify DE
*qushi*_n</N></V> ，_w **<P>***duiyu*_p <V>*cujin*_v <N><N&>*guoji*_n
trend as.for step.up international
*shehui*_n *de*_u *youhao*_a *hezuo*_vn</N&> *he*_c <N+>*gongtong*_b
community DE friendly co-operation and shared

*fazhan*_vn</N+></N></V>**</P>** <V>*zuochu*_v *le*_u <N>*jiji*_a *de*_u
development make PERF constructive DE
*gongxian*_n</N></V> 。_w</S>
contribution
"These diplomatic activities suit our goal of maintaining peace and development, meet the needs of global diversification, and contribute to enhancing our co-operation with other countries."

(25) <S N="109"><N>李_nr 鹏_nr</N> **<P>**对_p <S><N>他们_r</N> <Ja>倾心_ad</Ja> <V>照顾_v <N>下一代_n</N></V></S>**</P>** <V>表示_v <N>肯定_an</N></V> 。_w</S>
<S N="109"><N>*Li*_nr *Peng*_nr</N> **<P>***dui*_p <S><N>*tamen*_r</N>
Li Peng as.for they
<Ja>*qingxin*_ad</Ja> <V>*zhaogu*_v <N>*xiayidai*_n</N></V></S>**</P>**
devotedly nurture next.generation
<V>*biaoshi*_v <N>*kending*_an</N></V> 。_w</S>
express praise
"Li Peng complimented them on their dedication in taking good care of their children."

3.5.1.10 Adverbial prepositional phrase (Pa)

An adverbial prepositional phrase functions as an adjunct in a sentence. Semantically, it is typically used as an adverbial of time, reason, circumstances, place, etc.

(26) <S N="37">**<Pa>**在_p <N>这_r 辞旧迎新_l 的_u 美好_a 时刻_n</N>**</Pa>** ，_w <N>我_r</N> <V>祝_v <N>大家_r</N> <S><S&><N>新年_t</N> <J>快乐_a</J></S&> ，_w <S+><N>家庭_n</N> <J>幸福_a</J></S+></S></V> ！_w</S>
<S N="37">**<Pa>***zai*_p <N>*zhe*_r *cijiuyingxin*_l
on this farewell.the.past.and.welcome.the.future
*de*_u *meihao*_a *shike*_n</N>**</Pa>** ，_w <N>*wo*_r</N> <V>*zhu*_v
DE joyful occasion I wish
<N>*dajia*_r</N> <S><S&><N>*xinnian*_t</N> <J>*kuaile*_a</J></S&> ，
both.of.us New.Year happy

_w <S+><N>*jiating*_n</N> <J>*xingfu*_a</J></S+></S></V> ！_w</S>
family blessed
"On this joyful occasion of celebrating the New Year, I wish everyone a happy New Year and a blessed family."

(27) <S N="15">**<Pa>**通过_p <S><N>高层_n</N> <V>互访_v</V></S>**</Pa>** ，_w <N>中国_ns 与_p 美国_ns 、_w 俄罗斯_ns 、_w 法国_ns 、_w 日本_ns 等_u 大国_n</N> <V>确定_v 了_u <N><N&><双方_n 关系_n 未来_t 发展_v 的_u> 目标_n</N&> 和_c <N+>指导_vn 方针_n</N+></N></V> 。_w</S>

<S N="15">**<Pa>***tongguo*_p <S><N>*gaoceng*_n</N>
through senior.government.officials
<V>*hufang*_v</V></S>**</Pa>** ，_w <N>*Zhongguo*_ns *yu*_p
visit.each.other China with
*Meiguo*_ns 、_w *Eluosi*_ns 、_w *Faguo*_ns 、_w *Riben*_ns *deng*_u
America Russia France Japan etc.
*daguo*_n</N> <V>*queding*_v *le*_u <N><N&><*shuangfang*_n *guanxi*_n
giant.nations ensure PERF one.another relationship
*weilai*_t *fazhan*_v *de*_u> *bubiao*_n</N&> *he*_c <N+>*zhidao*_vn
future develop DE goal and guidance
*fangzhen*_n</N+></N></V> 。_w</S>
scheme

"Through frequent visits of Chinese officials to these countries, the United States, Russia, France and Japan have laid down definite goals and concrete plans to enchance co-operation with China."

(28) <S N="45">**<Pa>**在_p <N><<国际_n 金融_n 危机_n 的_u> 风浪_n 波及_v 许多_m 国家_n 的>_u 情况_n 下_f</N>**</Pa>** ，_w <N>我国_n</N> <V>保持_v 了_u <N><金融_n 形势_n 和_c 整个_m 经济_n 形势_n 的_u> 稳定_a 发展_vn</N></V> 。_w</S>

<S N="45">**<Pa>***zai*_p <N><<*guoji*_n *jinyong*_n *weiji*_n *de*_u>
in international financial crisis DE
*fenglang*_n *boji*_v *xuduo*_m *guojia*_n *de*>_u *qingkuang*_n
storm affect plenty.of countries DE circumstances
*xia*_f</N>**</Pa>** ，_w <N>*woguo*_n</N> <V>*baochi*_v *le*_u
under our.country maintain PERF

<N><*jinyong*_n *xingshi*_n *he*_c *zhengge*_m *jingji*_n *xingshi*_n *de*_u>
financial situation and whole economic situation DE
*wending*_a *fazhan*_vn</N></V> 。_w</S>
stable development
"In the situation where many countries suffered from the global financial crisis, China still maintained a steady development in both finance and economy."

(29) <S N="99">**<Pa>**在_p <N>控制室_n</N>**</Pa>** ，_w <N><N&>李_nr 鹏_nr</N&> 与_p <N+>职工_n 们_k</N+></N> <R>一一_d</R> <V>握手_v</V> ，_w <P>向_p <N>大家_r</N></P> <V>表示_v <Vo>慰问_v</Vo></V> 。_w</S>

<S N="99">**<Pa>***zai*_p <N>*kongzhishi*_n</N>**</Pa>** ，_w
in control.station
<N><N&>*Li*_nr *Peng*_nr</N&> *yu*_p <N+>*zhigong*_n
Li Peng with co-workers
*men*_k</N+></N> <R>*yiyi*_d</R> <V>*woshou*_v</V> ，_w <P>*xiang*_p
PL one.by.one hold.hands to
<N>*dajia*_r</N></P> <V>*biaoshi*_v <Vo>*weiwen*_v</Vo></V> 。_w</S>
them express compliments
"In the control station, Li Peng held hands with every member of staff and expressed his compliments to them."

3.5.1.11 Adverb phrase (R)

An adverb phrase consists of an adverb or a group of words in which an adverb is the head of the phrase.

(30) <S N="16"><N><中国_ns 与_p 周边_n 国家_n 和_c 广大_b 发展中国家_l 的_u> 友好_a 合作_vn</N> **<R>**进一步_d**</R>** <V>加强_v</V> 。_w</S>

<S N="16"><N><*Zhongguo*_ns *yu*_p *zhoubian*_n *guojia*_n *he*_c
China with neighbouring countries and
*guangda*_b *fazhanzhongguojia*_l *de*_u> *youhao*_a
all.over.the.world developing.countries DE friendly
*hezuo*_vn</N> **<R>***jinyibu*_d**</R>** <V>*jiaqiang*_v</V> 。_w</S>
co-operation further strengthen
"The co-operation between China and her surrounding countries and developing countries was further strengthened."

(31) <S N="35"><N>中国_ns</N> **<R>**永远_d**</R>** <V>是_v <V>维护_v <N><世界_n 和平_n 与_c 稳定_an 的_u> 重要_a 力量_n</N></V></V> 。_w</S>

<S N="35"><N>*Zhongguo*_ns</N> **<R>***yongyuan*_d**</R>** <V>*shi*_v
China forever be

<V>*weihu*_v <N><*shijie*_n *heping*_n *yu*_c *wending*_an *de*_u>
safeguard world peace and stability DE

*zhongyao*_a *liliang*_n</N></V></V> 。_w</S>
important power

"China has long been playing a vital role in maintaining world peace and stability."

(32) <S N="29">但是_c ，_w <N>世界_n</N> **<R>**还_d 不_d**</R>** <J>安宁_a</J> 。_w</S>

<S N="29">*danshi*_c ，_w <N>*shijie*_n</N> **<R>***hai*_d *bu*_d**</R>**
however peace still not

<J>*anning*_a</J> 。_w</S>
tranquil

"Yet, the world is not in peace."

3.5.1.12 Sentence (S)

A sentence is the maximal syntactic constituent into which a text is subdivided (Leech et al., 1996: §Sentence). By orthographic definition, in both English and Chinese, it is typically marked by a final full stop or some other terminal punctuation. For parsing purposes in this research, an item is labelled as a sentence if it (a) has an independent syntactic status; (b) is included in another sentence as in a transcript of directly quoted speech; (c) is embedded in a phrase, i.e. it is a clause-like unit with a subject and a verb.

(33) **<S N="8">**<N>国民经济_n</N> <V>保持_v 了_u <N>< "_w 高_a 增长_vn 、_w 低_a 通胀_j "_w 的_u> 良好_a 发展_vn 态势_n</N></V> 。_w**</S>**

<S N="8"><N>*guominjingji*_n</N> <V>*baochi*_v *le*_u <N><"_w
national.economy maintain PERF

*gao*_a *zengzhang*_vn 、_w *di*_a *tongzhang*_j ”_w *de*_u> *lianghao*_a
high growth low inflation DE good
*fazhan*_vn *taishi*_n</N></V> 。_w**</S>**
development trend
"Our country maintains a high growth rate and low inflation rate in the economy."

(34) <S N="110"><N>他_r</N> <V>说_v ：_w **<S>** "_w <N>人_n</N> <J>老_a 了_y</J> ，_w <V>照顾_v 照顾_v <N>后代_n</N></V> <R>也_d</R> <V>是_v <N>一_m 件_q <可以_v 带_v 来_v 快乐_a 的_u> 事_n</N></V> ，_w <R>当然_d</R> ，_w <P>对_p <N>孩子_n 们_k</N></P> <V>不能_v 溺爱_v</V> ，_w <V>要_v <Vo>让_v <S><N>他们_r</N> <Ja>健康_ad</Ja> <V>成长_v</V></S></Vo></V> 。_w ”_w**</S>**</V></S>

<S N="110"><N>*ta*_r</N> <V>*shuo*_v ：_w **<S>**"_w <N>*ren*_n</N>
he said people
<J>*lao*_a *le*_y</J> ，_w <V>*zhaogu*_v *zhaogu*_v
become.old PERF nurture nurture
<N>*houdai*_n</N></V> <R>*ye*_d</R> <V>*shi*_v <N>*yi*_m *jian*_q
next.generation also be one CL
<*keyi*_v *dai*_v *lai*_v *kuaile*_a *de*_u> *shi*_n</N></V> ，_w
can bring come happiness DE matter
<R>*dangran*_d</R> ，_w <P>*dui*_p <N>*haizi*_n *men*_k</N></P>
of.course as.for children PL
<V>*buneng*_v *niai*_v</V> ，_w <V>*yao*_v <Vo>*rang*_v
cannot spoil have.to let
<S><N>*tamen*_r</N> <Ja>*jiankang*_ad</Ja>
them healthily
<V>*chengzhang*_v</V></S></Vo></V> 。_w ”_w**</S>**</V></S>
grow
"He said, 'when we grow older, we take delight in rearing our next generation. But we must bear in mind that we cannot spoil them.'"

(35) <S N="105">同时_c ，_w <R>也_d</R> <V>希望_v **<S>**<N>你们_r</N> <Ja>安全_ad</Ja> <V>生产_v</V> 、_w <R>经济_ad</R> <V>调度_v</V> ，_w <V>实现_v <N><经济_n 增长_vn 方式_n 的_u> 转变_vn</N></V>**</S>**</V> 。_w ” _w</S>

<S N="105">*tongshi*_c ，_w <R>*ye*_d</R> <V>*xiwang*_v
in.the.meantime also hope

<S><N>*nimen*_r</N> <Ja>*anquan*_ad</Ja> <V>*shengchan*_v</V> 、_w
you safely produce

<R>*jingji*_ad</R> <V>*tiaodu*_v</V> ，_w <V>*shixian*_v <N><*jingji*_n
economically adjust realise economy

*zengzhang*_vn *fangshi*_n *de*_u> *zhuanbian*_vn</N></V>**</S>**</V> 。
growth mode DE change

_w ”_w</S>

"In the meantime, I hope you could take note of safety measures in manufacturing, improve productivity and keep up with any changes in our economy."

In this scheme, since embedded clauses in a phrase are marked by <S> elements, the "clause" category is not used except adverbial clause and correlative clause, both of which are formally distinguished from simple sentences. Adverbial clauses are generally identified by some sign of their dependence on the superordinate clause or sentence such as an introductory subordinating conjunction whereas simple sentences are not. As for correlative clauses, as Chao (1968: 121) points out, the correlative adverbs 越 *yue*… 越 *yue*… "the more…, the more…" make it impossible for the coordinated parts of correlative clauses to be independent sentences, and to this extent the sentence label would be misleading.

3.5.1.13 Verb phrase (V)

There is disagreement over the scope of the verb phrase, focussed upon whether or not it should include only its verb or its verb and complement (Leech et al., 1996: §Verb phrase; Kahrel et al., 1997: 240). Including the verb complement in the verb phrase evidently has an advantage as this will make the structure of the verb phrase conform to the basic assumption of most of the existing generative syntactic theories, including the theoretical frameworks I compared in section 3.4.2.1, e.g. GB, LFG, HPSG, etc., in which binary branching of phrasal structures is the norm, as shown in (36a). Excluding the verb complement from the verb phrase will result in ternary branching nodes as in (36b).

(36a)

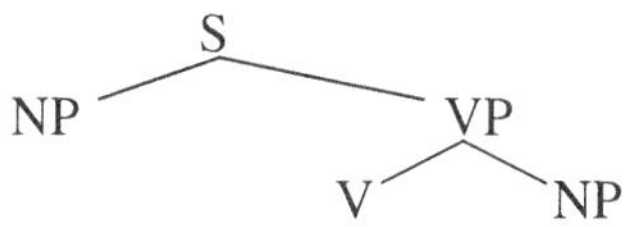

(36b)

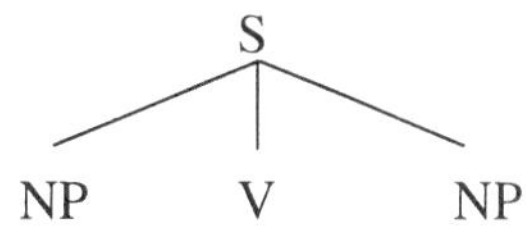

In (36a) and (36b), branching nodes are of different types: in (36a) there are binary branching nodes such as S and VP, which dominate two elements, while in (36b) S is a ternary branching node, which dominates three constituents, in contrast to its counterpart in (36a). As Haegeman (1994: 138–144) notes, there are further advantages to adopting a grammar which allows only binary branching: such a grammar is more aesthetically satisfying, and is more constrained in the sense that lots of imaginable representations are ruled out. I therefore decided in my annotation scheme to include the complements of the verb in the verb phrase. In other words, a verb phrase in this parsing scheme includes the words that are verbs and verb complements. A merit of this approach is that the relative levels of the constituents can be shown more clearly, while adjuncts and peripheral adverbials (mostly adverb phrases in my treebank) are left at the sentence level.

(37) <S N="11"><N><N&>民主_a 法制_n 建设_vn</N&> 、_w <N+>精神文明_n 建设_vn</N+> 和_c <N+>其他_r 各项_r 事业_n</N+></N> <R>都_d</R> **<V>**有_v <N>新_a 的_u 进展_vn</N>**</V>** 。_w</S>

<S N="11"><N><N&>*minzhu*_a *fazhi*_n *jianshe*_vn</N&> 、_w
democratic system establishment

<N+>*jingshenwenming*_n *jianshe*_vn</N+> *he*_c <N+>*qita*_r
moral.standards establishment and other

*gexiang*_r *shiye*_n</N+></N> <R>*dou*_d</R> **<V>***you*_v
various.kinds.of undertaking all have

<N>*xin*_a *de*_u *jinzhan*_vn</N>**</V>** 。_w</S>
new DE progress

"We have made good progress in developing democracy and moral standards and other undertakings."

3.5.1.14 Adverbial verb phrase (Va)

An adverbial verb phrase functions as a modifier to a verb or an adjunct to a sentence.

(38) <S N="70"><N>江_nr 泽民_nr 同志_n</N> <Na>最近_t</Na> **<Va>**强调_vd**</Va>** <V>指出_v</V> ，_w <V>要_v <R>大力_d</R> <V>倡导_v <N><说实话_l 、_w 办_v 实事_n 、_w 鼓_v 实劲_n 、_w 讲_v 实效_n 的_u> 作风_n</N></V></V> ，_w <Ja>坚决_ad</Ja> <V>制止_v <N><追求_v 表面文章_l> ，_w <搞_v 花架子_n> 等_u 形式主义_n</N></V> ，_w <Ja>坚决_ad</Ja> <V>杜绝_v <N><脱离_v 群众_n> 、_w <脱离_v 实际_n> 、_w <浮躁_a 虚夸_v> 等_u 官僚主义_n</N></V> 。_w</S>

<S N="70"><N>*Jiang*_nr *Zemin*_nr *tongzhi*_n</N> <Na>*zuijin*_t</Na>
Jiang Zemin comrade recently
<Va>*qiangdiao*_vd**</Va>** <V>*zhichu*_v</V> ，_w <V>*yao*_v
strongly point.out have.to
<R>*dali*_d</R> <V>*changdao*_v <N><*shuoshihua*_l 、_w *ban*_v
highly encourage tell.the.truth do
*shishi*_n 、_w *gu*_v *shijing*_n 、_w *jiang*_v *shixiao*_n *de*_u>
useful.work gather energy focus.on effectiveness DE
*zuofeng*_n</N></V></V> ，_w <Ja>*jianjue*_ad</Ja> <V>*zhizhi*_v
attitude persistently prohibit
<N><*zuiqui*_v *biaomianwenzhang*_l> ，_w <*gao*_v *huajiazi*_n> *deng*_u
follow superficiality make flower.rack etc.
*xingshizhuyi*_n</N></V> ，_w <Ja>*jianjue*_ad</Ja> <V>*dujue*_v
formalities persistently eliminate
<N><*tuoli*_v *qunzhong*_n> 、_w <*tuoli*_v
be.out.of.tune.with general.public be.out.of.tune.with
*shiji*_n> 、_w <*fuzao*_a *xukua*_v> *deng*_u
pragmatism impatient exaggerated etc.
*guanliaozhuyi*_n</N></V> 。_w</S>
red.tape

"Jiang Zemin has recently emphasised that we should encourage an effective and efficient working atmosphere and get rid of unnecessary formalities and red tape."

(39) <S N="89">**<Va>**演出_v 结束_v 后_f**</Va>** ，_w <N><N&>江_nr 泽民_nr 等_u 党_n</N&> 和_c <N+>国家_n 领导人_n</N+></N> <V>走_v 上_v <N>舞台_n</N></V> ，_w <Ja>亲切_ad</Ja> <V>会见_v 了_u <N><参加_v 演出_v 的_u> 全体_n 人员_n</N></V> ，_w <V><V&>祝贺_v <Vo>演出_v 成功_a</Vo></V&> ，_w 并_c <V+><P>与_p <N>他们_r</N></P> 合影_v <Vo>留念_v</Vo></V+></V> 。_w</S>

<S N="89">**<Va>***yanchu*_v *jieshu*_v *hou*_f**</Va>** ，_w
performance finish after
<N><N&>*Jiang*_nr *Zemin*_nr *deng*_u *dang*_n</N&> *he*_c
Jiang Zemin etc. the.Party and
<N+>*guojia*_n *lingdaoren*_n</N+></N> <V>*zou*_v *shang*_v
country leader step on
<N>*wutai*_n</N></V> ，_w <Ja>*qinqie*_ad</Ja> <V>*huijian*_v *le*_u
stage sincerely meet PERF
<N><*canjia*_v *yanchu*_v *de*_u> *quanti*_n
participate.in performance DE the.whole.group.of
*renyuan*_n</N></V> ，_w <V><V&>*zhuhe*_v <Vo>*yanchu*_v
performers compliment performance
*chenggong*_a</Vo></V&> ，_w *bing*_c <V+><P>*yu*_p
successful and with
<N>*tamen*_r</N></P> *heying*_v <Vo>*liunian*_v</Vo></V+></V> 。
them take.photo as.a.memento
_w</S>

"After the performance finished, Jiang Zemin's Communist Party and other leaders stepped onto the stage, met the performers and complimented them on their success and took photographs with them."

3.5.1.15 Verbal object (Vo)

This parsing label is specific to Chinese. As Norman (1988: 163) notes, "Chinese, like a number of other East Asian languages, is an aspect and not a tense language". This means that unlike English, Chinese verbs in themselves lack any distinction of finiteness and nonfiniteness (Rai-Chu, 1982: 78 ff.). In cases where a main verb takes another verb as direct object, English and Chinese verbs behave differently. While in

English the second verb is either an infinitive preceded by *to* or an *-ing* participle (Quirk and Greenbaum, 1973: 361; Faraci, 1974; Jones, 1985; Biber et al., 1999) as in example (40a), Chinese verbs do not show any morphological changes when they are used as direct object of another verb as in example (40b).

(40a) I like talking. Or I like to talk.

(40b) 我 喜欢说话。

wo *xihuan* *shuohua*

I like talk

"I like talking. Or I like to talk."

In other words, English verbs can easily be distinguished from their verbal objects by tense whereas Chinese verbs cannot. In order to explicitly mark this distinction between a main verb and its verbal object in Chinese, which will otherwise be lost due to no visible morphological difference between them, I decided to use a parsing label, *Vo*, to refer to verbal objects in Chinese.[17] Hence, besides having a nominal direct object, a verb in Chinese can take another verbal element (verb or verb phrase) as its object. This verbal object is enclosed in the <Vo> element and is included in the bracketing of the main verb, as illustrated in examples (41) and (42).

(41) <S N="62"><N>我们_r</N> **<V>**要_v <Ja>更_d 好_a 地_u</Ja> **<Vo>** 坚持_v <N> "<_w 两手抓_l 、_w 两手_m 都_d 要_v 硬_a "_w 的_u> 方针_n</N>**</Vo></V>** 。_w</S>

<S N="62"><N>*women*_r</N> **<V>***yao*_v <Ja>*geng*_d *hao*_a *de*_u</Ja>

we have.to more good ADVL

<Vo>*jianchi*_v <N>"<_w *liangshouzhua*_l 、_w *liangshou*_m *dou*_d

insist.on both.hands.hold.sth both.hands all

*yao*_v *ying*_a "_w *de*_u> *fangzhen*_n</N>**</Vo></V>** 。_w</S>

need.to stiff DE objective

"We must closely follow the principle of perseverance in an undertaking."

17 Verbal objects in Chinese are different from English nominal clauses in the sense that the former is only used as an object to a verb, while the latter can function both as subject and object in a clause/sentence.

(42) <S N="104"><Na>现在_t</Na> ，_w <N>我们_r 的_u 首都_n</N> <R>
已经_d</R> <V>结束_v 了_u <N><拉_v 闸_n 限_v 电_n 的_u>
历史_n</N></V> ，_w **<V>**希望_v **<Vo>**依靠_v <N>大家
_r</N>**</Vo></V>** ，_w <V>使_v <N><拉_v 闸_n 限_v 电_n 的_u>
历史_n</N> <V><R>永远_d 不再_d</R> 重演_v</V></V> 。_w </S>

<S N="104"><Na>*xianzai*_t</Na> ，_w <N>*women*_r *de*_u
at.present our GEN
*shoudu*_n</N> <R>*yijing*_d</R> <V>*jieshu*_v *le*_u <N><*la*_v *zha*_n
capital.city already end PERF pull barrier
*xian*_v *dian*_n *de*_u> *lishi*_n</N></V> ，_w **<V>***xiwang*_v
limit electricity DE history hope
<Vo>*yikao*_v <N>*dajia*_r</N>**</Vo></V>** ，_w <V>*shi*_v <N><*la*_v
count.on you make pull
*zha*_n *xian*_v *dian*_n *de*_u> *lishi*_n</N> <V><R>*yongyuan*_d
barrier limit electricity DE history forever
*buzai*_d</R> *chongyan*_v</V></V> 。_w </S>
never repeat

"Nowadays, a limited supply of electricity no longer occurs. However, I hope everybody can do their best to avoid a repetition of this event."

However, verb phrases with a verbal object are distinct from verb phrases with an auxiliary and a main verb. The main verb is not taken to be the verbal object of the auxiliary verb and thus no <Vo> element is used as in (43) and (44) where the auxiliaries are highlighted in grey colour, as opposed to the examples of verb phrases having a verbal object as shown in (41) and (42) above.

(43) <S N="12"><N>我们_r</N> <R>十分_m[18]</R> <V>关注_v <N><最近_t
一个_m 时期_n 一些_m 国家_n 和_c 地区_n 发生_v 的_u> 金融
_n 风波_n</N></V> ，_w <N>我们_r</N> <V>相信_v <S><Pa>通过_p
<N><N&><这些_r 国家_n 和_c 地区_n 的_u> 努力_an</N&> 以及
_c <N+>有关_v 的_u 国际_n 合作_vn</N+></N></Pa> ，_w <N>情况
_n</N> **<V>**会_v <R>逐步_d</R> 得到_v <N>缓解
_vn</N>**</V>**</S></V> 。_w</S>

18 The tag "m" for numeral is erroneously assigned in the PFR Chinese Corpus; it should be "d", an adverb.

<S N="12"><N>*women*_r</N> <R>*shifen*_m[19]</R> <V>*guanzhu*_v

we very be.concerned.about

<N><*zuijin*_t *yige*_m *shiqi*_n *yixie*_m *guojia*_n *he*_c *diqu*_n

recent one period.of.timesome countries and regions

*fasheng*_v *de*_u> *jinyong*_n *fengbo*_n</N></V> ，_w

happen DE financial storm

<N>*women*_r</N> <V>*xiangxin*_v <S><Pa>*tongguo*_p

we believe through

<N><N&><*zhexie*_r *guojia*_n *he*_c *dequ*_n *de*_u> *nuli*_an</N&>

these countries and regions DE efforts

*yiji*_c <N+>*youguan*_v *de*_u *guoji*_n *hezuo*_vn</N+></N></Pa>，

and related DE international co-operation

_w <N>*qingkuang*_n</N> **<V>***hui*_v <R>*zhubu*_d</R> *dedao*_v

situation will gradually obtain

<N>*huanjie*_vn</N>**</V>**</S></V> 。_w</S>

alleviation

"We are deeply concerned about the recent financial crises in some regions and countries, and believe that the situation will soon be alleviated through the efforts made by these places and help from other nations."

(44) <S N="75"><N>英雄_n 的_u 中国_ns 人民_n</N> <P>在_p <N><以_p 江_nr 泽民_nr 同志_n 为_v 核心_n 的_u> <N><N&>党中央_nt 坚强_a 领导_vn</N&> 和_c <N+>党_n 的_u <十五大_j 精神_n> 指引_v 下_f</N+></N></N></P> ，_w <Ja>更_d 高_a 地_u</Ja> <V>举起_v <N>邓小平理论_n 的_u 伟大_a 旗帜_n</N></V> ，_w <团结_a 一致_a> ，_w <Ja>扎实_ad</Ja> <V>工作_v</V> ，_w <R>奋勇_d</R> <V>前进_v</V> ，_w <R>一定_d</R> **<V>**能够_v 创造_v 出_v <N><更加_d 辉煌_a 的_u> 业绩_n</N>**</V>** ！_w</S>

<S N="75"><N>*yingxiong*_n *de*_u *Zhongguo*_ns *renmin*_n</N> <P>*zai*_p

hero DE China citizens at

<N><*yi*_p *Jiang*_nr *Zemin*_nr *tongzhi*_n *wei*_v *hexin*_n *de*_u>

with Jiang Zemin comrade to.be core DE

<N><N&>*Dangzhongyang*_nt *jianqiang*_a *lingdao*_vn</N&> *he*_c

central.government harsh leadership and

19 The tag "m" for numeral is erroneously assigned in the PFR Chinese Corpus; it should be "d", an adverb.

<N+>*dang*_n *de*_u <*shiwuda*_j *jingshen*_n> *zhiyin*_v
the.Party's GEN 15.primary principles guidance
*xia*_f</N+></N></N></P> ，_w <Ja>*geng*_d *gao*_a *de*_u</Ja>
under more high DE
<V>*juqi*_v <N>*Dengxiaopinglilun*_n *de*_u *weida*_a
hold the.principles.of.Deng.Xiaoping DE great
*qizhi*_n</N></V> ，_w <*tuanjie*_a *yizhi*_a> ，_w <Ja>*zhashi*_ad</Ja>
flag united together hard
<V>*gongzuo*_v</V> ，_w <R>*fenyong*_d</R> <V>*qianjin*_v</V> ，_w
work bravely proceed
<R>*yiding*_d</R> **<V>***nenggou*_v *chuangzao*_v *chu*_v <N><*gengjia*_d
certainly can create out more
*huihuang*_a *de*_u> *yeji*_n</N>**</V>** ！_w</S>
magnificent DE success

"Under the leadership of Jiang Zemin and his Communist Party and with the help of the Party's 15 guidelines, we should unite to closely follow Deng Xiaoping's principles, strive hard in our work and we will soon achieve great success."

In my parsing guidelines, I chose to adopt Li and Thompson's (1989: 182–183) list of Chinese auxiliary verbs because these auxiliary verbs are convincingly demonstrated by Li and Thompson to share a set of distributional properties that distinguish them from other grammatical categories such as verbs and adverbs. These include the following commonly used forms:

(45) 应该 *yinggai*, 应当 *yingdang*, 该 *gai* — "ought to, should"
能 *neng*, 能够 *nenggou*, 会 *hui*, 可以 *keyi* — "be able to"
能 *neng*, 可以 *keyi* — "has permission to"
敢 *gan* — "dare"
肯 *ken* — "be willing to"
得 *dei*, 不须 *buxu*, 不要 *buyao*, 不得 *budei* — "must, ought to"
会 *hui* — "will, know how"

3.5.1.16 Initial (&) and non-initial conjunct (+)

Any of the above parsing tags may be used with "&" and "+" to indicate coordination. The first coordinate element will carry "&" sign. Subsequent ones will have "+", placed after both medial punctuations and coordinating conjunctions (if any).

(46) <S N="13">总的来说_c ，_w <N>**<N&>**中国_ns 改革_v**</N&>** 和_c **<N+>**发展_v 的_u 全局_n**</N+>**</N> <V>继续_v <Vo>保持_v 了_u <N>稳定_an</N></Vo></V> 。_w</S>

<S N="13">*zongdelaishuo*_c ，_w <N>**<N&>***Zhongguo*_ns
on.the.whole China
*gaige*_v**</N&>** *he*_c **<N+>***fazhan*_v *de*_u *quanju*_n**</N+>**</N>
reform and development DE situation
<V>*jixu*_v <Vo>*baochi*_v *le*_u <N>*wending*_an</N></Vo></V> 。
continue maintain PERF stability
_w</S>

"On the whole, China's reform and development keep on progressing steadily."

(47) <S N="67"><N>这_r</N> <V>是_v <P>把_p <N>党_n 的_u 方针_n 、_w 政策_n</N></P> <落到实处_l></V> ，_w <V>使_v <Vo>**<Vo&>**改革_v**</Vo&>** 和_c **<Vo+>**建设_v**</Vo+>**</Vo> <Vo>取得_v <N>胜利_vn 的_u 重要_a 保证_vn</N></Vo></V> 。_w</S>

<S N="67"><N>*zhe*_r</N> <V>*shi*_v <P>*ba*_p <N>*dang*_n *de*_u
this be BA the.Party's GEN
*fangzhen*_n 、_w *zhengce*_n</N></P> <*luodaoshichu*_l></V> ，_w
objective policy realise
<V>*shi*_v <Vo>**<Vo&>***gaige*_v**</Vo&>** *he*_c
make reform and
<Vo+>*jianshe*_v**</Vo+>**</Vo> <Vo>*qude*_v <N>*shengli*_vn *de*_u
construction obtain success DE
*zhongyao*_a *baozheng*_vn</N></Vo></V> 。_w</S>
important guarantee

"This is to safeguard the implementation of the Communist Party's policy and success in the country's reform and development."

(48) <S N="5">**<S&>**<N>[中国_ns 政府_n]nt</N> <Ja>顺利_ad</Ja> <V>恢复_v <P>对_p <N>香港_ns</N></P> <Vo>行使_v <N>主权_n</N></Vo></V>**</S&>** ，_w 并_c **<S+>**<P>按照_p <N>< “_w 一国两制_j ”_w 、_w “_w 港人治港_l ”_w 、_w 高度_d 自治_v 的_u> 方针_n</N></P> <V>保持_v <N>香港_ns 的_u 繁荣_an 稳定_an</N></V>**</S+>** 。_w</S>

<S N="5">**<S&>**<N>[*Zhongguo*_ns *Zhengfu*_n]nt</N> <Ja>*shunli*_ad</Ja>
China government successfully
<V>*huifu*_v <P>*dui*_p <N>*Xianggang*_ns</N></P> <Vo>*xingshi*_v
resume to Hong.Kong exercise
<N>*zhuquan*_n</N></Vo></V>**</S&>** ，_w *bing*_c **<S+>**<P>*anzhao*_p
sovereignty and according.to
<N><“_w *yiguoliangzhi*_j ”_w 、_w “_w *gangrenzhigang*_l ”_w 、
one.country.two.systems people's.ruling.themselves
_w *gaodu*_d *zizhi*_v *de*_u> *fangzhen*_n</N></P> <V>*baochi*_v
highly autonomous DE objective maintain
<N>*Xianggang*_ns *de*_u *fanrong*_an *wending*_an</N></V>**</S+>** 。
Hong.Kong DE prosperity stability
_w</S>

"The Chinese government has succeeded in resuming its sovereignty over Hong Kong and maintaining the prosperity and stability of Hong Kong, according to the objectives of 'one country two systems', 'Hong Kong people ruling themselvels' and 'high degree of autonomy'."

3.5.2 Issues arising from the application of the scheme

Even if a basic parsing scheme for annotation is made explicit, many issues may arise when the scheme is applied to corpus data (Sampson, 1987: 94ff.). Throughout the entire parsing process, choices had to be made as such issues arose. These choices will be documented and explained in this section. The decisions were then adhered to consistently in the annotation of similar cases thereafter. In the following subsections, I will discuss the issues that arose and illustrate them with examples drawn from the sample treebank.

3.5.2.1 Underspecification – Use of unlabelled bracketings

Brackets may be left unlabelled in cases where a particular grouped sequence of words cannot fit in to any of the existing phrase or clause categories. Examples of constituents enclosed in unlabelled brackets are given below from (a) to (e).

(a) Multi-word premodifiers of noun phrases marked by the particle 的 *de* (see also section 3.6.2.3):

e.g. <N><全国_n 各族_r 的_u> 人民_n</N> <N><*quanguo*_n *gezu*_r *de*_u> *renmin*_n</N> "people from different ethnic groups throughout the country";

e.g. <N><同_p 联合国_nt 和_c 其他_r 国际_n 组织_n 的_u> 协调_vn</N> <N><*tong*_p *Lianheguo*_nt *he*_c *qita*_r *guoji*_n *zuzhi*_n *de*_u> *xietiao*_vn</N> "the compromise between the United Nations and other international organisations";

e.g. <N><最近_t 一个_m 时期_n 一些_m 国家_n 和_c 地区_n 发生_v 的_u> 金融_n 风波_n</N> <N><*zuijin*_t *yige*_m *shiqi*_n *yixie*_m *guojia*_n *he*_c *diqu*_n *fasheng*_v *de*_u> *jinyong*_n *fengbo*_n</N> "the recent financial crises happened in some countries and districts";

e.g. <N+><<V><V&>保护_v 环境_n</V&> 、_w <V+>消除_v 贫困_an</V+> 、_w <V+>打击_v 国际_n 犯罪_vn</V+></V> 等_u 方面_n 的_u> 国际_n 合作_vn</N+> <N+><<V><V&>*baohu*_v *huanjing*_n</V&> 、_w <V+>*xiaochu*_v *penkun*_an</V+> 、_w <V+>*daji*_v *guoji*_n *fanzui*_vn</V+></V> *deng*_u *fangmian*_n *de*_u> *guoji*_n *hezuo*_vn</N+> "worldwide co-operation on such matters as environmental protection, the elimination of poverty and a crackdown on international crime".

As stated in section 3.4.1, those grammatical constructions marked by the particle *de* as in (a) above are highly controversial: some scholars refer to them as relative clauses (e.g. Li and Thompson, 1989: 579ff.; Aoun and Li, 1993; Chiu, 1993; Wu, 2000; Xue et al., 2000) or appositive clauses (Chu and Chi, 1999: 226), while others do not agree with either approach (e.g. Chao, 1968; Zhu, 1982 and 2000; Liu, 2003). Moreover, using some catch-all label, such as "*de* constructions", does not help either because the particle *de* in itself is vague in its functions: it can be a genitive marker, a marker of nominalisation and an adjectival marker (see section 3.4.1). It is therefore not easy to agree upon how the *de* constructions are defined and instantiated in texts. Having considered that there is to date no consensus on this issue of how *de* constructions should be analysed, and any invented label that attempts to refer to them will act as a locus of controversy and disagreement, I decided not to set up a new label for them in my parsing scheme and thus these constructions were enclosed by unlabelled brackets in the treebank.

(b) Serial verb constructions which are used as if they were compound verbs (see also section 3.6.2.4):

e.g. <坚持_v 奉行_v> <*jianchi*_v *fengxing*_v> "insist on following";
e.g. <指挥_v 演奏_v> <*zhihui*_v *yanzou*_v> "lead and perform";
e.g. <看望_v 慰问_v> <*kanwang*_v *weiwen*_v> "visit and send regards to …".

As will be explained in more detail in section 3.6.2.4, some serial verb constructions are problematic in that their status of being serial verbs is dubious. Given no in-depth investigations of whether or not they are actually serial verbs or compound verbs that have been carried out as yet, these constructions were left unlabelled in my treebank.

(c) Serial adjective constructions:

e.g. <团结_a 一致_a> <*tuanjie*_a *yizhi*_a> "be united together";
e.g. <圆满_a 成功_a> <*yuanman*_a *chenggong*_a> "perfectly successful".

For the same reason as in (b), since it is not clear whether these serial adjective constructions are compound adjectives, I left them unlabelled.

(d) Idioms/set phrases which are used idiosyncratically as if they were single-word nouns or verbs (see also section 3.6.2.2):

e.g. <大势所趋_i ，_w 民心所向_l> <*dashisuoqu*_i ，_w *minxinsuoxiang*_l> "urged by the trend, supported by general public";
e.g. <大气磅礴_i ，_w 波澜壮阔_i> <*diqibangbo*_i ，_w *bolanzhuangkuo*_i> "powerful wind, fierce waves";
e.g. <流光溢彩_l ，_w 火树银花_i> <*liuguangyicai*_l ，_w *huoshuyinhua*_i> "filled with colourful lights, magnificent".

In cases like (d) above, idioms or set phrases can function as predicate in a sentence. However, as will be discussed in section 3.6.2.2, even if context is taken into consideration, it is not obvious whether these idiomatic expressions function as a nominal predicate or a verbal predicate, both of which are allowed in the Chinese syntax (Chao, 1968: 90). They were thus not enclosed in the <V> element nor <N> element in the treebank and left unlabelled instead.

(e) Coordinated verbs with shared direct object:

e.g. <V><学习_v 和_c 掌握_v> <N>党_n 的_u 十五大_j 精神_n</N></V> <V><*xuexi*_v *he*_c *zhangwo*_v> <N>*dang*_n *de*_u *shiwuda*_j *jingshen*_n</N></V> "learn and master the Communist Party's 15 principles";

e.g. <V><尊重_v 、_w 认识_v 和_c 掌握_v> <N>客观_a 规律_n</N></V> <V><*zhuanzhong*_v 、_w *renshi*_v *he*_c *zhangwo*_v> <N>*keguan*_a *guilü*_n</N></V> "respect, understand and master what we learn in our daily life".

In the examples given in (e) above, two or more transitive verbs in coordination share the same direct object. The coordinated verbs (except the last one) are not constituent-like in the sense that they do not constitute a complete verb phrase structure because the following shared object does not come immediately after them. I did not therefore apply the usual practice of marking conjuncts by enclosing them in the <V&> and <V+> elements, which are only used for coordinated verbs or verb phrases with complete verb phrase structure (Eyes and Leech, 1993: 53; Sampson, 1995: 310f.; Leech et al., 1996: §Coordination). Since it is also not worthwhile to set up a new parsing label to mark such a non-frequent phenomenon, I decided to put these verbal segments into unlabelled brackets.

3.5.2.2 Bracketing of multi-word constituents

The unlabelled bracketing facility evidently has its uses in skeleton parsing as it allows analysis to proceed where labelling decisions are not obvious or straightforward. Nevertheless, for some multi-word adverb phrases containing two adverbs (e.g. <R>还_d 不_d</R> <R>*hai*_d *bu*_d</R> "not…though"; <R>永远_d 不再_d</R> **<R>***yongyuan*_d *buzai*_d</R> "never forever"; <R>一直_d 都_d</R> **<R>***yizhi*_d *dou*_d</R> "constantly"), and multi-word attributive adjectival phrases containing an adjective premodified by at least one adverb (e.g. <J>非常_d 重要_a 的_u</J> **<J>***feichang*_d *zhongyao*_a *de*_u</J> "very important"; <J>很_d 不_d 平凡_a 的_u</J> **<J>***hen*_d *bu*_d *pingfan*_a *de*_u</J> "very extraordinary; <J>十分_m 高兴_a</J> <J>*shifen*_m *gaoxing*_a</J> "very happy"), though Eyes and Leech (1993: 53) chose to put them into unlabelled brackets, they were labelled in my treebank. The reason for this is that their internal structure is clear, having a head (adjective or adverb) being modified by another adverb.

3.5.2.3 Bracketing of single-word constituents

As suggested in the EAGLES Recommendations for the Syntactic Annotation of Corpora, Version of 11th March 1996 (Leech et al., 1996), it is considered preferable to bracket single-word constituents where they show their phrasal status by the possibility of adding modifiers or replacing them by a multi-word phrase as in (49), or where they are in coordination with other multi-word constituents as in (50).

(49) <N>人民_n 生活_vn</N> **<R>**进一步_d**</R>** **<V>**改善_v**</V>**
<N>*renmin*_n *shenghuo*_vn</N> **<R>***jinyibu*_d**</R>** **<V>***gaishan*_v**</V>**
citizens life further improve
"the life of the citizens is further improved"

(50) <N>**<N&>**全党_n**</N&>** 和_c **<N+>**全国_n 各族_r 人民_n**</N+>**</N>
<N>**<N&>***quandang*_n**</N&>** *he*_c **<N+>***quanguo*_n
the.whole.Communist.Party and the.whole.country
*gezu*_r *renmin*_n**</N+>**</N>
various.kinds.of.ethnic.groups citizens
"the Communist Party and the citizens of varied ethnic groups throughout the country"

In example (49), the phrase brackets delimiting the adverb 进一步 *jinyibu* "further" and the main verb 改善 *gaishan* "improve" are meant to indicate the potential phrasal status of these words, because of the possibility of adding another adverb (e.g. 再 *zai* “again”) before the former or replacing the latter with a multi-word verb phrase (e.g. 得到改善 *dedao gaishan* “have got (it) improved”). In example (50), the equivalence of the two conjuncts can be represented in the bracketing, though the initial conjunct is a noun and the final conjunct is a noun phrase.

3.5.2.4 Punctuation

Generally speaking, I included punctuation within the bracketing. As for phrase/sentence-initial and phrase/sentence-final punctuations, I enclosed them within the parsing bracketing, as in (51):

(51) <P>为_p **<N>**“_w 两手抓_l 、_w 两手_m 都_d 要_v 硬_a ” _w**</N>**</P> <V>提供_v 了_u <N>新_a 的_u 理论_n 根据 _n</N></V>

<P>*wei*_p **<N>**“_w *liangshouzhua*_l 、_w *liangshou*_m *dou*_d *yao*_v
for both.hands.hold.sth both.hands all have.to
*ying*_a ”_w**</N>**</P> <V>*tigong*_v *le*_u <N>*xin*_a *de*_u *lilun*_n
stiff provide PERF new DE theoretical
*genju*_n</N></V>
grounds
“provide new theoretical evidence for the principle of perseverance in an undertaking”

As regards medial punctuation marks, typically commas, I attached them to the highest available node in the parse tree, thus these punctuation marks can be used as delimiters of major constituents, as in (52):

(52) <S N="5">**<S&>**<N>[中国_ns 政府_n]nt</N> <Ja>顺利_ad</Ja> <V>恢复 _v <P>对_p <N>香港_ns</N></P> <Vo>行使_v <N>主权 _n</N></Vo></V>**</S&>** ，_w 并_c **<S+>**<P>按照_p <N>< “_w 一国 两制_j ”_w 、_w “_w 港人治港_l ”_w 、_w 高度_d 自治_v 的 _u> 方针_n</N></P> <V>保持_v <N>香港_ns 的_u 繁荣_an 稳定 _an</N></V>**</S+>** 。_w</S>

<S N="5">**<S&>**<N>[*Zhongguo*_ns *zhengfu*_n]nt</N> <Ja>*shunli*_ad</Ja>
China government successfully

<V>*huifu*_v <P>*dui*_p <N>*Xianggang*_ns</N></P> <Vo>*xingshi*_v
resume to Hong.Kong exercise
<N>*zhuquan*_n</N></Vo></V>**</S&>** ，_w *bing*_c **<S+>**<P>*anzhao*_p
sovereignty and according.to
<N><“_w *yiguoliangzhi*_j ”_w 、_w “_w *gangrenzhigang*_l ”_w 、
one.country.two.systems people’s.ruling.themselves
_w *gaodu*_d *zizhi*_v *de*_u> *fangzhen*_n</N></P> <V>*baochi*_v
highly autonomous DE objective maintain
<N>*Xianggang*_ns *de*_u *fanrong*_an *wending*_an</N></V>**</S+>** 。
Hong.Kong DE prosperity stability
_w</S>

“The Chinese government has succeeded in resuming its sovereignty over Hong Kong and maintaining the prosperity and stability of Hong Kong, according to the objectives on ‘one country two systems’, ‘Hong Kong people ruling themselvels’ and ‘high degree of autonomy’.”

3.5.2.5 Ambiguity

Linguistic forms are often ambiguous. My annotation scheme, however, did not contain any notation for representing ambiguity explicitly with which the human analyst selects one possible sense for a form and represents it. I decided not to explicitly mark an ambiguous form because even if a given item has more than one reading, the human analyst will not recognise this in the course of parsing and just annotate the item with the interpretation that seems initially most plausible. In fact, similar problems were encountered in the production of the Penn Chinese Treebank and the annotators of the treebank did not annotate ambiguities either (Xue et al., 2000: 173–178). They believed that in each case one of these ambiguous readings was unlikely and thus they annotated assuming the more plausible reading. In this regard, my treebank may appear unsatisfactory in connection with research on different kinds of ambiguity.

With such a detailed and carefully articulated parsing scheme and guidelines, I can now proceed to describe the actual process of skeleton parsing and difficulties encountered in the process of parsing.

3.6 The process of skeleton parsing

3.6.1 The basic concept of skeleton parsing

The basic idea of skeleton parsing, as Garside and McEnery (1993: 19) demonstrate, is that the treebanker marks only those syntactic structures which seem "intuitively obvious", rather than keeping track of a particular reference grammar. In the course of skeleton parsing, I inserted a nested set of brackets around a sequence of word tokens which appeared to be intuitively correct to group as a single unit. I then assigned to each of these units (i.e. sentence constituents) a label from the set of categories specified in my parsing scheme. An excerpt of the PFR Skeleton Treebank is provided in the following figure.

```
<ORIGINALMP>19980101-01-001-013_m</ORIGINALMP>  <S N="28"><V>环顾_v  <N>全球
_n</N></V>  ，_w  <N><日益_d  密切_a  的_u>  世界_n  经济_n  联系_vn</N>  ，_w  <N>日新月
异_i  的_u  科技_n  进步_vn</N>  ，_w  <R>正在_d</R>  <P>为_p  <N><各国_r  经济_n  的_u>  发
展_vn</N></P>  <V>提供_v  <N>历史_n  机遇_n</N></V>  。_w</S>  <S N="29">但是_c  ，_w  <N>
世界_n</N>  <R>还_d  不_d</R>  <J>安宁_a</J>  。_w</S>  <S N="30"><N><南北_n  之间_f  的_u>
贫富_n  差距_n</N>  <V>继续_v  <Vo>扩大_v</Vo></V>  ；_w  <N>局部_b  冲突_vn</N>  <时有发
生_l>  ；_w  <N><<不_d  公正_a  不_d  合理_a  的_u>  旧_a  的_u>  国际_n  政治_n  经济_n  秩
序_n</N>  <R>还_d</R>  <V>没有_v  <N>根本_a  改变_vn</N></V>  ；_w  <N>发展中国家_l</N>
<P>在_p  <N>激烈_a  的_u  国际_n  经济_n  竞争_vn  中_f</N></P>  <R>仍_d</R>  <V>处于_v
<N>弱势_n  地位_n</N></V>  ；_w  <N>人类_n  的_u  <N><N&>生存_vn</N&>  与_c  <N+>发展
_vn</N+></N></N>  <R>还_d</R>  <V>面临_v  <N>种种_q  <N><N&>威胁_vn</N&>  和_c  <N+>挑
战_vn</N+></N></N></V>  。_w</S>  <S N="31"><N><和平_n  与_c  发展_vn  的_u>  前景_n</N>
<V>是_v  <J>光明_a  的_u</J></V>  ，_w  <N>２１_m  世纪_n</N>  <R>将_d</R>  <V>是_v  <N><
充满_v  希望_n  的_u>  世纪_n</N></V>  。_w</S>  <S N="32">但_c  <N>前进_v  的_u  道路_n</N>
<V><V><V&>不会_v</V&>  <R>也_d</R>  <V+><R>不_d</R>  可能_v</V+></V>  <一帆风顺
_i></V>  ，_w  <N>矢键_n</N>  <V>是_v  <S><N>世界_n  各国_r  人民_n</N>  <V>要_v  <J>进一
步_d  团结_a  起来_v</J></V></S></V>  ，_w  <V><V><V&><R>共同_d</R>  推动_v</V&>  <V+><R>
早日_d</R>  建立_v</V+></V>  <N><公正_a  合理_a  的_u>  国际_n  政治_n  经济_n  新_a  秩序
 n</N></V>  。 w</S>
```

Figure 4: An excerpt of the PFR Sample Skeleton Treebank.

3.6.2 Difficulties in skeleton parsing Chinese text

It is noteworthy here to discuss the major difficulties that I encountered in the course of skeleton parsing a sample text taken from my corpus, as this illuminates some of the peculiarities of the Chinese language.

3.6.2.1 *Ba* constructions

Firstly, 把 *ba* constructions make the parse of a verb phrase incomplete. The *ba* construction is a widely discussed topic in the grammar of Chinese (see, for instance, Li and Thompson, 1989: 463–491; Chen, 1990; Kit, 1992; Zou, 1993; Xia and Wu, 1996; Li, 1997; Xue et al., 2000; Li, 2001). In general, the structure of the *ba* construction is expressed and underlined in (53): a *ba* sentence has a subject, followed by *ba* and the *ba* noun phrase (i.e. the NP directly following *ba*) followed by a verb.

(53) subject   <u>*ba*   NP</u>   verb

In my PFR treebank, 104 instances of the *ba* construction were found, which fall into three types of this construction. The general pattern of *ba* sentences is to place the direct object of the following verb immediately after *ba* as in example (54).

(54) <P>把_p **<N$_i$>**电厂_n**</N$_i$>**</P> <V>建_v 好_a</V> **Ø$_i$**
<P>*ba*_p **<N$_i$>***dianchang*_n**</N$_i$>**</P> <V>*jian*_v *hao*_a</V> **Ø$_i$**
BA electricity.supply.station build well
"build an electricity supply station"

Typically, a transitive verb should follow the pattern "<V>…<N>…</N></V>". However, the verb[20], 建_v 好_a, *jian-hao*, "build well, build in good shape" that follows the *ba* construction lacks a direct object, which is equivalent to the *ba* noun phrase, i.e. *ba* NP$_i$ verb Ø$_i$, where Ø$_i$ denotes the empty position of the preposed verb object that shares the same reference as the prepositional complement of *ba*. In other words, the structure of the verb phrase following the *ba* construction is in the form of <V>…</V> rather than the canonical form mentioned before.

More complicated *ba* constructions involve the occurrence of two following verbs and a passivised verb. In cases like (55) where two

20 建_v 好_a, *jian-hao* "build well, build in good shape" is a compound verb. More specifically, it is a verb-complement (V-R) compound (Chao, 1968: 435 ff.). The resultative complement 好 *hao* "good" is bound to and follows the verb 建 *jian* "build" and expresses the result of the action of the verb.

different transitive verbs follow the *ba* construction, it is not immediately obvious whether that the prepositional complement of *ba* co-refers to the object of the first verb (改编 *gaibian* "be adapted for") or that of the second one (为 *wei* "be changed as"). Since the second verb already takes a direct object (器乐曲 *qiyuequ* "acoustics of musical instruments"), the *ba* noun phrase must be co-referential with the object of the first verb.

(55) <P>把_p **<N$_i$>**<广大_b 听众_n 耳熟能详_i 的_u> 歌曲_n**</N$_i$>**</P>
<V>改编_v **Ø**$_i$ <V>为_v <N>器乐曲_n</N></V></V>
<P>*ba*_p **<N$_i$>**<*guangda*_b *tingzhong*_n *ershunengxiang*_i *de*_u>
BA general audience familiar DE
*gequ*_n**</N$_i$>**</P> <V>*gaibian*_v **Ø**$_i$ <V>*wei*_v
songs change to.be
<N>*qiyuequ*_n</N></V></V>
acoustics.of.musical.instruments
"change those popular songs into acoustic versions"

In less obvious cases like (56), however, it is impossible to locate any empty position that co-refers to the *ba* complement. The verb 带入 *dairu* "bring to" that follows the *ba* construction is used causatively without any visible passivisation. As Norman (1988: 164) notes, Chinese verbs do not make any distinction between the active (or unaccusative) and passive (or causative). The *ba* noun phrase 人们 *renmen* "people" therefore actually refers to the logical subject of the verb.

(56) <P>把_p <N>人们_n</N></P> <V>带入_v <N>迷人_a 的_u 艺术_n 境地_n</N></V>
<P>*ba*_p <N>*renmen*_n</N></P> <V>*dairu*_v <N>*miren*_a *de*_u
BA people bring.into fascinating DE
*yishu*_n *jingdi*_n</N></V>
imaginary world
"bring people into a fascinating imaginary world"

3.6.2.2 Idioms or set phrases

The use of idioms (tagged "i") or set phrases (tagged "l") as if they were nouns and verbs is also problematic. Noun-like idioms and set phrases are illustrated in example (57) and verb-like set phrases in example (58). To my knowledge, the grammatical categories of this kind of idiomatic expressions have not been documented so far.

(57) <N>今晚_t 的_u 长安街_ns</N> <流光溢彩_l ，_w 火树银花_i>
<N>*jinwan*_t *de*_u *Changanjie*_ns</N> <*liuguangyicai*_l ，_w
tonight DE Changan.Street filled.with.colourful.lights
*huoshuyinhua*_i>
bright.red.trees.with.silver.flowers
"Tonight the Changan Street was filled with colourful lights and really looked magnificent."

(58) <N>国民经济_n</N> <稳中求进_l>
<N>*guominjingji*_n</N> <*wenzhongqiujin*_l>
national.economy steadily.progress
"The national economy is progressing steadily."

That they can be used rather idiosyncratically as a noun or a verb makes it almost impossible for even a human analyst to determine the phrasal category of a given idiomatic expression: whether it is a noun phrase or a verb phrase. As in the above two examples, it is unclear whether the idiom/set phrase placed after the subject noun phrase is intended to function as a nominal expression or a verbal one. Unlike English, in which the subject must be followed by a verbal predicate, a Chinese predicate can be a verbal predicate, an adjectival predicate or a nominal predicate (Chao, 1968: 90). In the absence of further evidence of the categorial status of such segments, those idioms and set phrases occurring in the predicate position were left unlabelled in my treebank.

3.6.2.3 Lengthy premodifiers of a noun phrase

Unlike English, which favours the use of postmodification if a modifier of a noun phrase is long (Quirk and Greenbaum, 1973: 425; de Haan, 1991), Chinese prefers premodification to postmodification, regardless of the length of the modifier (cf. Liu et al., 1996: 265–274). It is thus common in the PFR treebank that a noun is qualified by a grammatical unit of over six words which is marked by the particle 的 *de* at the end, as in example (59). As stated in section 3.4.1, the particle 的 *de* is traditionally treated as a marker of modification.

(59) <N><中国_ns 与_p 周边_n 国家_n 和_c 广大_b 发展中国家_l 的_u> 友好_a 合作_vn</N>

<N><*Zhongguo*_ns *yu*_p *zhoubian*_n *guojia*_n *he*_c *guangda*_b
China with neighbouring countries and all.over.the.world

*fazhanzhongguojia*_l *de*_u> *youhao*_a *hezuo*_vn</N>
developing.countries DE friendly co-operation

"the co-operation between China and her surrounding countries and developing countries"

These lengthy premodifiers make the structure of the noun phrase in which they occur extremely difficult to interpret. Some premodifiers of this sort are complicated by the fact that they are further modified by another element marked by *de* in their internal structure, as in example (60).

(60) <N>党_n 的_u <<基本_a 路线_n 提出_v 的_u> 党_n 在_p 社会主义_n 初级_b 阶段_n 经济_n 、_w 政治_n 、_w 文化_n 的_u> 基本_a 纲领_n</N>

<N>*dang*_n *de*_u <<*jiben*_a *luxian*_n *tichu*_v *de*_u> *dang*_n *zai*_p
the.Party's GEN primary route mention DE the.Party at

*shehuizhuyi*_n *chuji*_b *jieduan*_n *jingji*_n 、_w *zhengzhi*_n 、_w
social.ideology initial stage economy politics

*wenhua*_n *de*_u> *jiben*_a *gangling*_n</N>
culture DE basic objectives

"the primary principles of the Communist Party on economy, politics and culture, which are also on a par with the Party's basic directions"

3.6.2.4 Serial verb constructions

Serial verb constructions in Chinese also increase the complexity of parsing. There is an immense literature on Chinese serial verb constructions (see, for instance, Li and Thompson, 1989: 594ff.; Lin and Soo, 1994; Liu, 1996). Generally speaking, a serial verb construction refers to a succession of two or more actions that share the same subject, as illustrated in the following concocted example.

(61) <N>我</N> <V>去 <N>朋友 家</N></V> <V>吃 <N>晚饭</N></V>
<N>*wo*</N> <V>*qu* <N>*pengyou* *jia*</N></V> <V>*chi*
I go.to friend home eat
<N>*wanfan*</N></V>
dinner
"I went to my friend's house to have dinner."

However, some of the serial verb constructions in my treebank do not conform to this general pattern of two successive verbs, each of which has a different direct object. Unlike ordinary serial verbs, the serial verbs, as shown in (62) and (63), do not take a direct object separately. They are more like compound verbs than serial verbs, though it is not clear that they can be fully assimilated to the former category. Evidence in support of this analysis comes from the fact that these verbs (i.e. 指挥_v 演奏_v *zhihui yanzou* "lead and perform" as in (62), and 坚持_v 奉行_v *jianchi fengxing* "insist and follow" as in (63)), functioning as if they were a single unit, take the same object, i.e. the following noun phrase.

(62) <V><指挥_v 演奏_v> 了_u <N>一_m 批_q 中外_j 名曲_n</N></V>
<V><*zhihui*_v *yanzou*_v> *le*_u <N>*yi*_m *pi*_q *zhongwai*_j
lead perform PERF one CL Chinese.and.western
*mingqu*_n</N></V>
popular.songs
"led and performed a variety of Chinese and western popular songs"

(63) <坚持_v 奉行_v> <N>独立自主_l 的_u 和平_n 外交_n 政策_n</N>
<*jianchi*_v *fengxing*_v> <N>*dulizizhu*_l *de*_u *heping*_n *waijiao*_n
insist.on follow independent DE peace diplomatic
*zhengce*_n</N>
policy
"insist on adopting an independent diplomatic policy in maintaining peace"

Besides sharing the same direct object, another clue that tends to prove that the two verbs are actually used as a compound verb is the suffixation of the morpheme 了 *-le*, as highlighted in (62). The verbal *-le* has generally been taken as an aspect marker, indicating completion (Norman, 1988: 163; Xiao, 2002), and it is attached to verbs and not to the objects of verbs (Chao, 1968: 247), excluding the possibility that the first verb takes the second verb (and the following noun phrase) as its object. Further research on clarifying their subcategorisation (whether they are serial or compound verbs) ought to be done in order to give a more precise parse.

3.7 Parses of adverbials and adverbial clauses

As stated in section 3.1, the annotation scheme that I used to manually parse the PFR treebank includes different sorts of adverbials: adverbial clauses (*Fa*), adverbial idioms/set phrases (*Ia*), adverbial adjective phrases (*Ja*), adverbial noun phrases (*Na*), adverbial prepositional phrases (*Pa*), adverb phrases (*R*) and adverbial verb phrases (*Va*). As adverb phrases, by definition, belong to the class of adverbials, they were not marked as "adverbial adverb phrases" in the scheme. A frequency table of these seven adverbial types occurring in the sample text under examination is given as follows:

Adverbial Type in PFR Sample Skeleton Treebank	**Frequency**
Adverbial Clause (*Fa*)	181
Adverbial Idiom/Set Phrase (*Ia*)	53
Adverbial Adjective Phrase (*Ja*)	352
Adverbial Noun Phrase (*Na*) – Temporal	713
Adverbial Noun Phrase (*Na*) – Non-temporal	44
Adverbial Prepositional Phrase (*Pa*) – Temporal	369
Adverbial Prepositional Phrase (*Pa*) – Non-temporal	524
Adverb Phrase (*R*)	2,208
Adverbial Verb Phrase (*Va*)	187
Total	**4,631**

Table 5: Frequency of seven adverbial types in the sample treebank.

Both the adverbial noun phrases and prepositional phrases are further split into temporal and non-temporal ones to specify their semantic functions, as the two kinds of adverbial are frequently employed to fulfil these functions. However, what I am particularly interested here is the adverbial clauses. In my treebank, there are altogether 181 adverbial clauses identified during manual skeleton parsing, three of which are illustrated in Figure 5; adverbial clauses in Chinese appear to be rare.

As I did not consider those clauses with no explicit subordinating marker as adverbial clauses proper in this book (see section 3.5.1.1), adverbial clauses found in the treebank are typically overtly marked by a *lianci* (连词), a conjunction[21], tagged "c". In each case the conjunction is a subordinating conjunction. This provides an important clue in the identification of adverbial clauses in the PFR Chinese Corpus as a whole. In the next chapter, I will discuss subordinating conjunctions and explain how to extract from the PFR corpus those adverbial clauses introduced by a subordinating conjunction.

<Fm><Fa>尽管_c <N>我们_r</N> <P>在_p <N>经济_n 社会_n 发展_v 中_f</N></P> <R>还_d</R> <V>面临_v <N>不少_m 困难_an</N></V></Fa> ，_w 但_c <N>我们_r</N> <V>有_v <N>邓小平理论_n 的_u 指引_vn</N></V> ，_w <V>有_v <N><改革_v 开放_v 近_a ２０_m 年_q 来_f> <N><N&>取得_v 的_u 伟大_a 成就_n</N&> 和_c <N+>积累_v 的_u 丰富_a 经验_n</N+></N></N></V> ，_w <R>还_d</R> <V>有_v <N>其他_r 的_u 各种_r 有利_a 条件_n</N></V> ，_w <N>我们_r</N> <R>一定_d</R> <V>能够_v 克服_v <N>这些_r 困难_an</N></V> ，_w <V>继续_v <稳步前进_l></V> 。_w</Fm>

<Fm><Fa>只要_c <N>我们_r</N> <R>进一步_d</R> <解放思想_i ，_w 实事求是_i> ，_w <V> 抓住_v <N>机遇_n</N></V> ，_w <开拓进取_l></Fa> ，_w <N><建设_v 有_v 中国_ns 特色_n 社会主义_n 的_u> 道路_n</N> 就_c <V>会_v <Fc>越_d 走_v 越_d 宽广_a</Fc></V> 。_w</Fm>

<Fm><Fa>只有_c <解放思想_i 、_w 实事求是_i></Fa> ，_w 才_c <V>能_v 冲破_v <N>各种_r <<不_d 切合_v 实际_n 的_u 或者_c 过时_a 的_u> 观念_n 的_u> 束缚_vn</N></V> ，_w <R>真正_d</R> <V>做到_v <Vo><尊重_v 、_w 认识_v 和_c 掌握_v> <N>客观_a 规律_n</N></Vo></V> ，_w <R>勇于_d</R> <V>突破_v</V> ，_w <R>勇于_d</R> <V>创新_v</V> ，_w <R>不断_d</R> <V>开创_v <N><社会主义_n 现代化_vn 建设_vn 的_u> 新_a 局面 n</N></V></Fm>

Figure 5: An illustration of adverbial clauses in the sample treebank.[22]

21 *Lianci* in Chinese vaguely refers to both coordinating and subordinating conjunctions. See Chapter Four, sections 4.2 and 4.3 for a critique of this notion.

22 The *pinyin* romanisations, the glosses and the English translations of these adverbial clauses were already given in examples (9), (3) and (2), respectively.

3.8 Conclusion: Quality control of the skeleton parsing process

In evaluating the success of an annotation project, Eyes and Leech (1993: 37–42) provide six essential criteria that can be used for evaluating my skeleton parsing scheme.

1. Consensual categories: The linguistic categories that were employed in my parsing scheme have been demonstrated, by comparison to seven syntactic theories, to represent grammatical features largely agreed upon by linguists, rather than features which are theory-specific or deeply controversial.
2. Overall coverage: My sample treebank represents a reasonable length of text (comprising about 100,000 word tokens or 2,500 sentences) to be manually parsed and could be re-used in future research.
3. Productivity: Productivity (i.e. the number of word tokens parsed within a reasonable length of time) was satisfactory with the simplified syntactic analysis provided by skeleton parsing.[23]
4. Accuracy: The output of the parsed sentences was cross-checked by several posteditors with a background in linguistics.[24] While one can never guarantee 100% accuracy, I believe the sample treebank to be highly accurate.
5. Uniformity of analysis: To demonstrate consistency of analysis, a concordance of the verb 要 *yao* "need" was drawn from my skeleton treebank. This verb always takes a verbal object, i.e. a verb functioning as the direct object of another verb, which is represented as *Vo* in my parsing scheme and is distinct from *V*, which stands for an independent verb phrase (see section 3.5.1.15). There are 252 instances of the verb *yao* in my treebank. In each case, it is

23 My skeleton treebank was completed in 6 months. The rate of manual skeleton parsing averages 500 words or 14 sentences a day.

24 An acknowledgment is due to the posteditors who corrected the manual skeleton parses of the sample treebank with skill and dedication: Gloria Lee, Candy Siu, Sara Wong and Sharon Wong.

followed by a verbal object consistently marked as *Vo* not *V*, as highlighted in the following figure.[25]

```
<V>注定_v  <Vo>要_v  <Vo>失败_v</Vo></Vo></V>
<V>要_v  <J>进一步_d  团结_a  起来_v</J></V>
<V>要_v  <Ja>更_d  好_a  地_u</Ja>  <Vo>坚持_v  <N><解放思想_i  、_w  实事求是_i  的_u>  思想_n  路线
_n</N></Vo></V>
<V>要_v  <Ja>更_d  好_a  地_u</Ja>  <Vo>坚持_v  <P 以_p  <N>经济_n  建设_vn</N></P>  <Vo>为_v  <N>中
心_n</N></Vo></Vo></V>
<V>要_v  <Vo>看_v  <Vo>能否_v  <P>把_p  <N>经济_n  工作_vn</N></P>  搞_v  上去_v</Vo></Vo></V>
<V>要_v  <Ja>切实_ad</Ja>  <P>把_p  <N>精力_n</N></P>  <Vo>集中_v  <Vo>到_v  <N><贯彻_v  落实_v  好
_a  中央_n  关于_p  今年_t  经济_n  工作_vn  的_u>  <N><N&>总体_n  要求_n</N&>  和_c  <N+>各项_r  重
要_a  任务_n</N+>  上_f  来_v</N></N></Vo></Vo></V>
<V>要_v  <Ja>更_d  好_a  地_u</Ja>  <Vo>坚持_v  <N> "<_w  两手抓_l  、_w  两手_m  都_d  要_v  硬_a  "
_w  的_u>  方针_n</N></Vo></V>
<V>要_v  <Ja>更_d  好_a  地_u</Ja>  <Vo>发扬_v  <N>求真务实_l  、_w  <密切_ad  联系_v  群众_n  的_u>
作风_n</N></Vo></V>
<V>要_v  <Vo>发扬_v  <N>这样_r  的_u  好_a  作风_n</N></Vo></V>
<V>要_v  <Vo>尊重_v  <N>群众_n  的_u  意愿_n</N></Vo></V>
<V>要_v  <R>大力_d</R>  <Vo>倡导_v  <N><说实话_l  、_w  办_v  实事_n  、_w  鼓_v  实劲_n  、_w  讲_v
实效_n  的_u>  作风_n</N></Vo></V>
<V>要_v  <Vo>坚守_v  <N>岗位_</N></Vo></V>
<V>要_v  <Vo>让_v  <S><N>他们_r</N>  <Ja>健康_ad</Ja>  <V>成长_v</V></S></Vo></V>
```

Figure 6: A concordance of the verb *yao*.

6. Linguistic validity: One of the aims of carrying out a skeleton parsing on a sample text of the PFR Chinese Corpus is to gain a better understanding of how to precisely locate adverbial clauses in a piece of POS tagged text. In written Chinese, adverbial clauses are typically overtly marked by subordinating conjunctions (or subordinators) of various sorts. Hence in the next chapter, I will describe in more detail the role of subordinators that are commonly employed in introducing adverbial clauses.

25 The verb *yao* can take an adjectival direct object, as shown in one instance of the concordance extracted. A vast majority of adjectives may function as verbs in Mandarin Chinese by taking aspect markers (e.g. *-guo* "experiential aspect", *-le* "perfective aspect", etc.) or directional complements (e.g. *qilai* "inchoative"). See Li and Thompson (1989: 141–147).

Chapter Four

Subordinators in Adverbial Clauses

4.1 Introduction

Following from the characteristic of Chinese adverbial clauses as shown in the PFR skeleton treebank, this book will focus on adverbial clauses which are overtly marked by a subordinating conjunction or an adverbial subordinator. In Chinese, several clauses can be juxtaposed in a sentence without being introduced by either a coordinator or a subordinator to mark their grammatical relations (Chu and Chi, 1999: 248–249). As a general rule, these clauses are more likely to be taken as coordinate clauses than subordinate clauses (cf. Li and Thompson, 1989: 631). Some Chinese scholars (Rai-Chu, 1982: 21–30; Liu et al., 1996: 505–513; Chu and Chi, 1999: 248f.; among others), however, argue that as long as a clause shows any semantic relations such as condition, reason, concession, etc., the clause must be an adverbial subordinate clause to another clause of the same sentence, even though it is not overtly marked by a subordinator. I did not follow this approach in my book because there is no conclusive morphosyntactic evidence in the Chinese language to prove that a clause under consideration is an adverbial subordinate clause rather than a coordinate clause and an independent sentence (cf. Chao, 1968: 104–106). In English, when an adverbial subordinate clause is not introduced by a subordinator, it must take the form of a non-finite clause such as *-ing* clause, *to*-infinitive clause, etc. (Quintero, 2002: 33–38). Chinese adverbial clauses, however, do not have such explicit morphological marking (Norman, 1988: 163; Hu et al., 2001). In the absence of any overt marking of the adverbial clause, the only way of identifying the adverbial clause is to rely on semantic relations, as noted above (Rai-Chu, 1982: 21–30; Liu et al., 1996: 505–513; Chu and Chi, 1999: 248f.). Since it is somewhat subjective to rely solely on semantic relations in identifying adverbial subordinate clauses and those quantitative analyses drawn from research of this sort would become very unreliable, I decided to focus only on the adverbial clause which is overtly marked by a subordinating conjunction and to exclude those "headless" adverbial clauses (i.e. adverbial clauses without an introductory subordinator) in my book. I will therefore discuss in detail the identification of *adverbial subordinators* in this chapter.

4.2 Problems with the PFR tagset

In the annotation scheme of the PFR Chinese Corpus, there is no such category as subordinator. Rather, the vague category *conjunction* tagged "c" is used to refer to both the coordinating and subordinating conjunctions, as is common in Chinese grammars (see, for example, Zhu, 1982; Lu and Ma, 1990, among others). These grammars typically state that any word which marks the grammatical relation between clauses, no matter whether it is a coordinate relation or a subordinate relation, is generally subsumed under the catch-all term 连词 *lianci*, more or less equivalent to a conjunction in English. This concept is so general that very few scholars have attempted to distinguish subordinating conjunctions from coordinating conjunctions and thus not many analyses have as yet addressed the issue of subordinators in adverbial clauses, the notable exceptions being Chao (1968: 113–114) and Wu (1982: 250ff.).

However, not all of the Chinese tagging systems neglect the distinction between coordinator and subordinator. The CKIP tagset is a case in point. As reviewed in Gao (1997), the CKIP tagset was designed by the Chinese Knowledge Information Processing (CKIP) Group at Academia Sinica in Taiwan. This tagset consists of 32 categories, including separate entries for coordinating conjunction and subordinating conjunction. Another noteworthy Chinese tagging system (Qin, 1998) is the Jasmine Chinese tagging system developed at the Chinese University of Hong Kong, comprising 47 word categories and 25 punctuation marks. Though it does not distinguish subordinators from coordinators, it insightfully proposes the distinction between a clause connector and a phrase connector, on which I would like to expand in the following section.[1]

1 For a detailed critique of these two main tagsets for Chinese, see Piao (2000: 54–59).

4.3 Suggested modifications to the PFR tagset with respect to tag "c"

For the purposes of my research, the most vital distinction is evidently the one between a coordinating conjunction and a subordinating conjunction. Hence, the catch-all term conjunction, as used in the PFR annotation scheme, needs to be sub-divided into these two major subcategories. Moreover, as will be demonstrated shortly, the coordinating conjunction is further split into three subdivisions i.e. intraclausal coordinating conjunction, interclausal coordinating conjunction and textual connective. In the following subsections, unless specified otherwise, all of the illustrative examples are taken from the PFR skeleton treebank as the syntactic information marked in the treebank is useful for explaining the properties of conjunctions.

4.3.1 Intraclausal coordinating conjunctions

As its name suggests, an intraclausal coordinating conjunction is typically used to link a variety of phrases in the same clause such as 和 *he* "and", 与 *yu* "and" and 而 *er* "and", etc. These phrases can be a noun phrase as in examples (1) and (2), a verb phrase as in example (3), and an adjective phrase as in example (4).

(1) <N><N&>两岸_n 经济_n 文化_n 交流_vn</N&> 和_c <N+>人员_n 往来_vn</N+></N>

<N><N&>*lianggan*_n	*jingji*_n	*wenhua*_n	*jiaoliu*_vn</N&>	***he*_c**
across.the.border	economic	cultural	exchange	and

<N+>*renyuan*_n	*wanglai*_vn</N+></N>
official	visit

"cross-straits economic and cultural exchange and official visits"

(2) <N>钢琴_n 与_c 管弦乐队_n 作品_n 《_w 东方_f 之_u 珠_Ng 》_w</N>

<N>*gangqin*_n ***yu*_c** *guanxianyuedui*_n *zuopin*_n 《_w *Dongfang*_f
piano and orchestra work Orient's
*Zhi*_u *Zhu*_Ng 》_w</N>
GEN pearl
"piano and orchestral versions of the song 'Pearl of the Orient'"

(3) <V><学习_v 和_c 掌握_v> <N>党_n 的_u 十五大_j 精神_n</N></V>

<V><*xuexi*_v ***he*_c** *zhangwo*_v> <N>*dang*_n *de*_u
learn and master the.Communist.Party's GEN
*shiwuda*_j *jingshen*_n</N></V>
15.primary principles
"learn and master the Communist Party's 15 primary principles"

(4) <N><度过_v 了_u 非凡_z 而_c 辉煌_a 的_u> １９９７年_t</N>

<N><*duguo*_v *le*_u *feifan*_z ***er*_c** *huihuang*_a *de*_u>
go.through PERF extraordinary and magnificent DE
１９９７*nian*_t</N>
year.of.1997
"passed an extraordinary and magnificent year of 1997"

4.3.2 Interclausal coordinating conjunctions

An interclausal coordinating conjunction is used to show a wide range of relations (e.g. addition, concession, result, simultaneity in time, etc.) between two adjacent clauses of the same sentence. Many examples of this sort of coordinator can be identified in my sample skeleton treebank e.g. 并 *bing* "and", 但是 *danshi* "but", 因此 *yinci* "therefore", 同时 *tongshi* "in the meantime", etc.

(5) <S N="112"><S&><Pa>在_p <N><N&>郭_nr 家_n</N&> 和_c <N+>闫_nr 家_n</N+></N></Pa> ，_w <N>李_nr 鹏_nr</N> <R>都_d</R> <Ja>具体_a 地_u</Ja> <V>了解_v 了_u <N><他们_r 退休_v 后_f 的_u> 生活_vn 保障_vn 问题_n</N></V></S&> ，_w 并_c <S+><P>与_p <N>一些_m 老_a 职工_n</N></P> <Na>一起_s</Na> <V>回忆_v 起_v 了_u <N><当年_t 建设_v 电厂_n 的_u> 情景_n</N></V> 。_w</S+></S>

<S N="112"><S&><Pa>*zai*_p <N><N&>*Guo*_nr *jia*_n</N&> *he*_c
at Guo home and
<N+>*Yan*_nr *jia*_n</N+></N></Pa> ，_w <N>*Li*_nr *Peng*_nr</N>
Yan home Li Peng
<R>*dou*_d</R> <Ja>*juti*_a *de*_u</Ja> <V>*liaojie*_v *le*_u
both in.detail ADVL understand PERF
<N><*tamen*_r *tuixiu*_v *hou*_f *de*_u> *shenghuo*_vn *baozhang*_vn
their retire after DE living pension
*wenti*_n</N></V></S&> ，_w ***bing*_c** <S+><P>*yu*_p <N>*yixie*_m
difficulty moreover with some
*lao*_a *zhigong*_n</N></P> <Na>*yiqi*_s</Na> <V>*huiyi*_v *qi*_v *le*_u
old co-workers together conjure up PERF
<N><*dangnian*_t *jianshe*_v *dianchang*_n *de*_u>
past build electricity.supply.station DE
*qingjing*_n</N></V> 。_w</S+></S>
memories

"In Guo's and Yan's homes, Li Peng gained an understanding of their life and difficulties after retirement. He also chatted with some other elderly staff and recalled the days when the electricity supply station was being built."

(6) <S N="29">但是_c ，_w <N>世界_n</N> <R>还_d 不_d</R> <J>安宁_a</J> 。_w</S>

<S N="29">***danshi*_c** ，_w <N>*shijie*_n</N> <R>*hai*_d *bu*_d</R>
however world still not
<J>*anning*_a</J> 。_w</S>
tranquil

"Yet, the world is not in peace."

(7) <S N="72">因此_c ，_w <N>各级_r 领导_n 干部_n</N> <R>务必_d</R> <V>牢记_v <N><全心全意_i 为_p 人民_n 服务_v 的_u> 宗旨_n</N></V> ，_w <P>在_p <N>勤政廉政_l 、_w 艰苦奋斗_i 方面_n</N></P> <以身作则_i> ，_w <V>当_v <N>好_a 表率_n</N></V> 。_w</S>

<S N="72">***yinci_c*** ，_w <N>*geji*_r *lingdao*_n *ganbu*_n</N>
therefore at.each.level leading official
<R>*wubi*_d</R> <V>*laoji*_v <N><*quanxinquanyi*_i *wei*_p *renmin*_n
necessarily bear.in.mind whole-heartedly for citizens
*fuwu*_v *de*_u> *zongzhi*_n</N></V> ，_w <P>*zai*_p
provide.service DE mission in
<N>*qinzhenglianzheng*_l 、_w *jiankufendou*_i *fangmian*_n</N></P>
diligence.and.integrity perseverance aspects
<*yishenzuoze*_i> ，_w <V>*dang*_v <N>*hao*_a *biaoshuai*_n</N></V> 。
set.an.example act.as good example
_w</S>

"Hence, heads at all levels of leadership must bear in mind that they serve the citizens wholeheartedly and demonstrate integrity and perseverance in order to set a good example."

(8) <S N="105">同时_c ，_w <R>也_d</R> <V>希望_v <S><N>你们_r</N> <Ja>安全_ad</Ja> <V>生产_v</V> 、_w <R>经济_ad</R> <V>调度_v</V> ，_w <V>实现_v <N><经济_n 增长_vn 方式_n 的_u> 转变_vn</N></V></S></V> 。_w ”_w</S>

<S N="105">***tongshi_c*** ，_w <R>*ye*_d</R> <V>*xiwang*_v
meanwhile also hope
<S><N>*nimen*_r</N> <Ja>*anquan*_ad</Ja> <V>*shengchan*_v</V> 、_w
you safely produce
<R>*jingji*_ad</R> <V>*tiaodu*_v</V> ，_w <V>*shixian*_v <N><*jingji*_n
economically adjust realise economy
*zengzhang*_vn *fangshi*_n *de*_u> *zhuanbian*_vn</N></V></S></V> 。
growth mode DE change
_w ”_w</S>

"In the meantime, I hope you could take note of safety measures in manufacturing, improve productivity and keep up with any changes in our economy."

4.3.3 Textual connectives

As noted above, the relations marked by an interclausal coordinating conjunction hold within two or three clauses in the same sentence. Textual connectives, however, tend to highlight the relations among clauses which occur in a larger context or in the preceding discourse. They are typically used to recapitulate or conclude the preceding discourse. Although only one instance, 总的来说 *zong de lai shuo* "on the whole", was found in the sample of the PFR skeleton treebank as shown in the following example, many other examples can be found throughout the corpus such as 综上所述 *zong shang suo shu* "to summarise", 具体地说 *juti de shuo* "to put it in more detail", 换而言之 *huan er yan zhi* "in other words", 由此可见 *you ci ke jian* "judging from all these", etc.

(9) <S N="13">总的来说_c ，_w <N><N&>中国_ns 改革_v</N&> 和_c <N+>发展_v 的_u 全局_n</N+></N> <V>继续_v <Vo>保持_v 了_u <N>稳定_an</N></Vo></V> 。_w</S>

<S N="13">***zongdelaishuo*****_c** ，_w <N><N&>*Zhongguo*_ns
on.the.whole China

*gaige*_v</N&> *he*_c <N+>*fazhan*_v *de*_u *quanju*_n</N+></N>
reform and develop DE situation

<V>*jixu*_v <Vo>*baochi*_v *le*_u <N>*wending*_an</N></Vo></V> 。
go.on maintain PERF stability

_w</S>

"On the whole, China's reform and development keep on progressing steadily."

4.3.4 Subordinating conjunctions or adverbial subordinators

Adverbial subordinators, frequently called "subordinating conjunctions" in grammars (e.g. Quirk and Greenbaum, 1973; Kortmann, 1997: 56; Altenberg and Tapper, 1998; Kortmann, 1998), are typically regarded as "words which specify some semantic interclausal (or: circumstantial, adverbial) relation between the subordinate clause over which they operate and the modified matrix clause" (Kortmann, 1998: 457). To put it another way, an adverbial subordinator refers to a word that marks an adverbial subordinate clause for its semantic relation to the main clause.

The major aim in establishing a catalogue of defining properties of adverbial subordinators needs to be a successful delimitation of the latter from other functionally analogous grammatical categories such as adverb and coordinator. In my book, the working definition of adverbial subordinator entails two criteria. Firstly, an adverbial subordinator introduces a clause which must be linked to (i.e. dependent on) another clause in the same sentence. Secondly, the two clauses must not be in coordination. One of the major differences between a coordinate clause and a subordinate clause is that the information expressed by the subordinate clause is likely to be placed in the background with respect to the main clause, while the information expressed by two coordinate clauses is of equal importance (Lakoff, 1971; Quirk and Greenbaum, 1973: 919; Winter, 1982; Martin, 1983; Hoey, 1986; Hoey and Winter, 1986; Johannessen, 1998). As an example of the first criterion, 可是 *keshi* "but" is not considered as a subordinator in my book as it can introduce a clause which is able to occur independently, as shown in example (10), though it is typically used in concert with a genuine subordinator, 虽然 *suiran* "although". As an example of the second criterion, 既 *ji* "not only" is not a subordinator as it must be linked to a coordinate clause introduced by 又 *you* "but also" in the same sentence, as illustrated in example (11).

(10) 可是_c ，_w 父母_n 靠_p 平时_t 省吃俭用_i ，_w 过年_v 时_Ng 也_d 要_v 为_p 我_r 和_c 妹妹_n 做_v 一_m 身_q 新衣_n 。_w (19980125)

***keshi*_c**	，_w	*fumu*_n	*kao*_p	*pingshi*_t	*shengchijianyong*_i	，_w	
however		parents	by.means.of	daily	save.money.on.expenditure		
*guonian*_v	*shi*_Ng	*ye*_d	*yao*_v	*wei*_p	*wo*_r	*he*_c	
Chinese.New.Year	occasion	yet	want.to	for	me	and	
*meimei*_n	*zuo*_v	*yi*_m	*shen*_q	*xinyi*_n	。_w (19980125)		
sister	make	one	CL	new.clothes			

"However, by cutting down on food and necessities, my parents bought new clothes for me and my younger sister for the Chinese New Year."

(11) 要_v 加强_v 基层_n 干部_n 队伍_n 的_u 建设_vn ，_w 既_c 要_v 抓好_v 对_p 现有_v 干部_n 队伍_n 的_u 培训_vn ，_w 提高_v 他们_r 的_u 素质_n ，_w 又_c 要_v 注重_v 培养_v 新_a 的_u 人才_n 。_w (19980110)

*yao*_v *jiaqiang*_v *jiceng*_n *ganbu*_n *duiwu*_n *de*_u *jianshe*_vn ，_w
want.to strengthen basic.level official troop DE development

ji_c *yao*_v *zhuahao*_v *dui*_p *xianyou*_v *ganbu*_n *duiwu*_n *de*_u
not.only have.to grasp as.regards current official troop DE

*peixun*_vn ，_w *tigao*_v *tamen*_r *de*_u *suzhi*_n ，_w *you*_c
training enhance their GEN quality but.also

*yao*_v *zhuzhong*_v *peiyang*_v *xin*_a *de*_u *rencai*_n 。_w (19980110)
have.to emphasise train new DE people.of.high.calibre

"To strengthen our troop, not only do we need to provide training to serving officers, but we also need to place emphasis on recruiting new blood of high calibre."

4.4 Subordinators in the PFR Chinese Corpus

4.4.1 Identification of adverbial subordinators

In the previous section, I have provided a detailed account of the properties of conjunctions in Chinese. The category needs to be split into four subdivisions, namely intraclausal coordinating conjunction, interclausal coordinating conjunction, textual connective and subordinating conjunction/adverbial subordinator, to address the range of properties that a conjunction may have. However, as the major aim of this book is to give both a quantitative and qualitative account of adverbial subordinate clauses in written Chinese, the distinction between a coordinating conjunction and a subordinating conjunction is the distinction focussed upon by my book. Consequently I do not explore the remaining subcategories of conjunction i.e. intraclausal coordinating conjunction, interclausal coordinating conjunction and textual connective.

4.4.2 Results

In the PFR Chinese Corpus, there are 175 distinct Chinese word forms which were tagged as 连词 *lianci* "conjunction".

Broadly speaking, most of the Chinese *lianci* are coordinators which function intraclausally, interclausally and textually. The most common ten *lianci* in written Chinese are coordinating conjunctions rather than subordinating ones. Five of the *lianci*, though tagged as "conjunction", were taken as adverbs in this book: these are 便 *bian* "then", 才 *cai* "then", 就 *jiu* "then", 宁愿 *ningyuan* "would rather" and 宁 *ning* "would rather". One of the most important syntactic differences between a conjunction and an adverb is that the former (not the latter) can either precede or follow the subject of the clause in which it occurs (Chao, 1968: 791; Wong, 2002). These five words were attested in the corpus to occur only after the subject. They were therefore considered as adverbs. After eliminating the coordinating conjunctions and adverbs from the list, 57 subordinating conjunctions can be found, as outlined in the following table.

甭管 *bengguan* “no matter what”
不单 *budan* “in addition to”
不管 *buguan* “no matter what”
不论 *bulun* “whether or, whatever”
不论是 *bulunshi* “whether or, whatever”
不说 *bushuo* “let alone …”
除非 *chufei* “unless”
从而 *conger* “in order that; as a result”
而是 *ershi* “rather”
故 *gu* “so that”
果真 *guozhen* “supposing that”
何况 *hekuang* “not to mention …”
假如 *jiaru* “supposing that”
假若 *jiaruo* “supposing that”
即便 *jibian* “even if”
尽管 *jinguan* “even though”
既然 *jiran* “since, as”
即使 *jishi* “even if”
就是 *jiushi* “even if”
哪怕 *napa* “even if”
且不说 *qiebushuo* “let alone …”
任 *ren* “no matter what”
如 *ru* “if”
如果 *ruguo* “if”
若 *ruo* “if”
若果 *ruoguo* “if”
若是 *ruoshi* “if”
如若 *ruruo* “if”
尚且 *shangqie* “even”
虽 *sui* “though”
虽然 *suiran* “although”
虽说 *suishuo* “while admitting that …”
随着 *suizhe* “as soon as”
倘 *tang* “supposing that”
倘若 *tangruo* “supposing that”
万一 *wanyi* “in case”
无论 *wulun* “whether or, whatever”
无论是 *wulunshi* “whether or, whatever”
要 *yao* “assuming that”
要不是 *yaobushi* “if not, otherwise”
要是 *yaoshi* “assuming that”
以 *yi* “in order that”
以便 *yibian* “in order that”
以免 *yimian* “in order that… not…”
因 *yin* “because”
因为 *yinwei* “because”
以致 *yizhi* “as a result”
以至于 *yizhiyu* “consequently”
由于 *youyu* “owing to the fact that”
与其 *yuqi* “rather than”
与其说 *yuqishuo* “rather than say that”
只是 *zhishi* “except that”
之所以 *zhisuoyi* “why there is a consequence of”
只要 *zhiyao* “provided that”
只有 *zhiyou* “only if”
纵 *zong* “even if”
纵使 *zongshi* “even if”

Table 6: The inventory of 57 adverbial subordinators in Chinese.

These subordinators generally exhibit two properties. Firstly, most of the Chinese adverbial subordinators are *correlative subordinators* (Quirk and Greenbaum, 1973: 313–314; Biber et al., 1999: 86): they are combinations of two markers, one (a subordinating conjunction) occurring in the subordinate clause, and the other (either an adverb or a conjunction) occurring in the superordinate clause. For example, 如果 *ruguo* "if" usually occurs with an adverb 就 *jiu* "then"; 虽然 *suiran* "although" is typically followed by a coordinating conjunction 但 *dan* "but"; 不单 *budan* "not only" and 尚且 *shangqie* "even" have the same correlative adverb 更 *gen* "even". An adverbial subordinator can have diverse correlates and those correlates are not obligatory. Take 尽管 *jinguan* "even though" as an example. It has a range of correlatives such as 但是 *danshi* "but", 可是 *keshi* "but", 却 *que* "but", 然而 *raner* "yet", 仍然 *rengran* "still", 还是 *haishi* "still", 而 *er* "but" (cf. Hou, 1998: 331 ff.) and a null correlative (i.e. *jinguan* does not have a correlative which occurs in the main clause), as illustrated in the following table.

Correlatives	**Frequency of Occurrence**
*Null correlative	8
但 *dan* "but" (conjunction)	88
但是 *danshi* "but" (conjunction)	10
都 *dou* "still" (adverb)	2
而 *er* "but" (conjunction)	2
还是 *hashi* "still" (adverb)	2
可 *ke* "but" (conjunction)	1
可是 *keshi* "but" (conjunction)	1
却 *que* "but" (adverb)	3
然而 *raner* "yet" (conjunction)	3
仍 *reng* "still" (adverb)	8
仍然 *rengran* "still" (adverb)	2
尚 *shang* "still" (adverb)	1
也 *ye* "still" (adverb)	1
Total:	**132**

* A null correlative refers to the fact that no correlative is found in the main clause.

Table 7: The list of correlatives of the adverbial subordinator *jinguan.*

Secondly, the adverbial subordinators can express a wide range of meanings such as condition (e.g. *ruo* 若 "if", 要是 *yaoshi* "if", etc.), reason/cause (e.g. 因为 *yinwei* "because", 由于 *youyu* "due to", etc.), result (e.g. 之所以 *zhisuoyi* "as a result", 故 *gu* "therefore", etc.), purpose (e.g. 从而 *conger* "in order to", 以便 *yibian* "in order to", etc.), and concession (e.g. 即使 *jishi* "even if", 就是 *jiushi* "even if" etc.), roughly reflecting different types of adverbial clauses. The semantic types of adverbial clauses in written Chinese will be discussed at length in the next chapter.

4.5 Using Java programming: The extraction of sentences containing adverbial subordinators

As adverbial clauses in Chinese are overtly marked by a subordinating conjunction, it is essential to extract those sentences having adverbial subordinators in order to identify the adverbial clause. Given an adverbial subordinator, something as simple as the "Find" facility of a word processor can easily identify the subordinator within a piece of text. However, the problem with this searching tool is that it can only look for one subordinator at one time: for a piece of text, I needed to search 57 times for the occurrence of 57 different subordinators which I identified earlier. This procedure would be repeated depending on how many texts I have to examine. Furthermore, this search facility merely spots the position of the subordinator in the text and does not automatically extract the sentence(s) in which the subordinator occurs. Hence the extraction of these subordinator-loaded sentences needs to be done manually. As a word processor's search function does not offer a very good resource for processing my corpus data to meet my research question, I decided to write a computer program to extract those sentences in which an adverbial subordinator occurs, as shown in the following figure.

Figure 7: An output of the Subordinator Extractor.

4.6 Chapter summary

The PFR annotation scheme and similar Chinese tagsets have a shortcoming in that they do not distinguish a subordinating conjunction from a coordinating conjunction. This is also reflected in traditional grammars for Chinese in which the catch-all category 连词 *lianci* "conjunction" does not express this distinction. Hence, in this book, it was proposed that a conjunction should be further split into four subcategories, namely, intraclausal coordinating conjunction, interclausal coordinating conjunction, textual connective and subordinating conjunction in order to capture all properties of conjunctions in Chinese. However, as my book is concerned with the adverbial subordinate clause, this categorisation covers cases not relevant to my research question. Hence, only the distinction between a coordinator and a subordinator is used in this work. A total of 175 conjunctions were identified in the PFR Chinese Corpus. To classify a given item as an adverbial subordinator, two defining criteria have to be fulfilled: firstly, it introduces a clause which must be linked to another clause in the same sentence; secondly, the two clauses are not in coordination.

From the list of conjunctions found in my corpus, I identified 57 adverbial subordinators, most of which are correlative subordinators: they take either an adverb or a conjunction as their correlative. An adverbial subordinator can have more than one correlative and the correlative is not obligatory. Moreover, the adverbial subordinator can express a wide range of meanings such as condition, concession, reason/cause, result, purpose, etc., possibly reflecting different types of adverbial clauses. After I obtained a list of subordinators, I developed a Java program to extract those sentences in which these subordinators occur in order to identify the adverbial clause, which is overtly marked by a subordinating conjunction. The program design is based on the idea that the computer can spot the occurrence of any of these subordinators in a text and display only those sentences containing the adverbial subordinator. In the next chapter, I will examine these subordinator marked sentences closely and identify the adverbial clauses and discuss their semantic roles.

Chapter Five

A Typology of Adverbial Clauses in Written Chinese

5.1 Introduction

Studies touching upon the semantic analysis of adverbial clauses to date have largely been concerned with the English language (Quirk et al., 1985: 1045–1123, Thompson and Longacre, 1985; Givón, 1993: 285–315 and 2001: 330–351; Quintero, 2002), though Chao (1968) and Wang (1995) are notable exceptions which are based on Chinese language data. However, both Chao and Wang chose to impose a relatively coarse categorisation which includes only five semantic classes of adverbial clause, namely temporal clauses, place clauses, conditional clauses, concessive clauses and causal clauses. The information offered by such a relatively coarse set of categories would be rather sparse and unable to fully capture the entire range of variety of semantic roles exhibited by adverbial clauses. For this reason, it is necessary to extend the scope of the semantic analysis of Chinese adverbial clauses and make more refined distinctions.

As the review in Chapter Two (section 2.3.2.1) has shown to some extent already, Quintero (2002) offers a corpus-informed (LOB Corpus) typology of English adverbial clauses within the framework of Functional Grammar (FG): in FG, there are four semantic hierarchies (i.e. Entity Type, Time Dependency, Factuality and Presupposition) that can be used in establishing an exhaustive typology of adverbial subordinate clauses. This study initially appears to be a good theoretical framework on which to base my typology of Chinese adverbial clauses. However, Quintero's study is primarily aimed at proving the existence of a systematic relation between the verb forms (finite and non-finite verb forms) of adverbial clauses and the semantic types which these clauses designate via the application of these hierarchies: each of these hierarchies establishes that non-finite verb forms are more likely to occur in adverbial clauses of lower order[1] than of higher order[2]. As has been repeatedly emphasised in this book (see Chapter Two, section 2.3.2.3; Chapter Three, sections 3.4.1 and 3.5.1.1), there is no independent evidence for a finite/non-finite verb form distinction in Chinese (Rai-Chu, 1982: 78 ff.; Norman, 1988: 163; Hu et al., 2001). Hence, I decided not to follow Quintero's approach in classifying adverbial clauses, as it presupposes such a distinction. Rather, I would like to give a theory neutral, descriptive, corpus-based account of a semantic classification of adverbial clauses in Chinese. The present chapter is organised as follows: in section 5.2, I will describe the approach I used to identify the adverbial clauses in the PFR Chinese Corpus; in section 5.3, I will examine at length each of the semantic types of adverbial clauses in Chinese, list the subordinators which are responsible for expressing the meanings, and explain the use of different sorts of adverbial clauses on the basis of the corpus data, in contrast to what previous accounts of the adverbial clause type under consideration have said; section 5.4 concludes by recapitulating and summarising my findings.

5.2 Identification of adverbial clauses: Problem-oriented tagging

The approach adopted here is called *problem-oriented tagging*. This annotation method is distinctive from other common annotation types such as POS tagging and skeleton parsing; it is undertaken in response to a very specific research goal (de Haan, 1991; McEnery and Wilson, 2001). As de Haan (1991: 52) notes, problem-oriented tagging entails a procedure in which not all of the language materials in the corpus are tagged

1 For example, those adverbial clauses describing relation, individual or state of affairs such as clauses of purpose (introduced, e.g., by *in order to*), clauses of addition (introduced, e.g., by *apart from*) and clauses of substitution (introduced, e.g., by *rather than*).

2 For example, those adverbial clauses which are characterised by propositional content or speech act such as clauses of condition (introduced, e.g., by *if*) and clauses of concession (introduced, e.g., by *although*).

but only those parts that are relevant to the research question. In other words, problem-oriented tagging has two characteristics: (1) it is not exhaustive; (2) the annotation scheme is not a broad coverage scheme but consists of all of the relevant distinctions required by a particular research question (McEnery and Wilson, 2001: 68–69). In my case, this meant that only the sentences in which adverbial clauses introduced by a subordinating conjunction were found needed to be taken into consideration. These sentences were first extracted automatically from the corpus by running the Java program described in the previous chapter, and then annotated manually into two major parts, a main clause (delimited by the <Fm> element) and an adverbial clause (delimited by the <Fa> element), by applying the bracketing notation I devised for my treebank (see Chapter Three, sections 3.5.1.1 and 3.5.1.3). It is important to note that in the process of problem-oriented tagging, I considered and counted only those genuine adverbial clauses in which the subordinator was tagged correctly.

(1) 郑_nr 成功_nr 与其_c 属下_n 施_nr 琅_nr 的_u 关系_n 冲突_vn ，_w [...]
*Zheng*_nr *Chenggong*_nr ***yuqi*_c** *shuxia*_n *Shi*_nr *Lang*_nr *de*_u
Zheng Chenggong and.his subordinate Shi Lang DE
*guanxi*_n *chongtu*_vn ，_w [...]
relationship conflicts
"The conflicts between Zheng Chenggong and his subordinate Shi Lang, [...]"

(2) 关公_nr 戏_n 几乎_d 全_d 是_v 演_v 他_r 破_v 大敌_n 显_v 神威_n 的_u 勇猛_a 故事_n 的_u ，_w 只有_c 《_w 走麦城_n 》_w 演_v 了_u 他_r 的_u 不幸_n 。_w
*Guangong*_nr *xi*_n *jihu*_d *quan*_d *shi*_v *yan*_v *ta*_r
Guangong Chinese.opera almost all be perform he
*po*_v *dadi*_n *xian*_v *shenwei*_n *de*_u *yongmeng*_a *gushi*_n *de*_u ，
attack enemy show power DE courageous story PART
_w ***zhiyou*_c** 《_w *Zoumaicheng*_n 》_w *yan*_v *le*_u *ta*_r
only.have Chinese.opera.of.Zou.Maicheng perform PERF his
*de*_u *buxing*_n 。_w
GEN misfortune
"Almost all of the Chinese operas about Guan Gong are concerned with his heroic deeds, only the Zou Maicheng Opera portrays his misfortune."

In example (1) above, the highlighted "single word" 与其 *yuqi* is in fact made up of two separate words with completely different parts of speech: 与 *yu* "and" is a conjunction, and 其 *qi* "one's" is a pronoun referring to the personal name 郑成功 *Zheng Chenggong*, the subject of this sentence. These two words were incorrectly taken as a single unit and thus the tag assigned was wrong. As I am only interested in those sentences with *correctly POS tagged* subordinating conjunctions, this sort of sentence was excluded from my list of adverbial clauses. Similarly, in example (2), the single-word conjunction (which means "only if") should be re-analysed as two words involving an adverb followed by a verb, i.e. 只 *zhi* "only" + 有 *you* "have".

(3) 极_d 少数_m 因为_c 客观_a 原因_n 暂时_d 难以_d 落实_v 的_u [...]
*ji*_d *shaoshu*_m ***yinwei*_c** *keguan*_a *yuanyin*_n *zanshi*_d
extremely very.few because practial reasons temporarily
*nanyi*_d *luoshi*_v *de*_u [...]
hard implement PART
"Very few of them cannot be implemented for practical reasons for the time being [...]"

(4) 因为_c 气候_n 的_u 关系_n ，_w [...]
***yinwei*_c** *qihou*_n *de*_u *guanxi*_n ，_w [...]
because climate DE reason
"Due to the climate, [...]"

(5) 由于_c 货币_n 贬值_vn 的_u 因素_n ，_w [...]
***youyu*_c** *huobi*_n *bianzhi*_vn *de*_u *yinshu*_n ，_w [...]
because currency depreciation DE reason
"Owing to the depreciation of the currency, [...]"

(6) 我_r 不管_c [步长_nz 公司_n]nt 一_m 年_q 几_m 个_q 亿_m ，_w [...]
*wo*_r ***buguan*_c** [*Buchang*_nz *Gongsi*_n]nt *yi*_m *nian*_q *ji*_m
I do.not.care Buchang company one year several
*ge*_q *yi*_m ，_w [...]
CL hundred.million
"I do not care how many hundred millions the Buchang Company can make in one year, [...]"

In less straightforward cases, some words have multiple word class membership such as 因为 *yinwei* "because" and 由于 *youyu* "because", which can be either a preposition or a subordinating conjunction with the same form and meaning. They might easily be wrongly tagged as in examples (3) and (4) where *yinwei*, being followed by a noun phrase, must be a preposition, not a conjunction as originally stated. In example (5), *youyu* should be a preposition for the same reason. These sentences were also disregarded by me. On the other hand, the word 不管 *buguan* can refer either to a verb or a subordinating conjunction with different meanings. In example (6), it must be a verb, meaning "not care, ignore", not a conjunction which conveys the meaning "no matter what" or "whatever" because of two reasons. Semantically, the meaning of the verb is more compatible with the meaning of the clause/sentence than that of the conjunction. Morphosyntactically, the verbal predicate of the clause/sentence, following the subject pronoun 我 *wo* "I", would lack a main verb if the word under consideration was interpreted as a conjunction.

(7) 巩固_v ，_w 就是_c 坚持_v 基本_a 思路_n ，_w 保持_v 好_a 的_u 工作_vn 态势_n ；_w […]

*gonggu*_v ，_w ***jiushi*_c** *jianchi*_v *jiben*_a *silu*_n ，_w *baochi*_v
consolidate that.is stick.at primary way.of.thinking maintain

*hao*_a *de*_u *gongzuo*_vn *taishi*_n ；_w […]
good DE job attitude

"Consolidation means sticking at primary objectives and maintaining a good attitude to a job; […]"

More subtle cases involve the use of the same word form for both adverb and conjunction as shown in example (7) above. It is particularly easy to confuse an adverb with a conjunction as both can assume a clause-medial position i.e. between the subject and the predicate. The distinction between an adverb and a conjunction in Chinese lies in the distributional fact that a conjunction can be placed before the subject and after it, while an adverb can only be put after the subject (Chao, 1968: 791; Wong, 2002). In example (7), the word in question occurs after the subject. This does not offer a clear indication as to whether the word concerned is a conjunction or an adverb as both of them can occur after the subject. However, when I looked at the meaning of the sentence, I found that the word must be an adverb, meaning "exactly", which differs drastically from the meaning "even if" when it is used as a conjunction. I decided therefore that the original tagging in the corpus was wrong and disregarded this sentence.

(8) 由于_p 各国_r 目前_t 尚_d 难_ad 断定_v ４５_m 海里_q 内_f 是否_v 有_v 油_n ，_w [...]

***youyu*_p**	*geguo*_r		*muqian*_t		*shang*_d	*nan*_ad	
because	each.country		for.the.time.being		yet	hard	
*duanding*_v	4 5 _m	*haili*_q	*nei*_f	*shifou*_v	*you*_v	*you*_n	，
confirm	45	sea.miles	within	whether.or.not	have	petroleum	

_w [...]

"Since all nations are uncertain about whether there is any potential source of petroleum within 45 nautical miles, [...]"

While those sentences having words misinterpreted as adverbial subordinators were disregarded by me, sentences with genuine adverbial subordinators which were not mistaken for subordinating conjunctions and incorrectly tagged were manually edited and added to my data. As shown in example (8) above, the word 由于 *youyu* "because", introducing a clause, must be an adverbial subordinator though it was wrongly marked as a preposition in cases such as (8). All such examples were manually corrected by me. As the words erroneously tagged as adverbial subordinators were omitted from my data and those manually-edited, genuine, adverbial subordinators were added to my data, the frequency of occurrence of individual correctly-tagged subordinators in my data is different from that used in Chapter 4 which is merely a count on the occurrence of the subordinators (either correctly or incorrectly) tagged with a conjunction tag. Below is a revised frequency of occurrence of subordinators as used in the PFR Chinese Corpus based upon my hand corrected data.

Subordinator	Frequency	Subordinator	Frequency
甭管 *bengguan*	1	虽然 *suiran*	173
不单 *budan*	3	虽说 *suishuo*	6
不管 *buguan*	39	随着 *suizhe*	1
不论 *bulun*	23	倘 *tang*	7
不论是 *bulunshi*	9	倘若 *tangruo*	7
不说 *bushuo*	1	万一 *wanyi*	1
除非 *chufei*	1	无论 *wulun*	60
从而 *conger*	172	无论是 *wulunshi*	30
而是 *ershi*	177	要 *yao*	1
故 *gu*	7	要不是 *yaobushi*	3
果真 *guozhen*	1	要是 *yaoshi*	8
何况 *hekuang*	7	以 *yi*	257
假如 *jiaru*	12	以便 *yibian*	6
假若 *jiaruo*	2	以免 *yimian*	9
即便 *jibian*	14	因 *yin*	16
尽管 *jinguan*	132	因为 *yinwei*	116
既然 *jiran*	9	以致 *yizhi*	9
即使 *jishi*	64	以至于 *yizhiyu*	5
就是 *jiushi*	3	由于 *youyu*	189
哪怕 *napa*	6	与其 *yuqi*	2
且不说 *qiebushuo*	2	与其说 *yuqishuo*	1
任 *ren*	3	只是 *zhishi*	25
如 *ru*	38	之所以 *zhisuoyi*	46
如果 *ruguo*	308	只要 *zhiyao*	143
若 *ruo*	33	只有 *zhiyou*	115
若果 *ruoguo*	2	纵 *zong*	1
若是 *ruoshi*	7	纵使 *zongshi*	1
如若 *ruruo*	1		
尚且 *shangqie*	3		
虽 *sui*	99		

Table 8: Frequency of occurrence of adverbial subordinators.

5.3 Semantic classes of adverbial clauses

In the PFR Chinese Corpus, 2,417 adverbial clauses were identified. For the classification of adverbial clauses, their semantic roles were taken into consideration. I assume that the basic meaning of the subordinator determines the semantic class of the adverbial clause for the purpose of this book. This assumption is shared by the previous literature on adverbial clauses which assumes that the semantic roles of adverbial clauses are identical to that of their subordinators (e.g. Chao, 1968: 113–124; Quirk et al., 1985: 1077–1118; Thompson and Longacre, 1985: 177; Hengeveld, 1998: 356–358; Kortmann, 1998: 457–468). Kortmann (1998: 457), for instance, explicitly states that adverbial subordinators perform the task of marking the semantic relation between the adverbial clause and the main clause. Thus his study of adverbial clauses in the languages of Europe aims to solve the question "which adverbial subordinators in language X are used for the marking of interclausal relations A, B, C [...]?" (*ibid*: 464). Using this assumption, I began my analysis by looking closely at the meanings of the subordinating conjunctions in turn. While subordinators are subsumed under existing, general, semantic categories in the literature (see, for example, Quirk et al. 1985; Thompson and Longacre, 1985) e.g. purpose, cause/reason, condition, concession, etc., not all of the commonly used semantic classes include subordinators. Hence, only those categories that are representative of the meaning of subordinators were considered in my study and irrelevant semantic categories were disregarded. In cases where a subordinator could not fit in to any semantic domains discussed in the literature, a new categorial label representing the semantic type of the adverbial clause was coined to encode the meaning of the problematic subordinator. Whilst almost all of the adverbial subordinators identified in my data bear out the assumption I initially made i.e. adverbial clauses inherit semantic meaning from their subordinators, an exception to this generally held assumption arises in the data. The adverbial subordinatorN *conger* can introduce adverbial clauses with two different semantic roles, namely purpose and result (see section 5.3.3). Quirk et al. (1985: 1077) have addressed this problem by saying that "[s]emantic analysis of adverbial clauses is complicated by the fact that many subordinators introduce clauses with different meanings; for example, a *since*-clause may be temporal or causal" and "some clauses combine meanings, for example time with purpose or result".[3] However, the adverbial clauses marked by the adverbial subordinator *conger* do not combine meanings i.e. purpose with result as Quirk et al. (*ibid*) claim would happen; rather, they alternate between purpose and result and manifest themselves clearly in either one semantic role or the other in my data. In this book, therefore, the semantic classification of adverbial clauses is exhaustive in the sense that all of the adverbial subordinators identified in my corpus can be subsumed separately into a range of semantic categories that represent their basic meaning(s) and hence determine the semantic class of adverbial clause.

As noted above, the semantic categories used in this study are informed by previous accounts of the interclausal semantic relations of adverbial clauses. These categories are in fact attested in a wide spectrum of languages by some typological studies of adverbial subordination. The main semantic functions commonly occurring in a sample of some 50 languages are, according to Kortmann (1998: 464ff.), time, cause/reason, condition, concession, contrast, result, purpose, degree/extent, exception/restriction, manner, similarity, comment/accord, comparison, instrument/means, proportion, place, substitution, preference, concomitance and addition. Thompson and Longacre (1985: 177) recognise twelve basic types of adverbial clause for a variety of languages: those of time, location and manner (which can be replaced by a single word adverb), purpose, reason, circumstantial, simultaneous, conditional, concessive, substitutive, additive and absolutive adverbial clauses. Two recent typological accounts of the semantic classification of adverbial clauses, namely Croft (2001: ch. 9) and Cristofaro (2003: ch. 6) are largely inspired by these two prior studies and therefore adopt similar categorial labels to refer to more or less the same kinds of semantic relations. The present analysis is an application of these four typologically-oriented categorisations with extensions where necessary. Hence

3 For example, *before*-clauses may imply purpose and result as well as time as in *I had to put my complaint in writing before they would take any action*. ['... so that they would take some action and with the result that they took action'; also 'They wouldn't take any action until I put my complaint in writing.'], quoted from Quirk et al. (1985: 1081).

the terminology adopted in this book should be generally accepted. In what follows, I will give an outline of which relations were taken to constitute the semantic field of the interclausal adverbial relations by classifying adverbial clauses into eleven interclausal domains with accompanying semantic characterisations and illustrative examples drawn from the PFR corpus.

5.3.1 Clauses of time

Broadly speaking, an adverbial subordinate clause of time relates the time of the situation described in its clause to the time of the situation described in the main clause (Givón, 1993: 287–290; Artstein, 2003; Lin, 2003). The temporal relationship between the main clause and the subordinate clause can typically fall into one of three time relationships. Using English examples for illustrative purposes, the time of the main clause can be previous to (e.g. *before*, *until*, etc.), subsequent to (e.g. *after*, *as soon as*, etc.), or simultaneous with (e.g. *as long as*, *while*, etc.) the time of the adverbial clause (Quirk and Greenbaum, 1973: 322–323; Dorr and Gaasterland, 2002).

In my findings, only one subordinating conjunction was identified (see Table 9), as shown in example (9). This simple example has the situation in the main clause occurring after that in the subordinate clause introduced by 随着 *suizhe* "as soon as". The scarcity of certain features one may wish to observe is a known problem in corpus studies (see Beal's (2000) review of Häcker (1999)) and perhaps inevitable given the finite size of a corpus. Yet what appears to be rather surprising and incompatible with previous analyses is that in the PFR corpus I discovered only one example of a time relationship realised by an adverbial clause. The answer to this conundrum lies in an observation by Chao (1968: 119ff.) who claims that temporal clauses in Chinese are marked by…以前 … *yiqian* "before …", …以后 … *yihou* "after…", and …的时候 …*de shihou* "when …", which express the three kinds of time relationship as noted with reference to English above.

(9) <Fm ID= "19980105" ><Fa>随着_c 生产_vn 规模_n 扩大_v</Fa> ，_w 分摊_v 到_v 单个_b 产品_n 上_f 的_u 厂房_n 设备_n 、_w 经营_vn 管理_vn 等_u 固定_vn 成本_n 就_d 会_v 减少_v 。_w</Fm>

<Fm ID="19980105"><Fa> ***suizhe*_c** *shengchan*_vn *guimo*_n
as.soon.as production scale

*kuoda*_v</Fa> ，_w *fentan*_v *dao*_v *dange*_b *chanpin*_n *shang*_f
expand spend reach individual product aspect

*de*_u *changfang*_n *shebei*_n 、_w *jingying*_vn *guanli*_vn *deng*_u
DE factory facilities operation management etc.

*guding*_vn *chengben*_n *jiu*_d *hui*_v *jianshao*_v 。_w</Fm>
fixed costs then will reduce

"In the wake of the expansion of production, the costs expended on the manufacturing facilities and management and administration for a single item are lower."

Temporal Clause

Adverbial Subordinator	Frequency of Occurrence
随着 *suizhe*	1
Total:	**1**

Table 9: Temporal clause and its adverbial subordinator.

Given that Chao makes this claim, the fact that I found so few temporal adverbial clauses is yet more perplexing. A closer observation of Chao's claim reveals, however, that the expressions referred to by him are not adverbial clauses at all. I would, rather, consider them typically as being noun phrases. They may also, however, be prepositional phrases when they are marked explicitly by the preposition 当 *dang* "being right" or 在 *zai* "being at", where the preposition signals the proximity in time of the two situations described in the subordinate clause and the main clause. The two words 以前 *yiqian* "before" and 以后 *yihou* "after" have not as yet been documented as function words but are not accepted as adverbial subordinators in Chinese (see, for example, Lu and Ma, 1990; Hou, 1998). They are time words per se, i.e. nouns (Lü, 1999; cf. Smith and Erbaugh,

2001).[4] Moreover, "… 的时候 *…de shihou* 'when …'" is a noun phrase in which the head noun 时侯 *shihou* "the moment" is pre-modified by the element marked by the particle 的 *de* (Zhu, 1982 and 2000). Chao's three temporal expressions are therefore adverbial noun or prepositional phrases functioning as adverbials, not adverbial clauses as such. What follows from Chao's analysis is that there are three strategies used in written Chinese for expressing the three time relationships (i.e. time before, time after and same time), namely adverbial noun phrases, adverbial prepositional phrases and adverbial clauses. However, the former two strategies are dominant, thereby leading to a very low frequency for the temporal adverbial clause. In the PFR corpus, the adverbial noun and prepositional phrases marked by *yiqian*, *yihou* and *de shi hou* are employed 19 times, 81 times and 90 times respectively to indicate the time of the main clause to be previous to, subsequent to and simultaneous with the time of the adverbial clause. As Chao's clauses of time are in fact temporal adverbial noun phrases or adverbial prepositional phrases rather than temporal adverbial clauses, and it is these adverbial noun and prepositional phrases in Chinese that take the burden of the relative expression of time, not the adverbial clause, it follows that temporal clauses in Chinese are limited in frequency by a preference for using adverbial noun/prepositional phrases to express temporal relation. One possible caveat I should add to this observation, however, is that this finding comes from the single genre expressed by the PFR corpus. Later in this book (see Chapter Seven, section 7.2 and Chapter Eight, section 8.3.2), I will return to this observation to access whether it holds across a range of genres and speech and writing. For now I will assume that temporal adverbial clauses, while observable, are rare.

4 The nominal uses of *yiqian* "in the past" and *yihou* "in the future" are shown in the following two invented examples.
(i) 我以前不喜欢吃辣。*wo* ***yiqian*** *bu xihuan chi la* "I didn't like eating spicy food in the past."
(ii) 我以后都不会来烦你。*wo* ***yihou*** *dou bu hui lai fan ni* "I won't bother you any more."

5.3.2 Clauses of cause or reason

As their name suggests, clauses of cause or reason (Altenberg, 1984; Rissanen, 1989, 1998, and 1999; Biber et al., 1999: 821; Claridge and Walker, 2001) identify a cause, reason, or motivation for a state of affairs or an action. They express either a direct or an indirect reason relationship between them and their associated main clauses. There are generally four types of adverbial subordinate clause that convey a direct reason relationship with the main clause with respect to such dimensions as cause and effect, reason and consequence, motivation and result, and circumstances and consequence (Quirk et al., 1985: 1103–1107). They are most commonly introduced by the conjunctions such as 由于 *youyu* "owing to the fact that" (see examples (10), (11), (12), (14) and (15)), 因为 *yinwei* "because" (see examples (17) to (19)), 因 *yin* "because" (see example (16)), and 既然 *jiran* "since, as" (see example (13)) as shown by my corpus data. On the other hand, an indirect reason relationship, as Quirk et al. (1985: 1104) note, refers to the fact that "the reason is not related to the situation in the main clause but is a motivation for the implicit speech act of the utterance" as in *Percy is in Washington, for he phoned me from there.* ["Since he phoned from there, I can tell you that Percy is in Washington."][5]. However, I could not obtain any evidence of this use of reason clauses in the PFR corpus. Hence, in the following subsections, I will concentrate on the four different kinds of direct reason relationship between the causal clause and the main clause.

5.3.2.1 Cause and effect

By cause and effect, what is meant is that there is a natural and objective connection in the real world between the state or action described in the adverbial clause and that in the main clause, as illustrated in examples (10) and (11). The frequency of causal clauses showing this relationship is given in Table 10a.

5 This example was taken from Quirk et al. (1985: 1104).

(10) <Fm ID= "19980107" ><Fa>由于_c 它们_r 是_v 近亲_n ，_w 不能_v 联姻_v</Fa> ，_w 公园_n 无_v 1_m 只_q 小_a 虎_n 出世_v 。_w</Fm>

<Fm ID= "19980107" ><Fa>***youyu***_c *tamen*_r *shi*_v *jinqin*_n ，_w
because they be close.relatives

*buneng*_v *lianyin*_v</Fa> ，_w *gongyuan*_n *wu*_v 1_m *zhi*_q *xiao*_a
cannot mate park have.not 1 CL small

*hu*_n *chushi*_v 。_w</Fm>
tiger be.born

"As the tigers are close relatives, they cannot mate with each other and thus no tiger cub has been born in the zoo yet."

(11) <Fm ID= "19980118" ><Fa>由于_c 终年_n 气温_n 较_d 低_a</Fa> ，_w 牛_n 羊_n 生长_v 缓慢_a ，_w 肉质_n 细嫩_a ，_w 鲜美_a 可口_a ，_w</Fm>

<Fm ID= "19980118" ><Fa>***youyu***_c *zhongnian*_n *qiwen*_n *jiao*_d
because perennial temperature relatively

*di*_a</Fa> ，_w *niu*_n *yang*_n *shengzhang*_v *huanman*_a ，_w
low cattle sheep grow slow

*rouzhi*_n *xinen*_a ，_w *xianmei*_a *kekou*_a ，_w</Fm>
quality.of.meat tender fresh delicious

"Because of the relatively low annual temperature in this district, cattle and sheep grow slowly and thus their meat is fresh, tender and delicious."

Causal or Reason Clauses
(Cause and Effect)

Adverbial Subordinators	**Frequency of Occurrence**
由于 *youyu*	19
因为 *yinwei*	12
因 *yin*	2
既然 *jiran*	1
Total:	**34**

Table 10a: Causal or reason clause (i.e. cause and effect) and its adverbial subordinators.

5.3.2.2 Reason and consequence

In this kind of causal clause, the connection between reason and consequence is less natural and objective than that in the first kind of causal clause as noted above. They can only be derived logically from our general knowledge or common sense relating to the situation described in the subordinate clause. What is said in the adverbial clause presents one of a number of possible reasons that yield the consequent state or action as denoted in the main clause. Instead of a natural connection, there is a logical relationship between the adverbial clause and the main clause, as illustrated in examples (12) and (13). Table 10b gives the frequency of reason-and-consequence causal clauses.

(12) <Fm ID= "19980109" ><Fa>由于_c 快餐_n 不仅_c 受到_v 埃及_ns 上班族_n 的_u 青睐_vn ，_w 而且_c 也_d 方便_v 家庭_n 或_c 亲朋_n 聚会_v</Fa> ，_w 于是_c 快餐业_n 的_u 势头_n 有如_v 雨后春笋_i ，_w 竞争_v 越来越_d 激烈_a 。_w</Fm>

<Fm ID= "19980109" ><Fa> ***youyu***_c *kuaican*_n *bujin*_c *shoudao*_v
because fast.food not.only face
*Aiji*_ns *shangbanzu*_n *de*_u *cinglai*_vn ，_w *erqie*_c *ye*_d *fangbian*_v
Egypt working.people DE appeal but.also also convenient
*jiating*_n *huo*_c *qinpeng*_n *juhui*_v</Fa> ，_w *yushi*_c *kuicanye*_n
family or relatives get-together then fast.food.industy's
*de*_u *shitou*_n *youru*_v *yuhouchunsun*_i ，_w *jingzheng*_v *yuelaiyue*_d
GEN popularity as.if in.full.bloom competition more
*jilie*_a 。_w</Fm>
fierce

"Because fast food shops attract plenty of working people in Egypt and make it convenient for holding gatherings of family and relatives, new shops are mushrooming all over the country, resulting in fierce competition."

(13) <Fm ID= "19980113" ><Fa>人们_n 对_p 客观_n 事物_n 规律_n 的_u 认识_n 既然_c 是_v 个_q 过程_n ，_w 不_d 可能_v 一下子_m 完成_v</Fa> ，_w 那么_c ，_w 在_p 工作_v 中_f 一波三折_i 总是_d 难免_v 的_u 。_w</Fm>

<Fm ID= "19980113" ><Fa> *renmen*_n *dui*_p *keguan*_n *shiwu*_n *guilü*_n
people in.regard.to objective matters routine
*de*_u *renshi*_n ***jiran***_c *shi*_v *ge*_q *guocheng*_n ，_w *bu*_d *keneng*_v
DE knowledge since be CL process not possible
*yixiazi*_m *wancheng*_v</Fa> ，_w *name*_c ，_w *zai*_p *gongzuo*_v
at.a.glance complete then at work
*zhong*_f *yibosanzhe*_i *zongshi*_d *nanmian*_v *de*_u 。_w</Fm>
within obstacles nevertheless hard.to.avoid PART
"Since one's perception of the world is accumulated as time goes by, in the course of learning how the world works, it is very likely to come across hurdles of different sorts."

Causal or Reason Clauses
(Reason and Consequence)

Adverbial Subordinators	**Frequency of Occurrence**
由于 *youyu*	95
因为 *yinwei*	58
因 *yin*	10
既然 *jiran*	8
Total:	**171**

Table 10b: Causal or reason clause (i.e. reason and consequence) and its adverbial subordinators.

5.3.2.3 Motivation and result

The third type of adverbial clause of reason expresses a motivation for doing something. In other words, what is mentioned in the subordinate clause offers a motivation for the action or state in the main clause to take place; there is neither an objective nor a logical relationship existing between the motivation in the adverbial clause and the resulting action in the matrix clause, as shown in examples (14) and (15). The frequency of clauses of reason of this type is given in Table 10c.

(14) <Fm ID= "19980109" ><Fa>由于_c 重视_v 写_v 出_v 人物_n 在_p 二难_b 困境_n 中_f 的_u 行动_vn 和_c 抗争_vn ，_w 以及_c 现实_n 中_f 的_u 个人_n 尊严_n 和_c 集体_n 尊严_n 等_u 范畴_n 的_u 艺术_n 形象_n</Fa> ，_w 在_p 一定_b 意义_n 上_f ，_w 这些_r 作品_n 已_d 开始_v 超越_v 『_w 新_a 写实_b 小说_n 』_w 。_w</Fm>

<Fm ID= "19980109" ><Fa> ***youyu***_c *zhongshi*_v *xie*_v *chu*_v *renwu*_n
because emphasise write out character
*zai*_p *ernan*_b *kunjing*_n *zhong*_f *de*_u *xingdong*_vn *he*_c
in dilemma situation within DE behaviour and
*kangzheng*_vn ，_w *yiji*_c *xianshi*_n *zhong*_f *de*_u *geren*_n
conflict and reality within DE individual
*zhuanyan*_n *he*_c *jiti*_n *zhuanyan*_n *deng*_u *fanchou*_n *de*_u *yishu*_n
dignity and collective dignity etc. aspects DE artistic
*xingxiang*_n</Fa> ，_w *zai*_p *yiding*_b *yiyi*_n *shang*_f ，_w
image at certain meaning aspect
*zhexie*_r *zuopin*_n *yi*_d *kaishi*_v *chaoyue*_v 『_w *xian*_a
this.kind.of works already start go.beyond contemporary
*xieshi*_b *xiaoshuo*_n 』_w 。_w</Fm>
realistic novel

"As writers always emphasise the need to portray a character's behaviour and mental conflicts in the face of dilemma, and build images of individual and collective dignity in reality, their works are gradually going beyond the contemporary realistic writing style."

(15) <Fm ID= "19980116" ><Fa>也许_d 由于_c 长_v 得_u 丑_a</Fa> ，_w 我_r 一向_d 不_d 喜_v 照镜子_v ，_w</Fm>

<Fm ID= "19980116" ><Fa> *yexu*_d ***youyu***_c *zhang*_v *de*_u
perhaps because look COMP
*chou*_a</Fa> ，_w *wo*_r *yixiang*_d *bu*_d *xi*_v *zhaojingzi*_v ，_w</Fm>
ugly I ever not like look.at.mirror

"I do not like looking at myself in the mirror, possibly because I am not good-looking."

Causal or Reason Clauses (Motivation and Result)

Adverbial Subordinators	**Frequency of Occurrence**
由于 *youyu*	9
因为 *yinwei*	6
因 *yin*	0
既然 *jiran*	0
Total:	**15**

Table 10c: Causal or reason clause (i.e. motivation and result) and its adverbial subordinators.

5.3.2.4 Circumstances and consequence

The fourth type of reason clause suggests that in view of the circumstances described in the subordinate clause, we can make an inference in the light of this fact and come to the conclusion that the consequence in the main clause will happen, as illustrated in examples (16) and (17). This kind of reason clause appears to be akin to the second, reason-and-consequence, kind of reason clause in that both of them rely on an inference of a logical relationship between the adverbial clause and the main clause. However, the logical relationship tends to be much weaker in the former (cf. Quirk et al., 1985: 1104): the consequence in the circumstances-and-consequence causal clauses is assumed to have occurred as in example (16), or about to take place as in example (17), while the consequence in the reason-and-consequence causal clauses has already been realised as in examples (12) and (13) above. I decided therefore to differentiate between circumstances-and-consequence causal clauses and reason-and-consequence causal clauses in my book. Table 10d shows the frequency of clauses of reason of this type in the PFR corpus.

(16) <Fm ID= "19980126"><Fa>许多_m 发展中国家_l 因_c 经济_n 结构_n 问题_n 的_u 困扰_vn 和_c 经济_n 增长_vn 速度_n 减慢_v ，_w 以及_c 股市_n 处于_v 起步_v 发展_v 之中_f</Fa> ，_w 因而_c 市场_n 的_u 资金_n 容量_n 小_a ，_w 交易_vn 产品_n 单一_a ，_w 机构_n 投资量_n 少_a ，_w 私人_n 投资_v 过_d 多_a ，_w</Fm>

<Fm ID= "19980126"><Fa> *xuduo*_m *fazhanzhongguojia*_l ***yin***_c
many developing.countries because
*jingji*_n *jiegou*_n *wenti*_n *de*_u *kunrao*_vn *he*_c *jingji*_n
economic structure problem DE worry and economic
*zengzhang*_vn *sudu*_n *jianman*_v ，_w *yiji*_c *gushi*_n *chuyu*_v
growth rate slow.down and stock.market remain
*qibu*_v *fazhan*_v *zhizhong*_f ，_w</Fa> *yiner*_c *shichang*_n *de*_u
infancy develop in.progress.of therefore market's GEN
*zijin*_n *rongliang*_n *xiao*_a ，_w *jiaoyi*_vn *chanpin*_n *danyi*_a ，_w
capital capacity little exchange product limited
*jigou*_n *touziliang*_n *shao*_a ，_w *siren*_n *touzi*_v *guo*_d
company chance.of.investment little private investment too
*duo*_a ，_w</Fm>
much

"Since many developing countries are hindered by structural deficiencies in their economic systems and slow economic growth, the stock markets of these countries are in their infancy and thus market funds are of insufficient quantity, the diversity of exchanged products is limited, investments made by firms are rare, and individual investments are excessive."

(17) <Fm ID= "19980120"><Fa>[马来西亚_ns 航空_n 公司_n]nt 因为_c 政府_n 缩减_v 开支_n 和_c 节省_v 外汇_n</Fa> ，_w 正_d 计划_v 将_p ２０_m 架_q 波音_nz 飞机_n 的_u 交货_vn 日期_n 推迟_v ５_m 年_q 。_w</Fm>

<Fm ID= "19980120"><Fa>[*Malaixiya*_ns *Hangkong*_n *Gongsi*_n]nt
Malayisa Airlines company
yinwei_c *zhengfu*_n *sujian*_v *kaizhi*_n *he*_c *jiesheng*_v
because government reduce expenditure and save
*waihui*_n</Fa> ，_w *zheng*_d *jihua*_v *jiang*_p ２０_m *jia*_q
foreign.currency.reserves PROG plan BA 20 CL
*boyin*_nz *feiji*_n *de*_u *jiaohuo*_vn *riqi*_n *tuichi*_v ５_m *nian*_q 。
Boeing aircrafts' GEN delivery date delay 5 years
_w</Fm>

"Because the Malaysian government reduced its expenditure to save its reserves of foreign currencies, Malaysia Airlines is currently planning to postpone the delivery date of twenty Boeing aircraft for five years."

Causal or Reason Clauses
(Circumstances and consequence)

Adverbial Subordinators	Frequency of Occurrence
由于 *youyu*	66
因为 *yinwei*	40
因 *yin*	4
既然 *jiran*	0
Total:	**110**

Table 10d: Causal or reason clause (i.e. circumstances and consequence) and its adverbial subordinators.

It is interesting to note that the causal subordinator 因为 *yinwei* can be placed both clause-initially (i.e. before the main clause) as in example (18), and clause-finally (i.e. after the main clause) as in example (19), while the other three causal subordinators tend to occur before the main clause they are associated with, as shown in Table 10e below.

(18) <Fm ID= "19980109" ><Fa>因为_c 历史_n 上_f 的_u 仿制者_n 后来_t 成为_v 了_u 名家_n</Fa> ，_w <Fa>更_d 因为_c 仿制_vn 年代_n 也_d 已_d 久远_z</Fa> ，_w 历史_n 上_f 的_u 许多_m 仿制品_n 也_d 相当_d 珍贵_a 。_w</Fm>

<Fm ID= "19980109" ><Fa> ***yinwei***_c *lishi*_n *shang*_f *de*_u *fangzhizhe*_n
because history aspect DE forger
*houlai*_t *chengwei*_v *le*_u *mingjia*_n</Fa> ，_w <Fa>*geng*_d ***yinwei***_c
later become PERF master.craftsman further because
*fangzhi*_vn *niandai*_n *ye*_d *yi*_d *jiuyuan*_z</Fa> ，_w *lishi*_n *shang*_f
forgery age also already far.away history aspect
*de*_u *xuduo*_m *fangzhipin*_n *ye*_d *xiangdang*_d *zhengui*_a 。_w</Fm>
DE many replica also remarkably precious

"Since historically forgers were master craftsmen, many historical forgeries are remarkably valuable."

(19) <Fm ID= "19980107" >他_r 受到_v 了_u 热烈_a 的_u 欢迎_vn ，_w
<Fa>因为_c 在_p 他_r 到来_v 之前_f ，_w 这里_r 还_d 没有_v
一个_m 专业_n 农业_n 工作者_n</Fa> 。_w</Fm>
<Fm ID= "19980107" > *ta*_r *shoudao*_v *le*_u *relie*_a *de*_u
he receive PERF warm DE
*huanying*_vn ，_w <Fa>***yinwei***_c *zai*_p *ta*_r *daolai*_v *zhiqian*_f ，_w
reception because at he arrive prior.to
*zheli*_r *hai*_d *meiyou*_v *yige*_m *zhuanye*_n *nongye*_n
here yet have.not one professional farming
*gongzuozhe*_n</Fa> 。_w</Fm>
worker
"He received a warm reception when he got there because, prior to his arrival, there wasn't a farm expert in the district."

Causal or Reason Clauses

Adverbial Subordinators	Frequency (Clause-initially)	Frequency (Clause-finally)	Total Frequency
由于 *youyu*	189	0	189
因为 *yinwei*	55	61	116
因 *yin*	15	1	16
既然 *jiran*	9	0	9
Total:	**268**	**62**	**330**

Table 10e: Causal or reason clause (i.e. clause-initially and clause-finally) and its adverbial subordinators.

5.3.3 Clauses of purpose

Like reason clauses, purpose clauses (Thompson, 1985; Di Eugenio, 1993) provide explanations for the occurrence of a given state or action. They are distinct from reason clauses in that they express an event which must be unrealised at the time of the main clause event whereas causal clauses express an event which may have been realised at the time of the main event (Thompson and Longacre, 1985: 185). Subordinators of purpose are 以 *yi*, 从而 *conger* and 以便 *yibian*, all of which mean "in order that", as shown in examples (20), (21) and (22) respectively. Negative purpose is expressed by 以免 *yimian* "in order that…not…" as in example (23). Table 11 shows the frequency of occurrence of purpose clauses in the PFR corpus.

(20) <Fm ID= "19980108" >我国_n 必须_d 尽快_d 改变_v 传统_a 的_u 农业_n 生产_vn 要素_n 配置_vn 方式_n ，_w 不断_d 增加_v 资本_n 和_c 技术_n 投入_vn ，_w <Fa>以_c 提高_v 农产品_n 的_u 科技_n 含量_n 和_c 附加_vn 价值_n</Fa> 。_w</Fm>

<Fm ID="19980108"> *woguo*_n *bixu*_d *jinkuai*_d *gaibian*_v
our.country must as.soon.as.possible change
*chuantong*_a *de*_u *nongye*_n *shengchan*_vn *yaosu*_n *peizhi*_vn
traditional DE agriculture production essential facility
*fangshi*_n ，_w *buduan*_d *zengjia*_v *ziben*_n *he*_c *jishu*_n
modes continuously increase capital and technology
*touru*_vn ，_w <Fa>***yi***_c *tigao*_v *nongchanpin*_n *de*_u
involvement by.means.of boost farming.goods DE
*keji*_n *hanliang*_n *he*_c *fujia*_vn *jiazhi*_n</Fa> 。_w</Fm>
technology component and additional value

"Our country should step up modifications in agricultural production and constantly increase the use of capital and advanced technology so as to enhance the technological value of our farming goods."

(21) <Fm ID= "19980114" >俄_j 与_p 其他_r 大国_n 首脑_n 将_d 进行_v 一_m 系列_q 新_a 的_u 会晤_vn ，_w <Fa>从而_c 继续_v 推动_v 大国_n 关系_n 的_u 调整_vn</Fa> 。_w</Fm>

<Fm ID="19980114"> *E*_j *yu*_p *qita*_r *daguo*_n *shounao*_n *jiang*_d
Russia with other giant.nations leader soon
*jinxing*_v *yi*_m *xilie*_q *xin*_a *de*_u *huiwu*_vn ，_w <Fa>***conger***_c
engage.in one series.of new DE dialogue in.order.that
*jixu*_v *tuidong*_v *daguo*_n *guanxi*_n *de*_u *tiaozheng*_vn</Fa> 。_w</Fm>
continue step.up giant.nation relationship DE regulation

"Russia and other heads of state or governments will hold a series of talks in order to continue to step up the regulation of diplomatic relations."

(22) <Fm ID= "19980121" >欧盟_j 财政部长_n 们_k 鼓励_v 意大利_ns 严格_ad 执行_v 财政_n 预算_n ，_w <Fa>以便_c 到_p ２０００ 年_t 时_Ng 将_p 其_r 财政_n 赤字_n 降_v 到_v 只_d 占_v 国内_s 生产总值_n 的_u １·８％_m</Fa> 。_w</Fm>

<Fm ID="19980121"> *Oumeng*_j *caizhengbuzhang*_n *men*_k *guli*_v
European.Union financial.minister PL encourage
*Yidali*_ns *yange*_ad *zhixing*_v *caizheng*_n *yusuan*_n ，_w
Italy strictly implement fiscal budget
<Fa>***yibian***_c *dao*_p ２０００*nian*_t *shi*_Ng *jiang*_p *qi*_r
in.order.that in year.of.2000 at.that.time BA its
*caizheng*_n *chizi*_n *jiang*_v *dao*_v *zhi*_d *zhan*_v
financial deficits reduce up.to only account.for
*guonei*_s *shengchanzongzhi*_n *de*_u １·８％_m</Fa> 。_w</Fm>
gross national product DE 1.8%

"The financial minister of the European Union encouraged the Italian government to strictly enforce its financial budget in order to reduce its financial deficits to just 1.8% of the gross national product in 2000."

(23) <Fm ID= "19980103" >世界_n 各国_r 都_d 应当_v 从_p 亚洲_ns 金融_n 危机_n 中_f 吸取_v 有益_a 的_u 经验_n 教训_vn ，_w <Fa>以免_c 重蹈覆辙_i</Fa> 。_w</Fm>

<Fm ID="19980103"> *shijie*_n *geguo*_r *dou*_d *yingdang*_v *cong*_p
world each.nation all must from
*Yazhou*_ns *jinyong*_n *weiji*_n *zhong*_f *xiqu*_v *youyi*_a *de*_u
Asian financial crisis within gain beneficial DE
*jingyan*_n *jiaoxun*_vn ，_w <Fa>***yimian***_c *chongdaofuzhe*_i</Fa> 。
experience lessons in.order.that get.into.the.same.trouble
_w</Fm>

"Nations all over the world should draw lessons from the Asian financial crisis so as not to get into the same trouble."

Purpose Clauses

Adverbial Subordinators	Frequency of Occurrence
以 *yi*	257
从而 *conger*	76
以免 *yimian*	9
以便 *yibian*	6
Total:	**348**

Table 11: Purpose clause and its adverbial subordinators.

It is worth noting that as shown in examples (24) and (25) below, the adverbial subordinator 从而 *conger* is also commonly used to express a consequence or result in the subordinate clause over which it operates. Unlike the clause of purpose, the clause of result is typically accompanied by the perfective aspect marked by 了 *-le* (McEnery and Xiao, 2002: 215–217 and 2003: 368 ff.; Xiao, 2002; Xiao and McEnery, 2004), as in example (24). In the PFR Chinese Corpus, *conger* is used to introduce a result clause almost as frequently as it is used to introduce a purpose clause, although it is used slightly more frequently in the result clause than in the purpose clause. The frequency of *conger* occurring in these two semantic types of adverbial clause is given in the following table.

	Frequency of Occurrence
从而 *conger* used in purpose clause	76 (44.2%)
从而 *conger* used in result clause	96 (55.8%)
Total	**172 (100%)**

Table 12: Frequency of occurrence of *conger* used in purpose clause and result clause.

(24) <Fm ID= “19980118” >教育_vn 资源_n 不能_v 优化_v 配置_n 和_c 充分_ad 利用_v ，_w 造成_v 很_d 大_a 浪费_vn ，_w <Fa>从而_c 影响_v 了_u 整体_n 教育_vn 质量_n 和_c 办学_vn 效益_n</Fa> 。_w</Fm>

<Fm ID=“19980118”> *jiaoyu*_vn *ziyuan*_n *buneng*_v *youhua*_v *peizhi*_n
education resources cannot preferentially allocate

*he*_c *chongfen*_ad *liyong*_v ，_w *zaocheng*_v *hen*_d *da*_a
and sufficiently make.use.of cause very great
*langfei*_vn ，_w <Fa>***conger***_c *yingxiang*_v *le*_u *zhengti*_n
waste as.a.result affect PERF entire
*jiaoyu*_vn *zhiliang*_n *he*_c *banxue*_vn *xiaoyi*_n</Fa> 。_w</Fm>
education quality and teaching effectiveness
"Education resources, if they are not allocated preferentially and exploited properly, will run to waste and eventually adversely influence the quality of education and teaching effectiveness."

(25) <Fm ID= "19980121" >由于_p 东南亚_ns 金融_n 危机_n 和_c 其他_r 因素_n 的_u 影响_vn ，_w 世界_n 石油_n 市场_n 的_u 需求量_n 反而_d 减少_v ，_w <Fa>从而_c 导致_v 石油_n 价格_n 连续_ad 下滑_v</Fa> 。_w</Fm>
<Fm ID="19980121"> *youyu*_p *Dongnanya*_ns *jinyong*_n *weiji*_n *he*_c
due.to South.East.Asian financial crisis and
*qita*_r *yinsu*_n *de*_u *yingxiang*_vn ，_w *shijie*_n *shiyou*_n
other factors DE influence world petroleum
*shichang*_n *de*_u *xuqiuliang*_n *faner*_d *jianshao*_v ，_w
market's GEN demand in.contrast reduce
<Fa>***conger***_c *daozhi*_v *shiyou*_n *jiage*_n *lianxu*_ad
as.a.result cause petroleum price continuously
*xiahua*_v</Fa> 。_w</Fm>
drop
"Due to the impact of the South East Asian financial crisis and other related factors, the demand for petroleum in the global market was reduced, resulting in a continuous drop in the market value of petroleum."

5.3.4 Clauses of result

Clauses of result (Quirk and Greenbaum, 1973: 328; White, 1997) are introduced by 从而 *conger* "as a consequence", 之所以 *zhisuoyi* "why there is a consequence of …", 以致 *yizhi* "as a result", 故 *gu* "so that" and 以至于 *yizhiyu* "consequently", as shown in examples (26) to (29). As noted above, the desired result named in a purpose clause has not been or has yet to be achieved. However, in the result clause, the result, either desirable or undesirable, has been achieved. The adverbial conjunction 之所以 *zhisuoyi* differs from other conjunctions as it introduces a result clause that must be placed clause-initially, followed by the main clause which gives the reason for such a result, as illustrated in example (26).[6] Table 13 gives the frequency of clauses of result in the PFR corpus.

(26) <Fm ID= "19980118" ><Fa>便士_n 邮票_n 之所以_c 成为_v 邮票_n 拍卖行_n 标价_n 最高_a 的_u 珍品_n</Fa> ，_w 还_d 因为_p 它_r 是_v 世界_n 上_f 唯一_d 在_p 票面_n 上_f 印_v 有_v "_w 邮局_n "_w 字样_n 的_u 邮票_n 。_w</Fm>

<Fm ID="19980118"><Fa> *bianshi*_n *youpiao*_n ***zhisuoyi***_c
pence stamp why.there.is.a.consequence.of
*chengwei*_v *youpiao*_n *paimaihang*_n *biaojia*_n *zuigao*_a
become stamp auction.firm price the.most.expensive
*de*_u *zhenpin*_n</Fa> ，_w *hai*_d *yinwei*_p *ta*_r *shi*_v *shijie*_n
DE commodity also due.to it be world
*shang*_f *weiyi*_d *zai*_p *piaomian*_n *shang*_f *yin*_v *you*_v "_w
scope only on stamp.surface scope print have
*youju*_n "_w *ziyang*_n *de*_u *youpiao*_n 。_w</Fm>
post.office print DE stamp

"The reason why the penny stamp has become the most valuable commodity in auction houses is that it is the only stamp in the world that has the words 'post office' printed on its cover."

(27) <Fm ID= "19980109" >日_j 、_w 美_j 监管_vn 当局_n 在_p 历次_b 检查_vn 中_f 均_d 未_d 发现_v 这些_r 问题_n ，_w <Fa>以致_c 未能_v 及时_ad 督促_v 其_u 建立_v 健全_v 内部_f 控制_vn 制度_n ，_w 使_v 巨额_b 亏损_n 长期_d 隐瞒_v</Fa> 。_w</Fm>

6 The subordinating conjunction *zhisuoyi* was treated as a unit in the original annotation. While *zhi* is a genitive suffix in classical Chinese, similar to modern *de*, it can no longer be used independently in modern Chinese and can only appear in some fixed expressions such as *zhisuoyi*.

<Fm ID="19980109"> Ri_j 、_w Mei_j jianguan_vn dangju_n zai_p
Japan America regulatory body in
lici_b jiancha_vn zhong_f jun_d wei_d faxian_v zhexie_r
previous inspections within all yet discover these
wenti_n ，_w <Fa>yizhi_c weineng_v jishi_ad ducu_v qi_u jianli_v
problems consequently cannot promptly advise its set.up
jianquan_v neibu_f kongzhi_vn zhidu_n ，_w shi_v
healthy internal monitoring mechanism cause
jue_b kuisun_n changqi_d yinman_v</Fa> 。
large.amount.of.money loss for.a.long.time cover.up
_w</Fm>

"The regulatory bodies of Japan and the United States did not notice in all their previous inspections any of these problems and, as a result, did not promptly call for the establishment of an internal monitoring mechanism, thereby concealing tremendous deficits for a long period of time."

(28) <Fm ID= "19980125" >过年_v 对_p 中国_ns 人_n 来说_u 是_v 如此_r 的_u 重要_a ，_w <Fa>以至于_c 许多_m 中国_ns 人_n 以己度人_i ，_w 自然_d 就_d 会_v 问_v ：_w 外国人_n 是_v 怎么_r 过年_v 的_u</Fa> ？_w</Fm>

<Fm ID="19980125"> guonian_v dui_p Zhongguo_ns ren_n
Chinese.New.Year for Chinese people
laishuo_u shi_v ruci_r de_u zhongyao_a ，_w <Fa>yizhiyu_c
generally.speaking be such DE important as.a.result
xuduo_m Zhongguo_ns ren_n yijiduren_i ，_w ziran_d jiu_d hui_v
many Chinese people presuppose naturally then will
wen_v ：_w waiguoren_n shi_v zenme_r guonian_v
ask westerners be how.to celebrate.the.New.Year
de_u</Fa> ？_w</Fm>
PART

"The new year celebrations are so important to Chinese that many Chinese people take its importance for granted and ask how westerners celebrate theirs."

(29) <Fm ID= “19980119” >殖民主义者_n 将_p 大批_m 黑人_n 奴隶_n 从_p 沿海_f 一带_n 贩卖_v 到_v 北美_ns ，_w <Fa>故_c 贝宁_ns 被_p 称为_v “_w 奴隶_n 海岸_n ” _w</Fa> 。_w</Fm>

<Fm ID=“19980119”> *zhiminzhuyizhe*_n *jiang*_p *dapi*_m *heiren*_n
colonialists BA plenty.of black
*nuli*_n *cong*_p *yanhai*_f *yidai*_n *fanmai*_v *dao*_v *Beimei*_ns ，_w
slaves from coastal areas sell to North.America
<Fa>*gu*_c *Beining*_ns *bei*_p *chengwei*_v “_w *Nuli*_n
consequently Benin PASSIVE become Slaves
*Haian*_n ”_w</Fa> 。_w</Fm>
Coast

“The colonialists took a large number of black slaves form the coastal area of Benin and sold them to the North Americans, and consequently Benin was named the ‘Coast of Slaves’.”

Result Clauses

Adverbial Subordinators	**Frequency of Occurrence**
从而 *conger*	96
之所以 *zhisuoyi*	46
以致 *yizhi*	9
故 *gu*	7
以至于 *yizhiyu*	5
Total:	**163**

Table 13: Result clause and its adverbial subordinators.

5.3.5 Clauses of preference or substitutive clauses

In their study which produced a typological analysis of adverbial clauses, Thompson and Longacre (1985: 199 ff.) demonstrated that some languages have subordinating markers for signalling the replacement of one event by another one. English uses such forms as *instead of*, *rather than* and *sooner than* for this purpose, while in Chinese, 与其 *yuqi* “rather than” as in example (30) and 与其说 *yuqishuo* “rather than say that” as in example (31), are used as the subordinating markers for introducing these adverbial substitutive clauses. Quirk et al. (1985: 1111–1112) use the term "clauses of preference" to refer to the same kind of adverbial relation. The frequency of occurrence of substitutive clauses is given in Table 14.

(30) <Fm ID= "19980103" ><Fa>与其_c 挤_v 在_p 名人_n 屋_n 外_f 的_u "_w 钥匙孔_n "_w 费力_a 地_u 窥寻_v 隐秘_n</Fa> ，_w 莫若_c 到_p 张_nr 安惠_nr 女士_n 推开_v 的_u 这_r 扇_q 人生_n 窗牖_n 前_f ，_w 默默_d 眺望_v ，_w 细细_d 究_d 想_v 。_w</Fm>

<Fm ID="19980103"><Fa> ***yuqi***_c *ji*_v *zai*_p *mingren*_n *wu*_n *wai*_f
rather.than stand at celebrity house outside
*de*_u "_w *yaoshikong*_n "_w *feili*_a *de*_u *kuixun*_v
DE the.hole.of.a.padlock painstakingly ADVL observe.in.secret
*yinmi*_n</Fa> ，_w *moruo*_c *dao*_p *Zhang*_nr *Anhui*_nr *nüshi*_n
secrets would.rather reach Zhang Anhui Ms
*tuikai*_v *de*_u *zhe*_r *shan*_q *rensheng*_n *chuangyou*_n *qian*_f ，_w
open DE this CL life window in.front.of
*momo*_d *tiaowang*_v ，_w *xixi*_d *jiu*_d *xiang*_v 。_w</Fm>
quietly look.around carefully research think.about

"Rather than stand outside the world of celebrities and explore what it is like, we could take a close look at Ms Zhang Anhui's book on being a renowned person and then ponder on the meaning of life."

(31) <Fm ID= "19980124" ><Fa>与其说_c 是_v 一_m 间_q 会客室_n</Fa> 不如说_c 是_v 一_m 间_q 简朴_a 别致_a 的_u 书房_n 。_w</Fm>

<Fm ID="19980124"> <Fa> ***yuqishuo***_c *shi*_v *yi*_m *jian*_q
rather.than.say.that be one CL
*huikeshi*_n</Fa> *burushuo*_c *shi*_v *yi*_m *jian*_q *jianpu*_a *biezhi*_a
conference.room would.rather be one CL simple delicate
*de*_u *shufang*_n 。_w</Fm>
DE study.room

"Rather than say that it is a conference room, we would take it as a simple but delicate study room."

Substitutive Clauses

Adverbial Subordinators	**Frequency of Occurrence**
与其 *yuqi*	2
与其说 *yuqishuo*	1
Total:	**3**

Table 14: Substitutive clause and its adverbial subordinators.

5.3.6 Clauses of contrast

A clause of contrast (cf. Ford, 2000) is introduced by the adverbial subordinator 而是 *ershi* "rather". Those contrastive adverbial clauses introduced by 而是 *ershi* "rather" interact with negation in an interesting way: they are typically associated with negative main clauses i.e. the main clauses that contain negated verb forms such as 不是 *bushi* "not", 没有 *meiyou* "have not", 并非 *bingfei* "not just", 不能 *buneng* "cannot", etc., and negation adverbs such as 从不 *congbu* "never", 不再 *buzai* "no longer", 不仅仅 *bujinjin* "not merely", 絶不 *juebu* "absolutely not", 未 *wei* "not yet", etc., as illustrated in examples (32) to (35). Table 15 gives the frequency of occurrence of clauses of contrast in the PFR corpus.

(32) <Fm ID= "19980113" >[泰国_ns 政府_n]nt 和_c 人民_n 面对_v 严峻_a 的_u 经济_n 形势_n ，_w 没有_d 被_p 困难_an 吓倒_v ，_w <Fa>而是_c 同心同德_i ，_w 群策群力_i ，_w 共_d 渡_v 难关_n</Fa> 。_w</Fm>

<Fm ID="19980113">[*Taiguo*_ns *Zhengfu*_n]nt *he*_c *renmin*_n
Thailand government and citizens
*miandui*_v *yanjun*_a *de*_u *jingji*_n *xingshi*_n ，_w *meiyou*_d
face tough DE economic situation have.not
*bei*_p *kunnan*_an *xiadao*_v ，_w <Fa>***ershi***_c
PASSIVE difficulty be.scared rather
*tongxintongde*_i ，_w *quncequnli*_i ，_w *gong*_d *du*_v
pool.one's.wisdom plan.and.work.together together go.through
*nanguan*_n</Fa> 。_w</Fm>
ordeal

"In the face of the tough economic situation, the Thai government and its citizens were not overwhelmed by adversity. Rather they pooled their wisdom and efforts to get through the crisis."

(33) <Fm ID= "19980116" >这_r 不_d 是_v 我_r 多_d 聪明_a ，_w <Fa>而是_c 试卷_n 上_f 的_u 那_r 点_q 东西_n ，_w 早就_d 在_p 我_r 的_u 肚子_n 里_f 了_y</Fa> 。_w</Fm>

<Fm ID="19980116"> *zhe*_r *bu*_d *shi*_v *wo*_r *duo*_d *congming*_a ，
this not be I how clever

_w <Fa>***ershi***_c *shijuan*_n *shang*_f *de*_u *na*_r *dian*_q *dongxi*_n ，
rather exam.papers aspect DE that CL stuff

_w *zaojiu*_d *zai*_p *wo*_r *de*_u *duzi*_n *li*_f *le*_y</Fa> 。_w</Fm>
in.advance in my GEN stomach inside PART

"This is not because I am clever, but the questions of the examination paper can easily be solved by my prior awareness of the problem."

(34) <Fm ID= "19980115" >目标_n 不仅仅_d 是_v 廉洁_an ，_w <Fa>而是_c 要_v 在_p 党内_s 、_w 政府_n 内_f 建立_v 和_c 形成_v 一_m 种_q 廉政_n 勤政_n 机制_n</Fa> 。_w</Fm>

<Fm ID="19980115"> *mubiao*_n *bujinjin*_d *shi*_v *lianjie*_an ，_w
goal not.only be integrity

<Fa>***ershi***_c *yao*_v *zai*_p *dangnei*_s 、_w *zhengfu*_n *nei*_f *jianli*_v
rather have.to in inside.the.Party government inside set.up

*he*_c *xingcheng*_v *yi*_m *zhong*_q *lianzheng*_n *qinzheng*_n
and form one CL intergrity diligence

*jizhi*_n</Fa> 。_w</Fm>
mechanism

"Our goal is not simply integrity but is to create a mechanism to monitor people's compliance with integrity at work in both the Communist Party and the Chinese government."

(35) <Fm ID= "19980125" >其_r 意义_n 已_d 不再_d 局限_v 于_p 敬_v 海神_n 、_w 求_v 平安_an ，_w <Fa>而是_c 成为_v 庆祝_v 新年_t 的_u 一_m 项_q 大众_n 活动_vn</Fa> 。_w</Fm>

<Fm ID="19980125"> *qi*_r *yiyi*_n *yi*_d *buzai*_d
its significance already not.only
*juxian*_v *yu*_p *jing*_v *haishen*_n 、_w *qiu*_v *pingan*_an ，
be.restricted.to at worship God.of.Sea pray.for safety
_w <Fa>***ershi***_c *chengwei*_v *qingzhu*_v *xinnian*_t *de*_u *yi*_m
rather become celebrate New.Year DE one
*xiang*_q *dazhong*_n *huodong*_vn</Fa> 。_w</Fm>
CL popular activity

"Holding this event is no longer just for worshipping the god of the sea and praying for seamen's safety. It has become one of the major activities of the Lunar New Year celebrations."

Contrastive Clauses

Adverbial Subordinator	Frequency of Occurrence
而是 *ershi*	177
Total:	**177**

Table 15: Contrastive clause and its adverbial subordinator.

5.3.7 Clauses of addition

In Chinese, the adverbial subordinators which express one state of affairs in addition to another as in clauses of addition (Thompson and Longacre, 1985: 200; Quintero, 2000: 65) are 何况 *hekuang* "not to mention …", 不单 *budan* "in addition to …", 且不说 *qiebushuo* "let alone …", and 不说 *bushuo* "let alone …". Interestingly, the subordinating conjunction 何况 *hekuang*, as shown in example (36), differs from the other three conjunctions in that the adverbial clause of addition on which it operates occurs in the final position of the sentence i.e. after the main clause[7], while others are placed clause-initially i.e. be-

7 One possible explanation for this positional pattern is that the material that is placed near the end of the sentence is believed to be an elaboration of that mentioned in the initial position (Chafe, 1980 and 1987; Altenberg, 1984; Abraham, 1991; Kirkpatrick, 1993; Wang, 2002). As a corollary, the adverbial clauses introduced by 何况 *hekuang* are put at the end position in the sentence i.e. after the main clause to provide further information to modify the matrix clause.

fore the main clause, as illustrated in examples (37) to (39). The frequency of clauses of addition is given in Table 16.

(36) <Fm ID= “19980124” >很多_m 人_n 连_u 不_d 加_v 标点_n 的_u 文言文_n ，_w 未必_d 读_v 得_u 断_v ，_w <Fa>何况_c 其他_r</Fa> ？_w</Fm>

<Fm ID=“19980124”> henduo_m ren_n lian_u bu_d jia_v biaodian_n
many people even not add punctuation
de_u wenyanwen_n ，_w weibi_d du_v de_u duan_v ，_w
DE classical.Chinese not.yet comprehend COMP well
<Fa>***hekuang***_c qita_r</Fa> ？_w</Fm>
not.to.mention others

“Many people can barely understand the unpunctuated writings of classical Chinese, let alone read other archaic styles of writing.”

(37) <Fm ID= “19980125” > “_w <Fa>签署_v 这项_r 协定_n 不单_c 代表_v 我们_r 在_d 合作_v 打击_v 跨_v 境_Ng 犯罪_v 方面_n 取得_v 良好_a 进展_vn ，_w</Fa> 同时_c 亦_d 向_p 国际_n 社会_n 发出_v 一个_m 有力_a 的_u 信息_n ，_w 就_d 是_v [香港_ns 特别_a 行政区_n]ns 继续_v 享有_v 法治_n 。_w ”_w</Fm>

<Fm ID=“19980125”>“_w <Fa>qianshu_v zhexiang_r xieding_n
sign this agreement
budan_c daibiao_v women_r zai_d hezuo_v daji_v kua_v jing_Ng
not.only represent we at co-operate combat cross border
fanzui_v fangmian_n qude_v lianghao_a jinzhan_vn</Fa> ，_w
crime aspect obtain good progress
tongshi_c yi_d xiang_p guoji_n shehui_n fachu_v yige_m
meanwhile also face international community issue one
youli_a de_u xinxi_n ，_w jiu_d shi_v [Xianggang_ns Tebie_a
forceful DE message that.is. be Hong.Kong Special
Xingzhengqu_n]ns jixu_v xiangyou_v fazhi_n 。_w ”_w</Fm>
Adminstrative.Region continue enjoy rule.of.law

“In addition to signposting our success in combating cross-border crimes in collaboration with the mainland, by signing this agreement, we would like to forcefully prove that the Hong Kong Special Administrative Region continues (after handover) to enjoy the rule of law.”

(38) <Fm ID= “19980112” ><Fa>且不说_c 遇_v 上_v 抢劫_v 或_c 偷车贼_n 这_r 类_q 让_v 人_n 心惊_v 的_u “_w 大_a 麻烦_an ”_w</Fa> ，_w 单_d 是_v 一些_m 可能_v 出现_v 的_u “_w 小_a 麻烦_an ”_w 就_d 够_v 你_r 受_v 的_u ，_w</Fm>

<Fm ID=“19980112”><Fa> ***qiebushuo***_c *yu*_v *shang*_v *qiangjie*_v
let.alone encounter up robbery

*huo*_c *touchezei*_n *zhe*_r *lei*_q *rang*_v *ren*_n *xinjing*_v *de*_u “_w
or car.theft this CL make people scare DE

*da*_a *mafan*_an ”_w</Fa> ，_w *dan*_d *shi*_v *yixie*_m *keneng*_v
big trouble only be some possible

*chuxian*_v *de*_u “_w *xiao*_a *mafan*_an ”_w *jiu*_d *gou*_v *ni*_r
appear DE small trouble then enough you

*shou*_v *de*_u ，_w</Fm>
suffer.from PART

“You may suffer from some minor trouble, not to mention those disastrous incidents such as robbery and car theft.”

(39) <Fm ID= “19980109” ><Fa>不说_c 别的_r</Fa> ，_w 单_d 看_v 病床_n 边_f 相互_d 倾诉_v 彼此_r 的_u 感觉_n ，_w 他_r 在_p 语言_n 不_d 流畅_a 的_u 状态_n 中_f 还_d 能_v 同_p 你_r 交心_v ，_w 互相_d 谈_v 到_v 对方_n 的_u 优点_n ：_w</Fm>

<Fm ID=“19980109”><Fa> ***bushuo***_c *biede*_r</Fa> ，_w *dan*_d *kan*_v
let.alone others only see

*bingchuang*_n *bian*_f *xianghu*_d *qingsu*_v *bici*_r *de*_u *ganjue*_n ，
sick-.bed rim both chat each.other’s GEN feeling

_w *ta*_r *zai*_p *yuyan*_n *bu*_d *liuchang*_a *de*_u *zhuangtai*_n
he at language not fluent DE state

*zhong*_f *hai*_d *neng*_v *tong*_p *ni*_r *jiaoxin*_v ，_w *huxiang*_d
within still can with you share both

*tan*_v *dao*_v *duifang*_n *de*_u *youdian*_n ：_w</Fm>
discuss.about reach each.other’s GEN merits

“Lying on his sick-bed, and speaking painstakingly with a slight stutter, he could still pour out his innermost feelings and share yours, and talk about virtues, let alone other things related to him.”

Additive Clauses

Adverbial Subordinators	Frequency of Occurrence
何况 *hekuang*	7
不单 *budan*	3
且不说 *qiebushuo*	2
不说 *bushuo*	1
Total:	**13**

Table 16: Additive clause and its adverbial subordinators.

5.3.8 Clauses of exception

Clauses of exception (Quirk et al., 1985: 1102–1103) are introduced by the subordinating conjunction 只是 *zhishi* "except that". The situations named by these adverbial clauses are considered to be exceptions to the situations described in the main clauses, as shown in examples (40) and (41). The frequency of occurrence of clauses of exception in the PFR corpus is given in Table 17.

(40) <Fm ID= "19980127" >开始_v 很_d 长_a 一_m 段_q 时间_n ，_w 电力_n 不足_a ，_w 时有时停_l ，_w <Fa>只是_c 在_p 夏种_vn 秋收_vn 大忙时节_l 、_w 元旦_t 春节_t 喜庆_v 之_u 时_Ng ，_w 才_c 能_v 尽情_d 使用_v</Fa> 。_w</Fm>

<Fm ID="19980127"> *kaishi*_v *hen*_d *chang*_a *yi*_m *duan*_q
begin very long one CL
*shijian*_n ，_w *dianli*_n *buzhu*_a ，_w *shiyoushiting*_l ，_w
period.of.time electricity.supply insufficient sudden.blackout
<Fa>***zhishi*** c *zai*_p *xiazhong*_vn *qiushou*_vn
except.that during summer.cultivation autumn.harvest
*damangshijie*_l 、_w *yuandan*_t *chunjie*_t
grand.celebrations Chinese.New.Year.Eve Chinese.New.Year
*xiqing*_v *zhi*_u *shi*_Ng ，_w *cai*_c *neng*_v *jinqing*_d
happy DE period.of.time then can fully
*shiyong*_v</Fa> 。_w</Fm>
use

"In the beginning we had to come to terms with limited electricity supply and sudden blackouts for quite a long period of time. However we could enjoy a full supply of electricity during grand celebrations such as summer plantings, autumn harvests, the New Year Eve and Lunar New Year."

(41) <Fm ID= "19980116" >应景_vn 作品_n 倒是_d 数量_n 可观_a ，_w
<Fa>只是_c 没有_v 什么_r 保留_vn 价值_n</Fa> 。_w</Fm>

<Fm ID="19980116"> *yingjing*_vn *zuopin*_n *daoshi*_d *shuliang*_n
suit.the.theme works yet amount
*keguan*_a ，_w <Fa>***zhishi***_c *meiyou*_v *shenme*_r *baoliu*_vn
substantial except.that have.not somewhat reserve
*jiazhi*_n</Fa> 。_w</Fm>
value
"There are a huge number of works that suit our theme, though none are valuable."

Exception Clauses

Adverbial Subordinator	**Frequency of Occurrence**
只是 *zhishi*	25
Total:	**25**

Table 17: Exception clause and its adverbial subordinator.

5.3.9 Clauses of condition

Clauses of condition (Bhatt and Pancheva, 2001; Ippolito, 2003) are used to convey the meaning that the situation in the main clause is dependent on that in the adverbial clause. The adverbial subordinators used to mark these conditional clauses are, in descending order of frequency of occurrence (see Table 18a), 如果 *ruguo* "if" (see examples (42), (45), (47), (49) to (51), (62) and (63)), 只有 *zhiyou* "only if", 只要 *zhiyao* "provided that", 如 *ru* "if", 即使 *jishi* "even if" (see example (55)), 若 *ruo* "if" (see example (43)), 即便 *jibian* "even if" (see example (56)), 假如 *jiaru* "supposing that" (see example (44)), 就是 *jiushi* "even if" (see example (57)), 若是 *ruoshi* "if", 要是 *yaoshi* "assuming that", 倘若 *tangruo* "supposing that" (see examples (46) and (61)), 倘 *tang* "supposing that" (see example (48)), 哪怕 *napa* "even if" (see example (58)), 要不是 *yaoshibu* "if not, otherwise" (see examples (53) and (54)), 除非 *chufei* "unless" (see example (52)), 果真 *guozhan* "supposing that", 假若 *jiaruo* "supposing that", 若果 *ruguo* "if", 纵 *zong* "even if" (see example (59)), 要 *yao* "assuming that", 如若 *ruguo* "if", 纵使 *zongshi* "even if" (see example (60)), and 万一 *wanyi* "in case".[8]

Conditional Clauses (Overall Frequency)

Adverbial Subordinators	Frequency of Occurrence
如果 *ruguo*	308
只要 *zhiyao*	143
只有 *zhiyou*	115
即使 *jishi*	64
如 *ru*	38
若 *ruo*	33
即便 *jibian*	14
假如 *jiaru*	12
要是 *yaoshi*	8
若是 *ruoshi*	7
倘 *tang*	7
倘若 *tangruo*	7
哪怕 *napa*	6
就是 *jiushi*	3
要不是 *yaobushi*	3
若果 *ruoguo*	2
假若 *jiaruo*	2
万一 *wanyi*	1
如若 *ruruo*	1
果真 *guozhen*	1
要 *yao*	1
除非 *chufei*	1
纵 *zong*	1
纵使 *zongshi*	1
Total:	**779**

Table 18a: Conditional clause and its adverbial subordinators (overall frequency).

8 The constraints of space have prevented me from providing the examples of all the conditional subordinating conjunctions in this section.

5.3.9.1 Open conditions

There are four different types of condition on which the main clause is dependent. A majority of conditional clauses (i.e. 84%, or 653 occurrences out of a total of 779 occurrences, of conditional clauses) belong to the first type of condition, the so-called open condition. An open, real, condition (Adams, 1970; Stalnaker, 1975; Gärdenfors, 1979) typically leaves unresolved the question of the fulfilment or non-fulfilment of the condition. Thus it is unclear whether the consequent main clause is in fact applied or not, as shown in examples (42) to (44). The frequency of open conditionals is given in Table 18b.

(42) <Fm ID= "19980105" ><Fa>如果_c 届时_d 没有_v 竞争_vn 能力_n</Fa> ，_w 这些_r 企业_n 就_d 会_v 成为_v 集团_n 的_u "_w 包袱_n "_w 。_w</Fm>

<Fm ID="19980105"><Fa> ***ruguo***_c *jieshi*_d *meiyou*_v *jingzheng*_vn
if at.that.time have.not competition
*nengli*_n</Fa> ，_w *zhexie*_r *qiye*_n *jiu*_d *hui*_v *chengwei*_v
ability these enterprises then will become
*jituan*_n *de*_u "_w *baofu*_n "_w 。_w</Fm>
mother.company's GEN burden

"If they are no longer competitive in the market in the future, these fledgeling enterprises will become a burden to their mother company."

(43) <Fm ID= "19980108" ><Fa>若_c 要_v 真正_d 下功夫_v 研制_v 民族_n 特色_n 产品_n</Fa> ，_w 毕竟_d 需要_v 较_d 长_a 的_u 开发_vn 周期_n ，_w 还有_v 一定_b 市场_n 风险_n 。_w</Fm>

<Fm ID="19980108"><Fa> ***ruo***_c *yao*_v *zhenzheng*_d *xiagongfu*_v
if have.to really put.effort.into.sth.
*yanzhi*_v *minzu*_n *tese*_n *chanpin*_n</Fa> ，_w *bijing*_d *xuyao*_v
produce culture peculiar products nevertheless need
*jiao*_d *chang*_a *de*_u *kaifa*_vn *zhouqi*_n ，_w *haiyou*_v *yiding*_b
relatively long DE exploration period also certain
*shichang*_n *fengxian*_n 。_w</Fm>
market risk

"If (we) take pains to develop products which are peculiar to our culture, we will go through a longer developmental phase and encounter greater market risk."

(44) <Fm ID= “19980125” ><Fa>假如_c 议会_n 三_m 天_q 内_f 对_p 政府_n 通过_v 了_u 不信任案_n</Fa> ，_w 政府_n 就_d 解散_v ；_w</Fm>

<Fm ID=“19980125”><Fa>***jiaru***_c *yihui*_n *san*_m *tian*_q *nei*_f *dui*_p
if parliament three days within to
*zhengfu*_n *tongguo*_v *le*_u *buxinrenan*_n</Fa> ，_w *zhengfu*_n *jiu*_d
government pass PERF bill.of.no.confidence government then
*jiesan*_v ；_w</Fm>
dissolve

"If the parliament endorses a vote of no confidence within three days, the government will dissolve."

Conditional Clauses (Open Condition)

Adverbial Subordinators	Frequency of Occurrence
如果 *ruguo*	288
只要 *zhiyao*	143
只有 *zhiyou*	115
如 *ru*	37
若 *ruo*	31
假如 *jiaru*	9
要是 *yaoshi*	6
若是 *ruoshi*	7
倘 *tang*	5
倘若 *tangruo*	4
若果 *ruoguo*	2
假若 *jiaruo*	2
万一 *wanyi*	1
如若 *ruruo*	1
果真 *guozhen*	1
要 *yao*	1
Total:	**653**

Table 18b: Conditional clause (i.e. open condition) and its adverbial subordinators.

5.3.9.2 Hypothetical conditions

The second type of condition, hypothetical or unreal condition (Bhatt and Pancheva, 2001), on the other hand, explicitly expresses the meaning that the condition is not fulfilled and hence proves the consequent main clause to be false i.e. the main event does not take place, as illustrated in examples (45) to (51).

(45) <Fm ID= "19980111" ><Fa>如果_c 没有_d 竞争_v</Fa> ，_w 谁_r 也_d 不_d 会_v 把_p 可能_v 得到_v 的_u 那_r 一_m 份_q 利润_n 拱手_vd 让_v 人_n 。_w</Fm>

<Fm ID="19980111"><Fa> ***ruguo***_c *meiyou*_d *jingzheng*_v</Fa> ，_w
if have.not competition

*shui*_r *ye*_d *bu*_d *hui*_v *ba*_p *keneng*_v *dedao*_v *de*_u *na*_r
who also not will BA can gain DE that

*yi*_m *fen*_q *lirun*_n *gongshou*_vd *rang*_v *ren*_n 。_w</Fm>
one CL profits willingly give others

"If there were not any competition, no company would agree to forgo their potential profits to their rivals."

(46) <Fm ID= "19980109" ><Fa>倘若_c 果真_d 情投意合_i</Fa> ，_w 当然_d 可以_v 结合_v 。_w</Fm>

<Fm ID="19980109"><Fa> ***tangruo***_c *guozhen*_d *qingtouyihe*_i</Fa> ，
assuming.that really sincere.and.compatible

_w *dangran*_d *keyi*_v *jiehe*_v 。_w</Fm>
of.course can marry

"If a pair of lovers were sincere in their affection and compatible to each other, they should definitely get married."

(47) <Fm ID= "19980107" >"_w <Fa>如果_c 美国_ns 真心_d 希望_v 与_p 朝鲜_ns 改善_v 关系_n</Fa> ，_w 就_d 必须_d 放弃_v 对_p 我们_r 的_u 不_d 信任_v 和_c 敌视_v 政策_n "_w ，_w 采取_v 实际_a 行动_vn 。_w</Fm>

<Fm ID="19980107">"_w <Fa> ***ruguo***_c *Meiguo*_ns *zhenxin*_d *xiwang*_v
if America sincerely hope

yu_p Zhaoxian_ns gaishan_v guanxi_n</Fa> ，_w jiu_d bixu_d
with Korea improve relationship then necessarily
fangqi_v dui_p women_r de_u bu_d xinren_v he_c dishi_v
give.up to us DE not believe and be.hostile
zhengce_n ”_w ，_w caiqu_v shiji_a xingdong_vn 。_w</Fm>
policy adopt feasible action
"If the United States genuinely intended to improve its relations with Japan, it would cease all distrustful and hostile policies towards the Japanese government."

(48) <Fm ID= "19980125" ><Fa>倘_c 亚洲_ns 金融_n 风暴_n 中_f 确_d 有_v 泡沫_n 作祟_v</Fa> ，_w 我们_r 倒_d 应该_v 引_v 为_v 借_v 镜_Ng 。_w</Fm>
<Fm ID="19980125"><Fa> **tang**_c Yazhou_ns jinyong_n fengbao_n
if Asian financial storm
zhong_f que_d you_v paomo_n zuosui_v</Fa> ，_w women_r
within surely have bubble.economy cause we
dao_d yinggai_v yin_v wei_v jie_v jing_Ng 。_w</Fm>
yet should quote to.be borrow mirror
"If the Asian financial crisis really stemmed from economic bubbles, we should draw lessons from it."

(49) <Fm ID= "19980116" > "_w <Fa>如果_c 那天_r 不_d 是_v 那么_r 晚_a 了_u 还_d 在_d 闲逛_v</Fa> ，_w 就_d 不_d 会_v 发生_v 意外_a 了_y 。_w "_w</Fm>
<Fm ID="19980116">"_w <Fa>**ruguo**_c natian_r bu_d shi_v name_r
if that.day not be such
wan_a le_u hai_d zai_d xianguang_v</Fa> ，_w jiu_d bu_d
late.at.night PERF still PROG wander.around then not
hui_v fasheng_v yiwai_a le_y 。_w "_w</Fm>
will happen accident PART
"If I had not wandered around so late at night, the accident would not have happened."

(50) <Fm ID= “19980115” > “_w <Fa>那时_r 如果_c 能_v 像_p 现在_t 这样_r 来_v 认识_v 和_c 理解_v 小平_nr 的_u 指示_n</Fa> ，_w 成果_n 会_v 大_a 得_u 多_a ！_w ” _w</Fm>

<Fm ID=“19980115”>“_w <Fa>*nashi*_r ***ruguo***_c *neng*_v *xiang*_p
at.that.time if can as

*xianzai*_t *zheyang*_r *lai*_v *renshi*_v *he*_c *lijie*_v *Xiaoping*_nr
at.present in.this.way come learn and interpret Xiaoping's
*de*_u *zhishi*_n</Fa> ，_w *chengguo*_n *hui*_v *da*_a *de*_u *duo*_a ！
GEN instructions influence will great COMP much
_w ”_w</Fm>

"If we had understood and interpreted Deng Xiaoping's instructions in this way, the policy would have been more influential."

(51) <Fm ID= “19980105” ><Fa>如果_c 早_ad 知道_v 要_v 交_v 这么_r 多_a 钱_n</Fa> ，_w 我_r 也_d 就_d 不_d 会_v 打_v 了_y 。_w</Fm>

<Fm ID=“19980105”><Fa> ***ruguo***_c *zao*_ad *zhidao*_v *yao*_v *jiao*_v
if in.advance know have.to pay
*zheme*_r *duo*_a *qian*_n</Fa> ，_w *wo*_r *ye*_d *jiu*_d *bu*_d *hui*_v
such much money I yet then not will
*da*_v *le*_y 。_w</Fm>
dial PART

"If I had known beforehand that I had to pay such a large sum of money, I would not have used the service to make phone calls."

The hypothetical conditional clauses in these sentences convey the following implications respectively:

(45a) Competitions will very probably occur.

(46a) The lovers will very probably not be sincere in their love.[9]

9 Although the example given in isolation is not able to show it clearly, it does carry this implication when context is taken into account. In the context, the author discusses the love affair between two of his/her friends; both of them are not entirely sincere. While one of the lovers just wants to have casual relationship, the other

(47a) The United States presumably does not intend to improve her relationship with Korea.[10]

(48a) The Asian crisis presumably does not result from a bubble economy effect.[11]

(49a) We certainly did wander around late at night.

(50a) We certainly did not understand and interpret Deng's instructions in the way we are doing now.

(51a) We certainly did not realise that we had to pay a lot for the phone call service.

In different hypothetical conditions, the falsity of the proposition expressed by the associated main clause varies with respect to certainty (Quirk et al., 1985: 1091–1092). For future time reference as in (45) and (46), the condition is contrary to *expectation* as in (45a) and (46a); for present time reference as in (47) and (48), it is contrary to *assumption* as in (47a) and (48a); for past time reference as in (49) through (51), it is contrary to *fact*, i.e. counterfactual as in (49a) to (51a). In this case, the falsity of the proposition in the main clause is certain as the main event did not actually happen, while the former two cases merely indicate a probable falsity of the main clause proposition. Table 18c gives the frequency of hypothetical conditionals in the PFR corpus.

intends to lead a better life by means of marriage. Hence, example (46) is an ironic remark.

10 In the context, the author blames the U.S. for her lack of strong determination in improving her ties with Korea. It is said in the preceding discourse that while many rounds of talks have been held over the past year, little progress was made; the key to success consists in the U.S. government's attitude.

11 In the context, the author attempts to account for the occurrence of Asian financial crisis in 1998. S/he discusses a range of possible factors behind the scene and s/he tends to attribute the crisis to bad management rather than bubble economy effect.

Conditional Clauses (Hypothetical Condition)

Adverbial Subordinators	Frequency of Occurrence
如果 *ruguo*	18
如 *ru*	1
若 *ruo*	1
假如 *jiaru*	3
要是 *yaoshi*	2
倘 *tang*	2
倘若 *tangruo*	2
Total:	**29**

Table 18c: Conditional clause (i.e. hypothetical condition) and its adverbial subordinators.

5.3.9.3 Negative conditions

Negative conditionals (Wright and Hull, 1986; Montolío, 2000), the third type of conditional, are those conditional clauses marked by adverbial subordinators 除非 *chufei* "unless" and 要不是 *yaobushi* "if not, otherwise". These two negative conditional markers differ from each other in their implication of the occurrence of the main event. Firstly, a necessary condition is given by using 除非 *chufei* in the adverbial clause: the main event will not happen if the necessary condition is not fulfilled (Hou, 1998: 92–94), as shown in example (52). Secondly, the negative conditionals introduced by 要不是 *yaobushi* are always associated with a main clause which is counterfactual, i.e. the event described in the main clause did not happen, as highlighted in examples (53) and (54). The frequency of negative conditionals in the PFR corpus is given in Table 18d.

(52) <Fm ID= "19980101" ><Fa>除非_c 美国_ns 缴_v 清_a 欠款_n</Fa> ，_w 否则_c 不_d 可能_v 重_d 开_v 谈判_v 。_w</Fm>

<Fm ID="19980101"><Fa> ***chufei*_c** *Meiguo*_ns *jiao*_v *qing*_a
unless America settle completely
*qiankuan*_n</Fa> ，_w *fouze*_c *bu*_d *keneng*_v *chong*_d *kai*_v
debts otherwise not can afresh open
*tanpan*_v 。_w</Fm>
talk

"Unless the United States settles all its debts, the talks will not be renewed."

(53) <Fm ID= “19980121” > “_w <Fa>要不是_c 小孩_n 寄信_v 来_v</Fa> ，_w 我们_r 都_d 不_d 知道_v 老大爷_n 还_d 做_v 了_u 这么_r 一_m 件_q 好事_n 。_w ” _w</Fm>

<Fm ID=“19980121”>“_w <Fa>***yaobushi***_c *xiaohai*_n *jixin*_v
if.not children send.letter

*lai*_v</Fa> ，_w *women*_r *dou*_d *bu*_d *zhidao*_v *laodaye*_n
come we all not know respectable.old.man

*hai*_d *zuo*_v *le*_u *zheme*_r *yi*_m *jian*_q *haoshi*_n 。_w ”_w</Fm>
yet do PERF such one CL favour

“If the children had not sent us a letter, we would not have realised that the respectable old man had done us such a big favour.”

(54) <Fm ID= “19980101” ><Fa>要不是_c 受_v 种族_n 隔离_vn 制度_n 的_u 影响_vn</Fa> ，_w 南非_ns 同_p 中国_ns 建交_v 早已_d 实现_v 。_w</Fm>

<Fm ID=“19980101”><Fa> ***yaobushi***_c *shou*_v *zhongzu*_n *geli*_vn
if.not suffer.from ethnic isolation

*zhidu*_n *de*_u *yingxiang*_vn</Fa> ，_w *Nanfei*_ns *tong*_p
policy DE influence South.Africa with

*Zhongguo*_ns *jianjiao*_v *zaoyi*_d *shixian*_v 。_w</Fm>
China build.diplomatic.ties already realise

“If South Africa had not been influenced by the policy of ethnic isolation, it would have established diplomatic ties with China.”

Conditional Clauses (Negative Condition)

Adverbial Subordinators	Frequency of Occurrence
要不是 *yaobushi*	3
除非 *chufei*	1
Total:	**4**

Table 18d: Conditional clause (i.e. negative condition) and its adverbial subordinators.

5.3.9.4 Concessive conditions

The fourth type of condition gives rise to an intriguing group of conditional clauses, concessive conditionals (König, 1986; von Fintel, 1999). The term "concessive conditional" is used by Thompson and Longacre (1985: 196ff.) to refer to "clauses analogous to 'even if' clauses in English coding the relation 'frustrated implication'". They are referred to in terms of "condition" and "concession" because of two reasons: firstly, adverbial clauses usually express an open condition (see section 5.3.9.1 of this chapter), i.e. whether the condition is fulfilled is not known and thus it is not clear whether the proposition of the main clause is true or not, hence the use of the term "condition"; secondly, even if the condition is fulfilled and thus the event in the main clause occurs, the nature of the main event is surprising and contrary to expectations, hence the use of the term "concession". These concessive conditionals are introduced by subordinators such as 即使 *jishi*, 即便 *jibian*, 就是 *jiushi*, 哪怕 *napa*, 纵 *zong* and 纵使 *zongshi*, as shown in examples (55) to (60) respectively. The frequency of concessive conditionals is given in Table 18e.

(55) <Fm ID= "19980116" ><Fa>即使_c 仿造_v 了_u 外形_n</Fa> ，_w 也_d 无法_v 伪造_v 符合_v 产品_n 的_u 防伪_vn 密码_n 。_w</Fm>

<Fm ID="19980116"><Fa>***jishi***_c *fangzao*_v *le*_u *waixing*_n</Fa> ，_w
even.if forge PERF look
*ye*_d *wufa*_v *weizao*_v *fuhe*_v *chanpin*_n *de*_u *fangwei*_vn
yet cannot forge suit merchandise DE anti-piracy
*mima*_n 。_w</Fm>
password
"Even if you can forge the merchandise, you cannot forge the anti-piracy passwords correctly."

(56) <Fm ID= "19980121" ><Fa>即便_c 偶尔_d 办_v 错_a 一_m 件_q 事_n</Fa> ，_w 群众_n 也_d 是_v 会_v 谅解_v 你_r 的_u 。_w</Fm>

<Fm ID="19980121"><Fa>***jibian***_c *ouer*_d *ban*_v *cuo*_a *yi*_m
even.if occasionally do wrong one

*jian*_q *shi*_n</Fa> ，_w *qunzhong*_n *ye*_d *shi*_v *hui*_v
CL matter general.public yet be will
*liangjie*_v *ni*_r *de*_u 。_w</Fm>
forgive you PART
"Even if you occasionally make a mistake, people will forgive you."

(57) <Fm ID= "19980109" ><Fa>就是_c 上级_n 任命_v 个_q 总经理_n 之_u 职务_n</Fa> 也_d 不能_v 接受_v 了_y ，_w</Fm>
<Fm ID="19980109"><Fa>***jiushi***_c *shangji*_n
even.if higher.management
*renming*_v *ge*_q *zongjingli*_n *zhi*_u *zhiwu*_n</Fa> *ye*_d
appoint CL managing.director DE position yet
*buneng*_v *jieshou*_v *le*_y ，_w</Fm>
cannot accept PART
"Even if you were promoted to managing director, you could not accept the offer."

(58) <FmID= "19980114" ><Fa>哪怕_c 是_v 由于_p 第三者_n 的_u 原因_n 造成_v 的_u 旅客_n 人身_n 伤亡_vn</Fa> ，_w 铁路_n 运输_vn 企业_n 也_d 要_v 承担_v 赔偿_vn 责任_n 。_w</Fm>
<FmID="19980114"><Fa> ***napa***_c *shi*_v *youyu*_p *disanzhe*_n *de*_u
even.if be due.to third.party DE
*yuanyin*_n *zaocheng*_v *de*_u *lüke*_n *renshen*_n
reason cause DE tourist body
*shangwang*_vn</Fa> ，_w *tielu*_n *yunshu*_vn *qiye*_n *ye*_d *yao*_v
injuries railway transport firm yet need.to
*chengdan*_v *peichang*_vn *zeren*_n 。_w</Fm>
bear compensation responsibility
"Even if the commuters were injured or died as a result of third party actions, the railway and transport firm should be held responsible for the insurance costs incurred."

(59) <Fm ID= "19980103" > "_w 裹尸马革_l 英雄_n 事_n ，_w <Fa>纵_c 死_v</Fa> 终_d 令_v 汗_n 竹_Ng 香_a "_w</Fm>

<Fm ID="19980103">"_w *guohumage*_l *yingxiong*_n *shi*_n ，_w
ride.a.horse hero matter

<Fa>***zong***_c *si*_v</Fa> *zhong*_d *ling*_v *han*_n *zhu*_Ng
even.if die finally make sweat bamboo

*xiang*_a "_w</Fm>
flourish

"Even if you die, your heroic deeds will eventually be recorded for posterity."

(60) <Fm ID= "19980107" ><Fa>纵使_c 无_v 福_n 为_v 母_Ng</Fa> ，_w 也_d 可以_v 付出_v 母亲_n 般_u 的_u 爱_v 。_w</Fm>

<Fm ID="19980107"><Fa> ***zongshi***_c *wu*_v *fu*_n *wei*_v
even.if have.not blessing become

*mu*_Ng</Fa> ，_w *ye*_d *keyi*_v *fuchu*_v *muqin*_n *ban*_u *de*_u
mother yet can offer mother like DE

*ai*_v 。_w</Fm>
love

"Even if you are not blessed with a child, you can offer maternal affection to homeless children."

Conditional Clauses (Concessive Condition)

Adverbial Subordinators	**Frequency of Occurrence**
即使 *jishi*	64
即便 *jibian*	14
哪怕 *napa*	6
就是 *jiushi*	3
纵 *zong*	1
纵使 *zongshi*	1
Total:	**89**

Table 18e: Conditional clause (i.e. concessive condition) and its adverbial subordinators.

5.3.9.5 Indirect conditions

The four conditions mentioned above are more clearly conditional by comparsion to two types of peripheral conditional clause, namely rhetorical conditional clauses[12] and indirect conditional clauses[13] (Quirk et al., 1985: 1094ff.). I could not find any instances of rhetorical conditionals in the PFR corpus. It is a rare conditional type (Quirk et al., 1985: 1095; Mizutani, 2000) so this is hardly surprising. However, I did identify some potential uses of conditional clauses expressing an indirect condition, as shown in examples (61) to (63) below.

(61) <Fm ID= "19980123" ><Fa>倘若_c 有人_r 问_v 我_r ，_w 印象_n 最_d 深_a 的_u 是_v 什么_r</Fa> ？_w 我_r 要_v 告诉_v 他_r ：_w 是_v 手_n ，_w 是_v 几千_m 名_q 官兵_n 的_u 几千_m 双_q 手_n 。_w </Fm>

<Fm ID="19980123"><Fa> ***tangruo***_c *youren*_r *wen*_v *wo*_r ，_w
supposing.that people ask me
*yinxiang*_n *zui*_d *shen*_a *de*_u *shi*_v *shenme*_r</Fa> ？_w *wo*_r
impression most deep DE be what I
*yao*_v *gaosu*_v *ta*_r ：_w *shi*_v *shou*_n ，_w *shi*_v
want.to tell him be hands be
*jiqian*_m *ming*_q *guanbing*_n *de*_u *jiqian*_m *shuang*_q
several.thousand CL soldiers' GEN several.thousand CL
*shou*_n 。_w </Fm>
hands

"If someone asks me about the deepest impression of the troop, I will tell them – hands, the hands belonging to thousands of soldiers."

12 As Quirk et al. (1985: 1094–1095) note, there are two types of rhetorical conditional clauses: (a) if the proposition in the main clause is clearly false, the proposition in the conditional clause is shown to be false (e.g. *If they're Irish, I'm the Pope.* ["Since I'm obviously not the Pope, they're certainly not Irish."]); (b) if the proposition in the conditional clause is clearly true, the proposition in the main clause is shown to be true (e.g. *He's ninety if he's a day.* ["If you'll agree that he's at least a day old, perhaps you'll take my word that he's ninety."]).

13 Broadly speaking, the indirect conditional clause is a conventional expression of politeness which seeks the hearer's permission before the speaker makes an utterance (Quirk et al., 1985: 1095 ff.), for instance, *If I may say so, your work is not well written.*

(62) <Fm ID= “19980131” ><Fa>如果_c 让_v 我_r 回答_v</Fa> ，_w 我_r 想_v 首先_d 是_v 那些_r 不_d 上档次_l 的_u 记者_n ，_w <Fm ID= “19980131” >他们_r 不_d 是_v 以_p 天下_n 为_v 己任_n ，_w <Fa>而是_c 像_v 苍蝇_n 一样_u ，_w 紧紧_d 叮_v 着_u “_w 星_n ”_w 们_k 不_d 放_v ，_w 捧_v 一些_m 臭_a 脚_n ，_w 制造_v 一些_m 绯闻_n 来_v 提高_v 自己_r 的_u 知名度_n</Fa></Fm> ；_w</Fm>

<Fm ID=“19980131”><Fa> ***ruguo***_c *rang*_v *wo*_r *huida*_v</Fa> ，_w
if let me reply
*wo*_r *xiang*_v *shouxian*_d *shi*_v *naxie*_r *bu*_d *shangdangci*_l *de*_u
I think first.of.all be those not respectable DE
*jizhe*_n ，_w <Fm ID=“19980131”> *tamen*_r *bu*_d *shi*_v *yi*_p
journalists they not be as.regards
*tianxia*_n *wei*_v *jiren*_n ，_w <Fa>*ershi*_c *xiang*_v *cangying*_n
world be one’s.responsibility rather be.akin.to fly
*yiyang*_u ，_w *jinjin*_d *ding*_v *zhe*_u “_w *xing*_n ”_w *men*_k
the.same closely spy PROG celebrities PL
*bu*_d *fang*_v ，_w *peng*_v *yixie*_m *chou*_a *jiao*_n ，_w *zhizao*_v
not release hold some smelly feet make.up
*yixie*_m *feiwen*_n *lai*_v *tigao*_v *ziji*_r *de*_u
some gossip serve.a.purpose enhance oneself’s GEN
*zhimingdu*_n</Fa></Fm> ；_w</Fm>
reputation
“If I may say so, first of all, I dislike the paparazzi. They never take their eyes off celebrities and they make up gossip about them in order to enhance their own reputation.”

(63) <Fm ID= “19980118” ><Fa>如果_c 上帝_n 存在_v 的话_u</Fa> ，_w 在_p 法国_ns ，_w 这个_r 上帝_n 就_d 是_v 政府_n ；_w</Fm>

<Fm ID=“19980118”><Fa> ***ruguo***_c *Shangdi*_n *cunzai*_v
if god exist
*dehua*_u</Fa> ，_w *zai*_p *Faguo*_ns ，_w *zhege*_r *Shangdi*_n *jiu*_d
so.to.speak in France this god then
*shi*_v *zhengfu*_n ；_w</Fm>
be government
“If god is real, government is god in France.”

The conditions in examples (61) and (62) are dependent on the implicit speech act "I am telling you, if I may, that …". In conventional politeness in conversations, the speaker makes an utterance of assertion dependent on obtaining proper permission from the hearer, though the fulfilment of that condition is conventionally taken for granted (Levinson, 1983: 263–276; Brown and Levinson, 1987: 162–164). Previous analyses of properties of spoken and written language have demonstrated that features which have been identified as characterising a spoken style may be borrowed by writers for stylistic purposes (Tannen, 1982a and 1982c; Chafe and Danielewicz, 1987). The Chinese writers of the newspaper articles included in the PFR corpus adopt similar strategies to those identified by Tannen and Chafe and Danielewicz to gain a reader's attention, as shown in examples (61) and (62). Yet in example (63), the conditional clause does not express the implicit speech act as occurs in examples (61) and (62); rather, it expresses uncertainty about the extralinguistic knowledge required by the reader to correctly interpret the sentence. The three conditional clauses in examples (61) to (63) are taken to be *indirect* because the situation of the main clause is not directly dependent on that of the conditional clause: the occurrence of the main event is not a direct consequence of the fulfilment of the condition in the conditional clause. Table 18f gives the frequency of indirect conditional clauses in the PFR corpus.

Conditional Clauses (Indirect condition)

Adverbial Subordinators	Frequency of Occurrence
如果 *ruguo*	2
若 *ruo*	1
倘若 *tangruo*	1
Total:	**4**

Table 18f: Conditional clause (i.e. indirect condition) and its adverbial subordinators.

5.3.10 Clauses of concession

5.3.10.1 Simple concessive clauses

A simple concessive clause (Couper-Kuhlen and Thompson, 2000; Crevels, 2000; König and Siemund, 2000; Kim, 2002) is one which makes a concession against which the proposition in the main clause is contrasted. More specifically, the meaning of concessive sentences can be characterised as follows: the situation in the main clause is contrary to expectation in the light of what is said in the concessive clause (cf. Haspelmath and König, 1998: 584–593). In Chinese, clauses of concession are introduced by the adverbial subordinators 虽然 *suiran* "although", 尽管 *jinguan* "even though", 虽 *sui* "though" and 虽说 *suishuo* "while admitting that…", as illustrated in examples (64) to (67). The frequency of simple concessive clauses is given in Table 19a.

(64) <Fm ID= "19980111" ><Fa>冷战_n 虽_c 已_d 结束_v</Fa> ，_w 但_c 在_p 美国_ns 政界_n 、_w 军界_n 和_c 情报界_n 中_f ，_w 仍_d 有_v 不少_m 人_n 根深蒂固_i 地_u 坚持_v 冷战_n 思维_n ，_w 继续_v 把_p 俄罗斯_ns 看做_v 敌人_n 。_w</Fm>

<Fm ID="19980111"><Fa> *lengzhan*_n ***sui***_c *yi*_d *jieshu*_v</Fa> ，_w
cold.war though already finish

*dan*_c *zai*_p *Meiguo*_ns *zhengjie*_n 、_w *junjie*_n *he*_c
but in America political.arena military and

*qingbaojie*_n *zhong*_f ，_w *reng*_d *you*_v *bushao*_m
intelligence.agency among still have quite.a.number.of

*ren*_n *genshendigu*_i *de*_u *jianchi*_v *lengzhan*_n *siwei*_n ，_w
people deep-rooted ADVL insist.on cold.war way.of.thinking

*jixu*_v *ba*_p *Eluosi*_ns *kanzuo*_v *diren*_n 。_w</Fm>
continue BA Russia be.seen.as enemy

"Though the cold war ended, in the United States there were many people in the political arena, military and intelligence agency who still insisted on cold-war diplomacy towards Russia and perceived the Russians as their enemies."

(65) <Fm ID= "19980116" ><Fa>虽然_c 香港_ns 基础_n 良好_a ，_w 金融_n 体系_n 健全_a</Fa> ，_w 但是_c 过去_v 半_m 年_q 来_f 香港_ns 发生_v 的_u 不少_m 事情_n ，_w 尤其_d 是_v 亚洲_ns 金融_n 市场_n 再度_d 出现_v 的_u 紧张_a 局面_n ，_w 对_p 香港_ns 产生_v 了_u 负面_b 影响_vn ，_w 香港_ns 金融_n 市场_n 和_c 整个_b 经济_n 体系_n 受到_v 考验_v 。_w</Fm>

<Fm ID="19980116"><Fa> ***suiran***_c *Xianggang*_ns *jichu*_n
although Hong.Kong foundation
*lianghao*_a ，_w *jinyong*_n *tixi*_n *jianquan*_a</Fa> ，_w *danshi*_c
sound financial system healthy but
*guoqu*_v *ban*_m *nian*_q *lai*_f *Xianggang*_ns *fasheng*_v *de*_u
past half year onwards Hong.Kong happen DE
*bushao*_m *shiqing*_n ，_w *youqi*_d *shi*_v *Yazhong*_ns
quite.a.number.of incidents especially be Asian
*jinyong*_n *shichang*_n *zaidu*_d *chuxian*_v *de*_u *jinzhang*_a
financial market again emerge DE tense
*jumian*_n ，_w *dui*_p *Xianggang*_ns *chansheng*_v *le*_u *fumian*_b
situation to Hong.Kong create PERF negative
*yingxiang*_vn ，_w *Xiangguang*_ns *jinyong*_n *shichang*_n *he*_c
influence Hong.Kong financial market and
*zhengge*_b *jingji*_n *tixi*_n *shoudao*_v *kaoyan*_v 。_w</Fm>
whole economic system face challenge

"Although Hong Kong has a strong foundation and perfect financial system, the adverse circumstances that Hong Kong encountered over the past six months, especially the financial crisis in Asia, have posed a challenge to Hong Kong's financial market and economic system as a whole."

(66) <Fm ID= "19980128" ><Fa>这样_r 的_u 晚会_n 虽说_c 年年_q 都_d 有_v</Fa> ，_w 但_c 今年_t 从_p 内容_n 编排_vn 、_w 演出_vn 水准_n 到_p 服装_n 道具_n 都_d 很_d 令_v 人_n 耳目一新_i 。_w</Fm>

<Fm ID="19980128"><Fa> *zheyang*_r *de*_u *wanhui*_n ***suishuo***_c
this.kind.of DE soirée while.admitting.that
*niannian*_q *dou*_d *you*_v</Fa> ，_w *dan*_c *jinnian*_t *cong*_p
annually all have but this.year from

*neirong*_n *bianpai*_vn 、_w *yanchu*_vn *shuizhun*_n *dao*_p *fuzhuang*_n
content schedule performance standard to clothing
*daoju*_n *dou*_d *hen*_d *ling*_v *ren*_n *ermuyixin*_i 。_w</Fm>
property all very make people feel.refreshed
"Although a soirée of this sort is organised annually, this year's function has broken fresh ground in terms of schedule, quality of performance and stage property."

(67) <Fm ID= "19980127" ><Fa>尽管_c 联合国_nt 在_p 伊拉克_ns 进行_v 武器_n 核查_vn</Fa> ，_w 但_c 伊拉克_ns 现在_t 仍_d 拥有_v 生物武器_l 工厂_n ，_w 并且_c 还_d 在_d 秘密_ad 开工_v 。_w</Fm>

<Fm ID="19980127"><Fa>***jinguan***_c *Lianheguo*_nt *zai*_p *Yilake*_ns
even.though United.Nation in Iraq
*jinxing*_v *wuqi*_n *hecha*_vn</Fa> ，_w *dan*_c *Yilake*_ns *xianzai*_t
conduct weapon inspection but Iraq at.present
*reng*_d *yongyou*_v *shengwuwuqi*_l *gongchang*_n ，_w *bingqie*_c
still own biological.weapon factory also
*hai*_d *zai*_d *mimi*_ad *kaigong*_v 。_w</Fm>
still PROG secretly operate
"In spite of the regular military weapon inspections held by the United Nation, Iraq is still secretly engaged in the manufacture of biological weapons."

Simple Concessive Clauses

Adverbial Subordinators	**Frequency of Occurrence**
虽然 *suiran*	173
尽管 *jinguan*	132
虽 *sui*	99
虽说 *suishuo*	6
Total:	**410**

Table 19a: Simple concessive clause and its adverbial subordinators.

5.3.10.2 Alternative concessive clauses

Apart from simple concessive clauses, there are two other types of concessive clause, namely alternative concessive clauses and universal concessive clauses. Alternative concessive clauses (Quirk and Greenbaum, 1973: 326; Haspelmath and König, 1998: 594–604) are those adverbial clauses marked by the correlative sequence *whether ... or* which is made up of a pair of adverbial subordinators i.e. 无论 *wulun* … 还是 *haishi* …, 无论是 *wulunshi* … 还是 *haishi* …, 不论 *bulun* … 还是 *haishi* …, and 不论是 *bulunshi* … 还是 *haishi* …, as shown in examples (68) to (71). The correlative sequence provides two alternative conditions under which the same situation in the main clause applies. In other words, the concessive meaning in these clauses arises from implication that two contrasting conditions unexpectably result in the occurrence of the same main event. Table 19b gives the frequency of alternative concessive clauses in my corpus.

(68) <Fm ID= "19980112" ><Fa>无论_c 身_Ng 处_v 高位_n ，_w 还是_c 平头_n 百姓_n</Fa> ，_w 海内外_s 游子_n 心中_s 的_u 家_n 永远_d 在_v 生养_v 他_r 的_u 故乡_n 。_w</Fm>

<Fm ID="19980112"><Fa> ***wulun***_c *shen*_Ng *chu*_v *gaowei*_n ，_w
whether.or body situate high.management
haishi_c *pingtou*_n *baixing*_n</Fa> ，_w *haineiwai*_s *youzi*_n
whether.or ordinary citizen local.and.overseas lingerer
*xinzhong*_s *de*_u *jia*_n *yongyuan*_d *zai*_v *shengyang*_v *ta*_r *de*_u
in.the.heart DE home forever at be.born his GEN
*guxiang*_n 。_w</Fm>
place.of.birth

"Whether coming from a noble class or from the masses, overseas people always regard their birth place as home."

(69) <Fm ID= "19980125" ><Fa>无论是_c 繁华_a 的_u 都市_n ，_w 还是_c 偏远_a 的_u 乡村_n</Fa> ，_w 所到之处_l ，_w 无不_d 洋溢_v 着_u 欢快_a 的_u 节日_n 气氛_n 。_w</Fm>

<Fm ID="19980125"><Fa> ***wulunshi***_c *fanhua*_a *de*_u *doushi*_n ，_w
whether.or bustling DE city

haishi_c *pianyuan*_a *de*_u *xiangcun*_n</Fa> ，_w *suodaozhichu*_l ，
whether.or remote DE village everywhere
_w *wubu*_d *yangyi*_v *zhe*_u *huankui*_a *de*_u
without.exception be.filled.with PROG joyful DE
*jieri*_n *qifen*_n 。_w</Fm>
festival atmosphere
"Whether a bustling city or a village in the countryside, it is in festive mood."

(70) <Fm ID= "19980122" ><Fa>少数民族_n 干部_n 不论_c 在_p 数量_n 上_f ，_w 还是_v 在_p 队伍_n 结构_n 上_f</Fa> ，_w 都_d 还_d 不能_v 适应_v 客观_n 需要_vn 。_w</Fm>

<Fm ID="19980122"><Fa> *shaoshuminzu*_n *ganbu*_n ***bulun***_c *zai*_p
ethnic.minorities cadre whether.or at
*shuliang*_n *shang*_f ，_w ***haishi***_v *zai*_p *duiwu*_n *jiegou*_n
quantity aspect whether.or at troop arrangement
*shang*_f</Fa> ，_w *dou*_d *hai*_d *buneng*_v *shiying*_v *keguan*_n
aspect all still cannot meet practical
*xuyao*_vn 。_w</Fm>
needs
"Whether in terms of size or troop arrangements, the cadre of the ethnic minorities cannot meet practical needs."

(71) <Fm ID= "19980107" ><Fa>不论是_c 有_v 实力_n 的_u 企业_n 还是_c 个人_n</Fa> ，_w 他们_r 的_u 钱_n 都_d 是_v 辛辛苦苦_z 挣_v 来_v 的_u ，_w</Fm>

<Fm ID="19980107"><Fa> ***bulunshi***_c *you*_v *shili*_n *de*_u *qiye*_n
whether.or have ability DE enterprise
haishi_c *geren*_n</Fa> ，_w *tamen*_r *de*_u *qian*_n *dou*_d *shi*_v
whether.or individual their GEN money all be
*xinxinkuku*_z *zheng*_v *lai*_v *de*_u ，_w</Fm>
painstakingly earn come PART
"Whether operating a competitive enterprise of their own or working in a firm, people take pains to earn a living."

Alternative Concessive Clauses

Adverbial Subordinators	Frequency of Occurrence
无论是 *wulunshi* … 还是 *haishi* …	30
无论 *wulun* … 还是 *haishi* …	17
不论是 *bulunshi* … 还是 *haishi* …	9
不论 *bulun* … 还是 *haishi* …	2
Total:	**58**

Table 19b: Alternative concessive clauses and its adverbial subordinators.

5.3.10.3 Universal concessive clauses

The meaning that the same main event applies to the contrastive conditions described in the adverbial concessive clause may also be conveyed by empolying universal concessive clauses (Quirk and Greenbaum, 1973: 326; Haspelmath and König, 1998: 604–619), except that the number of opposing stated conditions involved in the contrast is unspecified rather than being expressly two. Hence, universal concessive clauses are those which signal a meaning like "no matter what" or "whatever", expressed by the subordinators such as 无论 *wulun*, 不论 *bulun*, 不管 *buguan*, 甭管 *bengguan*, and 任 *ren*, as shown in examples (72) to (76). These clauses typically contain some unspecified elements, usually an indefinite pronoun and a question word, e.g. 什么 *shenme* "what", 怎样 *zenyang* "how", 谁 *shui* "who", 如何 *ruhe* "how", 哪 *na* "which", 什么样 *shenmeyang* "what kind of", etc. The frequency of universal concessive clauses is given in Table 19c, whereas the overall frequency of concessive clauses is given in Table 19d.

(72) <Fm ID= "19980112" ><Fa>无论_c 在_p 哪个_r 商城_n 或_c 超市_n</Fa> ，_w 残疾人_n 都_d 享受_v 这种_r 特殊_a 优待_vn 。_w</Fm>

<Fm ID="19980112"><Fa> ***wulun***_c *zai*_p *nage*_r *shangcheng*_n *huo*_c
whatever in which shopping.mall or

*chaoshi*_n</Fa> ，_w *canjiren*_n *dou*_d *xiangshou*_v *zhezhong*_r
supermarket disabled all enjoy these

*teshu*_a *youdai*_vn 。_w</Fm>
special privileges
"Whatever shopping malls or supermarkets they go to, handicapped people will enjoy special privileges."

(73) <Fm ID= "19980108" ><Fa>不论_c 什么_r 情况_n 下_f</Fa> ，_w 都_d 要_v 坚持_v 报道_v 的_u 客观_an 、_w 公正性_n 。_w</Fm>
<Fm ID="19980108"><Fa> ***bulun***_c *shenme*_r *qingkuang*_n
whatever what.kind.of circumstances
*xia*_f</Fa> ，_w *dou*_d *yao*_v *jianchi*_v *baodao*_v *de*_u
under all have.to insist.on reporting DE
*keguan*_an 、_w *gongzhengxing* _n 。_w</Fm>
objectivity impartiality
"No matter what the circumstances, journalists should maintain objectivity and impartiality in their reporting."

(74) <Fm ID= "19980120" >老人_n ，_w <Fa>不管_c 他们_r 的_u 能力_n 大小_n ，_w 职位_n 高低_n</Fa> ，_w 都_d 为_p 自己_r 的_u 家庭_n 、_w 为_p 祖国_n 做出_v 了_u 奉献_vn 。_w</Fm>
<Fm ID="19980120"> *laoren*_n ，_w <Fa>***buguan***_c *tamen*_r
elderly whatever their
*de*_u *nengli*_n *daxiao*_n ，_w *zhiwei*_n *gaodi*_n</Fa> ，_w *dou*_d
GEN ability extent post seniority all
*wei*_p *ziji*_r *de*_u *jiating*_n 、_w *wei*_p *zuguo*_n *zuochu*_v
for oneself's GEN family for motherland make
*le*_u *fengxian*_vn 。_w</Fm>
PERF contribution
"No matter how capable they are or in which posts they serve, old people have played their part in contributing to their family and their country."

(75) <Fm ID= "19980109" ><Fa>甭管_c 东西_n 拍_v 得_u 多_d 臭_a</Fa> ，_w 主演_n 的_u 片酬_n 低_a 不_d 了_v ，_w 导演_n 的_u 谱儿_n 小_a 不_d 了_v 。_w</Fm>
<Fm ID="19980109"><Fa> ***bengguan***_c *dongxi*_n *pai*_v *de*_u *duo*_d
whatever stuff produce COMP how

*chou*_a</Fa> ，_w *zhuyan*_n *de*_u *pianchou*_n *di*_a *bu*_d
poor leading.role's GEN pay low not
*liao*_v</Fa> ，_w *daoyan*_n *de*_u *puer*_n *xiao*_a
complete director's GEN script indispensable
*bu*_d *liao*_v 。_w</Fm>
not complete
"No matter how poor the film is or how much the leading actor is paid, the director's script is indispensable."

(76) <Fm ID= "19980118" ><Fa>任_c 你_r 走_v 进_v 哪个_r 角落 _n</Fa> ，_w 保_v 你_r 不_d 会_v 发现_v 零乱_an 与_c 污浊 _an 。_w</Fm>
<Fm ID="19980118"><Fa> ***ren***_c *ni*_r *zou*_v *jin*_v *nage*_r
whatever you go enter.into which
*jiaoluo*_n</Fa> ，_w *bao*_v *ni*_r *bu*_d *hui*_v *faxian*_v *lingluan*_an
corner guarantee you not will discover mess
*yu*_c *wuzhuo*_an 。_w</Fm>
and filth
"Wherever you go, you will not spot any mess or filth."

Universal Concessive Clauses

Adverbial Subordinators	**Frequency of Occurrence**
无论 *wulun*	43
不管 *buguan*	39
不论 *bulun*	21
任 *ren*	3
甭管 *bengguan*	1
Total:	**107**

Table 19c: Universal concessive clause and its adverbial subordinators.

Concessive Clauses (Overall Frequency)

Adverbial Subordinators	Frequency of Occurrence
虽然 *suiran*	173
尽管 *jinguan*	132
虽 *sui*	99
无论 *wulun*	90
不管 *buguan*	39
不论 *bulun*	32
虽说 *suishuo*	6
任 *ren*	3
甭管 *bengguan*	1
Total:	**575**

Table 19d: Concessive clause and its adverbial subordinators (overall frequency).

5.3.11 Clauses of inference

In marking that two events are dependent on each other, inference clauses differ from conditional clauses in that the condition for the main event to take place has been fulfilled in an inference clause, while a conditional clause will either leave unresolved the question of the fulfilment or non-fulfilment of the condition (i.e. an open conditional; see section 5.3.9.1), or imply that the condition is/was/will not be fulfilled (i.e. a hypothetical conditional; see section 5.3.9.2). Furthermore, clauses of inference can be distinguished from clauses of concession because in the former the nature of this dependence is expected and the main clause event can easily be inferred given the accomplished condition stated in the adverbial clause, whereas in the latter the main clause is unexpected given the condition. As shown in the corpus data, the clause of inference is marked by the adverbial subordinator 尚且 *shangqie* "even", as illustrated in examples (77) and (78). The frequency of clauses of inference is given in Table 20.

(77) <Fm ID= "19980112" ><Fa>医疗_n 器械_n 管理_vn 走_v 在_p 全国_n 前_f 列_n 的_u 上海_ns 尚且_c 如此_r</Fa> ，_w 其他_r 一些_m 地方_n 更为_d 不堪_v 。_w</Fm>

<Fm ID="19980112"><Fa> *yiliao*_n *qixie*_n *guanli*_vn *zou*_v *zai*_p
medicine equipment management walk on
*quanguo*_n *qian*_f *lie*_n *de*_u *Shanghai*_ns ***shangqie***_c
across.the.country top list DE Shanghai even
*ruci*_r</Fa> ，_w *qita*_r *yixie*_m *defang*_n *gengwei*_d *bukan*_v 。_w</Fm>
as.such other several places even.more unbearable

"Even Shanghai, which offers the best service in the territory, cannot meet the worldwide standard for medical apparatus and instruments. Some other places are far worse."

(78) <Fm ID= "19980123" ><Fa>要_v 开辟_v 出_v 一_m 条_q 路_n 来_v 尚且_c 不易_a</Fa> ，_w 更何况_l 建寺_v 修_v 庙_n ！_w</Fm>

<Fm ID="19980123"><Fa> *yao*_v *kaipi*_v *chu*_v *yi*_m *tiao*_q *lu*_n
have.to construct out one CL road
*lai*_v ***shangqie***_c *buyi*_a</Fa> ，_w *genghekuang*_l *jiansi*_v
come even not.easy not.to.mention build.a.monastery
*xiu*_v *miao*_n ！_w</Fm>
renovate temple

"Even constructing a path in this dangerously steep area is enormously difficult, let alone building a monastery or renovating a temple."

Inference Clauses

Adverbial Subordinator	**Frequency of Occurrence**
尚且 *shangqie*	3
Total:	**3**

Table 20: Inference clause and its adverbial subordinator.

5.4 Chapter summary

In this chapter, I have provided an analysis of the semantic roles of the 2,417 adverbial clauses found in the PFR Chinese Corpus. Adverbial clauses in Chinese can be semantically subsumed into eleven classes: clause of time, clause of cause/reason, clause of purpose, clause of result, clause of preference or substitutive clause, clause of contrast, clause of addition, clause of exception, clause of condition, clause of concession and clause of inference. For each semantic class, I have analysed the sentences in the corpus and drawn frequency tables to illustrate the use of adverbial subordinators in conveying particular semantic meaning(s). The following table is a summary of the frequency of occurrence of individual interclausal semantic relations exhibited by Chinese adverbial clauses.

Semantic Classes of Adverbial Clauses	*Frequency of Occurrence*
Clause of Condition	779
Clause of Concession	575
Clause of Purpose	348
Clause of Cause or Reason	330
Clause of Contrast	177
Clause of Result	163
Clause of Exception	25
Clause of Addition	13
Clause of Inference	3
Clause of Preference	3
Clause of Time	1
Total:	2,417

Table 21: Interclausal semantic relations of adverbial clauses in Chinese.

Among these semantic categories, conditional and concessive clauses make up approximately half of the adverbial clauses studied and use a wide variety of subordinating conjunctions, while time, inference and preference clauses occur infrequently in the corpus (i.e. three or fewer examples each) and are introduced by no more than two adverbial subordinators. The adverbial subordinator 从而 *conger* "in order that" marks the apparent overlap between purpose clause and result clause as it can be used to introduce both the purpose clause and result clause in more or less the same frequency of occurrence in the corpus. Clauses of inference, on the other hand, form a semantic class in their own right as they are distinct from seemingly functionally alike conditional and concessive clauses. Furthermore, I indicated and attempted to explain some of the peculiarities with respect to actual usage in real-life data which were found in certain of these adverbial types; for instance, the clauses of contrast introduced by 而是 *ershi* "rather" interact interestingly with negation verb forms and negative adverbs occurring in the main clause.

Chapter Six

Non-overt Subjects of Chinese Adverbial Clauses: A Government and Binding Approach

6.1 Introduction

In this chapter, I will explore the non-overt subjects that occur in Chinese adverbial clauses (henceforth CACs). A non-overt subject, by definition, is an empty (or covert, null) category, i.e. a category which has no overt phonetic form, and hence which is inaudible or silent (Radford, 1997: 131). It generally refers to the subject of a finite clause that remains unexpressed lexically. A language that allows a subject to be omitted is referred to as a *pro-drop* language (Haegeman, 1994: 19). Chinese is a pro-drop language (Huang, 1989). Previous pro-drop analyses (Cordin, 1980; Belletti, 1982; Hyams, 1983; Åfarli, 1987; Adams, 1987; Philippaki-Warburton, 1987; Kouwenberg, 1990; Koktová, 1992; Joseph, 1994; Modesto, 2000) have concentrated primarily on the question of the correlation between morphological agreement and pro-drop: languages with rich inflectional agreement can allow for covert subjects as the verbs are sufficiently marked morphologically to show the intended subject. However, languages such as Chinese, Japanese and Korean do not have rich morphology yet they still allow for covert subjects (Ohso, 1976). Setting out to provide a solution for this problem, Huang (1984: 550ff.) proposes that there may be two separate explanations for pro-drop: whereas pro-drop in Romance languages, such as Italian, may be motivated by rich morphology, pro-drop in languages such as Chinese, Japanese and Korean may be motivated by the fact that these are topic-prominent languages in which structural subjects are not a basic requirement of the sentence.[1] The key motivation

1 Li and Thompson (1974 and 1976) argue persuasively for analysing Chinese as a topic-prominent language. Basically, the topic of a sentence is what the sentence is about. It always comes first in the sentence. While almost all English sentences

for Huang's work was the inability of accounts of pro-drop, developed on Romance languages, to account for pro-drop in Chinese. This mirrors the motivation for my work. Previous research on the distribution of non-overt subjects in linguistics has been based on morphologically rich languages (cf. Bodomo and Luke, 2001), and morphology has been the main component of the explanation of the distribution (Rögnvaldsson, 1993 (Icelandic); Aroonmanakun, 1997 (Thai); Bar-Shalom and Snyder, 1997 (Russian); Ackema, 2002 (German); Bennis, 2002 (Dutch)). These explanations cannot apply to Chinese. The main aim of this book is therefore to develop an explanation for the distribution of non-overt subjects in Chinese adverbial clauses.

Most accounts of pro-drop in Chinese are concerned with pro-drop in complement clauses of verbs (Battistella, 1985; Huang, 1987; Chen, 1990; Henry, 1990; Huang, 1995; among others), as shown in the following example adapted from Huang (1987: 329).

(1)	张三	说	[*e*	不	认识	李四]
	Zhangsan	*shuo*	[*e*	*bu*	*renshi*	*Lisi*]
	Zhangsan	say		not	know	Lisi

"Zhangsan said he does not know Lisi."

In example (1), the non-overt subject, represented as *e*, occurs in the complement clause that the verb 说 *shuo* "say" takes. As my book does not focus on complement clauses, I will not investigate the pro-drop phenomenon in these clauses further. Rather I would like to examine the non-overt subjects that occur in adverbial clauses because research to date has focussed on complement clauses at the expense of adverbial clauses. I wish to redress this imbalance. In doing so, I will adopt a Government and Binding (GB) approach. I chose to follow GB theory because this theory is one of the approaches that falls within the

must have a subject, it is difficult to identify the subject in a Chinese sentence: the subject is not marked by position, by agreement, or by any case marker; and it can be the agent of an action, or it can be the topic or whatever comes first in the sentence, or both (LaPolla, 1993). Since the definition of subject is so problematic in Chinese, several scholars such as Li and Thompson argue that though there may be a subject in Chinese, it does not play an important role in the Chinese grammar; they suggest that the concept of topic appears to be relatively more significant in analysing the structure of sentences in the language.

principles and parameters (P&P) family of theories (van Valin, 2001: 193). GB is based on the idea of universal grammar or UG (Chomsky, 1981b: 7), and consequently the principles it proposes are intended to be linguistic universals, that is universal properties of the grammars of human languages. Variation between different languages is captured in terms of *parameters* (Chomsky, 1981c). One of the parameters is the *pro-drop parameter* which characterises languages like Chinese, in which subjects can be dropped, as noted above. This suggests that GB theory is particularly suited to frame an investigation of non-overt subjects in Chinese[2] as a solution to the pro-drop question is central to the theory. Other examples of principles-and-parameters syntactic theories include the Minimalist Program (Chomsky, 1995a and 1995b) and Generalised Phrase Structure Grammar (Gazdar et al., 1985). However, I did not follow these approaches because a typology of empty categories is more thoroughly explained using the GB framework (e.g. Haegeman, 1994: 431–479) than using these theories (Marantz, 1995: 352–354; Harbert, 1995: 217–233; Borsley, 1999: 175–187).

Other theories of syntax that do not take the P&P approach e.g. Relational Grammar (RelG), Lexical-Functional Grammar (LFG), Head-driven Phrase Structure Grammar (HPSG), Role and Reference Grammar (RRG), Functional Grammar (FG) and Optimality Theory (OT) are unsuitable for use in this book also. Relational Grammar (Perlmutter and Postal, 1977; Perlmutter, 1980 and 1983), a descendant of Transformational Grammar or TG (Chomsky, 1965), represents clause structure in terms of grammatical relations subject, direct object and indirect object. It postulates a number of general principles constraining possible relational networks and hence possible syntactic structures in human languages. One of the most important ones is the *Final 1 Law*[3] which states that every clause has a subject. However, it ignores the question of why a subject can be omitted in the first place, and takes

2 Quite a large number of previous analyses of Chinese syntax are based on the application of GB theory; see, for example, Aoun (1984), Lee (1987), Lu (1988), Yu (1988), Pan (1989), Tang (1989), Gasde (1990), Li (1990), Huang (1991), Juffs (1991), Li (1991), Zhou (1991), Yang (1992), Cole et al. (1993), Xie (1997), Li (1998), among many others.

3 *Final 1 Law*: there must be a 1 [i.e. subject] in every final stratum [i.e. syntactic structure] (Blake, 1990: 13).

for granted that there must be an NP as subject which in some instances is covert (Blake, 1990: 13). Yet it provides a detailed account of passivisation by its principle *1 Advancement Exclusive Law* (1AEX) which limits the number of advancements of an NP to be the subject to one in a clause (Blake, 1990: 30). Like RelG, Lexical-Functional Grammar (Bresnan, 1978, 1982a, 1994 and 2001) was developed from TG, as did Head-driven Phrase Structure Grammar (Pollard and Sag, 1987 and 1994; Sag and Wasow, 1999). In LFG and HPSG, the lexicon is very important and thus the strengths of these two theories are their analyses of grammatical-relation-changing phenomena, like passive and dative shift, which crucially involve the lexicon, and their exclusive use of the notions of TOPIC and FOCUS[4]. Hence the notion of "adjunct", my main interest, is relegated to a less important position in these theories. Furthermore, like RelG, LFG and HPSG presuppose that every clause must have a SUBJ (i.e. subject) with little theoretical justification in terms of constraints to bear out this postulation. Consequently, I rejected the use of the RelG, LFG and HPSG frameworks in this book.

Role and Reference Grammar (Foley and van Valin, 1977 and 1984; van Valin, 1993; van Valin and LaPolla, 1997) is concerned with the interaction of syntax, semantics and discourse-pragmatics in grammar. It shares a great deal with Functional Grammar (Dik, 1978, 1989 and 1997). RRG rejects both grammatical-relations-based representations such as those used in RelG and LFG, and X-bar-type constituent-structure representations as in GB (see section 6.1.1 below) because it is argued that neither type is universally valid, and that a syntactic theory should capture all of the universal features of clauses without imposing features on languages in which there is no evidence for them (van Valin and LaPolla, 1997). This theory seems to be a promising theoretical framework on which to base my research as it presupposes that languages vary in their representation of a grammatical relation or function e.g. subject. However, there are two features that make RRG (and FG) unsuitable for use in my book. Firstly, the notion *operators* play a central

4 The terms "topic" and "focus" are used to refer to discourse functions. Generally speaking, the *topic* element denotes an entity which has been established in the discourse context and the *focus* is information about one or more topical participants that is new in the context (Bresnan, 2001: 96–98).

part in the theory. Operators such as aspect (e.g. perfective, imperfective/ progressive/durative), negation, tense and illocutionary force (i.e. whether the utterance is a question, statement or command) are used in the theory. Operators have scope over different layers of the clause: aspect is a nuclear operator, which modifies the predicate only; tense and illocutionary force are clausal operators; and negation can be an operator modifying the predicate or the clause. These operators are not relevant to my research. Secondly, RRG has a very different view of grammatical relations from other theories: it does not employ the traditional grammatical relations of subject, direct object and indirect object as theoretical constructs as happens in LFG; rather, it adopts a single construction-specific grammatical relation known as the *privileged grammatical argument*, which covers all kinds of subject, direct object and indirect object in a single category, and thus does not particularly well address those syntactic phenomena related to a certain grammatical relation such as the omission of a subject and its control in adjunct clauses. Hence, I rejected the use of RRG and FG in my work also.

The final theoretical framework to be mentioned is Optimality Theory (Archangeli and Langendoen, 1997). It is not a theory as such and is, rather, a way of organising the rules, principles and constraints of a theory in a hierarchy. These constraints are violable: a violation of a higher-ranked constraint is more significant than that of a lower-ranking constraint and a sentence showing such violation may be rejected i.e. it is ungrammatical. The constraints are assumed to be universal, and cross-linguistic variation is reflected in different rankings that different languages impose on them. As OT is just a way of organising grammatical constraints, the theoretical constructs to be ranked must come from a substantive syntactic theory. As noted earlier, GB has a pro-drop parameter to address cross-linguistic variation and a PRO theorem to license the omission of a subject in a clause. It thus lends itself well to the analysis of the distribution of non-overt subjects in Chinese adverbial clauses. Since no theoretical frameworks appear to better suit my research question than GB, I decided to use the GB framework in my book. In the following section, I will introduce the basic concepts that underlie GB and the way phrase structure is treated in this book.

6.1.1 An introduction to Government and Binding Theory

Government and Binding Theory was developed initially by Chomsky (1981a, 1982 and 1986) and is in a sense the immediate descendant of Transformational Grammar or TG (Horrocks, 1987: 68ff.), which was put forth in the 1960s (Chomsky, 1957). An important aspect of GB is that it assumes that there are no construction-specific rules (Chomsky, 1981a: 2). This is an important departure from TG: while TG has rules (or transformations) of, say, passive and question formation, GB avoids this. Thus the TG approach to passivisation is to set up a rule which makes an object a subject (Radford, 1988). In contrast, what we find in GB theory is not a rule of passivisation but rather a set of structural parameters which impose *constraints* (Sells, 1985: 25ff.; Horrocks, 1987: 74–92) on the range of structural variations applying across languages as a whole. In other words, GB proposes that the grammar itself consists of a series of "modules" that contain constraints and principles which govern the well-formedness of the output sentences (Chomsky, 1981a: 5ff.).

Another fundamental concept in GB theory is *X-bar theory* which was developed in the 1970s (Jackendoff, 1977). It provides principles for the projection of phrasal categories from lexical categories and imposes conditions on the hierarchical organisation of categories in the form of a general schema, as shown in the syntactic representation (2).

(2)

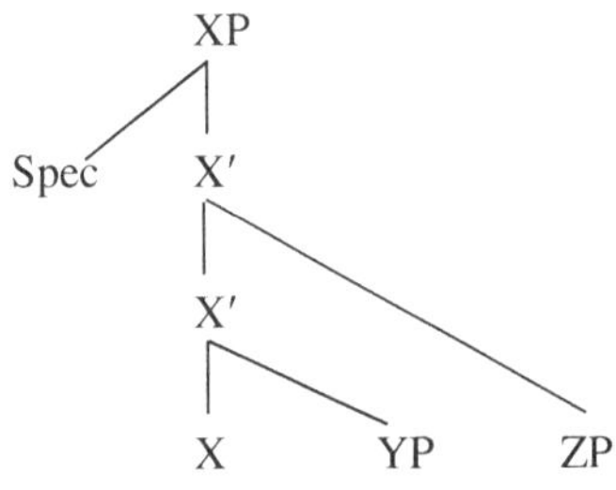

The central core of X-bar theory is to make explicit the fact that phrasal constituents have heads upon which the other elements of the constituents in question are dependent. In the syntactic representation (2), heads (X) are terminal nodes, which dominate lexical words; complements (YP) combine with X to form X′-projections; adjuncts (ZP) combine with X′ to form X′-projections. The specifier (Spec) combines with the topmost X2 to form the maximal projection XP.[5]

Besides the basic X-bar structures, the functional nodes of IP and CP are also used in this book. IP refers to both finite and infinitival clauses, depending on the content of the node INFL, which is a terminal node signifying the inflectional morphology of the verb, affixes and infinitival *to* (Haegeman, 1994: 114ff.). CP refers to either a finite or non-finite clause introduced by a complementiser (Webelhuth, 1995: 52ff.). Complementisers, represented as C, such as *whether*, *if*, *that* and *for* in English introduce a sentence (IP): C selects an IP-complement. The choice of the type of IP depends on the choice of C. The complementisers *that* and *if* select a finite clause as their complement; *for* selects an infinitival clause and *whether* selects either type of clause (Radford, 1997: 54ff.).

Other important theoretical constructs within GB such as the theta criterion, extended projection principle (EPP) and control theory will be explained later in this chapter when they become relevant to the discussion (sections 6.2.1, 6.2.2 and 6.2.3 respectively). For the remainder of this chapter, in section 6.2, I will show that the non-overt subject of Chinese adverbial clause, represented as PRO, is syntactically significant and has anaphoric and pronominal features. PRO may be referentially dependent on, or controlled by, another NP in the sentence according to control theory (Bresnan, 1982b). Section 6.3 examines the distribution of PROs: a non-overt subject occurs in an ungoverned position; when it is ungoverned, it is licensed (Chomsky, 1986b). In section 6.4, I will explain some of the properties of control. In section 6.5, I will examine the occurrence and distribution of PROs in the eleven semantic types of Chinese adverbial clauses I established in the last chapter. Section 6.6 gives a summary of the major findings discussed in this chapter.

5 See Radford (1997: 89–93) for a detailed description of specifiers.

6.2 The motivation for the presence of PRO in Chinese adverbial clauses and the control theory

6.2.1 The theta criterion

In Government and Binding Theory, the thematic or argument structure (Radford, 1997: 324–329) associated with lexical items must be represented, or saturated, in the syntax (Haegeman, 1994: 73), as stated in the theta criterion:

(3) Theta criterion

(3a) Each argument is assigned one and only one theta role.

(3b) Each theta role is assigned to one and only one argument.

The theta roles of a predicate, i.e. the arguments which the predicate takes, are represented in a grid-format, and the assignment of thematic roles is indicated by means of referential indices which are associated with thematic roles. For example, the verb 解决 *jiejue* "solve" is a two-place predicate: it requires the presence of two arguments in its thematic structure, as illustrated in the theta grid (4). In the GB literature, the subject is usually referred to as the *external argument*, i.e. the argument that is external to the VP, and the direct object is usually referred to as the *internal argument*, i.e. the argument that is internal to the VP (van Valin, 2001: 194). Hence, in the adverbial clause of example (5),[6] the internal argument of the verb 解决 *jiejue* "solve", the patient of the activity, is realised by the NP 金融危机 *jinrong weiji* "financial crisis", while the external argument, the agent of the activity, is not overtly realised.

(4) 解决 *jiejue* "solve": verb

Agent NP	Patient NP
?	j

6 All of the examples in this chapter are taken from the PFR Chinese Corpus unless indicated otherwise.

(5) <Fm ID= "19980114" >印尼_ns 人民_n 树立_v 信心_n <Fa>以_c 解决_v [金融_n 危机_n]j</Fa> 。_w</Fm>

<Fm ID="19980114"> *Yinni*_ns *renmin*_n *shuli*_v *xinxin*_n <Fa>*yi*_c
Indonesia citizens build.up confidence in.order.that
*jiejue*_v [*jinrong*_n *weiji*_n]j</Fa> 。_w</Fm>
solve financial crisis

"The Indonesian people should build up confidence to get over the financial crisis."

The theta criterion allows the arguments of a predicate to be syntactically represented. I will therefore interpret the adverbial clause in example (5) as if there were an external argument, and argue that the adverbial clause contains a non-overt subject, i.e. an implicit subject which is syntactically "present" in the sentence and which interacts with the other constituents of the sentence. In Government and Binding Theory, the non-overt subject of non-finite clause is conventionally represented by the element *PRO* (Chomsky, 1981a: 20). In this book, I use the same symbol, PRO, to refer to the non-overt subject of adverbial clause in Chinese because, as will be shown in section 6.3, both the PRO of Chinese adverbial clause and that of non-finite clause have the same distribution, i.e. they occur in ungoverned positions. Some scholars (e.g. Huang, 1992; Xue et al., 2000: 145ff.) assert, however, that PRO in Chinese can only be used to refer to the subject of infinitival clause. Since there is no conclusive evidence to support a finite vs. non-finite distinction in Chinese (Norman, 1988: 163; Hu et al., 2001), their arguments for the definition of PRO based primarily on such a distinction are at best contingent, and have been characterised as detrimental to attempts at offering a real picture of non-overt subjects in Chinese (Battistella, 1985: 338). I will not therefore follow their approach and will use the empty category PRO to refer to the non-overt subjects in CACs.

It is also important to note that for non-overt NPs, the previous literature (e.g. Jaeggli and Safir, 1989; Haegeman, 1994: 431–483) has in fact distinguished four possible types of non-overt NP, namely NP-traces, *wh*-traces, PRO, and *pro*. NP-traces are left by A-movement (Postal, 1974; Koster, 1978), i.e. moving to an argument position such as [Spec, IP]. This occurs, for example, in passivisation where the logical object NP is raised to the subject position. *Wh*-traces are produced by A′-movement (van Riemsdijk, 1978; Toman, 1981; Rizzi, 1982; Rudin, 1988), i.e. moving to a non-argument position such as [Spec, CP]. This occurs, for example, in the derivation of interrogative sentences where a *wh*-constituent moves to [Spec, CP], and in the formation of relative clauses. The non-overt subject of example (5) is obviously not a trace, there being no A- or A′-movement: A-movement involves just one thematic role shared between the trace and its antecedent (Chomsky, 1981a: 56), but a non-overt subject can be assigned a theta role, as explained above, resulting in two thematic roles; moreover, a subject position is an argument position (or A-position) to which a theta role is assigned (Haegeman, 1994: 115) and thus it is impossible for a non-overt subject to undergo an A′-movement, which involves movement to a non-argument position (or A′-position). It would also not be reasonable to assimilate this null element with *pro*. PRO and *pro* are distinct empty categories (Borer, 1980; Rizzi, 1986) and differ in their distribution: *pro* is found in governed positions as in complement clauses where the complementisers can govern it, while PRO must be ungoverned (Haegeman, 1994: 454). As will be demonstrated in section 6.3, the non-overt subject of CAC is ungoverned. Since only PRO fits in with my analysis of the non-overt subject of the adverbial clause, I will not pursue the other three empty categories. My focus is solely on PRO for the non-overt subjects being studied here. Furthermore, referring to the example (5) above, PRO in example (5) is understood to be semantically identical with the main clause subject (Sells, 1985: 74–75; Horrocks, 1987: 134), which is 印尼人民 *Yinni renmin* "the Indonesian people". The interpretation of PRO will be discussed in more detail in sections 6.2.3 and 6.4.

6.2.2 The extended projection principle (EPP)

The extended projection principle (EPP) requires that all predicates must have subjects; in structural terms, it means that all VPs must be associated with an external argument (Chomsky, 1982: 8–10). In other words, it says that all projections of IP have a subject, i.e. [Spec, IP] must be projected (Haegeman, 1994: 68–69).

(6) Extended projection principle: S → NP – AUX – VP

(6a)

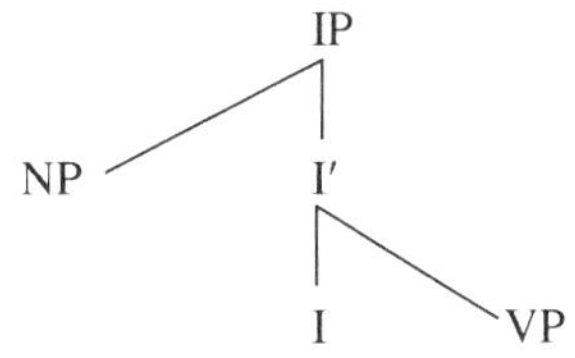

Hence, the example (5) above should have the syntactic structure (7) which contains a non-overt [Spec, IP].

(7)

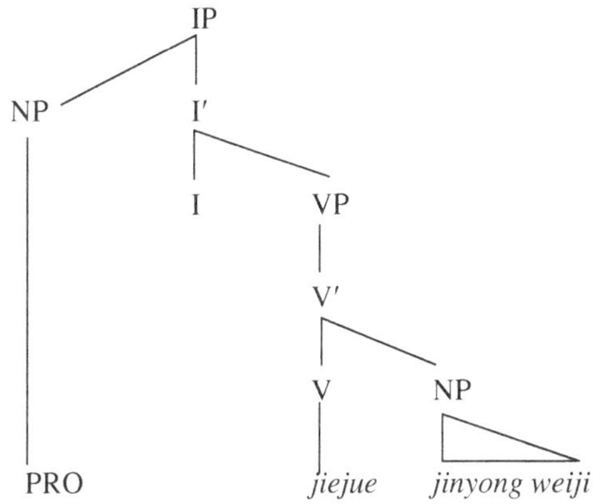

6.2.3 The features of PRO and the control theory

I have posited in the preceding subsections that an adverbial clause without an overt subject has a non-overt subject represented as PRO. PRO is *anaphoric*: depending on the context, PRO may be taken to refer to a specific referent. In example (8), PRO is like an anaphor; it is dependent on a full NP (i.e. an antecedent) for its interpretation. However, PRO is also *pronominal*: a covert subject may be interpreted as equivalent to a pronoun as in example (9). Hence, I propose that PRO in Chinese is an NP with anaphoric and pronominal properties but not simultaneously (cf. Chomsky, 1982: 78).

(8) <Fm ID= "19980106" ><Fa>尽管_c **PRO**$_i$ 遭受_v 了_u 金融_n 危机_n</Fa> ，_w [亚洲_ns 经济_n]$_i$ 今年_t 仍然_d 有望_v 增长_v 6%_m ，_w 明年_t 增长_v 6·1%_m 到_v 7·5%_m 。_w</Fm>

<Fm ID="19980106"><Fa>*jinguan*_c **PRO**$_i$ *zaoshou*_v *le*_u *jinyong*_n
even.though PRO face PERF financial
*weiji*_n</Fa> ，_w [*Yazhou*_ns *jingji*_n]$_i$ *jinnian*_t *rengran*_d
crisis Asia economy this.year still
*youwang*_v *zengzhang*_v 6%_m ，_w *mingnian*_t *zengzhang*_v
anticipate grow 6% next.year grow
6·1%_m *dao*_v 7·5%_m 。_w</Fm>
6.1% up.to 7.5%

"In spite of being hit by the financial crisis, the Asian economy is still expected to grow by 6% this year and by 6.1% to 7.5% next year."

(9) <Fm ID= "19980105" ><Fa>如果_c **PRO**$_i$ 早_ad 知道_v 要_v 交_v 这么_r 多_a 钱_n</Fa> ，_w [我_r]$_i$ 也_d 就_d 不_d 会_v 打_v 了_y 。_w</Fm>

<Fm ID="19980105"><Fa>*ruguo*_c **PRO**$_i$ *zao*_ad *zhidao*_v *yao*_v
if PRO in.advance know have.to
*jiao*_v *zheme*_r *duo*_a *qian*_n</Fa> ，_w [*wo*_r]$_i$ *ye*_d *jiu*_d *bu*_d
pay such much money I yet then not
*hui*_v *da*_v *le*_y 。_w</Fm>
will dial PART

"If I had known beforehand that I had to pay such a large sum of money, I would not have used the service to make phone calls."

According to the *control theory* (Chomsky, 1980 and 1986a: 124–131; Williams, 1980 and 1992; Bresnan, 1982b; Manzini, 1983; Koster, 1984; Speas, 1997; Lyngfelt, 2000), when PRO is interpreted as referentially dependent on another NP in the same sentence, as in the above examples, it is controlled by that NP.

> The term *control* is used to refer to a relation of referential dependency between an unexpressed subject (the *controlled* element) and an expressed or unexpressed constituent (the *controller*). The referential properties of the controlled element [...] are determined by those of the controller. (Bresnan, 1982b: 372)

In examples (8) and (9), PRO is controlled by the main clause subject NP 亚洲经济 *Yazhou jingji* “Asian economy” and 我 *wo* “I” respectively. In the cases where PRO is not controlled by another NP and refers freely, as in example (10), PRO can have an arbitrary reading, known as arbitrary PRO, represented as PRO$_{arb}$ (Chomsky, 1981a: 75).

(10) <Fm ID=“19980125”><Fa>如_c **PRO$_{arb}$** 大_d 吃_v 活_a 鱼_n</Fa> ，_w 则_c 是_v 希望_v 自己_r 和_c 家人_n 像_v 活_a 鱼_n 那样_r 灵活_a ，_w 去_v 驾驭_v 生活_vn ，_w 去_v 取得_v 自由_an 和_c 成功_an ！_w</Fm>

<Fm ID=“19980125”><Fa>*ru*_c **PRO$_{arb}$** *da*_d *chi*_v *huo*_a
if PRO greatly eat living

*yu*_n</Fa> ，_w *ce*_c *shi*_v *xiwang*_v *ziji*_r *he*_c *jiaren*_n
fish then be hope oneself and family

*xiang*_v *huo*_a *yu*_n *nayang*_r *linghuo*_a ，_w *qu*_v *jiayu*_v
be.like living fish as.ADJ.as lively go control

*shenghuo*_vn ，_w *qu*_v *qude*_v *ziyou*_an *he*_c *chenggong*_an ！_w</Fm>
life go obtain freedom and success

“If one is a big eater of raw fish, one wishes oneself and one’s family to be as lively as a fish, to live their life to the full and to pursue their freedom and success.”

PRO may also be dependent on implicit arguments. In example (11), PRO is not arbitrary in reference. Rather it is controlled by the implied agent of the passivised verb 装有 *zhuangyou* “install”.

(11) <Fm ID= “19980124” >活动_vn 看台_n 的_u 底部_f 装有_v 气垫_n ，_w <Fa>以_c **PRO** 保护_v 跑道_n</Fa> 。_w</Fm>

<Fm ID=“19980124”>*huodong*_vn *kantai*_n *de*_u *dibu*_f *zhuangyou*_v
activity stage DE bottom install

*qidian*_n ，_w <Fa> *yi*_c **PRO** *baohu*_v *paodao*_n</Fa> 。_w</Fm>
a.cushion.of.air in.order.to PRO protect running.track

“The bottom of the activity stage was installed with a cushion of air so as to protect the running tracks.”

In this section, I have demonstrated that the non-overt subject of adverbial clause is syntactically represented as PRO, having anaphoric and pronominal properties. The null subject is always controlled by the main clause subject NP which may be a specific referent or a pronoun. In the next two sections, I will discuss the conditions or contexts in which PRO is admitted or licensed, and how its interpretation is determined.

6.3 The distribution of PROs and the PRO theorem

In the *PRO theorem* (Chomsky, 1981a: 56; Haegeman, 1994: 272ff.) of Government and Binding Theory, it is claimed that PRO is restricted to ungoverned positions. PRO is admitted or *licensed* (Borer, 1980 and 1989; Chomsky, 1986b; Rizzi, 1986; Rothstein, 1992), i.e. legitimated in certain positions, if it is ungoverned. PRO is in complementary distribution with overt NPs (Harbert, 1995: 217–220): where PRO is allowed, overt NPs are excluded; where overt NPs are allowed, PRO is excluded. Chinese adverbial clauses support the PRO theorem in that the non-overt subjects in CACs must occur in ungoverned positions, as will be demonstrated shortly.

(12) <Fm ID= "19980102" ><Fa>只有_c **PRO**$_i$ 实现_v 祖国_n 统一_v</Fa> ，_w [台湾_ns]$_i$ 才能_v 有_v 更_d 大_a 的_u 发展_vn 和_c 前途_n 。_w</Fm>

<Fm ID="19980102"><Fa>*zhiyou*_c **PRO**$_i$ *shixian*_v *zuguo*_n
only.if PRO realise motherland
*tongyi*_v</Fa> ，_w [*Taiwan*_ns]$_i$ *caineng*_v *you*_v *geng*_d *da*_a
unification Taiwan can have more great
*de*_u *fazhan*_vn *he*_c *qiantu*_n 。_w</Fm>
DE development and prospects
"Only if she can realise the unification between China and her, will Taiwan have greater development and prospects."

(13) <Fm ID= "19980129" ><Fa>由于_c **PRO**$_i$ 受_v 东亚_ns 金融_n 危机_n 的_u 影响_vn</Fa> ，_w [１９９７年_t 全球_n 跨国_b 旅游_vn]$_i$ 人数_n 为_v ６·１６６３５亿_m 人_n ，_w 比_p 上_f 一_m 年度_n 减少_v ３·８%_m 。_w</Fm>

<Fm ID="19980129"><Fa>*youyu*_c **PRO**$_i$ *shou*_v *Dongya*_ns
because PRO face East.Asia

*jinrong*_n *weiji*_n *de*_u *yingxiang*_vn</Fa> ，_w [１９９７*nian*_t
financial crisis DE influence year.of.1997

*quanqiu*_n *kuaguo*_b *lüyou*_vn]$_i$ *renshu*_n *wei*_v ６·１６６３５
globe worldwide tourism number be 6.16635

*yi*_m *ren*_n ，_w *bi*_p *shang*_f *yi*_m
one.hundred.million people BI previous one

*niandu*_n *jianshao*_v ３·８%_m 。_w</Fm>
year drop 3.8%

"As tourism was adversely affected by the East Asian financial crisis, the number of tourists in 1997 was just 6.16635 hundred million, dropping 3.8% as compared with last year."

Before proceeding to explain why PRO in CACs is ungoverned, I would first like to briefly delineate the concepts of c-command and government in GB theory, as they are vital to my argument that PRO must be ungoverned.

6.3.1 C-command and government

Chomsky (1986b: 8) proposes the following definition of c-command (14).

(14) C-command
A c-commands B if and only if A does not dominate B and every X that dominates A also dominates B.

The dominance relation between nodes relates to whether one node occurs higher up in the structure than another (Radford, 1997: 99–100); the higher node dominates the lower node. If there is a maximal projection XP which dominates two given nodes A and B and A does not dominate B, then it is said that the node A m-commands, rather than c-commands, the node B. Using the notion of m-command, Chomsky (1986b: 8) proposes that government[7] be defined as in (15).

(15) Government
A governs B if and only if
(i) A is a governor; and
(ii) A m-commands B; and
(iii) no barrier intervenes between A and B.
Maximal projections are barriers to government.
Governors are heads.

For illustrative purposes, the adverbial clause in the example (12) above is represented in its syntactic structure (16). In (16), V m-commands the NP 祖国统一 *zhuguo tongyi* "the unification of the entire country" because V does not dominate the NP and the VP that dominates V also dominates the NP. Since there is no barrier intervening between V and the NP, the verb 实现 *shixian* "realise" governs the NP, which is its direct object.

(16)

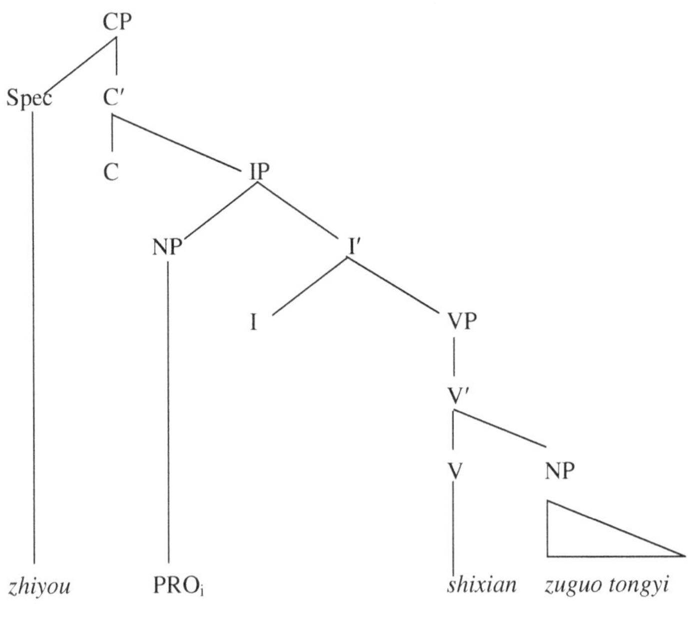

7 See also Lasnik and Saito (1984) for the notion of government.

Similarly, in the adverbial clause of example (13), which has the same syntactic representation, (17), as in (16), the verb 受 *shou* "suffer as a result of" m-commands and thus governs its direct object NP *Dongya jinrong weiji de yinxiang* "the impact of the East Asian financial crisis".

(17)

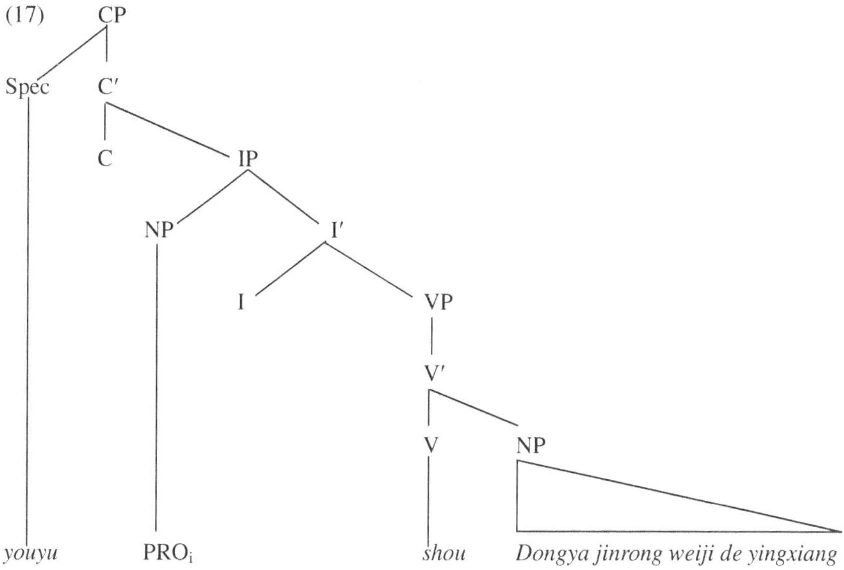

6.3.2 The PRO theorem: PRO must be ungoverned

As demonstrated in the preceding subsection, in both of the syntactic structures (16) and (17), the verbs, 实现 *shixian* "realise" and 受 *shou* "suffer as a result of", respectively, govern the following NP in the respective adverbial clauses. However, the verbs cannot govern PRO$_i$ as they cannot m-command it: the VP that dominates V does not dominate PRO$_i$. The only constituent that can govern PRO$_i$ is C because C m-commands PRO$_i$: C does not dominate PRO$_i$ and the CP that dominates C also dominates PRO$_i$. Moreover, there is no barrier between C and PRO$_i$: in spite of being a maximal projection, IP is assumed not to be a barrier to outside government. I, the head of the infinitival IP, is a functional head which has the feature composition [-AGR,

-Tense][8]. Haegeman (1994: 168) notes that this non-finite I is "weak" and thus it is not a governor and its projection IP cannot block outside government. Chinese lacks both of the features AGR and Tense entirely (Huang, 1984). As a corollary, I in Chinese is even "weaker" than non-finite I in English. It is therefore reasonable to assume that IP is not a barrier and cannot block the government of its specifier NP, PRO_i, by the head C (cf. Battistella, 1985).

However, C does not dominate any lexical item in the syntactic structures (16) and (17); the adverbial subordinators, 只有 *zhiyou* "only if" and 由於 *youyu* "because", in (16) and (17) respectively, are not dominated by C but are generated under [Spec, CP][9]. Adverbial clauses function only as adjuncts in the sentences in my corpus. Thus the adverbial subordinators cannot be complementisers because they do not introduce a complement clause (Biber et al., 1999: 85); rather they are used to overtly mark the adjunct clauses. Since no lexical word is inserted under a node C, which is the only constituent that can m-command and govern PRO_i, PRO_i in (16) and (17) are ungoverned.

It is important to point out that in the literature, PRO is assumed to occur in non-case-marked positions because nonfinite I cannot assign nominative case to the subject position of a nonfinite clause (Martin, 1996, 1999 and 2001). Thus it seems at first sight that the distribution of PROs is regulated by Case Theory[10] (Ouhalla, 1999: 183–224) rather than Government Theory. However, there are reasons to believe that the opposite is true: the distribution of PROs is explained by Government Theory rather than Case Theory. In GB theory, case-marked positions are governed positions since case is assigned under government (Chomsky, 1981a: 49ff.). But not all positions which are governed are also case-marked. The object position of passive verbs is an instance of a position that is governed but not case-marked. Passive verbs do not

8 The head of an IP, INFL or I, is posited to dominate the tense feature (Tense) and the agreement features for person and number (AGR) associated with V (Chomsky, 1982: 85–86; Radford, 1997: 54, 512).

9 [Spec, CP] can be occupied by maximal projections (Radford, 1997: 268–282). Thus this analysis would mean that Chinese adverbial subordinators are maximal projections (cf. Haegeman, 1994: 275).

10 Case Theory takes the form of a Case Filter which can be formulated like this: *NP if NP has phonetic content and has no case (Chomsky, 1981a: 49).

assign case to their object; the accusative case of the base transitive verb is "absorbed" by the passive morpheme (Chomsky, 1981a: 117ff.). So positions that are governed but non-case-marked represent the real test for determining whether the distribution of PROs is regulated by Case Theory or Government Theory. My hypothesis is as follows: if PRO cannot occur in a position that is governed but non-case-marked, it follows that PRO is excluded from governed positions rather than case-marked positions. After examining my corpus data, I found that PRO cannot occur in the object position of passives. If PRO is excluded from case-marked positions rather than governed positions, there is no reason why it should not occur in the object position of passives, which is non-case-marked. The absence of a possible controller for PRO is unlikely to be the reason it is excluded since PRO can assume an arbitrary reading. Therefore my hypothesis that PRO is excluded from governed positions rather than case-marked positions is proved to be true. But one of the major issues still to be resolved is the status of PRO with respect to the case requirement or case filter (Chomsky, 1981a: 175): an NP is ungrammatical if it has no case. There are at least two kinds of proposal for it. Chomsky (1982: 86 and 1986a) and Chomsky and Lasnik (1993) suggest that PRO can be assumed to have "inherent case" or "null case". This implies that PRO is not dependent on any case assigner for its case to be assigned and hence it can occur in non-case-marked positions. The other accounts (Saito, 1983 and 1985; Kang, 1986; Kang 1988; Jang and Kim, 2001) are largely inspired by Chomsky's analysis: it is said that in most of the Asian languages such as Chinese, Korean and Japanese, nominative case is a "default case", i.e. nominative case is not assigned by INFL but assigned as a default case. Note that if PRO has default case, this case feature has to be matched with the case feature of the inflectional node I under Spec-head agreement (cf. Hendrick, 1995: 316–319). This entails that I is marked for the case feature, although not necessarily for the other agreement features such as person, number and gender features.

To conclude, CACs support the PRO theorem of Government and Binding Theory in that PRO in CACs occurs only in ungoverned positions and is thus properly licensed.

6.4 Properties of control in CACs

So far I have not discussed how we can arrive at the interpretation of PRO. I have merely established that sometimes PRO is controlled by an NP or an implicit argument, or it is not controlled by any element in the sentence and thus its interpretation is arbitrary. In this section, I will describe two things: (i) the contrast between obligatory control and optional control (section 6.4.1); (ii) the contrast between subject control and object control (section 6.4.2). I will also propose in section 6.4.3 that non-overt subjects in Chinese adverbial clauses can be controlled by an NP occurring in the context prior to the main clause they modify.

6.4.1 Obligatory control and optional control

Previous literature on control (e.g. Williams, 1980; Manzini, 1983; Chomsky, 1986a: 124–131) distinguishes two types of control: optional control as in examples (18) and (19), and obligatory control as in (20).

(18) <Fm ID= "19980102" ><Fa>只要_c **PRO** 先_d 画_v 好_a 牡丹_n</Fa> ，_w 其他_r 的_u 花卉_n 则_c 一_d 点_v 即_d 通_v ，_w 迎刃而解_i 。_w</Fm>

<Fm ID="19980102"><Fa>*zhiyao*_c **PRO** *xian*_d *hua*_v *hao*_a
given.that PRO early draw well
*Mudan*_n</Fa> ，_w *qita*_r *de*_u *huahui*_n *ze*_c *yi*_d *dian*_v
Chinese.flower.of.Mudan other DE flowers then once point.out
*ji*_d *tong*_v ，_w *yingrenerjie*_i 。_w</Fm>
at.once understand work.out.a.problem

"If one can manage to draw the Mudan flower, it will be easy for one to draw other flowers."

(19) <Fm ID= "19980107" ><Fa>不管_c **PRO**$_i$ 如何_r 变化_v</Fa> ，_w [中东_ns]$_i$ 和平_n 总_d 要_v 进行_v 下去_v 。_w</Fm>

<Fm ID="19980107"><Fa>*buguan*_c **PRO**$_i$ *ruhe*_r *bianhua*_v</Fa> ，
whatever PRO how change

_w [*Zhongdong*_ns]i *heping*_n *zong*_d *yao*_v *jinxing*_v *xiaqu*_v 。
Middle.East peace still have.to sustain go.down
_w</Fm>
"No matter what changes happen, peace in the Middle East has to be maintained."

(20) <Fm ID= "19980117" >[香港_ns]i 坚定_a 地_u 执行_v 港元_n 与_p 美元_n 相_d 联系_v 的_u 政策_n ，_w <Fa>从而_c **PRO**i 保证_v 了_u 港元_n 对_p 美元_n 汇率_n 的_u 基本_a 稳定_vn</Fa> 。_w</Fm>
<Fm ID="19980117">[*Xianggang*_ns]i *jianding*_a *de*_u *zhixing*_v
Hong.Kong consistently ADVL implement
*gangyuan*_n *yu*_p *meiyuan*_n *xiang*_d *lianxi*_v *de*_u *zhengce*_n ，
HK.dollars and US.dollars each.other peg DE policy
_w <Fa>*conger*_c **PRO**i *baozheng*_v *le*_u *gangyuan*_n *dui*_p
in.order.that PRO ensure PERF HK.dollars exchange
*meiyuan*_n *huilü*_n *de*_u *jiben*_a *wending*_vn</Fa> 。_w</Fm>
US.dollars rate DE primary stability
"Hong Kong consistently upholds the policy that the Hong Kong currency is pegged to the US dollar, thereby maintaining exchange rate stability."

In the examples (18) and (19), control is optional. In example (18), PRO is not controlled by anything in the sentence: it may be taken to have an arbitrary reading, or it may be taken as referring to a specific referent which has been established in the context. In example (19), PRO may be controlled by the NP 中东 *Zhongdong* "Middle East" in its specifier position or it may also have an arbitrary interpretation. In example (20), on the other hand, PRO must be controlled by the main clause subject 香港 *Xianggang* "Hong Kong" and cannot be arbitrary. Besides relying on the semantics of these sentences, Williams (1980) demonstrates that c-command requirement can distinguish obligatory control from optional control. In the case of obligatory control, the controller must c-command the controlled element. In the case of optional control, the controlled element is not required to be c-commanded by the controller.

(21)

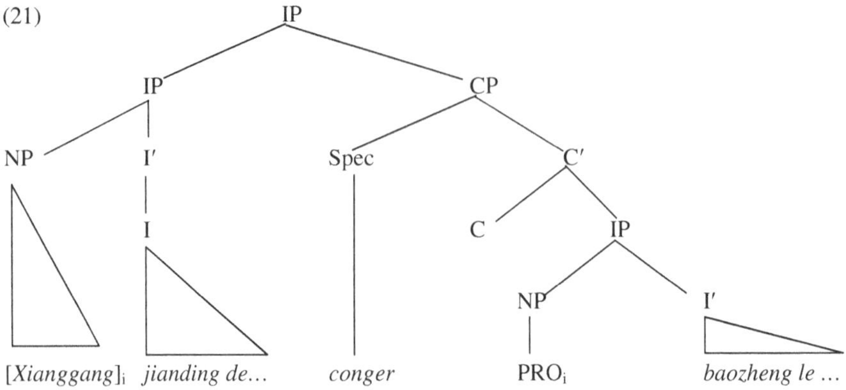

In the example of the obligatory control as in (20), the controller 香港 *Xianggang* "Hong Kong" c-commands its controlled element PRO_i because it does not dominate PRO_i and the IP that dominates it also dominates PRO_i, as can be seen from the syntactic structure in (21). It should be noted that the adverbial clause, the CP as a whole, is adjoined to the main clause in the operation conventionally referred to as *adjunction* (Chomsky, 1986b: 15–16), resulting in two maximal IP nodes. The lower IP, or the base maximal projection in Haegeman's (1994: 387) terms, is the original maximal projection which is the main clause. The higher IP dominates both the base maximal projection and the adjoined adverbial clause CP. This adjunction structure is different from the phrase structure, (2), having an adverb or an adverb phrase as an adjunct, as mentioned earlier in section 6.1.1. Radford (1997: 142–143) distinguishes two kinds of adverb, namely IP-adverbs (i.e. an adverb which modifies the sentence as a whole and is positioned internally within IP) and VP-adverbs (i.e. an adverb which modifies the main verb and is positioned internally within VP), and illustrates two properties of these two kinds of adverbial adjunct: firstly, they are adjoined to intermediate projections (like V-bar and I-bar); and secondly, they serve to expand a category into an extended category of the same type (i.e. an VP-adverb expands V′ into an extended V′, and an IP-adverb expands I′ into an extended I′). Hence, in GB, adverbial clauses and adverbs (and adverb phrases) are treated differently in structural terms (Haegeman, 1984; Larson, 1985): while adverbial clauses are adjoined to maximal projections (e.g. IP), adverbs or adverb phrases are adjoined to intermediate projections (e.g. V′ or I′).

(22)

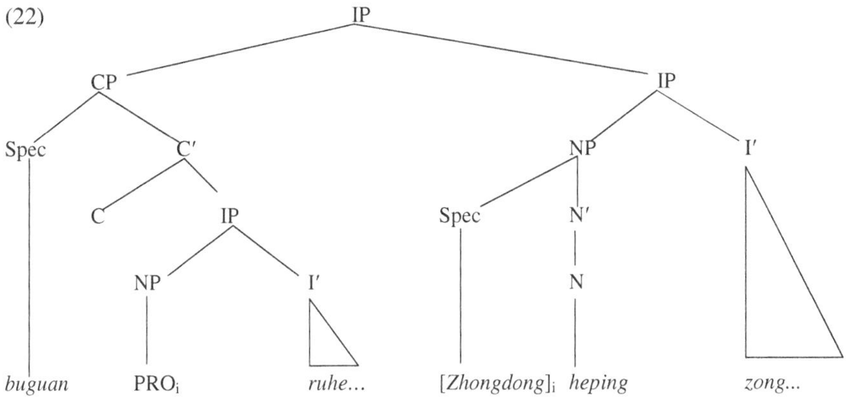

However, in the case of optional control, the situation is different, as illustrated in the syntactic representation (22) of example (19). In example (19), control is optional: PRO may be controlled by the specifier 中东 *Zhongdong* "Middle East" of the NP 中东和平 *Zhongdong heping* "peace in the Middle East", or it may have an arbitrary reading. The controller 中东 *Zhongdong* "Middle East" in (22) does not c-command PRO_i because there is a maximal projection NP which dominates the controller in its specifier position but does not dominate PRO_i.

6.4.2 Subject control and object control

In the example of obligatory control (20) and the examples (8), (9), (12) and (13) mentioned earlier, the controller of the non-overt subject in the adverbial clause is the main clause subject. However, sometimes the controller is the object NP in the associated matrix clause, as highlighted in examples (23) and (24). In example (23), PRO refers to, or is controlled by, the pronoun 你 *ni* "you", which is the direct object of the verb 諒解 *liangjie* "forgive" in the following main clause. Example (24) is taken to be an illustration of object control because the controller of PRO is the direct object 记者 *jizhe* "journalists" of the verb 让 *rang* "make" in the main clause, which co-refers to the PRO in the adverbial clause.

(23) <Fm ID= "19980121" ><Fa>即便_c **PRO**ᵢ 偶尔_d 办_v 错_a 一_m 件_q 事_n</Fa> ，_w 群众_n 也_d 是_v 会_v 谅解_v [你_r]ᵢ 的_u 。_w</Fm>

<Fm ID="19980121"><Fa>*jibian*_c **PRO**ᵢ *ouer*_d *ban*_v *cuo*_a
even.if PRO occasionally do wrong
*yi*_m *jian*_q *shi*_n</Fa> ，_w *qunzhong*_n *ye*_d *shi*_v *hui*_v
one CL matter people yet be will
*liangjie*_v [*ni*_r]ᵢ *de*_u 。_w</Fm>
forgive you PART

"Even if you make a mistake occasionally, people would forgive you."

(24) <Fm ID= "19980120" ><Fa>尽管_c **PRO**ᵢ 已_d 有_v 心理_n 准备_vn ，_w 福州_ns 漆器_n 的_u 龙头_n 企业_n ———_w [第一_m 脱胎_vn 漆器_n 厂_n]nt 的_u 破旧_an 与_c 逼仄_an</Fa> ，_w 仍_d 让_v [记者_n]ᵢ 吃惊_a 。_w</Fm>

<Fm ID= "19980120"><Fa>*jinguan*_c **PRO**ᵢ *yi*_d *you*_v *xinli*_n
even.though PRO already have psychological
*zhunbei*_vn ，_w *Fuzhou*_ns *qiqi*_n *de*_u *longtou*_n *qiye*_n
preparation Fuzhou.privince paint DE leading enterprise
———_w [*tiyi*_m *tuotai*_vn *qiqi*_n *chang*_n]nt *de*_u *pojiu*_an
the.First Breakthrough Paint Factory DE oldness
*yu*_c *bize*_an</Fa> ，_w *reng*_d *rang*_v [*jizhe*_n]ᵢ *chijing*_a 。_w</Fm>
and pressure still make journalists scare

"Although the journalists have had some expectations of how it looks, the leading paint factory in the industry – The First Breakthrough Paint Factory still surprises them by its ruin."

6.4.3 Control from outside main clause: A feature specific to non-overt subjects of Chinese adverbial clauses

In the preceding subsections, I have discussed how the non-overt subject of the adverbial clause can be controlled by (i) the main clause subject (ii) the object of the verb in the main clause. In addition, it is possible for it to assume an arbitrary reading without being controlled by an element in the same sentence. This reflects the general discussions about the interpretation of PRO in adverbial clauses claimed in control theory (Huang, 1984 and 1989; Haegeman, 1994: 277–278). However, apart from subject and object control and no control from the main clause, the non-overt subjects in Chinese adverbial clauses demonstrate yet another type of control which has been neglected in the previous literature: the controller of the PRO occurs in the context prior to the main clause. In other words, the control is from outside the sentence in which the non-overt subject occurs, as illustrated in examples (25) and (26).

(25) 19980106-12-007-005_m 一九八三年_t 十一月_t ，_w [刚刚_d 结束_v 新兵_n 训练_v 的_u 梁_nr 坤奠_nr]$_i$ 来到_v 了_u 永兴岛_ns 。_w 在_p 家里_s 肉_n 见_v 得_v 不_d 多_a 的_u 他_r ，_w <Fm><Fa>到_v 了_u 西沙_ns 后_f 虽然_c **PRO$_i$** 没有_v 蔬菜_n 吃_v</Fa> ，_w 但_c 肉_n 罐头_n 却_d 能_v 敞开_v 肚子_n 吃_v 个_q 够_v 。_w</Fm>

19980106-12-007-005_m 1983*nian*_t *shiyiyue*_t ，_w [*ganggang*_d
year.of.1983 November just
*jieshu*_v *xinbing*_n *xunlian*_v *de*_u *Liang*_nr *Kundian*_nr]$_i$ *laidao*_v
complete military training DE Liang Kundian arrive.at
*le*_u *Yongxingdao*_ns 。_w *Zai*_p *jiali*_s *rou*_n *jian*_v *de*_v *bu*_d
PERF Yongxing.Island at home meat see COMP not
*duo*_a *de*_u *ta*_r ，_w <Fm><Fa>*dao*_v *le*_u *Xisha*_ns *hou*_f
much DE he reach PERF Xisha after
*suiran*_c **PRO$_i$** *meiyou*_v *shucai*_n *chi*_v</Fa> ，_w *dan*_c *rou*_n
although PRO have.not vegetables eat but meat
*guantou*_n *que*_d *neng*_v *changkai*_v *duzi*_n *chi*_v *ge*_q *gou*_v 。
a.can.of.sth. yet can open stomach eat CL enough
_w</Fm>

"In November 1983, Liang Kundian, who had just finished his military training, arrived at Yongxing Island. Not having meat very often at home, he ate a lot of canned meat at Xisha, though he could not get vegetables there."

(26) 19980107-11-008-003_m 那_r 是_v １９８３年_t ，_w 怀着_v "_w 老三届_j "_w 未_d 圆_Vg 的_u 大学_n 梦_n ，_w 当时_t [已_d 进入_v ３５_m 岁_q 的_u 我_r]$_i$ ，_w 考_v 入_v 了_u [华南_ns 师范大学_n 函授_vn 学院_n]nt ，_w 成为_v 汉语言_n 文学系_n 的_u 一_m 名_q 学生_n 。_w <Fm><Fa>由于_c **PRO$_i$** 通过_p 工作_v 实践_v 感到_v 非_d 学_v 无以_d 建业_v ，_w 不_d 学_v 难_ad 有_v 后劲_n</Fa> ，_w 因此_c 比_p 少年_n 上学_v 时_Ng 勤奋_a 用功_a 多_a 了_y 。_w</Fm>

19980107-11-008-003_m *na*_r *shi*_v １９８３年_t ，_w *huaizhe*_v
that be year.of.1983 embrace
"_w *laosanjie*_j "_w *wei*_d *yuan*_Vg *de*_u *daxue*_n *meng*_n ，_w
previous yet fulfill DE university dream
*dangshi*_t [*yi*_d *jinru*_v ３５_m *sui*_q *de*_u *wo*_r]$_i$ ，_w
at.that.time already enter 35 years.old DE I
*kao*_v *ru*_v *le*_u [*Huanan*_ns *Shifandaxue*_n *Hanshou*_vn
be.admitted into PERF Huanan education.institute taught.programme
*Xueyuan*_n]nt ，_w *chengwei*_v *Hanyuyan*_n *Wenxuexi*_n
college become Chinese.language dept.of literature
*de*_u *yi*_m *ming*_q *xuesheng*_n 。_w <Fm><Fa>*youyu*_c **PRO$_i$**
DE one CL student because PRO
*tongguo*_p *gongzuo*_v *shijian*_v *gandao*_v *fei*_d *xue*_v *wuyi*_d
through work practice feel not learn not.possible
*jianye*_v ，_w *bu*_d *xue*_v *nan*_ad *you*_v *houjing*_n</Fa> ，_w
develop.a.career not learn hard have potential
*yinci*_c *bi*_p *shaonian*_n *shangxue*_v *shi*_Ng *qinfen*_a
therefore BI youth attend.school period.of.time diligent
*yonggong*_a *duo*_a *le*_y 。_w</Fm>
put.effort.into.sth. much PART

"It happened in 1983 that at the age of 35 I finally got a chance to study in a university, Huanan Shifan Daxue Hanshou Xueyuan, where I realised my dream of being a student in the Chinese Literature Department. As I learned from my work that the acquisition of knowledge is essential for developing a career, I worked much harder than I used to in secondary school."

In example (25), the NP *ganggang jieshu xinbing xunlian de Liang Kundian* "Liang Kundian, who had just finished military training" is the controller for the non-overt subject of the concessive clause in the following sentence. Similarly, in example (26), the PRO of the causal clause co-refers to the subject NP of the preceding sentence, *yi jinru 35 sui de wo* "I, at the age of 35". In both of these examples, the NP controller and PRO are placed in separate sentences. These instances and similar ones have thrown up two interesting facts about control for non-overt subjects and control theory. Firstly, as far as non-overt subjects in CACs are concerned, there are at least three distinct types of control, namely, main clause control (i.e. either subject NP or object NP in the main clause is the controller), control from outside the main clause (i.e. the controller occurs in previous context) and no control (i.e. PRO is not controlled by another NP and refers freely). The emergence of the type of control from outside the main clause can be explained by the fact that Chinese sentences in general do allow an NP established in previous context, and not the subject NP of the sentence in which any missing syntactic constituent occurs, to control co-referential constituent deletion: the subject NP does not necessarily control the co-reference of the deleted constituent; rather, any NPs in the context can be possible candidates for controller (Li and Thompson, 1976: 469–470; Tsao, 1979; Li, 1985; Chen, 1986). Secondly, control theory (see section 6.2.3) encounters significant difficulties when faced with attested language use. Although it seems to work well for some of the corpus data which conform to a syntactician's introspections about language, it becomes inadequate for much complex language data that emerges from real-life usage. The non-overt subject of the Chinese adverbial clause is a case in point. As can be seen from Table 22, 411 controllers of PRO in my corpus do not occur in the main clause as control theory claims should happen; as noted earlier (see section 6.2.3), the null subject is typically controlled by an NP in the same sentence. There are, however, 689 subject NP controllers and 12 object NP controllers of the main clause that conform to what is claimed in the theory; object control[11] is rare in written

11 For the record, object control takes place in 12 paragraphs in the PFR corpus, namely, 19980109-12-001-005, 19980110-01-002-003, 19980111-03-003-007, 19980113-09-005-006, 19980118-04-006-007, 19980120-09-006-004, 19980120-11-004-007, 19980121-09-004-006, 19980122-06-007-004, 19980123-06-002-004, 19980124-09-005-004, 19980124-10-008-003.

Chinese. This emerging, Chinese-specific, type of control clearly demonstrates the importance of adopting a corpus-based approach to theory: without such the abundance of language data provided in a corpus, I would have chosen example sentences from the corpus that support the published account of control theory and would have ignored a pattern which has yet to be discussed within the theory.

Semantic classes of CACs	**Main clause control**		**Control from outside main clause**	**No control i.e. arbitrary interpretation**	**No. of PRO**
	Subject control	***Object control***			
Clause of condition	79	5	**204**	143	431
Clause of purpose	241	3	**63**	35	342
Clause of concession	58	1	**97**	33	189
Clause of contrast	149	0	**6**	5	160
Clause of result	107	1	**0**	0	108
Clause of cause/reason	42	1	**33**	4	80
Clause of exception	9	0	**5**	0	14
Clause of addition	4	1	**2**	1	8
Clause of preference	0	0	**1**	1	2
Clause of inference	0	0	**0**	0	0
Clause of time	0	0	**0**	0	0
Total:	689	12	**411**	222	1,334

Table 22: Control types of PRO in CACs.

There is some relevant research in the literature which may help with the process of interpreting this unexpected finding; it is in line with Lambrecht's (1994: 184–185) *Principle of the Separation of Reference and Role (PSRR)*. PSRR states that a referential noun phrase can appear *elsewhere* rather than in the position assigned to it by the canonical sentence model built by a syntactic theory: in control theory, the noun phrase that a non-overt subject of adverbial clause co-refers to is expected to occur in either the structural subject position or the structural object position of the main clause. In other words, this principle allows the *referential* function of noun phrases to separate from the *role* they play as an argument (i.e. either an external argument or an internal argument of the main verb; see section 6.2.1) in a clause/sentence and thus they can be controllers for the non-overt subjects of adverbial clauses occurring in separate sentences. While the type of control in which the NP controller occurs outside the main clause is taken as an exception or anomaly in control theory, it is taken as a rule (i.e. PSRR) in the information-structure-based approach as demonstrated by Lambrecht. In the next section, I will present some empirical findings relating to the distribution of PROs across the semantic domains of adverbial clauses, and will demonstrate how the corpus-based theoretical approach and the information-structure-based approach can be combined into an integrated approach to explain the distribution of PROs in different types of adverbial clauses.

6.5 The occurrence of PROs in different semantic types of CACs

In this section, I will examine how overt NP subjects and non-overt ones are used in different semantic types of Chinese adverbial clauses. Section 6.5.1 explores the relationship between the semantic domains and subject types of CACs, and section 6.5.2 is concerned with the distribution of PROs in individual semantic types of adverbial clauses.

6.5.1 Relatedness between semantic types of CACs and subject types of CACs

There are 1,083 instances of overt NP subjects and 1,334 cases of PRO in the Chinese adverbial clauses in the PFR corpus. Non-overt subjects are annotated in the corpus – PROs are marked in the subject position of the adverbial clause and the possible controller for the PRO, which has the same reference as that of the PRO, is marked also. As illustrated in Table 23, it can be seen that the distribution of both overt NP subjects and PRO is uneven in that a certain type of adverbial clause shows a preponderance of overt NP subjects over PRO and vice versa. The occurrence of null subjects tends to depend on the semantic types of adverbial clauses. As the rationale of my investigating the research questions of this book (see Chapter One, section 1.2) has shown to some extent already, different semantic types of adverbial clauses would be expected to interact with the choice of overt NP subjects vs. PRO. In this regard, I hypothesise that the distribution of PROs varies across the semantic domains of adverbial clauses. To test this hypothesis, I used the log-likelihood (henceforth LL) test of significance (Oakes, 1998: 38; Rayson et al., 2004) rather than Pearson's chi-square test (Butler, 1985: 112–123; Woods et al., 1986: 139–144; Oakes, 1998: 24–29; Weiss, 2002a: 536–575; Weiss, 2002b: 640–679) or Fisher's exact probability test (Conover, 1980: 167–169; Siegel and Castellan, 1988: 102–111; Agresti, 1992: 134–136) to determine the statistical relatedness between the two variables, i.e. semantic types of CACs and subject types of CACs. I rejected Pearson's chi-square test as the test is not applicable in clauses of inference, preference and time: their frequency of occurrence is too low (i.e. no more than three instances in my corpus), resulting in an exceptionally low minimum expected count, i.e. less than zero. As the lowest expected frequency required for Pearson's chi-square test is five (Coakes and Steed, 2001: 208), I rejected chi-square as a measure of significance for use in my work. I rejected Fisher's exact test as inappropriate also. Fisher's exact test is usually used in place of the chi-square test for analysing small data samples, i.e. when the total sample size is less than 20 or the expected frequency count is less than 5 (cf. Howitt and Cramer, 2001: 121–123). While this test initially seemed to be a promising substitute for the chi-square test in my research, it proved to be unsuitable. Fisher's exact test is used to test statistically whether there is any relation between two variables with two levels or subcategories. One of my variables, as mentioned above, is the subject type of CAC, which has two levels i.e. overt NP subjects and non-overt ones (PRO). The other variable, the semantic type of CAC, however, has 11 levels as there are eleven semantic classes of adverbial clauses. Since Fisher's exact test is used for two variables with two levels, I rejected the use of this test and, rather, used the log-likelihood test of significance for my research. As will be demonstrated shortly, by calculating the LL values, preference for a certain subject type (either overt NP or PRO) is shown to depend statistically significantly on the interclausal semantic relations of adverbial clauses.

			Subject Types of CACs		
			Overt NP Subjects	PRO	Total
Semantic Types of CACs	Clause of Condition	Count	348	431	779
		% within Subject Types of CACs	32.1%	32.3%	32.2%
	Clause of Concession	Count	386	189	575
		% within Subject Types of CACs	35.6%	14.2%	23.8%
	Clause of Purpose	Count	6	342	348
		% within Subject Types of CACs	.6%	25.6%	14.4%
	Clause of Cause or Reason	Count	250	80	330
		% within Subject Types of CACs	23.1%	6.0%	13.7%
	Clause of Contrast	Count	17	160	177
		% within Subject Types of CACs	1.6%	12.0%	7.3%
	Clause of Result	Count	55	108	163
		% within Subject Types of CACs	5.1%	8.1%	6.7%
	Clause of Exception	Count	11	14	25
		% within Subject Types of CACs	1.0%	1.0%	1.0%
	Clause of Addition	Count	5	8	13
		% within Subject Types of CACs	.5%	.6%	.5%
	Clause of Inference	Count	3		3
		% within Subject Types of CACs	.3%		.1%
	Clause of Preference	Count	1	2	3
		% within Subject Types of CACs	.1%	.1%	.1%
	Clause of Time	Count	1		1
		% within Subject Types of CACs	.1%		.0%
Total		Count	**1083**	**1334**	**2417**
		% within Subject Types of CACs	100.0%	100.0%	100.0%

Table 23: Distribution of overt NP subjects and PRO in CACs

Significance Tests

	Value	df	Asymp. Sig. (2-sided)
Pearson Chi-Square	606.957	10	.000
Likelihood Ratio	**723.265**	**10**	**.000**
Linear-by-Linear Association	22.119	1	.000
N of Valid Cases	2417		

Table 24: Overall significance test results.

In Table 24, the log-likelihood statistic gives a value of 723.265. This LL value is much greater than the critical value for significance, 23.209, with 10 degrees of freedom at p <0.01 (Woods et al., 1986: 141; Oakes, 1998: 28). In examining the frequency counts in Table 23, I found that overt subjects are predominantly used in clauses of concession while null subjects are used in conditional clauses.

(27) <Fm ID= "19980129" ><Fa>尽管_c 专家_n 们_k 对_p 家电_j 价格_n 大战_n 不_d 无_v 担忧_vn</Fa> ，_w 但_c 消费者_n 从中_d 受益_v 已_d 是_v 不_d 争_v 的_u 事实_n 。_w</Fm>

<Fm ID="19980129"><Fa>*jinguan*_c **zhuanjia**_n **men**_k *dui*_p
even.though expert PL as.regards
*jiadian*_j *jiage*_n *dazhan*_n *bu*_d *wu*_v
household.electrical.appliances price war not have.not
*danyou*_vn</Fa> ，_w *dan*_c **xiaofeizhe**_n *congzhong*_d *shouyi*_v
worry but consumers from.this benefit
*yi*_d *shi*_v *bu*_d *zheng*_v *de*_u *shishi*_n 。_w</Fm>
already be not argue DE fact

"Although experts express concern over the impact of the price war in household electrical appliances, it is undeniable that consumers can benefit from competitive prices."

(28) <Fm ID= "19980102" ><Fa>虽然_c 亚洲_ns 出现_v 了_u 金融_n 风波_n</Fa> ，_w 但_c 香港_ns 经济_n 仍然_d 跨_v 步_n 向前_v 。_w</Fm>

<Fm ID="19980102"><Fa>*suiran*_c **Yazhou**_ns *chuxian*_v *le*_u
although Asia emerge PERF
*jinrong*_n *fengbo*_n</Fa> ，_w *dan*_c **Xianggang**_ns **jingji**_n
financial crisis but Hong.Kong economy
*rangran*_d *kua*_v *bu*_n *xiangqian*_v 。_w</Fm>
still cross step proceed

"Despite the Asian financial crisis, Hong Kong's economy still makes great strides."

Concessive clauses typically take more overt NP subjects than other types of adverbial clause because their subjects are usually different from that of the associated main clause, thereby excluding the possibility of the subject control of PRO from the main clause and favouring the use of overt NP subjects. As shown in the above examples, the highlighted subjects in the adverbial clause and main clause differ from each other: they refer to distinct entities in the discourse universe. In example (27), the subject of the concessive clause, 专家们 *zhuanjia men* "experts" is different from the subject of the main clause, 消费者 *xiaofeizhe* "consumers". Similarly, in example (28), the adverbial clause of concession has its subject, 亚洲 *Yazhou* "Asia", which is not identical to the subject of the main clause it modifies, 香港经济 *Xianggang jingji* "Hong Kong's economy".

Conditional clauses, on the other hand, are the type of adverbial clause in which the non-overt subjects are dominant. This is because PRO in conditional clauses can be controlled by the main clause subject, for instance, 中华民族 *Zhonghuaminzu* "Chinese people" as in example (29), or be controlled by the object NP of the verb in the main clause as in example (30), where PRO refers to the direct object 伊拉克 *Yilake* "Iraq" of the verb 教训 *jiaoxun* "punish" in the following main clause, or be controlled by an NP in previous context as in example (31), where PRO refers to the subject 我们 *women* "we" of the preceding sentence.

(29) <Fm ID= "19980127" ><Fa>只有_c **PRO**$_i$ 团结_a 起来_v</Fa> ，_w [中华民族_n]$_i$ 才_c 能_v 创造_v 更加_d 辉煌_a 的_u 明天_t 。_w</Fm>

<Fm ID="19980127"><Fa>*zhiyou*_c **PRO**$_i$ *tuanjie*_a *qilai*_v</Fa> ，_w
only.if PRO unite stand.up

[*Zhonghuaminzu*_n]$_i$ *cai*_c *neng*_v *chuangzao*_v *gengjia*_d
People's.Republic.of.China then can create more

*huihuang*_a *de*_u *mingtian*_t 。_w</Fm>
rosy DE tomorrow

"Only if we Chinese people unite can we make a better future."

(30) <Fm ID= "19980123" ><Fa>如果_c **PRO**$_i$ 做_v 不_d 到_v 这_r 一_m 点_q</Fa> ，_w 美国_ns "_w 决不_d 排除_v 采用_v 其它_r 手段_n "_w 教训_v [伊拉克_ns]$_i$ 。_w</Fm>

<Fm ID="19980123"><Fa>*ruguo*_c **PRO**$_i$ *zuo*_v *bu*_d *dao*_v *zhe*_r
if PRO do not COMP this

*yi*_m *dian*_q</Fa> ，_w *Meiguo*_ns "_w *juebu*_d *paichu*_v
one point America absolutely.not rule.out
*caiyong*_v *qita*_r *shouduan*_n "_w *jiaoxun*_v [*Yilake*_ns]ᵢ 。_w</Fm>
employ other strategies punish Iraq
"If Iraq did not commit itself to the above, the United States would punish Iraq by taking other measures."

(31) 因此_c [我们_r]ᵢ 决不能_v 因为_c 农业_n 连年_d 丰收_v 而_c 盲目_a 乐观_an ，_w 产生_v 松懈_a 、_w 麻痹_a 思想_n</Fm> 。_w <Fm ID= "19980112" ><Fa>如果_c **PRO**ᵢ 忽视_v 或_c 放松_v 了_u 农业_n</Fa> ，_w 一旦_d 出_v 了_u 问题_n ，_w 则_c 很_d 可能_v 几_m 年_q 都_d 缓_v 不_d 过_v 劲_n 来_v ，_w 势必_d 影响_v 整个_b 国民经济_n 的_u 持续_vn 健康_a 发展_vn 。_w</Fm>
*yinci*_c [*women*_r]ᵢ *quebuneng*_v *yinwei*_c *nongye*_n *liannian*_d
hence we absolutely.cannot because agriculture year.by.year
*fengshou*_v *er*_c *mangmu*_a *leguang*_an ，_w *changsheng*_v
good.harvests then blind optimistic establish
*songjie*_a 、_w *mabi*_a *sixiang*_n</Fm> 。_w <Fm
slack stiff thought
ID="19980112"><Fa>*ruguo*_c **PRO**ᵢ *hushi*_v *huo*_c *fangsong*_v *le*_u
If PRO neglect or slack.up PERF
*nongye*_n</Fa> ，_w *yidan*_d *chu*_v *le*_u *wenti*_n ，_w *ze*_c *hen*_d
agriculture.industry once emerge PERF problem then very
*keneng*_v *ji*_m *nian*_q *dou*_d *huan*_v *bu*_d *guo*_v *jing*_n *lai*_v ，_w
likely several years still slow.down not cross force come
*shibi*_d *yingxiang*_v *zhengge*_b *guominjingji*_n *de*_u *chixu*_vn
absolutely influence whole national.economy DE continuing
*jiankang*_a *fazhan*_vn 。_w</Fm>
healthy development
"Hence, we cannot overrate our success in the agriculture industry. If we slack off, once there is any problem, we cannot get it over within several years and this will adversely affect our economic growth."

6.5.2 Distribution of PROs across semantic domains of CACs

I have demonstrated in the previous section that the occurrence of both overt NP subjects and PRO is dependent on the semantic types of adverbial clauses, and overt NP subjects are dominant in concessive clauses whereas null subjects are most frequently used in conditional clauses. However, I have not addressed variations across individual semantic types of adverbial clauses in their use of overt and non-overt subjects. In this section I would, therefore, like to discuss the distribution of PROs in relation to different interclausal semantic domains in CACs.

Semantic Types of CACs	**Subject Types of CACs**		**LL values**
	Freq. of Overt NP Subjects	**Freq. of PRO**	**(1 d.f., $p < 0.01$)**
Clause of Condition	348 (44.7%)	431 (55.3%)	**8.86**
Clause of Concession	386 (67.1%)	189 (32.9%)	**68.88**
Clause of Purpose	6 (1.7%)	342 (98.3%)	**421.81**
Clause of Cause/ Reason	250 (75.8%)	80 (24.2%)	**91.93**
Clause of Contrast	17 (9.6%)	160 (90.4%)	**133.40**
Clause of Result	55 (33.7%)	108 (66.3%)	**17.55**
Clause of Exception	11 (44.0%)	14 (56.0%)	0.36
Clause of Addition	5 (38.5%)	8 (61.5%)	0.70
Clause of Inference	3 (100.0%)	0 (0.0%)	4.16
Clause of Preference	1 (33.3%)	2 (66.7%)	0.34
Clause of Time	1 (100.0%)	0 (0.0%)	1.39

Table 25: Results of log-likelihood tests on individual semantic types of CACs.

In Table 25, the calculated LL value is significant if it is greater than the critical value for significance, 6.635, with 1 degree of freedom (henceforth d.f.) at $p < 0.01$. Hence, there are significant differences in the frequency of overt NP and PRO subjects in clauses of condition, concession, purpose, cause or reason, contrast and result. It can be seen that purpose clauses, contrastive clauses and result clauses take more null subjects than overt ones because, like conditional clauses, their subjects are usually controlled by the main clause subject, as shown in examples (32), (33) and (34), respectively.

(32) <Fm ID= "19980106" >今年_t [泰国_ns 旅游_vn 机构_n]ᵢ 计划_v 在_p 上海_ns 设立_v 办事处_n ，_w <Fa>以_c **PROᵢ** 加强_v 泰_j 中_j 两_m 国_n 的_u 旅游_vn 合作_vn</Fa> 。_w</Fm>

<Fm ID="19980106">*jinnian*_t [*Taiguo*_ns *lüyou*_vn *jigou*_n]ᵢ *jihua*_v
this.year Thailand tourism organisation plan
*zai*_p *Shanghai*_ns *sheli*_v *banshichu*_n ，_w <Fa> *yi*_c **PROᵢ**
in Shanghai set.up office in.order.that PRO
*jiaqiang*_v *Tai*_j *Zhong*_j *liang*_m *guo*_n *de*_u *lüyou*_vn
step.up Thai Sino two nations DE tourism
*hezuo*_vn</Fa> 。_w</Fm>
co-operation

"This year Thailand's tourist association plans to set up an office in Shanghai in order to step up the co-operation between Thailand and China on promoting tourism."

(33) <Fm ID= "19980118" >[她_r]ᵢ 没有_d 坐_v 飞机_n ，_w <Fa>而是_c **PROᵢ** 乘坐_v 北京_ns 至_p 莫斯科_ns 的_u 国际_n 列车_n</Fa> 。_w</Fm>

<Fm ID="19980118">[*ta*_r]ᵢ *meiyou*_d *zuo*_v *feiji*_n ，_w <Fa>*ershi*_c
she have.not sit flight rather
PROᵢ *chengzuo*_v *Beijing*_ns *zhi*_p *Mosike*_ns *de*_u *guoji*_n
PRO ride.on Beijing to Moscow DE international
*lieche*_n</Fa> 。_w</Fm>
train

"She did not travel by plane but took a train from Beijing to Moscow."

(34) <Fm ID= "19980118" >[她_r 母亲_n]ᵢ 从_p 翻译_v 的_u 大量_m 作品_n 中_f 了解_v 了_u 中国_ns ，_w <Fa>从而_c **PROᵢ** 向往_v 中国_ns ，_w 想_v 去_v 中国_ns 看看_v</Fa> ，_w</Fm>

<Fm ID="19980118">[*ta*_r *muqin*_n]ᵢ *cong*_p *fanyi*_v *de*_u *daliang*_m
her mother from translated DE plenty.of
*zuopin*_n *zhong*_f *liaojie*_v *le*_u *Zhongguo*_ns ，_w
works within.which understand PERF China
<Fa>*conger*_c **PROᵢ** *xiangwang*_v *Zhongguo*_ns ，_w *xiang*_v *qu*_v
in.order.that PRO long.for China wish go.to

*Zhongguo*_ns *kankan*_v</Fa> ，_w</Fm>
China visit
"Her mother gained a fascinating insight into China from a number of translated works and thus she was eager to visit China."

Reason clauses, on the other hand, resemble concessive clauses and favour the use of overt NPs over PROs as their subjects. As shown in the following examples, the subject of the reason clause in examples (35) and (36) is not referentially dependent on that of the associated main clauses because both of them are different. In contrast, clauses of exception, addition, inference, preference and time do not show a marked preference for either subject type as their LL values are less than 6.635, the critical value for significance at p<0.01.

(35) <Fm ID= "19980129" > "_w 我们_r 希望_v 取得_v 切实可行_l 的_u 进展_vn ，_w <Fa>因为_c 目前_t 的_u 局势_n 已_d 极为_d 危险_a</Fa> " _w 。_w</Fm>
<Fm ID="19980129">"_w ***women*_r** *xiwang*_v *qude*_v *qieshikexing*_l
we hope obtain feasible
*de*_u *jinzhan*_vn ，_w <Fa>*yinwei*_c ***muqian*_t** ***de*_u** ***jushi*_n** *yi*_d
DE progress because at.present DE situation already
*jiwei*_d *weixian*_a</Fa> "_w 。_w</Fm>
extremely dangerous
"We wish to make good progress in the reform because the present situation has reached an alarming state."

(36) <Fm ID= "19980106" ><Fa>由于_c 竞争_v 激烈_a</Fa> ，_w 菲律宾_ns 国内_s 的_u 制造商_n 都_d 不_d 愿_v 提高_v 价格_n 。_w</Fm>
<Fm ID="19980106"><Fa>*youyu*_c ***jingzheng*_v** *jilie*_a</Fa> ，_w
because compete fierce
***Feilübin*_ns** ***guonei*_s** ***de*_u** ***zhizaoshang*_n** *dou*_d *bu*_d *yuan*_v
Philippines home DE manufacturers all not want.to
*tigao*_v *jiage*_n 。_w</Fm>
raise price
"Owing to fierce competition, the manufacturers in the Philippines do not want to raise the cost price."

6.5.3 An integrated account of the distribution of PROs in CACs[12]

As discussed in sections 6.5.1 and 6.5.2, clauses of condition, purpose, contrast and result take more PROs than overt subjects because PROs in these adverbial clauses can either be controlled by the main clause subject and/or object or be controlled by an NP in previous context, while clauses of concession and cause/reason take more overt subject than PRO because the subject of the adverbial clause is different from that of the main clause. In fact this distribution pattern can also be explained in terms of information structure (cf. Eckardt, 2003), or more specifically, *given information* and *new information* (Crystal, 1985: 136). In the following, I will propose that the management of given/new information acts as a constraint for the selection of subject type (either PRO or overt subject) in the adverbial clause.[13]

Information structure describes the manner in which information is provided to the addressee in discourse (Chafe, 1976, 1979, 1980, 1987 and 1994; Lambrecht, 1994; Master, 2002). The aspect of information structure that is particularly relevant to my research is *givenness* (Bock, 1977; Szwedek, 1977; Bing, 1981; Lee, 1990; Virtanen, 1992), i.e. the distinction between given information and new information. From the point of view of information structure in which the pragmatic structuring of a proposition in discourse is formally expressed (Lambrecht, 1994: 5–6)[14], *given information* is information that is assumed

12 This account was inspired by the Corpus Linguistics Research Group seminar held at Lancaster University (UK) in the spring of 2004. I would like to express my sincere thanks to three of the participants, Florencia Franceschina, Willem Hollmann and Amy Wang for their insightful comments, criticisms and suggestions on my talk.

13 Compare Li (2004). Based on written narrative texts taken from an influential novel, *Luotuo Xiangzi* by Lao She (1936), Li argues that clauses with sentence-initial zero NPs (i.e. non-overt NPs) function differently from those with sentence-initial overt NPs. While clauses headed by zero NPs have the function of *backgrounding* i.e. they form a base for narration in subsequent clauses by continuing and encapsulating what is said in the previous sentences, clauses having sententially initial overt NPs are more likely to play the role of *foreground* text.

14 There are three main categories of information structure: (i) *presupposition and assertion*: propositions are structured into portions which a speaker assumes an addressee already knows or does not yet know; (ii) *identifiability and activation*: at the time of producing an utterance, a speaker makes some assumptions about the sta-

by the speaker to be known to, assumed by, or inferable by, the addressee at the time of the speaker's utterance (Crystal, 1980: 161–162; Prince, 1981: 230; Levinson, 1983: 88; Quirk et al., 1985: 1360–1362). The non-overt subjects in clauses of condition, purpose, contrast and result are typically co-referential with (or controlled by) an NP in the main clause or in previous context, which serves as given information. These subjects can be seen, in Chafe's (1994: 99–115) terminology, as "light subjects", which encode given information and are redundant. The relatively high frequency of dropping the subject in these clauses as opposed to other types of adverbial clause is therefore understandable. *New information*, on the other hand, is information that is assumed by the speaker not to be known or assumed by the addressee, or has not been mentioned previously in the discourse (Crystal, 1980: 241; Levinson, 1983: 88; Quirk et al., 1985: 1361). A discourse entity characterised as such is referred to as a *brand-new referent* (Prince, 1981: 233, 235–236). A lexical subject of the main clause which differs from that of the adverbial clause, for example, can be seen as an NP with a brand-new referent (Kärkkäinen, 1996). Hence it is hardly surprising that the subject of the clauses of concession and cause/reason which is not identical to that of the associated main clause cannot be dropped, as shown in their relatively less frequent use of PRO.

In conclusion, the basic pattern of information structure as shown in the distribution of PROs and overt subjects in Chinese adverbial clauses is the presentation of given information by the use of PRO and the presentation of new information by the use of overt subject. I have also demonstrated that the information-structure-based approach can be combined with the corpus-based theoretical approach into an *integrated* account in which the distribution of PROs across the semantic domains of adverbial clauses can be adequately explained.

tuses of the mental representations of discourse referents in the addressee's mind; and (iii) *topic and focus*: a speaker assesses the predictability/unpredictability of the relations between propositions and their elements in a given discourse situation (Lambrecht, 1994: 6).

6.6 Chapter summary

By the theta criterion and the extended projection principle (EPP), Chinese adverbial clauses (or CACs) are proved to take a non-overt subject, represented as PRO in Government and Binding (GB) Theory. In this chapter, it is shown that PRO is characterised by anaphoric and pronominal properties. According to control theory, it may be referentially dependent on, or controlled by, another NP in the sentence or an implicit argument (e.g. the agent of the action in the main clause), or it is not controlled at all and its interpretation is arbitrary. Like the non-overt subject of non-finite clause in English, PROs in the CACs must occur in ungoverned positions. Hence, my corpus data supports the PRO theorem in GB theory which states that PRO must be ungoverned. When it is ungoverned, it is licensed for its occurrence. In some example sentences taken from the PFR Chinese Corpus, control is obligatory while in others it is optional. In the case of obligatory control, the controller (i.e. an NP in the main clause) must c-command the controlled element (i.e. the non-overt subject of the CAC). Both subject and object NPs in the matrix clause can be controllers. Moreover, PRO in Chinese adverbial clauses demonstrates that it can be controlled by an NP in a sentence prior to the main clause. The postulation of this type of control is verified by the Principle of the Separation of Reference and Role (PSRR).

In the PFR Chinese Corpus, there are 1,083 instances of overt NP subjects and 1,334 cases of PRO as used in CACs. By calculating the log-likelihood (LL) value between two variables, namely the semantic types of CACs and subject types of CACs, I found that the value is highly significant (i.e. LL = 723.265 > 23.209) and thus concluded that the distribution of non-overt subjects varies significantly across semantic domains of adverbial clauses. While overt subjects are typically preferred by concessive clauses, null subjects are overwhelmingly used in conditional clauses. Concessive clauses always have subjects which are different from that of their associated main clause, and thus disfavour the use of PRO, which typically requires a controller. Non-overt subjects, on the other hand, predominantly occur in conditional clauses because they can be properly controlled by the main clause subject, the object of the verb in the main clause or an NP in the context. Other types of adverbial clause also give statistically significant results in the use of overt and non-overt subjects: clauses of purpose, contrast and result show a preponderance of null subjects while clauses of reason favour overt ones. However, this difference in the distribution of subject types is not statistically significant in clauses of exception, addition, inference, preference and time. As an attempt to combine corpus-based theoretical approach with information-structure-based approach, the distribution pattern of PRO of adverbial clauses is explained in terms of given and new information: while the controller occurring in the main clause or previous context can be seen as given information and thus the non-overt subject of the adverbial clause which co-refers to it can commonly be omitted as in clauses of condition, purpose, contrast and result, the brand-new subject of the main clause which differs from the subject of the adverbial clause can be seen as new information and thus the latter cannot be dropped as in clauses of concession and cause/reason.

Chapter Seven

Semantic Classes and Non-overt Subjects of CACs in the Lancaster Corpus of Mandarin Chinese

7.1 Introduction

The Lancaster Corpus of Mandarin Chinese (LCMC) is used in this book in large part to offset four major drawbacks of the PFR Chinese Corpus. Firstly, the PFR corpus is made up of newswire texts only. Journalistic writing is only one form of written language (Biber, 1988: 69) and thus a body of journalistic texts can hardly be sufficiently representative of written language as a whole. The LCMC corpus is, however, a balanced corpus of Mandarin Chinese, modelling its sampling frame on that of the Freiburg-LOB Corpus of British English or FLOB (Hundt et al., 1998): it has 500 samples of 2,000 words each, taken from fifteen different text types, as shown in Table 26 (McEnery and Xiao, 2004b). Secondly, while the tagset of the LCMC corpus is basically identical to that of the PFR corpus (see Chapter Two, section 2.2.2.1), it uses five additional tags i.e. conjunction morpheme (*cg*), sentential punctuation (*ew*), locality morpheme (*fg*), preposition morpheme (*pg*) and descriptive morpheme (*zg*). In particular, the distinction between non-sentential punctuation (*w*) and sentential punctuation (*ew*) is vital as it eases the identification of individual sentences in which an adverbial clause occurs so that the reference of the non-overt subject of the adverbial clause can easily be tracked down. Furthermore, unlike the written texts in most of the extant Chinese corpora, including the PFR corpus, which are encoded in GB2312 using simplified Chinese characters, the texts of the LCMC corpus were encoded in Unicode (UTF-8) which can be used in non-Chinese operating systems and can be searched in Unicode-compliant concordancers such as the LCMC web concordancer (see section 7.1.1.1), *Xaira* version 1.0 (Burnard and

Todd, 2003)[1] and the *Wordsmith* Tools version 4.0 (Scott, 2003). As McEnery and Xiao (2004a) observe, a real problem in Asian corpus building is the existence of multiple and often competing encodings of Asian writing systems: the Chinese language can be encoded in GB2312, GB18030, HZ and Unicode. Xiao et al. (2004), however, recommend Unicode as the best encoding format, and support this by using two Unicode-compliant corpus tools that are available, *Xaira* and *Wordsmith* version 4, to explore the LCMC corpus. Given that the Unicode-encoded LCMC corpus can be explored efficiently with generally available corpus tools such as *Xaira* and *Wordsmith* 4 and its own web concordancer, it is of greater use than the PFR corpus in linguistic research, in particular in the investigation of complicated grammatical phenomena. I therefore decided to carry out an investigation of adverbial clauses in the LCMC to supplement my findings based on the PFR corpus. A final advantage of the LCMC corpus is that it is annotated with five levels of detail[2] in addition to POS tagging, notably including the annotation of sentence and paragraph boundary markers, without which I would have had to add these two levels of markup as I had to with the PFR corpus. In this chapter, I will apply the findings presented in the preceding chapters to the LCMC corpus in the hope of providing a more concrete description of adverbial clauses in written Chinese. This chapter is organised as follows: section 7.2 discusses the occurrence of the eleven semantic classes of Chinese adverbial clauses (CACs) in different text types; section 7.3 examines the distribution of non-overt subjects (PROs) across and within text types, and across the semantic domains of CACs. These results are compared to the results obtained on the basis of the PFR corpus to investigate whether the effect of adverbial semantic domain on the distribution of PROs as indicated in the previous chapter is indeed dependent on text type; section 7.4 discusses how the type of control of PRO is influenced by text type; section 7.5 summaries the findings presented in this chapter.

1 Xaira stands for "XML Aware Indexing and Retrieval Architecture".

2 The five levels of annotation in the LCMC corpus are, namely, (1) text category, (2) file identifier, (3) paragraph, (4) sentence and (5) word, punctuation/symbol and elements omitted in transcriptions.

Text Type	*Description*	*Tokens*
Category A	Press: reportage	88,000
Category B	Press: editorials	54,000
Category C	Press: reviews	34,000
Category D	Religion	34,000
Category E	Skills, trades and hobbies	76,000
Category F	Popular lore	88,000
Category G	Biographies and essays	154,000
Category H	Miscellaneous: reports and official documents	60,000
Category J	Science: academic prose	160,000
Category K	General fiction	58,000
Category L	Mystery and detective fiction	48,000
Category M	Science fiction	12,000
Category N	Adventure and martial arts fiction	58,000
Category P	Romantic fiction	58,000
Category R	Humour	18,000

Table 26: The list of text types in the LCMC corpus.

7.1.1 Methodological issues

In the previous chapters of this book, I used the PFR Chinese Corpus as a training corpus to gain insights into the use of adverbial clauses in written Chinese. I have explored various features of them, namely the use of a subordinating conjunction to mark the adverbial clause overtly (Chapter Three), the identification of 57 adverbial subordinators (Chapter Four), the classification of 2,417 adverbial clauses identified in the PFR corpus into eleven distinct interclausal semantic domains (Chapter Five) and the distribution of non-overt subjects within these semantic domains (Chapter Six). As noted above, all of the findings so far are based on the PFR corpus, a homogeneous collection of journalistic texts; these results cannot be generalised to written Chinese easily if at all (cf. Biber and Finegan, 1991: 211–213). As the distribution of both the adverbial clauses and their non-overt subjects may vary across text types, the LCMC corpus was used in my research as the test corpus in an attempt to offer a comprehensive account of adverbial clauses in written Chinese. The main procedures of exploiting the LCMC corpus for the purposes of this research are presented as follows.

7.1.1.1 The LCMC web concordancer

I used the LCMC web concordancer[3] for my search of adverbial clauses in the LCMC corpus. The discussion in Chapter Three (section 3.7) showed that Chinese adverbial clauses (CACs) are typically marked by adverbial subordinators and the discussion in Chapter Five (section 5.3) indicated that the semantic classes of adverbial clauses are commonly introduced by different adverbial subordinators, as highlighted in Table 27.

Semantic classes of CACs	**Adverbial subordinators**
Clauses of Time	随着 *suizhe*
Clauses of Cause/Reason	由于 *youyu*, 因为 *yinwei*, 因 *yin*, 既然 *jiran*
Clauses of Purpose	以 *yi*, 从而 *conger*, 以免 *yimian*, 以便 *yibian*
Clauses of Result	从而 *conger*, 之所以 *zhisuoyi*, 以致 *yizhi*, 故 *gu*, 以至于 *yizhiyu*
Clauses of Preference	与其 *yuqi*, 与其说 *yuqishuo*
Clauses of Contrast	而是 *ershi*
Clauses of Addition	何况 *hekuang*, 不单 *budan*, 且不说 *qiebushuo*, 不说 *bushuo*
Clauses of Exception	只是 *zhishi*
Clauses of Condition	如果 *ruguo*, 只要 *zhiyao*, 只有 *zhiyou*, 要是 *yaoshi*, 若是 *ruoshi*, 倘 *tang*, 倘若 *tangruo*, 哪怕 *napa*, 就是 *jiushi*, 要不是 *yaobushi*, 若果 *ruoguo*, 假若 *jiaruo*, 万一 *wanyi*, 如若 *ruruo*, 果真 *guozhen*, 要 *yao*, 除非 *chufei*, 即使 *jishi*, 如 *ru*, 若 *ruo*, 即便 *jibian*, 假如 *jiaru*, 纵 *zong*, 纵使 *zongshi*
Clauses of Concession	虽然 *suiran*, 尽管 *jinguan*, 虽 *sui*, 虽说 *suishuo*, 无论是 *wulunshi*, 无论 *wulun*, 不论是 *bulunshi*, 不论 *bulun*, 不管 *buguan*, 任 *ren*, 甭管 *benguan*
Clauses of Inference	尚且 *shangqie*

Table 27: Semantic classes of CACs and their respective adverbial subordinators.

3 See its website <http://corpus.nie.edu.sg/cgi-bin/lcmc/conc.pl> (accessed 15 May 2012).

I used the LCMC web concordancer for searching those adverbial clauses overtly marked by an adverbial subordinator. As illustrated in Figure 8, the adverbial subordinator Yg *ruguo* "if" was used as the search term across the fifteen text types of the LCMC corpus. This procedure was repeated until all of the adverbial subordinators identified in the PFR training corpus were searched for in the test corpus. As a result, I obtained a list of subordinator-marked (adverbial) clauses.

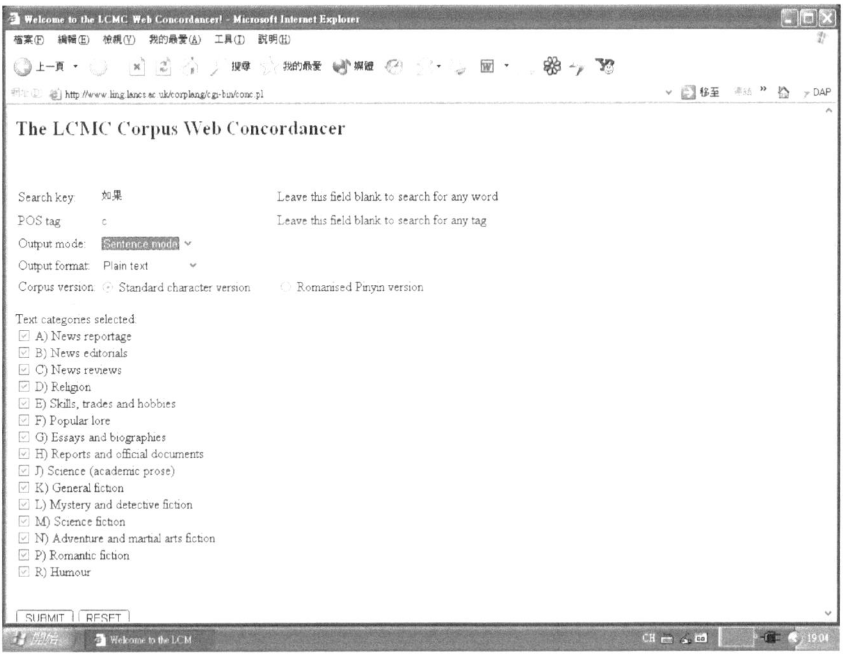

Figure 8: An illustration of the LCMC web concordancer.

7.1.1.2 Invalid adverbial clauses

I eliminated incorrect adverbial clauses from the list of subordinator-marked clauses obtained. There are three types of error causing these incorrect adverbial clauses to be drawn from the LCMC corpus by the concordancer. The first kind of error was already noted in Chapter Five (section 5.2) that some words of multiple word class membership may be misinterpreted as adverbial subordinators (e.g. 由于 *youyu* "because" can be a preposition and a conjunction) and the unwanted sentences retrieved by those words should be disregarded. On the other hand, the sentences in which genuine adverbial subordinators were annotated with the wrong tag were added to the data set manually. The second kind of error arises from the LCMC web concordancer itself: it cannot distinguish adverbial subordinators having identical final characters e.g. 要 *yao* "if" and 只要 *zhiyao* "only if", and 以 *yi* "in order to" and 之所以 *zhisuoyi* "the reason why…". The adverbial clauses introduced by these subordinators were therefore sorted by hand. The third kind of error is a result of four borderline adverbial subordinators. In both the PFR and LCMC corpora, four of the adverbial subordinators sporadically violate the first criterion of the operational definition of a subordinating conjunction, which states that the clause overtly marked by an adverbial subordinator must be linked to another clause(s) in the same sentence, as Chinese adverbial clauses function only as an adjunct. These are: 因为 *yinwei* "because", 从而 *conger* "in order to or as a result", 何况 *hekuang* "let alone" and 故 *gu* "therefore". These four subordinating conjunctions are at times used to introduce an independent sentence rather than a subordinate clause. However, I still considered them as subordinating conjunctions because in over sixty percent of their occurrences, these subordinators conform to the first operational criterion, as highlighted in Tables 28 and 29.

Borderline subordinators	因为 *yinwei*		从而 *conger*		何况 *hekuang*		故 *gu*	
Raw frequency	Freq.	%	Freq.	%	Freq.	%	Freq.	%
In independent sentence	63	35.2	5	2.8	4	36.4	2	22.2
In adverbial clause	116	**64.8**	173	**97.2**	7	**63.6**	7	**77.8**
Total	179	100	178	100	11	100	9	100

Table 28: Frequencies of borderline adverbial subordinators in independent sentences and adverbial clauses in the PFR corpus.

Borderline subordinators	因为 *yinwei*		从而 *conger*		何况 *hekuang*		故 *gu*	
Raw frequency	Freq.	%	Freq.	%	Freq.	%	Freq.	%
In independent sentence	68	32.5	2	2.8	7	38.9	6	31.6
In adverbial clause	141	**67.5**	69	**97.2**	11	**61.1**	13	**68.4**
Total	209	100	71	100	18	100	19	100

Table 29: Frequencies of borderline adverbial subordinators in independent sentences and adverbial clauses in the LCMC corpus.

7.1.1.3 Raw and normalised frequencies

As can be seen from Table 26, the fifteen text categories in the LCMC corpus are of different sizes. It is therefore impossible to compare the distribution of adverbial clauses within different text types on the basis of their raw frequencies. Hence, the frequency scores obtained need to be *normalised/standardised* to a common base in order to permit comparison across text types (McEnery et al., 2005: 47–48). A *normalised frequency* is a weighted frequency measure that allows for the easy and reliable comparison of data sets of different sizes (cf. Ball, 2002: 11). I initially chose to normalise frequencies to a common base of 10,000 word tokens because "the common base for normalisation must be comparable to the sizes of the corpora (or corpus segments) under consideration [...] as the results obtained on an irrationally enlarged or reduced common base are distorted" (McEnery et al., *ibid*). As the sizes of the fifteen text types included in the LCMC corpus range from 12K tokens to 160K tokens i.e. the average size of a text type is of approximately 60K tokens, it would be appropriate to normalise frequencies to a common base of 10K tokens. However, as shown in my PFR skeleton treebank (see Chapter Three, section 3.7), adverbial clauses are rare in written Chinese. With such a low frequency of occurrence, statistical tests of significance may not yield reliable results. Consequently, I decided to normalise frequencies to a common 100K-token base so as to avoid the potentially misleading outcomes resulting from significance tests relying on expected values less than 5. I assume that varying the common base for normalisation in this way will not distort the outcomes of the statistical tests significantly.

Take clauses of reason as an example. As shown in Table 30, the frequency of the reason clauses occurring in a text category was obtained by summing the frequencies of the four adverbial subordinators (i.e. *youyu*, *yinwei*, *yin* and *jiran*) responsible for introducing the clauses of reason in the text category. The frequency scores of individual text categories were then normalised to a common 100,000-word base so as to allow for the comparison of the distribution of reason clauses across text types.

Text types of LCMC	Raw frequency					Freq. per 100K tokens
	由于 *youyu*	因为 *yinwei*	因 *yin*	既然 *jiran*	Total	Total
Category A	11	3	1	2	17	19.3
Category B	12	8	0	1	21	38.9
Category C	9	1	0	0	10	29.4
Category D	9	6	0	11	26	76.5
Category E	23	13	4	4	44	57.9
Category F	31	22	0	3	56	63.6
Category G	20	20	0	8	48	31.2
Category H	7	0	1	0	8	13.3
Category J	96	39	3	8	146	91.3
Category K	0	6	0	5	11	19.0
Category L	10	5	0	6	21	43.8
Category M	2	0	0	5	7	58.3
Category N	2	5	2	10	19	32.8
Category P	5	8	0	5	18	31.0
Category R	1	5	0	4	10	55.6
Total:	238	141	11	72	462	46.2

Table 30: Raw and normalised frequencies of clauses of reason across text types.

7.1.1.4 Overt and non-overt subjects across semantic domains and text types

While the frequencies of adverbial clauses across text types can be found by performing a simple addition as illustrated above, the occurrences of overt and non-overt subjects were found via manual annotation. In this annotation process, each of the adverbial clauses identified in the LCMC corpus was carefully screened to track down any occurrence of a non-overt subject. The raw frequencies of occurrence of overt and non-overt subjects were obtained for different semantic domains and text types. The raw frequencies of both subject types across semantic domains were not normalised as the distribution of subjects across semantic domains is not based on text types but the LCMC corpus as a whole, as shown in Table 31, whereas the raw frequencies of overt and non-overt subjects across text types were normalised to a common base of 100K word tokens, as shown in Table 32.

Semantic classes of CACs	Raw frequency		
	Overt subjects	PROs	Total
Clause of Time	2	0	2
Clause of Cause or Reason	381	81	462
Clause of Purpose	18	90	108
Clause of Result	65	81	146
Clause of Preference	2	11	13
Clause of Contrast	17	193	210
Clause of Addition	11	6	17
Clause of Exception	39	4	43
Clause of Condition	589	612	1,201
Clause of Concession	509	267	776
Clause of Inference	3	0	3
Total:	1,636	1,345	2,981

Table 31: Raw frequencies of overt and non-overt subjects across semantic domains.

Text types of LCMC	Raw frequency			Freq. per 100K tokens		
	Overt subjects	PROs	Total	Overt subjects	PROs	Total
Category A	71	45	116	80.7	51.1	131.8
Category B	103	107	210	190.7	198.1	388.9
Category C	40	47	87	117.6	138.2	255.9
Category D	60	78	138	176.5	229.4	405.9
Category E	183	170	353	240.8	223.7	464.5
Category F	201	170	371	228.4	193.2	421.6
Category G	194	142	336	126.0	92.2	218.2
Category H	14	22	36	23.3	36.7	60.0
Category J	369	313	682	230.6	195.6	426.3
Category K	72	58	130	124.1	100.0	224.1
Category L	64	55	119	133.3	114.6	247.9
Category M	18	17	35	150.0	141.7	291.7
Category N	132	58	190	227.6	100.0	327.6
Category P	88	52	140	151.7	89.7	241.4
Category R	27	11	38	150.0	61.1	211.1
Total:	1,636	1,345	2,981	163.6	134.5	298.1

Table 32: Normalised frequencies of overt and non-overt subjects across text types.

7.2 Semantic domains of CACs and text types of LCMC

In this section, I will explore how the semantic domains of adverbial clauses interact with the text types of the LCMC corpus. As can be seen from Table 33, clauses of time (i.e. 2 occurrences) and clauses of inference (i.e. 3 occurrences) are rare, making it impossible to study the distribution of these two types of adverbial clause across the fifteen text categories of the LCMC corpus. This corroborates my initial observation based on the PFR corpus that temporal adverbial clauses rarely occur in written Chinese (see Chapter 5, section 5.3.1). Other semantic classes of adverbial clauses are, however, closely related to certain text types of written Chinese. Hence, in this section, I will examine the interaction between (i) conditional and concessive clauses and text categories A, B and C (section 7.2.1); (ii) reason and result clauses and text categories D and J (section 7.2.2); (iii) purpose clauses and text categories E and F (section 7.2.3). Each contrast will allow me to gain a better understanding of how semantic classes of adverbial clauses distribute across a range of genres in written Chinese.

7.2.1 The interaction between conditional and concessive clauses and categories A, B and C

As noted in Chapter Five (section 5.4), conditional and concessive clauses, among the eleven semantic categories of adverbial clauses in Chinese, make up almost half of the adverbial clauses studied in the PFR corpus. In the LCMC corpus, these two types of adverbial clause occur significantly more frequently than other semantic types (see Table 33).[4] By examining the distribution of conditional and concessive clauses in the press-related texts of the LCMC corpus, it was found that these two types of adverbial clause also dominate in press reportage, press editorials and press reviews (i.e. categories A, B and C) of the corpus. Table 34 shows the frequencies of adverbial clauses in both the PFR corpus and an *ad hoc* subcorpus composed of categories A, B and

4 The calculated log-likelihood (LL) value with 10 degrees of freedom (d.f.) is 5644.170, considerably greater than 29.59, the critical value for significance at $p<0.001$.

C of the LCMC corpus. It can be seen from Table 34 that conditional and concessive clauses occur at least twice as frequently as the other kinds of adverbial clause in the press-related texts of categories A, B and C.

Semantic classes of CACs	**Raw frequency**
Clauses of Time	2
Clauses of Cause or Reason	462
Clauses of Purpose	108
Clauses of Result	146
Clauses of Preference	13
Clauses of Contrast	210
Clauses of Addition	17
Clauses of Exception	43
Clauses of Condition	1,201
Clauses of Concession	776
Clauses of Inference	3
Total:	2,981
Log-likelihood (10 d.f.):	5644.170 (>29.59)

Table 33: Frequencies of adverbial clauses in the LCMC corpus.

Semantic Types of CACs	**PFR**		**LCMC (categories A, B and C)**	
	Raw freq.	**Freq. per 100K tokens**	**Raw freq.**	**Freq. per 100K tokens**
Clauses of time	1	0.1	0	0.0
Clauses of reason	330	29.4	48	27.3
Clauses of purpose	348	31.1	48	27.3
Clauses of result	163	14.5	28	15.9
Clauses of preference	3	0.3	3	1.7
Clauses of contrast	177	15.8	36	20.5
Clauses of addition	13	1.2	2	1.1
Clauses of exception	25	2.2	2	1.1
Clauses of condition	779	**69.5**	166	**94.3**
Clauses of concession	575	**51.3**	115	**65.3**
Clauses of inference	3	0.3	0	0.0
Total:	2,417	215.7	448	254.5

Table 34: Frequencies of adverbial clauses in the PFR corpus and categories A, B, and C of the LCMC corpus.

I therefore hypothesise that journalistic writing is marked by clauses of condition and concession. To test this hypothesis, I tested the statistical significance of the difference in the occurrence of these two types of adverbial clause between the journalistic texts of categories A, B and C and non-journalistic texts of other categories of the LCMC corpus (i.e. categories D, E, F, G, H, J, K, L, M, N, P, and R).

Adverbial semantic classes	**Freq. per 100K tokens Journalistic texts (Categories A, B and C)**	**Freq. per 100K tokens Non-journalistic texts (Categories D, E, F, G, H, J, K, L, M, N, P, R)**	**Fisher's Exact Test ($p<0.05$)**
Clauses of condition	94.3	125.6	0.747
Clauses of concession	65.3	80.2	

Table 35: Journalistic texts vs. non-journalistic texts in the LCMC corpus.

As Table 35 illustrates, conditional and concessive clauses are not a marked feature of journalistic writing; they do not occur significantly more frequently in journalistic texts than in non-journalistic texts.[5] This finding is in line with Biber et al. (1999: 823), who observe that in British English it is time and purpose clauses that are frequently used in news rather than conditional and concessive clauses: temporal clauses describe certain events in relation to others while clauses of purpose explain motivations behind events. In written Chinese, as shown in Table 36, conditional clauses are mostly used in category E (skills, trades and hobbies) for giving directions and instructions in hypothetical situations as in example (1), and concessive clauses are predominantly used in category N (adventure and martial arts fiction) for demonstrating a character's ability to handle some difficult events as in example (2). The LL values with 14 d.f. calculated on the basis of normalised frequencies for determining the distribution of clauses of condition and concession across text categories are 395.790 and 192.970 respectively, markedly greater than 36.12, the critical value for significance at $p<0.001$. This suggests that clauses of condition and concession are more frequently used in categories E and N than in other text categories.

5 The Fisher's Exact Test (see Chapter Six, section 6.5.1) gives a high probability value (or p-value), greater than 0.05, the p-value at the level of significance of 95 percent.

Text types of LCMC	Clauses of condition		Clauses of concession	
	Raw freq.	Freq. per 100K tokens	Raw freq.	Freq. per 100K tokens
Category A	43	48.9 (2.8%)	38	43.2 (3.9%)
Category B	82	151.9 (8.6%)	54	100.0 (9.0%)
Category C	41	120.6 (6.8%)	23	67.6 (6.1%)
Category D	39	114.7 (6.5%)	40	117.6 (10.6%)
Category E	195	**256.6 (14.5%)**	62	81.6 (7.3%)
Category F	185	210.2 (11.9%)	72	81.8 (7.4%)
Category G	119	77.3 (4.4%)	115	74.7 (6.7%)
Category H	13	21.7 (1.2%)	3	5.0 (0.5%)
Category J	218	136.3 (7.7%)	159	99.4 (8.9%)
Category K	58	100.0 (5.6%)	38	65.5 (5.9%)
Category L	45	93.8 (5.3%)	32	66.7 (6.0%)
Category M	13	108.3 (6.1%)	6	50.0 (4.5%)
Category N	76	131.0 (7.4%)	75	**129.3 (11.6%)**
Category P	55	94.8 (5.4%)	52	89.7 (8.1%)
Category R	19	105.6 (6.0%)	7	38.9 (3.5%)
Total:	1,201	120.1 (100%)	776	77.6 (100%)
LL scores (14 d.f.):	395.790		192.970	

Table 36: Clauses of condition vs. clauses of concession in the LCMC corpus.

(1) 白色 衬衣 经过 多次 穿 用 、洗涤 ，容易 发黄 ，<Fm><Fa>[[如果]] 经常 用 淘 米 水 浸 洗</Fa> ， 就 不易 发黄 了 。 </Fm>(LCMC_E.xml/sn="0016")

baise	*chenyi*	*jingguo*	*duoci*	*chuanyong*	*xidi*	*rongyi*
white	shirt	go.through	several.times	wear	wash	easy

fahuang	<Fm><Fa>***ruguo***	*jingchang*	*yong*	*taomishui*
turn.yellow	if	frequently	use	water.for.washing.rice

jinxi</Fa>	*jiu*	*bu*	*yi*	*fahuang*	*le*</Fm>
soak.and.wash	then	not	easy	turn.yellow	PART

"The white shirts easily become yellow after being washed several times, but if they are frequently soaked and washed in the water used for washing rice, they will not turn yellow so easily."

(2) <Fm><Fa>谭 公直 的 手 [[虽然]] 正在 开始 僵硬</Fa> ，但 两 人 功力 相差 太 远 ，媳妇 还是 扳 不 开 公公 的 手 。
</Fm>(LCMC_N.xml/sn="0021")

<Fm><Fa>*Tan Gong*		*zhi*	*de*	*shou*	***suiran***	*zhengzai*	
Tan Gong		straight	DE	hand	although	PROG	
kaishi	*jiangying*</Fa>	*dan*	*liangren*		*gongli*		*xiangcha*
begin	stiff	but	both.of.them		marial.arts.skill		differ
tai	*yuan*	*xifu*	*haishi*	*banbukai*		*Gonggong*	*de*
too	far.away	daughter.in.law	still	not.get.rid.of		Tan's	GEN
shou</Fm>							
hand							

"Although Tan Gong began to have difficulties in moving his hand, his daughter-in-law, being far less skilful and competent than Tan, still could not get rid of him."

7.2.2 The interaction between reason and result clauses and categories D and J

As can be seen from Table 37, reason and result clauses are most frequently used in category D (religion) and category J (scientific academic prose) of the LCMC corpus. A log-likelihood test of significance was used to determine the distribution of these two kinds of adverbial clause across genres on the basis of their normalised frequencies. The calculated LL score (14 d.f.) for clauses of reason is 162.094, considerably greater than the critical value for significance at $p<0.001$ (36.12), whereas the calculated LL score (13 d.f.) for clauses of result is 87.465, much greater than the critical value for significance at $p<0.001$ (34.53). Therefore, the statistical tests clearly indicate that reason and result clauses occur significantly more frequently within the two text categories under consideration. Category D is a collection of 17 texts taken from reference books on a range of mainstream religions in mainland China such as Buddhist and Taoist faiths. Most of the texts give details about the origin and development of the religions (e.g. *D03* and *D05*), and a few of them are concerned with the theory and ritual of a particular religion (e.g. *D08*, *D11* and *D13*) as well as the comparisons between different religious beliefs and ideologies (e.g. *D04*, *D09* and *D17*). Thus, clauses of reason and result are commonly used for describing the development of a religion as in examples (3) and (5), and are also employed for presenting the background/origin of an ideology (i.e. Confucianism) or a religion (i.e. Buddhism) as in examples (4) and (6) respectively.

Text types of LCMC	**Clauses of cause or reason**		**Clauses of result**	
	Raw freq.	**Freq. per 100K tokens**	**Raw freq.**	**Freq. per 100K tokens**
Category A	17	19.3 (2.9%)	4	4.5 (2.1%)
Category B	21	38.9 (5.9%)	18	**33.3 (15.6%)**
Category C	10	29.4 (4.4%)	6	17.6 (8.2%)
Category D	26	**76.5 (11.6%)**	11	**32.4 (15.2%)**
Category E	44	57.9 (8.7%)	15	19.7 (9.2%)
Category F	56	63.6 (9.6%)	13	14.8 (6.9%)
Category G	48	31.2 (4.7%)	8	5.2 (2.4%)
Category H	8	13.3 (2.0%)	4	6.7 (3.1%)
Category J	146	**91.3 (13.8%)**	47	**29.4 (13.8%)**
Category K	11	19.0 (2.9%)	5	8.6 (4.0%)
Category L	21	43.8 (6.6%)	6	12.5 (5.9%)
Category M	7	58.3 (8.8%)	2	16.7 (7.8%)
Category N	19	32.8 (5.0%)	6	10.3 (4.8%)
Category P	18	31.0 (4.7%)	1	1.7 (0.8%)
Category R	10	55.6 (8.4%)	0	0.0 (0.0%)
Total:	462	46.2 (100%)	4	4.5 (100%)
LL scores:	162.094 (14 d.f.)		87.465 (13 d.f.)	

Table 37: Frequencies of clauses of reason and result across text types.

(3) 但 在 另一方面 ，<Fm><Fa> [[由于]] 教会 在 历次 教案 中 获得 了 大量 ” 赔款 ” 和 种种 特权</Fa> ， 使 它 有 可能 在 各地 大肆 建盖 教堂 。</Fm>(LCMC_D.xml/sn="0065")

dan zai lingyifangmian <Fm><Fa>***youyu*** *jiaohui zai*
but at on.the.other.hand because church in
lici jiaoanzhong huode le daliang peikuan
previous lawsuits obtain PERF plenty.of compensations
he zhongzhong tequan</Fa> *shi ta you keneng zai*
and various.kinds.of privileges thereby it have possibility at
gedi dasi jiangai jiaotang</Fm>
worldwide on.a.large.scale build churches

"On the other hand, as the Church received a huge sum in compensations and privileges of various kinds from previous lawsuits, it could build a lot of churches worldwide."

(4) <Fm>但 儒学 不能 代替 和 包容 传统 宗教 ，<Fa>[[因为]] 儒学 是 一种 理论 形态 的 学术 文化 ， 宗教 祭祀 并非 儒学 题 中 应有 之义 ，儒学 的 重心 在 内 圣 外 王 之 学 ，自 有 其 发展 脉络 ，形成 独立 的 学 统</Fa> ；</Fm>(LCMC_D.xml/sn="0045")

<Fm>*dan* *ruxue* *buneng* *daiti* *he* *baorong* *chuantong*
but Confucian cannot replace and embrace traditional
zongjiao <Fa>***yinwei*** *ruxue* *shi* *yi* *zhong* *lilun* *xingtai*
religions because Confucian be one CL theory mode
de *xueshi* *wenhua* *zongjiao* *jisi* *bingfei* *ruxue* *ti*
DE academic culture religion ritual not Confucian assumption
zhong *yingyou* *zhi* *yi* *ruxue* *de* *zhongxin*
within should.have DE meaning Confucian's GEN focus
zai *neishengwaiwang* *zhi* *xue* *zi* *you* *qi*
on spiritual DE ideology itself have its
fazhang *mailuo* *xingcheng* *duli* *de*
development route form independent DE
xuetong</Fa></Fm>
ideology

"However, Confucianism cannot replace or represent traditional religions because unlike religions it is based on theory, does not employ ritual and has developed into an ideology in its own right."

(5) <Fm>在 这个 痛苦 的 探索 过程 中 ， 一些 人 以 皈依 宗教 作为 自己 的 精神 归宿 ， <Fa>[[从而]] 也 导致 了 宗教 的 复兴</Fa> 。</Fm>(LCMC_D.xml/sn="0073")

<Fm>*zai* *zhege* *tongku* *de* *tansuo* *guochengzhong* *yixie*
in this painful DE explore in.process.of some
ren *yi* *guiyi* *zongjiao* *zhuowei* *ziji* *de* *jingsheng*
people use follow religion serve.as their GEN spiritual
guisu <Fa>***conger*** *ye* *daozhi* *le* *zongjiao* *de*
shelter consequently also cause PERF religion DE
fuxing</Fa></Fm>
resurgence

"In the course of this painful adventure, a few of these people sought consolation in religious belief, bringing about the resurgence of religion."

(6) <Fm>6 年 中 经常 风餐露宿 ，" 日 食 一 麻 一 米 ，乃至 七 日 食 一 麻 一 米 " ，在 艰苦 的 修行 中 度过 ，<Fa>[[以致]] " 身形 消瘦 ，有 若 枯 木 " ，然而 却 一无所获</Fa> 。</Fm>(LCMC_D.xml/sn="0054")

<Fm>*liu* *nian* *zhong* *jingchang* *fengcanlusu* *ri* *shi*
six years within frequently live.in.the.wild day eat
yi *ma* *yi* *mi* *naizhi* *qi* *ri* *chi* *yi* *ma* *yi* *mi*
one sesame one rice and.then seven days eat one sesame one rice
zai *jianku* *de* *xiuxing* *zhong* *duguo*<Fa> ***yizhi***
in harsh DE training in.process.of go.through consequently
shengxing *xiaoshou* *you* *ruo* *ku* *mu* *raner* *que*
body.shape skinny have look.like dry wood yet but
yiwusuohuo</Fa></Fm>
in.vain

"Over the past six years, Buddha had lived in the wild. In the beginning, he ate a piece of sesame and rice each day, and later on he had sesame and rice once a week. Consequently he became very skinny but gained no insights into life."

On the other hand, in category J, there are a total of 80 academic texts covering a wide spectrum of science and social science topics such as medicine (e.g. *J01* and *J03*), computing (e.g. *J07*, *J08* and *J68*), engineering (e.g. *J11*, *J67* and *J69*), physics (e.g. *J09* and *J10*), biology, (e.g. *J19* and *J20*) sociology (e.g. *J18* and *J49*), economics (e.g. *J24*, *J27*, *J34* and *J36*), journalism (e.g. *J32*, *J38* and *J53*), management (e.g. *J74* and *J77*), finance (e.g. *J54* and *J73*), psychology (e.g. *J21* and *J75*), education (e.g. *J12* and *J56*), linguistics (e.g. *J23*, *J57* and *J60*), philosophy (e.g. *J48* and *J71*), Chinese literature (e.g. *J04*, *J79* and *J80*), etc. In these texts, causal clauses are frequently used for justifying the methodology of a piece of research as in examples (7) and (8) while result clauses are mainly used for presenting the findings of a piece of research as in examples (9) and (10). Apart from discussing research findings, clauses of result are also frequently used by the official Xinhua news agency and several local newspapers represented in category B (press editorials) of the LCMC corpus. Result clauses are used to present an editor's comments on the consequences of economic and political policies. As illustrated in examples (11) and (12), both of the examples are concerned with a commentator's opinions on global political events.

(7) <Fm><Fa>[[由于]] 要 针对 不同 的 需要</Fa> ， 语言 研究 的 目的 、 角度 和 侧重点 就 会 有所不同 ， 研究 方法 也 会 有所不同 。 </Fm>(LCMC_J.xml/sn="0010")

<Fm><Fa>***youyu*** *yao* *zhendui* *butong* *de* *xuyao*</Fa> *yuyan*
because have.to suit different DE needs language
yanjiu *de* *mudi* *jiaodu* *he* *cezhongdian* *jiu* *hui*
research DE purpose perspective and focus then will.be
yousuobutong *yanjiu* *fangfa* *ye* *hui* *yousuobutong*</Fm>
different research methodology also will.be different

"In an attempt to suit different purposes, linguistic analyses vary in their objectives, perspectives, focusses and methodologies."

(8) <Fm>在 词 处理 阶段 ， 我们 主要 解决 了 不 实行 分词 连写 的 汉语 的 词 处理 手段 问题 ， <Fa>[[因为]] 作为 语言 的 基础 毕竟 是 词 而 不 是 " 字 " </Fa> 。</Fm>(LCMC_J.xml/sn="0019")

<Fm>*zai* *ci* *chuli* *jieduan* *women* *zhuyao* *jiejue* *le*
at word handling stage we mainly solve PERF
bu *shixing* *fenci* *lianxie* *de* *hanyu* *de*
not put.into.use word.segmentation write DE Chinese.language DE
ci *chuli* *shouduan* *wenti* <Fa>***yinwei*** *zhuowei* *yuyan*
word handling strategy problem because serve.as language's
de *jichu* *bijing* *shi* *ci* *er* *bu* *shi*
GEN foundation nonetheless be word but not be
zi</Fa></Fm>
character

"In handling words, we have mainly focussed on the segmentation of words in Chinese as the basic unit of a language is the word not the character."

(9) <Fm>由于 它们 的 繁殖力 极 强 ， 生长 速度 极 快 ， 短期 内 就 会 产生 大量 的 后代 ， 所以 把 目的 基因 转入 这些 细菌 ， 就 能 在 短 时间 内 得到 大量 的 基因 拷贝 ，<Fa>[[从而]] 产生 大量 的 产物 </Fa> 。</Fm>(LCMC_J.xml/sn="0083")

<Fm>*youyu* *tamen* *de* *fanzhili* *ji* *qiang*
because their GEN reproductive.power extremely strong
shengzhang *sudu* *ji* *kui* *duanqi* *nei* *jiu*
growth rate extremely quick short.spell during then

hui *chansheng* *daliang* *de* *houdai* *suoyi* *ba* *mudi*
can produce plenty.of DE next.generation so.that BA target
jiyin *zhuangru* *zhexie* *xijun* *jiu* *neng* *zai* *duan*
genes inject.into these bacteria then can within short
shijian *nei* *dedao* *daliang* *de* *jiyin* *kaobei*
period.of.time during obtain plenty.of DE genes replica
<Fa>***conger*** *chansheng* *daliang* *de* *chanwu*</Fa></Fm>
consequently form plenty.of DE products

"Since they have strong reproductive power and a high growth rate and can reproduce within a short spell, if we inject our target gene into these bacteria, we will obtain, in a short period of time, a huge number of replicas of the target gene and this boosts productivity substantially."

(10) <Fm>有 个 连队 收看 电视 连续剧《 诽谤 》，片面 强调 看 节目 就 是 受 教育 ，不论 工作 多 忙 也 要 看到 底 ，<Fa>[[以致]] 有 １５ 次 推迟 早晨 起床 时间</Fa> 。</Fm>(LCMC_J.xml/sn="0024")

<Fm>*you* *ge* *liandui* *shoukan* *dianshi* *lianxuju*
there.exists CL military.officer watch TV drama.series
Feibang *pianmian* *qiangdiao* *kan* *jiemu* *jiushi*
Rumours on.the.screen emphasise watch TV.programme that.is
shou *jiaoyu* *bulun* *gongzhuo* *duo* *mang* *ye*
receive education no.matter job how busy yet
yao *kandaodi* <Fa>***yizhi*** *you* *15* *ci* *tuichi*
want.to watch.till.the.end as.a.result have 15 times delay
zaocheng *qichuang* *shijian*</Fa></Fm>
morning wake.up time

"One of the military officers watched the TV drama series entitled 'Rumours' which purported to be an educational programme and he watched it no matter how busy he was and thus he had got up late fifteen times."

(11) <Fm>人们 将 密切 注视 ， 日本 今后 将 以 何种 形式 扩大 自己 的 国际 影响 ， <Fa>[[从而]] 达到 成为 " 政治 大国 " 的 目的</Fa> 。</Fm>(LCMC_B.xml/sn="0056")

<Fm>*renmen* *jiang* *miqie* *zhushi* *Riben* *jinhou*
people very.soon closely pay.attention.to Japan in.future

jiang *yi* *hezhong* *xingshi* *kuoda* *ziji* *de* *guoji*
very.soon use which way expand its GEN international
yingxiang <Fa>***conger*** *dadao* *chengwei* *zhengzhi* *daguo*
influence consequently reach become political giant.nation
de *mudi*</Fa></Fm>
DE purpose
"People will see how Japan expands its influence over other nations and achieves its goal of being one of the largest countries in the world."

(12) 路透社 认为 ， <Fm><Fa>她 [[之所以]] 不 象 过去 讨论 成立 货币 联盟 时 那样 强烈 反对</Fa> ，其 原因 是 在 国内 政治 上 遇到 了 麻烦 ， 威信 下降 ， 希望 得到 其他 盟国 的 支持 ， 再说 ， 目前 政治 联盟 的 目标 尚 不 具体 ， 笼统 地 表示 支持 也 无 不可 </Fm>。(LCMC_B.xml/sn="0025")
Lutoushe *renwei* <Fm><Fa>*ta* ***zhisuoyi*** *bu* *xiang*
Reuters believe she the.reason.why not like
guoqu *taolun* *chengli* *huobi* *lianmeng* *shi*
in.the.past discuss set.up currency union at.that.time
nayang *qianglie* *fandui*</Fa> *qi* *yuanyin* *shi* *zai* *guonei*
that.way fiercely object her reason be at within.the.country
zhengzhishang *yudao* *le* *mafan* *weixin* *xiajiang*
politically-speaking face PERF trouble credibility drop
xiwang *dedao* *qita* *mengguo* *de* *zhichi* *zaishuo*
hope obtain other united.nations' GEN support what.is.more
muqian *zhengzhi* *lianmeng* *de* *mubiao* *shang* *bu*
for.the.time.being political coalition's GEN goal yet not
juti *longtong* *de* *biaoshi* *zhichi* *ye* *wu* *bu*
flesh.out ostensibly ADVL indicate support yet have.not not
ke</Fm>
possible
"Reuters news agency believed the reason why she did not object severely to the creation of currency unions as she did previously was that she had political troubles at home and her credibility dropped, and thus she wished to gain support from other nations; additionally, the objective of the plan was not made clear yet and her ostensible support was by no means inappropriate."

7.2.3 The interaction between purpose clauses and categories E and F

In the LCMC corpus, it was shown in Table 38 that purpose clauses are most frequently used in category E (i.e. skills, trades and hobbies) as in examples (13) and (14) and category F (i.e. popular lore) as in examples (15) and (16). The LL value with 9 d.f. for clauses of purpose calculated on normalised frequencies is 51.296, greater than the critical value for significance at $p<0.001$ (27.88), highlighting the fact that clauses of purpose are predominant in these two text categories.

Text types of LCMC	**Clauses of purpose**	
	Raw frequency	**Freq. per 100K tokens**
Category A	0	0.0 (0.0%)
Category B	10	18.5 (13.8%)
Category C	3	8.8 (6.6%)
Category D	5	14.7 (10.9%)
Category E	19	**25.0 (18.6%)**
Category F	22	**25.0 (18.6%)**
Category G	6	3.9 (2.9%)
Category H	8	13.3 (9.9%)
Category J	32	20.0 (14.9%)
Category K	1	1.7 (1.3%)
Category L	0	0.0 (0.0%)
Category M	0	0.0 (0.0%)
Category N	2	3.4 (2.5%)
Category P	0	0.0 (0.0%)
Category R	0	0.0 (0.0%)
Total:	108	10.8 (100%)
LL score (9 d.f.):	51.296	

Table 38: Frequencies of clauses of purpose across text types.

Category E contains 18 texts on a wide variety of topics which fall into three major categories, namely (a) hobbies e.g. fishing (*E02*), playing bridge (*E16*), playing badminton (*E18*), photography (*E32*), playing cards (*E38*), etc., (b) practical skills in various fields such as craft (*E37*) and home decoration (*E27* and *E36*), etc., and (c) tactics in trades and business such as stocks investment (*E13* and *E15*). On the other hand, category F is composed of texts relating to local culture such as celebrities (*F05* and *F13*), fashion (*F37*), marriage and family (*F07* and *F35*), overseas study (*F08*) and love affairs (*F16*, *F23* and *F24*), and texts relating to everyday life such as cosmetic preparations (*F10*), diet/health (*F39*, *F40* and *F41*), school (*F29*) and driving (*F01*). Hence, as illustrated in examples (13) and (14) respectively, clauses of purpose are used for giving instructions on mastering a hobby i.e. photography and explaining the practical skills needed in making a bird cage, while in examples (15) and (16), they are used, respectively, for offering guidance on interpersonal skills and giving advice on careers.

(13) <Fm>色彩 选配 得当 ， 能 给 人 以 清雅 大方 之 感 ， <Fa>[[从而]] 得到 艺术 上 的 享受</Fa> 。</Fm>(LCMC_E.xml/sn="0004")

<Fm>*secai* *xuanpei* *dedang* *neng* *gei* *ren* *yi*
colour pick.and.match properly can give people as.regards
qingya *dafang* *zhi* *gan* <Fa>***conger*** *dedao* *yishushang*
elegant generous DE impression in.order.that obtain aesthetical
de *xiangshou*</Fa></Fm>
DE pleasure

"If the colour is used properly, the work will look elegant and aesthetic."

(14) <Fm>洗刷 后 的 竹制 鸟笼 不能 任 烈日 下 暴晒 ， <Fa>[[以免]] 笼架 松散</Fa> 。</Fm>(LCMC_E.xml/sn="0046")

<Fm>*xicha* *hou* *de* *zhuzhi* *niaolong* *buneng* *ren*
wash after DE bamboo bird.cage cannot let
lieri *xia* *baoshai* <Fa>***yimian*** *longjia*
strong.sunlight under expose in.order.not.to parts.of.cage
songsan</Fa></Fm>
dismantle

"The washed bamboo bird cage should not be exposed to strong sunlight in order not to damage the cage."

(15) <Fm>他们 悄悄地 察看 着 你 的 脸 ， 察看 你 的 相貌 、 衣着 、 举止 ，倾听 着 你 的 言谈 和 回答 ，<Fa>[[从而]] 试 着 判定 你 是 个 怎样 的 人</Fa> 。</Fm>(LCMC_F.xml/sn="0048")

<Fm>*tamen* *qiaoqiaode* *chakan* *zhe* *ni* *de* *lian*
they quietly examine PROG your GEN face
chakan *ni* *de* *xiangmao* *yizhuo* *juzhi*
examine your GEN appearance clothing behaviour
qingting *ni* *de* *yantan* *he* *huida* <Fa>***conger***
listen.to your GEN talk and reply in.order.to
shi *zhe* *panding* *ni* *shi* *ge* *zenyang* *de* *ren*</Fa></Fm>
try PROG judge you be CL what.kind.of DE person
"They examined in secret your face, appearance, clothing and manner and listened to what you said and how you replied in order to gauge what sort of person you are."

(16) <Fm>在 明确 个人 的 职业 意向 及 心理 特点 后 ， 应 进一步 设法 了解 所 倾向 的 职业 要求 ， 培养 相 调节 自己 所 倾向 的 职业 所需 的 各种 心理 品质 ， <Fa>[[以免]] 今后 的 工作 处于 被动</Fa> 。</Fm>(LCMC_F.xml/sn="0046")

<Fm>*zai* *mingque* *geren* *de* *zhiye* *yixiang* *ji*
at realise individual's GEN career objective and
xinli *tedian* *hou* *ying* *jinyibu* *shefa*
psychological traits after should further make.every.effort.to
liaojie *suo* *qingxiang* *de* *zhiye* *yaoqiu*
understand belong.to.oneself intended DE career requirement
peiyang *xiang* *tiaojie* *ziji* *suo* *qingxiang*
foster accordingly adjust oneself belong.to.oneself intended
de *zhiye* *suo* *xu* *de* *gezhong* *xinli*
DE career belong.to.oneself need DE various.kinds.of psychological
pinzhi <Fa>***yimian*** *jinhou* *de* *gongzhuo* *chuyu*
qualities in.order.not.to future DE work remain.in.a.state.of
beidong</Fa></Fm>
unmotivated
"After understanding one's career objective and personality traits, one should learn more about the requirements of the desired career and prepare one's mentality for it in order not to be unmotivated later at work."

To conclude this section, I have demonstrated that semantic classes of adverbial clauses and text categories are in a reciprocal relationship in that adverbial semantic classes have a propensity to occur in certain text categories (for example, clauses of condition and purpose are frequently used in category E for giving instructions), and different genres tend to prefer a particular semantic class of adverbial clauses (for example, academic prose takes more clauses of reason to explain research methodological issues).

7.3 The distribution of PROs across text types and semantic domains

In this section, I will examine how overt and non-overt subjects are used in adverbial clauses across text categories and across the semantic domains of adverbial clauses, by comparison to the results obtained from the PFR training corpus.

7.3.1 Text type and choice of subject

Table 39 shows the distribution of overt and non-overt subjects in different text types. I tested the statistical significance of the relatedness between text category and choice of subject, both *across* and *within* text types. As the text categories are of different sizes, the log-likelihood value for determining the distribution of subjects across text types was calculated on the basis of the normalised frequencies of subjects. However, the log-likelihood scores of individual text categories were calculated on the basis of the raw frequencies of overt and non-overt subjects, which both occur within the same text type. While the distribution of overt and non-overt subjects is significantly different across text types (the calculated LL value with 14 d.f. is 105.762, greater than 36.12, the critical value for significance at $p<0.001$), the distribution of subjects within certain text categories does not differ significantly at this level. Only category N indicates a significant outcome; its LL score with 1 d.f. (29.60) is greater than the critical value for significance

(10.83) at $p<0.001$.[6] Only if p is lessened to 0.05 do more significant results occur (when 3.841 becomes the critical value). At that level overt subjects occur more frequently in categories A, G, J, N, P and R. Of the fifteen text categories, only six genres were shown statistically to prefer one type of subject (i.e. overt subject) over the other (i.e. PRO) in adverbial clauses. Consequently, I would not claim that the relatedness between text type and choice of subject is of significance. However, this does not entirely exclude the influence of text type on the distribution of subjects, though that significance is only measurable at a lower level (95%). In the following, I will demonstrate that text types do play a role in the choice of subject in the adverbial clause.

Text	**Raw frequency**		**Freq. per 100K tokens**		**LL (1 d.f.)**
types	**Overt NP subjects**	**PRO**	**Overt NP subjects**	**PRO**	
A	71	45	80.7	51.1	**5.88**
B	103	107	190.7	198.1	0.08
C	40	47	117.6	138.2	0.56
D	60	78	176.5	229.4	2.35
E	183	170	240.8	223.7	0.48
F	201	170	228.4	193.2	2.59
G	194	142	126.0	92.2	**8.08**
H	14	22	23.3	36.7	1.79
J	369	313	230.6	195.6	**4.60**
K	72	58	124.1	100.0	1.51
L	64	55	133.3	114.6	0.68
M	18	17	150.0	141.7	0.03
N	132	58	227.6	100.0	**29.60**
P	88	52	151.7	89.7	**9.36**
R	27	11	150.0	61.1	**6.95**
Log-likelihood (LL) value (14 d.f.)			105.762		

Table 39: Subject types vs. text types.

6 Category N, *adventure and martial arts fiction*, is a distinctive language type in that the language used in most stories of this type is influenced by vernacular Chinese, i.e. modern Chinese styled to appear like classical Chinese. In this way, the use of adverbial clauses in this text category may be different from that in other text categories due to the difference between modern Chinese and classical Chinese. However, as the focus of my book is on adverbial clauses in modern Chinese, I will not explore this issue further in this book. Interested readers can refer to Wiebusch (2005) for a quantitative investigation of Chinese numeral classifiers based on historical corpora.

7.3.2 Adverbial semantic class and choice of subject

The discussion in Chapter Six (section 6.5) reported that the distribution of non-overt subjects of adverbial clauses varies significantly across semantic types of adverbial clauses. To recapitulate, clauses of concession and reason favour the use of overt subjects whereas clauses of condition, purpose, contrast and result prefer using null subjects. Table 40 shows the raw frequencies of overt and non-overt subjects of adverbial clauses in both the PFR and LCMC corpora.[7] While both subject types are slightly more frequent in the LCMC corpus than in the PFR corpus, the difference in the distribution of these two subject types between the two corpora is not statistically significant: Fisher's Exact Test fails to detect a significant difference even at the 95% level (p=2.105). Given that the distribution of subjects of adverbial clauses is not sensitive to genre variations (as noted in section 7.3.1), it is not surprising that the two corpora, which are structurally distinct from each other in terms of their composition of genres, show no statistically significant difference in the occurrence of overt and non-overt subjects of Chinese adverbial clauses. On the other hand, the semantic class of the adverbial clause plays a vital role in determining the distribution of subjects, as demonstrated in the previous chapter using the PFR corpus. As the PFR corpus contains a single genre i.e. journalistic writing, it is unclear whether or not the influence of adverbial semantic class on the distribution of overt and non-overt subjects depends on text type. I therefore decided to investigate this question by using the LCMC corpus. As the variation in genres has been proved to be insignificant in the distribution of subjects in the adverbial clause, I hypothesise that the effect of adverbial semantic domain on the distribution of subjects is not dependent on text type, i.e. a similar pattern of the distribution of overt subjects and non-overt ones (PROs) in certain semantic kinds of adverbial clauses can be found in both the PFR corpus (a homogenous corpus of journalistic texts) and the LCMC corpus (a balanced corpus of fifteen distinct text types). To test this hypothesis, I compared the distribution of both subject types (i.e. overt subject and PRO) within eleven semantic classes of adverbial clauses in the LCMC corpus. As

7 As both the PFR and LCMC corpora are of equal sizes, containing one million word tokens, normalisation of frequencies is not required.

illustrated in Table 41, the distribution of overt and non-overt subjects varies significantly across semantic domains (the LL value with 10 d.f. is 535.750, considerably greater than 29.59, the critical value for significance at $p<0.001$). Five semantic types of adverbial clauses give statistically significant results with the log-likelihood values (with 1 d.f.) greater than the critical value for significance at $p<0.001$ (10.83). Whilst overt subjects are most frequently used in clauses of concession and less frequently used in clauses of reason and exception, null subjects are overwhelmingly used in clauses of contrast and purpose.

Subject types	**PFR Corpus**	**LCMC Corpus**	**Fisher's Exact Test ($p<0.05$)**
Overt NP subjects	1,083	1,636	2.105
PROs	1,334	1,345	

Table 40: Frequencies of overt and non-overt subjects of adverbial clauses in PFR and LCMC.

Semantic types of CACs	**Raw frequency**		**LL (1 d.f.)**
	Overt NP subjects	**PROs**	
Clauses of time	2	0	2.77
Clauses of reason	381	81	**211.52**
Clauses of purpose	18	90	**52.40**
Clauses of result	65	81	1.76
Clauses of preference	2	11	6.86
Clauses of contrast	17	193	**173.06**
Clauses of addition	11	6	1.49
Clauses of exception	39	4	**33.00**
Clauses of condition	589	612	0.44
Clauses of concession	509	267	**76.74**
Clauses of inference	3	0	4.16
Log-likelihood (LL) value (10 d.f.)	535.750		

Table 41: Subject types vs. semantic types of CACs.

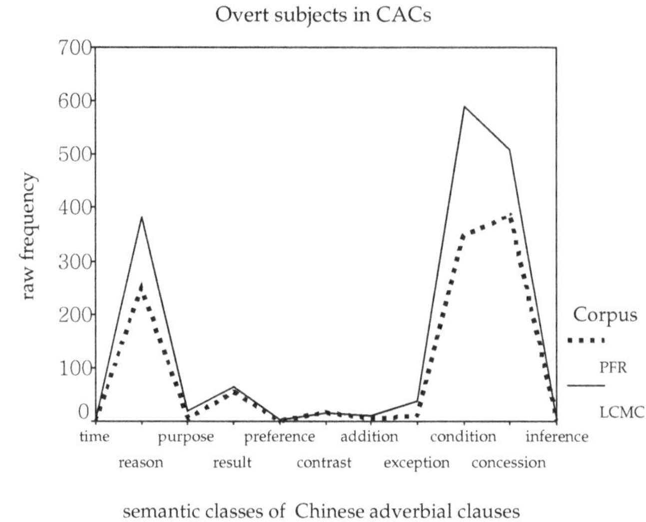

Figure 9: Contrasting overt subjects in PFR and LCMC.

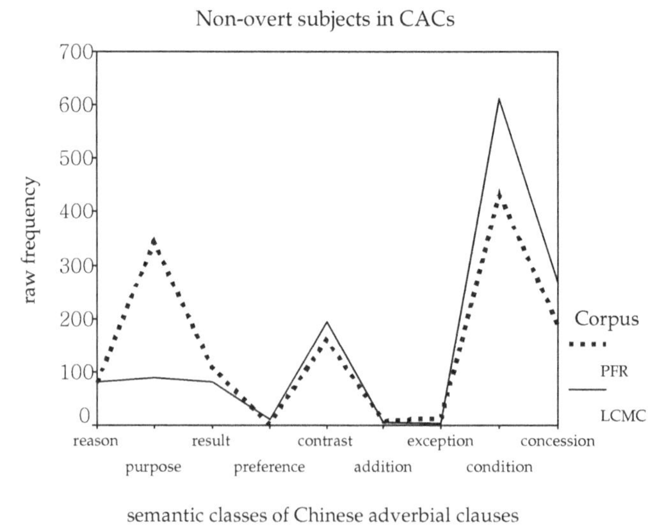

Figure 10: Contrasting non-overt subjects in PFR and LCMC.

LL scores for overt subjects vs. PROs					
Text types	**Semantic classes of CACs**				
	Cause/reason	***Purpose***	***Contrast***	***Exception***	***Concession***
A	**11.25**	0.00	**13.86**	2.77	**13.57**
B	6.06	**13.86**	**12.97**	0.00	9.23
C	1.65	0.34	5.55	0.00	0.04
D	3.95	1.93	9.75	0.34	0.40
E	**25.95**	2.64	**14.70**	1.39	1.62
F	**25.08**	2.98	5.78	4.16	0.89
G	**26.66**	2.91	8.71	**16.64**	4.63
H	**11.09**	**11.09**	0.00	0.00	0.34
J	3.17	**29.40**	**86.56**	8.32	**34.81**
K	2.36	1.39	**19.41**	1.39	6.95
L	2.38	0.00	2.94	4.16	6.34
M	7.72	0.00	5.55	2.77	0.00
N	**13.55**	2.77	0.34	5.55	**13.21**
P	5.88	0.00	9.70	0.00	**11.51**
R	0.40	0.00	0.00	2.77	1.33

Table 42: Contrasting the distribution of subjects across text types.

As far as the distribution of overt subjects is concerned, the results obtained from the PFR corpus can be perfectly mirrored in the data drawn from the LCMC corpus. As can be seen in Figure 9, the distribution patterns of overt subjects in the PFR and LCMC corpora are strikingly similar. However, as far as the distribution of non-overt subjects is concerned, two observations made on the basis of the LCMC corpus go against the results obtained from the PFR corpus. These two findings are telling arguments for the role of text type in the use of overt and non-overt subjects in the adverbial clause; this relationship should not be ignored simply because of the lack of significance when text type and choice of subject are contrasted (see section 7.3.1). As shown in Figure 10, purpose clauses take remarkably less PROs in the LCMC corpus than in the PFR corpus, possibly because the majority (87%) of the non-overt subjects of the purpose clauses occur only in six of the text types in the LCMC corpus i.e. scientific academic prose (17%), press editorials (17%), skills/trades/hobbies (15%), popular lore (15%), reports and official documents (12%) and religion (11%). Whilst a fall in the use of non-overt subjects in clauses of purpose attaches some credence to the influence of text type on the distribution of subjects, the insignificant contrast between the distribution of overt and non-overt subjects in clauses of condition provides further evidence to support this influence. As shown in Table 41, conditional clauses do not show a preponderant use of PRO in the LCMC corpus (the calculated LL value with 1 d.f. is 0.44, much smaller than the critical value for significance, 10.83, at $p<0.001$). If the semantic domains of adverbial clauses had imposed an influence on the occurrence of PROs irrespective of genre variations, conditional clauses, which were proved to favour the use of non-overt subjects in the PFR corpus, would have taken significantly more PROs than overt subjects in the LCMC corpus. Thus it is necessary to examine more closely the five adverbial clause types which, as noted above, give significant results on their choice of subject, with the aim of identifying any difference in the distribution of subjects across genres in these adverbial semantic domains. Table 42 shows the log-likelihood scores of individual text categories in the contrast of overt and non-overt subjects, where statistically significant values are highlighted.[8] As illustrated in the table, the contrast between the distribution of overt and non-overt subjects in the five adverbial semantic classes under consideration is marked only in certain text types, and the influence of text type is most appreciable in clauses of exception in which the difference in the distribution of these two kinds of subject is significant only in category G. Hence, I rejected the null hypothesis and conclude that the effect of semantic domain on the distribution of subjects depends on text type. While text types do not have a direct influence on the distribution of PROs as indicated by the non-significant results between text type and subject type, they do indeed have an indirect influence on how the semantic domains of adverbial clauses determine the distribution of subjects in the adverbial clause. In the following section, I will investigate how text type influences the choice of referential controllers for PRO in CACs.

8 As both the overt and non-overt subjects of a particular kind of adverbial clause occur in the same text category, the log-likelihood test of significance was computed on the basis of the raw frequencies of the subjects. The calculated LL value (with 1 d.f.) is significant if it is greater than 10.83, the critical value for significance at $p<0.001$.

7.4 Types of control of PRO and text types

The discussion of the properties of control of PRO in Chapter Six, section 6.4 brings out three distinct types of control for Chinese non-overt subjects: a non-overt subject of the Chinese adverbial clause is controlled by either an NP (subject or object) in the main clause or an NP outside the main clause i.e. in previous context, or it is not controlled by any NP and refers freely. While more or less the same number of non-overt subjects occur in both the PFR and LCMC corpora, the distribution of their controllers is different in the two corpora.

Chinese corpora	Main clause control		Control outside main clause	No control i.e. arbitrary interpretation	No. of PRO
	Subject control	*Object control*			
PFR	689 (52%)	12 (1%)	411 (31%)	**222 (17%)**	1,334 (100%)
LCMC[9]	436 (32%)	32 (2%)	424 (32%)	**453 (34%)**	1,345 (100%)

Table 43: Types of control of PRO in PFR and LCMC.

As can be seen in Table 43, subject control from the main clause slightly dominates the other two types of control in the PFR corpus. However, in the LCMC corpus, these three types of control average out in their distribution, with more or less the same frequency of occurrence. The effect of averaging out the three kinds of control of PRO in the LCMC corpus is caused by a surge in the use of non-overt subjects (PRO_{arb}) which are not controlled by any element in the sentence and thus take an arbitrary reading, i.e. 453 instances in the LCMC corpus, the double of 222 instances in the PFR corpus. While more "arbitrary" non-overt subjects appear, there is a relatively reduced use of main clause subject control. In Figure 11, a drop in the use of main clause subject controllers can be clearly seen, as opposed to a rise in "no control" in the

9 For the record, object control in the LCMC corpus occurs in various text types, namely category B (*yinwei*, *jishi* and *ruo*), category C (*zhiyou*), category D (*yimian*), category E (*yimian*, *conger* (2) and *sui*), category F (*youyu*, *conger* (2), *ruguo*, *zhiyao*, *zhiyou* and *chufei*), category G (*youyu*, *yinwei*, *zhiyao*, *suiran*, *sui* and *buguan*), category J (*yimian*, *conger* and *suiran*), category K (*ruguo* and *napa*), category N (*ru*, *ruoshi* and *buguan*), and category P (*ruguo* and *yaoshi*).

LCMC corpus. As highlighted in Table 44, the evident growing use of PRO_{arb} is shown in clauses of condition, which have 314 cases of PRO_{arb} in the LCMC corpus, compared to 143 cases in the PFR corpus. More specifically, it was shown in Table 45 that clauses of condition take the greatest number of PRO_{arb} in category E among the fifteen text types of the LCMC corpus. This category comprises a wide range of articles on practical skills and hobbies. In articles of this sort, authors give instructions for how to manage a particular skill or hobby. As has been mentioned in section 7.2.1, conditional clauses are frequently employed in this genre to create a hypothetical situation in which the author provides an explanation. In these situations, there is no specific referent intended to be the reader. As a result, non-overt subjects with an arbitrary interpretation are overwhelmingly used in text type E, as illustrated in examples (17) and (18).

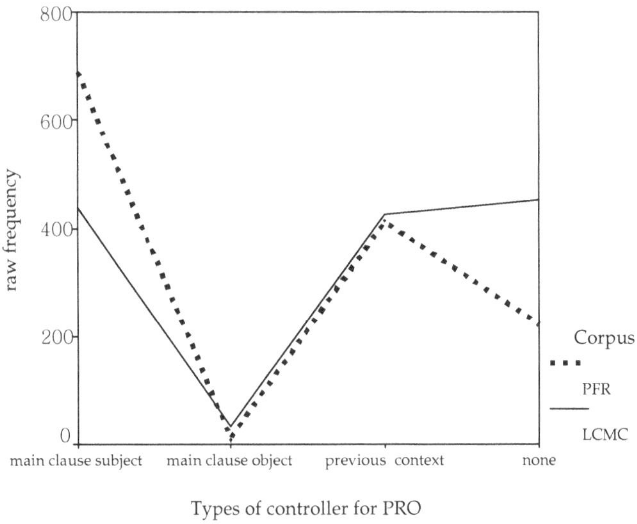

Figure 11: Contrasting types of controller for PRO in PFR and LCMC.

Non-overt subjects with an arbitrary interpretation (PRO_{arb})		
Semantic Classes of CACs	**PFR Corpus**	**LCMC Corpus**
Clause of Time	0	0
Clause of Cause or Reason	4	17
Clause of Purpose	35	21
Clause of Result	0	13
Clause of Preference	1	2
Clause of Contrast	5	1
Clause of Addition	1	4
Clause of Exception	0	3
Clause of Condition	**143**	**314**
Clause of Concession	33	78
Clause of Inference	0	0
Total:	222	453

Table 44: Distribution of PRO_{arb} across semantic types of CACs in PFR and LCMC.

Text Types	Semantic Domains of Chinese Adverbial Clauses										
	Time	*Cause*	*Purpose*	*Result*	*Preference*	*Contrast*	*Addition*	*Exception*	*Condition*	*Concession*	*Inference*
A	0	0	0	0	0	0	1.1	0	11.4	4.5	0
B	0	3.7	0	1.9	1.9	0	0	0	38.9	1.9	0
C	0	0	0	0	0	0	0	0	35.3	17.6	0
D	0	14.7	0	0	0	0	0	5.9	50.0	29.4	0
E	0	1.3	6.6	2.6	0	0	0	0	**103.9**	13.2	0
F	0	2.3	4.5	0	0	0	1.1	0	48.9	10.2	0
G	0	0.6	0	0	0	0	0	0	14.9	4.5	0
H	0	0	1.7	0	0	0	0	0	3.3	0	0
J	0	1.9	6.9	6.3	0.6	0.6	0	0	46.9	11.9	0
K	0	0	0	0	0	0	1.7	0	41.4	5.2	0
L	0	2.1	0	0	0	0	2.1	0	20.8	6.3	0
M	0	0	0	0	0	0	0	0	25.0	0	0
N	0	1.7	0	0	0	0	0	0	6.9	10.3	0
P	0	0	0	0	0	0	0	1.7	12.1	3.4	0
R	0	5.6	0	0	0	0	0	0	5.6	0	0

Table 45: Distribution of PRO_{arb} across semantic domains of CACs and text types of LCMC.

(17) <Fm><Fa>[[如果]] **PRO**$_{arb}$ 递 钩 后 ， 没 见 鱼 上钩</Fa> ， 要 上 下 提 拉 钓钩 ， 以此 诱 鱼 和 显示 钓饵 可见度 。 </Fm>(LCMC_E.xml/sn="0023")

<Fm><Fa>***ruguo*** **PRO**$_{arb}$ *di gou hou mei jian yu*
if PRO hold hook after have.not see fish
shanggou</Fa> *yao shangxia ti la diaogou yici*
being.caught have.to up.and.down raise pull hookthereby
you yu he xianshi diaoer kejiandu</Fm>
attract fish and show bait visibility

"If (you) hold the hook and do not see any fish being caught, (you) should move the hook up and down in order to attract prey and monitor the bait."

(18) <Fm><Fa>[[若]] **PRO**$_{arb}$ 用 洗衣机 洗衣</Fa> ，只要 在 洗衣 缸 里 放 一 杯 醋 ， 洗衣粉 泡沫 就 会 消失 ， 不会 溢出 机 外 。 </Fm>(LCMC_E.xml/sn="0004")

<Fm><Fa>***ruo*** **PRO**$_{arb}$ *yong xiyiji xiyi*</Fa>
if PRO use washing.machine wash.clothes
zhiyao zai xiyigang li fang yi bei
given.that in drum.of.washing.machine inside put one CL
cu xiyifen paomo jiu hui xiaoshi buhui
vinegar washing.powder foam then will disappear will.not
yichu ji wai</Fm>
splash.outmachine outside

"If (you) apply washing powder, (you) can pour a cup of vinegar into the drum of the washing machine so that the foam of the powder will disappear and will not spill out."

7.5 Chapter summary

In this chapter, I used the Lancaster Corpus of Mandarin Chinese (LCMC), which is a balanced corpus containing fifteen distinct text types of written Chinese, as a test corpus and the PFR corpus as a training corpus. I examined the interrelationship between the semantic domains of Chinese adverbial clauses (CACs) and the text types of the LCMC corpus. I also investigated how the non-overt subjects (PROs) of adverbial clauses are used in written Chinese and explored the influence of semantic domain and text type on the distribution of PROs in the adverbial clause.

In both the PFR and LCMC corpora, conditional and concessive clauses are the most common of the eleven semantic types of adverbial clauses. In a close examination of the press texts of the LCMC corpus exclusively (i.e. categories A, B and C), it is clear that conditional and concessive clauses also dominate all other semantic domains in these text categories. A hypothesis drawn from this is that journalistic texts are marked by conditional and concessive clauses. However, a statistical test of significance on the difference in the occurrence of these two kinds of adverbial clause between journalistic texts (of categories A, B and C) and non-journalistic texts (of the remaining categories in the LCMC) indicated that the difference is not significant. Hence, while conditional and concessive clauses are commonly used in press texts, they are not a marked feature of journalistic writing. Rather, they are most frequently used, respectively, in categories E (skills, trades and hobbies) and N (adventure and martial arts fiction). Other semantic classes of adverbial clauses also have a propensity to occur in certain text types of the corpus. Clauses of reason and result are closely related to categories D and J. Category D is chiefly concerned with the history of mainstream religions in mainland China and thus reason and result clauses are used to describe the origin and development of a religion, whereas category J is a collection of various science and social science academic texts. Thus reason clauses are commonly employed to give a rationale for adopting a particular research methodology and result clauses are used to present the research findings. As well as discussing research observations and results, result clauses are frequently used to give comments on the effects of political and economic events in category B which contains editorials from Xinhua news agency and local newspapers. Purpose clauses interact with category E (*ibid*) to give instructions for mastering a particular skill (e.g. craft and home decoration) and hobby (e.g. photography and fishing), as well as with category F (popular lore) to offer guidance on topics concerning local culture and daily life such as fashion, health, interpersonal communication skills, family, school and careers.

Whilst the distribution of subjects of adverbial clauses varies significantly across text types, overt and non-overt subjects do not differ significantly in their distribution within text types. This does not indicate, however, that text type does not influence the distribution of PROs in the adverbial clause. Results obtained from the PFR corpus have demonstrated that the distribution of non-overt subjects varies significantly across semantic domains of adverbial clauses: while non-overt subjects are used predominantly in clauses of condition, purpose, contrast and result, overt subjects are mostly used in concessive and causal clauses. In the LCMC corpus, the use of overt subjects confirms the results obtained from the PFR corpus, i.e. they occur significantly more frequently in clauses of concession, reason and exception. On the other hand, null subjects are used mostly in clauses of contrast and purpose. In contrast to the results obtained earlier from the PFR corpus, conditional clauses do not show a marked difference in the use of either subject type, though they were proved statistically to take significantly more PROs than overt subjects in the PFR corpus. One possible explanation is that text type has an influence on the distribution of PROs: in the five adverbial clause types which, as noted above, show a preference for a particular type of subject, the contrast between the distribution of overt and non-overt subjects is marked only in certain text categories of the LCMC corpus. This suggests that the effect of the semantic domains of adverbial clauses on the distribution of PROs, as shown in both the PFR and LCMC corpora, does indeed depend on text type. In other words, the distribution of PROs is a result of the semantic domains of adverbial clauses which is determined by text type.

Of the three distinct types of control of PRO identified in the PFR corpus (i.e. main clause control, control from previous context and no control), while main clause subject control slightly dominates in the corpus, these three kinds of control have more or less the same frequency of occurrence in the LCMC corpus. This averaging-out effect is brought about by a doubled number of PRO_{arb} used in the LCMC (i.e. 453 occurrences) compared to that in PFR (i.e. 222 cases). The preponderant use of PRO_{arb} is evident in text type E, which employs a huge number of conditional clauses to create a hypothetical situation for teaching a particular skill or hobby. As articles of this nature are not intended for a particular group of readers, it does not come as a surprise that non-overt subjects with an arbitrary interpretation occur obtrusively in category E. Thus more occurrences of PRO_{arb} are found in the LCMC corpus than in the PFR corpus, which is made up of press materials only. This demonstrates how text type influences the choice of the type of control of PRO in CACs.

Chapter Eight

Semantic Classes and Non-overt Subjects of CACs in the CALLHOME Mandarin Chinese Transcripts Corpus

8.1 Introduction

In this chapter, I will examine spoken and written registers' use of adverbial clauses by comparing the behaviour of adverbial clauses in the fifteen text categories of the LCMC corpus to that in a spoken corpus of Mandarin Chinese (cf. Wang, 1998 and 1999). Many studies have explored the differences between spoken and written language for a range of languages, but not Chinese.[1] Hence findings from a contrastive study of adverbial clauses between spoken and written Chinese can be used to re-evaluate claims made in the literature about the differences between spoken and written discourse derived from the study of other languages.

The spoken Mandarin Chinese corpus[2] used in this chapter is the CALLHOME Mandarin Chinese Transcripts Corpus[3] (Wheatley, 1996; Huang et al., 1997; Zhan et al., 1998; Cieri, 2000; Cieri and Liberman,

1 For example, Pellegrino and Scopesi, 1978; Ochs, 1979; Olson, 1980; Rubin, 1980; Green and Morgan, 1981; Kroll and Vann, 1981; Scibner and Cole, 1981; Akinnaso, 1982; Chafe, 1982, 1985, 1986a and 1986b; Lakoff, 1982; Ong, 1982; Tannen, 1982a, 1982b, 1982c and 1985; Hinofotis, 1983; Redeker, 1984; Biber 1986a, 1986b, 1988 and 1992; Halliday, 1987 and 1989.

2 There are some other spoken Mandarin Chinese corpora available at the LDC. These are *broadcast speech corpora* (e.g. 1997 Mandarin Broadcast News Speech, TDT2 Mandarin Audio Corpus and TDT3 Mandarin Audio), and *telephone speech corpora* (e.g. CALLFRIEND Mandarin Chinese-Mainland Dialect, CALLFRIEND Mandarin Chinese-Taiwan Dialect, Hub-5 Mandarin Telephone Speech Corpus and 2001 HUB5 Mandarin Evaluation).

3 See the corpus website <http://www.ldc.upenn.edu/Catalog/LDC96T16.html> (accessed 15 May 2012).

2000; Lo et al., 2000; Shu et al., 2000; Zhang and Yamamoto, 2001; Cieri et al., 2002; Honal and Schultz, 2003; Lo et al., 2003; Meng et al., 2004). It was built in 1996 and consists of some 300,000 words of short, contiguous, speech segments, ranging from 5 to 10 minutes and taken from 120 unscripted telephone conversations between native speakers of Mandarin Chinese.

XML elements of annotation	*Description*
Fa	Adverbial subordinate clause (see section 8.2.1)
Fam	Adverbial-main clause (see section 8.2.2)
PRO	Non-overt subject (PRO)
PROarb	Arbitrary PRO (i.e. the interpretation of PRO is arbitrary)
Cs	Subject controller (i.e. the subject NP of the main clause which is co-referential with PRO)
Co	Object controller (i.e. the object NP of the verb in the main clause which is co-referential with PRO)
Cc	Contextual controller (i.e. an NP in previous context which is co-referential with PRO)

Table 46: The annotation scheme of CALLHOME.

As with the PFR and LCMC corpora (see Chapter 5, section 5.2; Chapter 7, section 7.1.1), I adopted a problem-oriented tagging approach to CALLHOME to annotate a range of features in the corpus designed to suit my research purposes. The annotation scheme is described in Table 46. The purpose of annotating these features was to ease my investigation of adverbial clauses and the non-overt subjects occurring in these clauses. In the remainder of this chapter, I will discuss how I identified the adverbial clause in spoken Chinese (section 8.2). The adverbial clause is more complex in spoken Chinese than in written Chinese. I will also examine in CALLHOME the distribution of adverbial clauses across their semantic classes by comparison to the distribution pattern in the narrative texts of the LCMC corpus (section 8.3). To demonstrate any similarities/differences between speech and writing regarding the use of non-overt subjects in adverbial clauses, I will compare the distribution of subjects of the adverbial clauses in the CALLHOME and LCMC corpora (section 8.4). Section 8.5 will give a summary of the findings presented in this chapter.

8.2 Definition of adverbial clauses in CALLHOME

Given that in written language an adverbial clause and its modified main clause typically occur in the same sentence, the canonical form for an adverbial clause in spoken language is that, as illustrated in examples (1) and (2), the adverbial clause and the main clause are uttered by the same speaker in a single turn[4] (i.e. more or less equivalent to a single sentence in the written language). However, as will be demonstrated shortly, some of the adverbial clauses identified in the CALLHOME corpus do not conform to this canonical expression format; in conversation, some adverbial clauses are set apart from the main clause that they modify and placed in different turns from the modified main clause. Section 8.2.1 examines those atypical adverbial subordinate clauses in speech, and explains their occurrence by addressing the features characterising spoken discourse as discussed in the literature on the differences between spoken and written language. Section 8.2.2, on the other hand, focusses on an adverbial clause type that cannot be found in written Chinese and is referred to as *adverbial-main clause* in this work.

Example (1)

180.08 182.62 A1: <Fm2>我 这 倒 不 不 需要 打 # 工 #, <Fa2>因为 我 在 学 校 当 <English_T_A> 嘛</Fa2> .</Fm2>

180.08 182.62 A1: <Fm2>*wo* *zhe* *dao* *bu* *bu* *xuyao* *da# gong #,*
I this yet not not have.to work
<Fa2>*yinwei* *wo* *zai* *xuexiao* *dang* *<English_T_A>*
because I stay at.school work.as teaching.assistant
ma</Fa2> .</Fm2>
PART
"I don't have to work outside because I am now working as a teaching assistant in the university."

4 In conversation, a turn can be a word, a phrase, a clause and a full sentence spoken at a time by an interlocutor (Nofsinger, 1991: 80).

Example (2)

172.86 175.89 B: <Fm2>很 难 就是 请假，<Fa2>因为 PRO2 还 呀，不好意思 请假，因为 都 是</Fa2> --</Fm2>

172.86 175.89 B: <Fm2>*hen*	*nan*	*jiushi*	*qingjia*,	<Fa2>*yinwei*		
very	hard	that.is	take.leave	because		
PRO2	*hai*	*a,*	*buhaoyisi*	*qingjia*,	*yinwei*	*dou*
PRO	still	PART	feel.sorry	take.leave	because	all
shi</Fa2> --</Fm2>						
be						

"(I) find it difficult to take leave, because (I) feel guilty, because all are […]"

8.2.1 Adverbial subordinate clauses of spoken Chinese

8.2.1.1 Other speaker interrupts

There are three kinds of adverbial subordinate clause which are characterised by the way they are expressed in spoken discourse as identified in the CALLHOME corpus. Firstly, as shown in examples (3) and (4), speaker A/B[5] at one end of the conversation was interrupted by the speaker at the other end; the other speaker produced minimal responses (e.g. *mm*, *uh*, etc.) to signal speaker A/B to proceed. On the other hand, as can be seen in examples (5) and (6), speaker A/B was interrupted by the other speaker(s) who asked questions to clarify the situation described in the conversation. In either case, speaker A/B was interrupted at the boundary between the adverbial clause and the main clause and thus the adverbial clause and the main clause are expressed in separate turns by the same speaker.

5 In the examples used in this chapter, speakers are labelled as *A* (i.e. the person calling from the U.S.), and *B* (i.e. the person overseas). If there is more than one speaker at one end of the conversation (e.g. the telephone is passed around, or multiple extensions are in use), each new speaker is identified by a number: for example, B stands for the first speaker on side B; B1 stands for a different speaker; B2 stands for yet another speaker.

Example (3)

476.06 480.28 A: <Fm2>那么 呢，但是 回，从 &美国& 回国 一趟 太 远 了
机票 是 太 贵，因为 –

<Fm2>*name* *le* *danshi* *hui* *cong* *Meiguo*
well PART but go.back from America
huiguo *yitang* *tai* *yuan* *le* *jipiao* *shi* *tai*
go.home once too far.away PART air.ticket be too
gui *yinwei* –
expensive because

"But it's a long distance for me to travel from the U.S. to the mainland, and the air ticket is expensive, because –"

476.40 476.75 B: 哎 .

ai
PART

"Uh."

480.55 483.82 A: <Fa2>&日本& 毕竟 很 近 嘛 ,&美& ,&美国& 太 远 了，
它 机票 很 贵</Fa2> .</Fm2>

<Fa2>*Riben* *bijing* *hen* *jin* *ma* *Mei*
Japan nevertheless very near PART America
Meiguo *tai* *yuan* *le* *jipiao* *hen*
America too far.away PART air.ticket very
gui</Fa2></Fm2>
expensive

"Japan is closer anyway. America is too far away from mainland China. The air ticket is expensive."

Example (4)

216.72 221.43 B: 恢复，就 一下子 去 了 嘛 ,<Fm2>我 是 心里 好象 很 难
接受 这 种 事实 .

huifu *jiu* *yixiazi* *qu* *le* *ma* <Fm2>*wo*
recover then suddenly pass.away PERF PART I
shi *xinli* *haoxiang* *hen* *nan* *jieshou* *zhe*
be in.spirit as.if very hard accept this
zhong *shishi*
CL fact

"(He) recovered and then passed away all of a sudden. I felt overwhelmed with grief and could not come to terms with his death."

221.46 221.85 A: 嗯 .
ng
PART
"Mm."

221.62 223.75 B: <Fa2>因为 我 原来 计划 暑假 里 嘛，跟 他 嘛，
<Fa2>*yinwei* *wo* *yuanlai* *jihua* *shujia* *li*
because I originally plan summer.vacation in
ma *gen* *ta* *ma*
PART with him PART
"Because this summer I planned to [...]"

224.02 227.71 B: 嗯，搞搞 就 吃 些 西瓜 啊，搞搞 绿豆 汤 啊，陪陪 他 啊</Fa2> .</Fm2>
<Fa2>*ng* *gaogao* *jiu* *chi* *xie* *xigua* *a*
PART make then eat some melon PART
gaogao *lüdou* *tang* *a* *peipei* *ta*
make green.beans soup PART accompany him
a</Fa2></Fm2>
PART
"mm, share some melon with him, make green bean soup for him, and be his companion."

Example (5)

714.44 715.94 A: <Fm2>经济 上 要 损失 一点 了 哈 ?
<Fm2>*jingji* *shang* *yao* *xunshi* *yidian*
economy aspect have.to lose a.bit
le *ha*
PART PART
"You have to spend some money. Haha."

716.56 718.38 B2: 哎，反正 也 无所谓 啦 . {laugh}
ai ***fanzheng*** ***ye*** ***wusuowei*** ***le***
PART anyway yet does.not.matter PART
"Oh, it doesn't matter anyway."

718.13 720.28 A: {laugh}

120.09 121.21 B: 没问题，是不是 啊？
meiwenti ***shibushi*** ***a***
no.problem is.it PART
"It isn't a problem, is it?"

120.17 124.36 A: <Fa2>因为 他 现在 就是说，现在 是 夏天 嘛，你 就 给 他 有 个 毛巾 被，什么的</Fa2> .</Fm2>
<Fa2>*yinwei* *ta* *xianzai* *jiushishuo* *xianzai* *shi*
because he now so.to.speak at.present be
xiatian *ma* *ni* *jiu* *gei* *ta* *you* *ge* *maojinbei*
summer PART you then for him have CL blanket
shenmede</Fa2></Fm2>
whatever
"Because it's summer so you'd better buy him a blanket or whatever."

Example (6)

532.06 534.86 B: <Fm2>并且 看 了 你们 的 照片，我们 非常 高兴 .
<Fm2>*bingqie* *kan* *le* *nimen* *de*
additionally read PERF your GEN
zhaopian *women* *feichang* *gaoxing*
photos we very happy
"And, after we saw your photos, we were very happy."

534.83 535.46 A: 怎么样？
zenmeyang
why
"Why?"

536.15 540.44 B: <Fa2>因为 那个 照片 看上 去 好象 在 一 个 非常 美丽 的 田野 里面</Fa2> .</Fm2>
<Fa2>*yinwei* *nage* *zhaopian* *kanshangqu* *haoxiang*
because those photos look.like as.if
zai *yi* *ge* *feichang* *meili* *de* *tianye*
in one CL very beautiful DE forest
limian</Fa2></Fm2>
inside
"Because it seemed to us that the photos were taken in front of a magnificent forest."

8.2.1.2 Speaker pauses

The second kind of adverbial subordinate clause found in the corpus demonstrates *fragmentation* in speech. As illustrated in examples (7) and (8), in spite of experiencing no interruption from the other speaker, speaker A/B still completed the utterance containing both the adverbial clause and the main clause in several turns, rather than in a single turn as occurs in the canonical form of the adverbial subordinate clause aforementioned. In comparing spoken and written language, Chafe (1982) observes that while written language is characterised by a high degree of integration, spoken language is characterised by fragmentation.[6] The difference between integration and fragmentation lies in the notion of *idea units* (Chafe 1985: 106–108; McNeill and Duncan, 2000; Spelman-Miller, 2002; Luoma, 2003: 12). An idea unit contains all the information a speaker/writer intends to convey in a piece of spoken/written discourse. The idea units in the written language are relatively longer and more complex than those in the spoken language. Writers tend to integrate more information into a single idea unit by means of morphosyntactic devices such as nominalisations, genitive subjects and objects, participles, attributive adjectives, conjoined phrases, series, sequences of prepositional phrases, complement clauses, and relative clauses as identified by Chafe (1982: 39–44), while speakers are less likely to use them because of the spontaneous and unplanned nature of conversation (Luoma, 2003: 13). Consequently, the idea units in the spoken language are typically expressed in the form of fragments or fragmented grammatical structures, reflecting in part the spurt-like nature of a speaker's thoughts. Thus the adverbial clause and the main clause in conversation tend to be expressed in separate turns rather than in a single turn.

6 The distinction between integration and fragmentation was further elaborated in Chafe and Tannen (1987), supported in Flowerdew (1993) and applied in Chevalier (2004).

Example (7)

569.78 572.86 A: <Fm2>反正 我 到 现在 吧，我 也 没 跟 他 正面 谈 这 件 事情，
<Fm2>*fanzheng wo dao xianzai ba wo ye*
anyway I up.to now PART I also
mei gen ta zhengmian tan zhe jian shiqing
have.not with him directly discuss.about this CL matter
"Anyway, I haven't talked to him directly about the whole thing up to now."

573.05 579.23 A: <Fa2>因为 我 那天 我 那天 打电话 我 我 我 给 &陈& 先 生 说，他 讲 说，这个 你 现在 先 别 谈</Fa2> ,</Fm2>
<Fa2>*yinwei wo natian wo natian da dianhua wo*
because I that.day I that.day dial telephone I
wo wo gei Chen xiansheng shuo ta jiang
I I for Chen Mr say he speak
shuo zhege ni xianzai bie tan</Fa2></Fm2>
say this you for.now do.not talk.about
"Because I phoned Mr Chen that day and he said I shouldn't talk about it then."

Example (8)

585.22 586.53 B: <Fm2>你 把 我的 信 啊，
<Fm2>*ni ba wo de xin a*
you BA my GEN letter PART
"My letter, you […]"

586.78 588.89 B: 看 个 两 遍，好不好？
kan ge liang bian haobuhao
read CL two times can.you
"read it twice, can you?"

588.86 592.22 B: <Fa2>因为 你 有的时候，把 我 信 上 的 意思 啊，没 闹 懂</Fa2> .</Fm2>
<Fa2>*yinwei ni youdeshihou ba wo xinshang de*
because you sometimes BA my letter DE
yisi a mei naodong</Fa2></Fm2>
meaning PART have.not understand
"Because sometimes you can't quite catch my meaning in the letter."

8.2.1.3 Other speaker main clause

The third kind of adverbial subordinate clause in spoken Chinese demonstrates yet another feature of speech i.e. *involvement* (Chafe, 1982 and 1986b; Oviatt and Cohen, 1989; Flowerdew, 1993). As shown in examples (9) and (10), speaker A uttered the main clause and speaker B uttered the adverbial clause or vice versa. In these cases, the adverbial clause and the main clause are in separate turns produced by two different interlocutors whereas in the second kind of adverbial subordinate clause, both the adverbial clause and the main clause are in separate turns produced by the same speaker. Biber et al. (1999: 771) refer to this phenomenon as "other speaker main clause" and acknowledge it as a feature specific to conversation as well as to dialog in fiction, where "speakers will co-construct clauses or clarify each other's speech so that one speaker adds an adverbial to another speaker's utterance". The emergence of this type of adverbial clause in spoken Chinese can be explained by the feature of involvement commonly occurring in speech. There are three different types of involvement associated with conversation identified by Chafe (1986b: 116–118): (i) involvement of the speaker with *himself/herself* in the use of first person pronouns; (ii) involvement of the speaker with the *hearer* by showing his/her concern for the dynamics of interaction with another person; (iii) involvement of the speaker with the *subject matter* by expressing a keen interest in the discussion topic. As can be seen from the following examples, the speakers demonstrate an acknowledgement of the flow of information by supplying the information needed i.e. the adverbial clauses of reason, in an attempt to make sure that communication channel is functioning well. These examples are therefore illustrations of the second kind of involvement as noted above.

Example (9)

292.68 295.00 A: <Fm2>那 &中国& [noise] 可能 开车 是 很 难 , 我 想 .

<Fm2>*na* *Zhongguo* *keneng* *kaiche* *shi* *hen nan*

that China perhaps driving be very hard

wo xiang

I think

"So it's hard to have a chance to drive in mainland China."

295.87 296.33 A: 现在 ((你)) -
xianzai *ni*
at.present you
"Now, you [...]"
296.12 297.71 B: <Fa2>因为 人 太 多 了</Fa2>, 哈 .</Fm2>
<Fa2>*yinwei* *ren* *tai* *duo* *le*</Fa2> *ha*</Fm2>
because people too many PART PART
"Because nowadays the population is huge."

Example (10)

530.42 532.95 B: <Fm2>反正 现在 就 做 个 老板，挺 稳当 的 这 种 .
<Fm2>*fanzheng* *xianzai* *jiu* *zuo* *ge* *laoban*
anyway nowadays now be CL shop.owner
ting *wendang* *de* *zhe* *zhong*
quite safe PART this kind
"Anyway it's quite safe nowadays to be an owner of a shop."
533.00 536.04 A: {laugh}
534.47 537.97 B: {laugh} 不 象 那时候，那么 焦头烂额 .
bu *xiang* *nashihou* *name* *jiaotoulane*
not like at.that.moment that risky
"It won't be as risky as it used to be."
537.93 541.86 A: 呃 . 对 . <Fa2>因为 都 熟 了 么 嚎，都 都 弄 顺 了 就 好 了</Fa2> .</Fm2>
e *dui* <Fa2>*yinwei* *dou* *shou* *le* *me*
PART right because all familiar PFRF PART
hao *dou* *dou* *long* *xun* *le*
PART all all work.out smooth PERF
jiu *hao* *le*</Fa2></Fm2>
then goodPART
"Oh, yes, because we are more familiar with it and things work out quite well."

8.2.2 Adverbial-main clauses of spoken Chinese

While an adverbial clause is always subordinated to the main clause of the same sentence (see section 8.2.1), an *adverbial-main clause* is not associated with a superordinate/main clause. The main clause is not explicitly stated in the discourse and can be inferred from the context, as illustrated in examples (11) and (12). Given that no evidence of their occurrence can be found in the two written Chinese corpora used in this book, adverbial-main clauses are considered as being a feature specific to spoken Chinese. These clauses, however, rarely occur in my data. Of the 1,139 adverbial clauses identified in my corpus, 33 instances are adverbial-main clauses, as opposed to 1,106 adverbial subordinate clauses.

Example (11)

203.84 207.01 A: 如果 我 现在 马上 又 能 再 给 你 另外 找 到 房子 的话，

ruguo wo xianzai mashang you neng zai
if I now at.once again can again
gei ni lingwai zhao dao fangzi dehua
for you alternatively find COMP house so.to.speak
"If I can find another apartment for you right away,"

206.99 209.47 A: 你 现在 能 不能 搬？还是 说，你 必需 在 那 住 一 个 月？

ni xianzai neng bu neng ban
you now can not can move.house
haishi shuo ni bixu zai na
or say you necessary in that.place
zhu yi ge yue
live one CL month
"can you move house now? Or you need to stay in your place for one month?"

210.93 214.35 B1: **<Fam2>**因为 他 定金 付 一 个 月，跟 他 讲 是 一 个 月 .**</Fam2>**

<Fam2>*yinwei ta dingjin fu yi ge yue gen*
because his deposit pay one CL month with

ta jiang shi yi ge yue</Fam2>
him say be one CL month
"Because his deposit was paid for one month. We agreed the deposit was for one month."

214.39 216.64 A: 呃，行，我 明白 你 意思 了 .{breath_noise} 嗯 .
{breath_noise}
e xing wo mingbai ni yisi le
PART okay I understand your meaning PART
ng
PART
"Okay, I understand now."

215.79 217.50 B1: 哎，我 看 你 这样子 好 了，
ai wo kan ni zheyangzi hao le
PART I see you this.way good PART
"Uh, that's it."

217.46 218.02 A: 嗯，
ng
PART
"Yeah."

Example (12)

239.30 242.76 A: &南京& 据说 有的人 很 热，到 四十 度，死 了 十 十几 个人 嗷，
Nanjing jushuo youderen hen re dao sishidu
Nanjing hearsay someone very hot reach 40.degrees.C
si le shi shiji ge ren ao
die PERF ten some.ten CL person PART
"It was said that many people in Nanjing felt very hot when the temperature reached 40 degrees Celsius. Some ten people died."

243.96 249.03 B1: <Fm2> &南京& 好象 我们 觉得 还好，前一阵子 说 是 比较 热，但是 <Fa2>我们 因为，
<Fm2>*Nanjing haoxiang women juede hai*
Nanjing look.like we think quite
Hao qianyizhenzi shuo shi bijiao re
Good recently say be comparatively hot

danshi <Fa2>*women* *yinwei*
but we because
"We are alright in Nanjing. Recently, it has been rather hot here but because we […]"

249.46 250.02 A: 不 出去，
bu chuqu
not go.out
"didn't go out."

250.05 253.86 B1: 不怎么 出去，在 家里，哎，我们 家 好象 房子 也 不怎么 热</Fa2>,</Fm2>
bu zenme chuqu zai jiali ai women
not somehow go.out at home PART our
jia haoxiang fangzi ye buzenme
home perhaps house yet not.really
re</Fa2></Fm2>
hot
"(We) didn't go out often and stayed at home. We didn't feel hot in the house."

251.80 252.13 A: 噢，
ao
PART
"Mm."

253.53 255.70 A: **<Fam2>**因为 我 看 报纸 上 说 有 十几 个人，**</Fam2>**
<Fam2>*yinwei wo kan baozhishang shuo you*
because I read newspaper say have
*shiji ge ren***</Fam2>**
some.ten CL people
"Because I learned from the newspaper that there were about ten people,"

254.40 254.68 B1: 这个 -
zhege
this
"About this […]"

In example (11), speaker A offered to help speaker B1 to find a house but B1 was reluctant to move out of his/her present house as one-month deposit had been paid. Prior to the occurrence of the adverbial-main clause (enclosed in the <Fam> element), A asked B1 whether s/he could move house as soon as another house was available. B1 did not give a clear indication that s/he could not move house (i.e. the main clause) and rather, explained why s/he could not do so (i.e. the adverbial clause of reason). Since the main clause is not explicitly expressed and it can be inferred from the context, the adverbial clause in this example is taken as an illustration of the adverbial-main clause. Example (12) is more complicated than example (11) because the main clause in the former is less obvious than that in the latter. Speakers A and B1 discussed about the recent soaring temperature in China's eastern city of Nanjing. The adverbial-main clause in this example is a causal clause which expresses the reason why A raised the issue and discussed and clarified the situation with B1. The main clause which states the consequence i.e. the clarification of the news about the heat wave is not explicitly spelled out and can only be inferred from the sequence of the information delivered in the context and from an interlocutor's general knowledge of the world.

To conclude this section, an adverbial clause in spoken Chinese basically takes one of the following two forms. First, an adverbial subordinate clause is expressed by the same speaker as in the main clause (i.e. *other speaker interrupts/speaker pauses*), or it is expressed by a different speaker from the main clause (i.e. *other speaker main clause*); in either case, the adverbial clause and the main clause are uttered in separate turns rather than in a single turn, in contrast to the fact that in written Chinese both the adverbial clause and the main clause occur in a single sentence. Second, an adverbial-main clause is not associated with a main clause which can be inferred from the context and is commonly omitted. In what follows, I consider the distribution of adverbial clauses in the CALLHOME corpus and report the similarities and differences between spoken and written Chinese in their use of adverbial clauses.

8.3 Distribution of adverbial clauses in CALLHOME

As discussed in the previous chapter (see sections 7.2.1 to 7.2.3), some text categories of the LCMC corpus show a marked preference for using a certain type of adverbial clause: (i) clauses of condition are typically used in category E (skills/trades/hobbies); (ii) clauses of purpose are commonly used in category E (*ibid*) and category F (popular lore); (iii) clauses of cause/reason and result are typically used in category D (religion) and category J (scientific academic prose). These general patterns may throw up some important differences in the behaviour of adverbial clauses in written and spoken Chinese. They may also reveal the differences between two major discourse types in written Chinese i.e. narrative and expository texts, as demonstrated below.

8.3.1 Narrative texts vs. expository texts in LCMC

In the LCMC corpus, *narrative text types* include the five fiction categories[7] plus humour, biography and press reportage whereas *expository text types* include reports/official documents, academic prose, skills/trades/hobbies, press reviews, press editorials, religion and popular lore (McEnery and Xiao, 2003: 369). Log-likelihood (LL) tests indicate that in the LCMC corpus, the differences between the distribution of adverbial clauses in narrative and expository texts are highly statistically significant (see Table 47).[8] Narrative texts are typically characterised by a relatively lower frequency of clauses of condition, purpose, result, cause/reason and contrast than expository texts.

7 The five fiction categories in the LCMC corpus are general fiction, mystery and detective fiction, science fiction, adventure and martial arts fiction and romantic fiction.

8 For one degree of freedom (henceforth d.f.), the calculated LL score must be greater than 10.83 for a difference to be statistically significant at $p<0.001$.

Semantic classes of CACs	Frequency in *narrative* texts (i.e. categories K-R, A & G) of LCMC	Frequency in *expository* texts (i.e. categories B-F, H & J) of LCMC	LL score (1 d.f., $p<0.001$)
Clauses of time	0	2	2.72
Clauses of cause/reason	**151**	**311**	**52.80**
Clauses of purpose	**9**	**99**	**85.62**
Clauses of result	**32**	**114**	**74.43**
Clauses of preference	6	7	0.05
Clauses of contrast	**71**	**139**	**20.82**
Clauses of addition	13	4	5.24
Clauses of exception	30	13	7.32
Clauses of condition	**428**	**773**	**92.41**
Clauses of concession	363	413	2.14
Clauses of inference	1	2	0.32
Total:	1,104	1,877	184.63

Table 47: Distribution of CACs in narrative and expository texts of LCMC.

8.3.2 Narrative texts of written Chinese vs. spoken Chinese

As narrative texts, notably fiction and humour, basically involve dialogue, they bear more resemblance to conversation than expository texts (Biber, 1988: 135–142). I therefore hypothesise that the distribution pattern of the semantic classes of adverbial clauses in narrative texts of written Chinese can also be found in spoken Chinese, when contrasted with expository texts. To test this hypothesis, I considered and contrasted the distribution of the eleven semantic types of adverbial clauses in spoken Chinese and that in expository texts.

Adverbial clause types	CALLHOME		LCMC		LL score
	Frequency	Freq. per 100K tokens	Frequency	Freq. per 100K tokens	(1 d.f., $p<0.001$)
Time	0	0	2	0	1.05
Cause/reason	**606**	**202**	**462**	**46**	**558.54**
Purpose	**0**	**0**	**108**	**11**	**56.67**
Result	**0**	**0**	**146**	**15**	**76.61**
Preference	1	0	13	1	2.55
Contrast	**0**	**0**	**210**	**21**	**110.19**
Addition	2	1	17	2	2.00
Exception	12	4	43	4	0.05
Condition	**476**	**159**	**1,201**	**120**	**25.34**
Concession	**42**	**14**	**776**	**78**	**199.14**
Inference	0	0	3	0	1.57
Total:	1,139	380	2,981	298	46.43

Table 48: Distribution of CACs in CALLHOME and LCMC.

As can be seen in Table 48, temporal adverbial clauses are non-existent in the CALLHOME corpus. This finding corroborates what I initially observed, i.e. that adverbial clauses of time are rare in the single genre of journalistic writing expressed by the PFR corpus (i.e. one occurrence; see Chapter Five, section 5.3.1) as well as in the fifteen written genres of the LCMC corpus (i.e. two occurrences; see Chapter Seven, section 7.2). Given that adverbial clauses of time are barely used in both the CALLHOME corpus and the two written Chinese corpora, temporal adverbial clauses are rare in both spoken and written Chinese. However, there are a significantly greater number of adverbial clauses found in CALLHOME than in the LCMC.[9] This finding is surprising as it is not in conformance with previous claims regarding differences between spoken and written language in that spoken language avoids elaborate syntactic relations among clauses such as subordination (O'Donnell, 1974; Kroll, 1977; Ochs, 1979: 66–68; Finegan, 1982;

9 The calculated LL value is 46.43, greater than the critical value for significance, 10.83, with 1 d.f. at $p<0.001$.

Tannen, 1982a: 3; Beaman, 1984; Gumperz et al., 1984; Chafe and Danielewicz, 1987: 87).[10] In other words, there is a strong tendency for speakers to produce simple, coordinated, clauses and to avoid the more elaborate interclausal relations found in writing. This tendency is tied to the disparate operative constraints associated with the two discourse modes. As Chafe and Danielewicz (1987: 86) note, speakers have to make choices very quickly when deciding what they want to say in spontaneous conversation, whereas writers have time to deliberate and even to revise their choices when they are not satisfied. Hence the relatively higher frequency of Chinese adverbial clauses in the CALLHOME spoken Chinese corpus in comparison to the LCMC written Chinese corpus is surprising. One possible explanation for this is that certain adverbial clause types are typically more common in spoken discourse than in written discourse, namely clauses of reason and clauses of condition, resulting in a greater number of adverbial clauses identified in CALLHOME. As can be seen in Table 48, the clauses of reason (i.e. 606 occurrences or 53%) and clauses of condition (i.e. 476 occurrences or 42%) account for 95 percent of the adverbial clauses in CALLHOME, while the two kinds of adverbial clauses make up just 56 percent of the adverbial clauses in the LCMC.

10 Poole and Field (1976), however, found that more subordinate clauses were used in speaking than in writing. Their findings may be due to the highly structured nature of the spoken data. Their speech samples were obtained individually from first-year undergraduates, who probably took the experiment very seriously, in an interview which contained questions on secondary school and university experience (e.g. *what are your impressions of life in a residential college?*). Their spoken data is therefore highly structured and exhibits more of the features of written language than that of spoken language.

Adverbial clause types	CALLHOME		LCMC (expository texts)		LL score
	Frequency	Freq. per 100K tokens	Frequency	Freq. per 100K tokens	(1 d.f., $p<0.001$)
Time	0	0	2	0	1.86
Cause/reason	**606**	**202**	**311**	**61**	**312.77**
Purpose	**0**	**0**	**99**	**20**	**92.18**
Result	**0**	**0**	**114**	**23**	**106.14**
Preference	1	0	7	1	2.47
Contrast	**0**	**0**	**139**	**27**	**129.42**
Addition	2	1	4	1	0.04
Exception	12	4	13	3	1.21
Condition	*476*	*159*	*773*	*153*	*0.42*
Concession	**42**	**14**	**413**	**82**	**187.42**
Inference	0	0	2	0	1.86
Total:	1,139	380	1,877	371	0.38

Table 49: Distribution of CACs in CALLHOME and LCMC (expository texts).

The wide use of causal and conditional clauses in spoken Chinese attaches credence to the claim by Biber et al. (1999: 820) that there are considerable differences in the preferred semantic categories of adverbial clauses across four registers in English, namely conversation, fiction, news and academic prose. They correctly observe that conditional clauses are most commonly used in conversation and causal clauses are common only in conversation. Biber et al. (*ibid*: 786) attribute conversation's greater use of reason and condition clauses to its concern for participants' actions in that these two kinds of adverbial clause often clarify the reasons for or conditions on an interlocutor's actions. Altenberg (1984: 39ff.) also found a preference for causal expressions in spoken data from the London-Lund Corpus as compared with written data from the Lancaster-Oslo/Bergen Corpus. The telephone conversations contained in the CALLHOME corpus centre on the life of the people who live/study/work overseas. Although speakers were not given any guideline concerning what they should talk about, most of them called family members or close friends. When these overseas people speak to their parents and/or friends, they usually describe how they get on in a foreign country. The talks are mostly concerned with their daily experiences; under what circumstances (i.e. adverbial clauses of condition) and for what reasons (i.e. adverbial clauses of reason) do they do things. In other words, speakers have to clarify and explain their actions frequently to the parties at the other end of the conversation. This explains why clauses of cause/reason and condition are used relatively more frequently in CALLHOME than in the LCMC in general (see Table 48), and in expository written texts in particular (see Table 49), although the occurrence of conditional clauses in CALLHOME does not differ significantly from that in expository texts.[11] However, what is at issue here is not the differing distribution of adverbial clauses between the CALLHOME corpus and the expository texts but the different use of adverbial clauses between conversation and narrative texts. As can be seen in Figure 12, clauses of condition occur significantly more frequently in spoken texts than in narrative texts.[12]

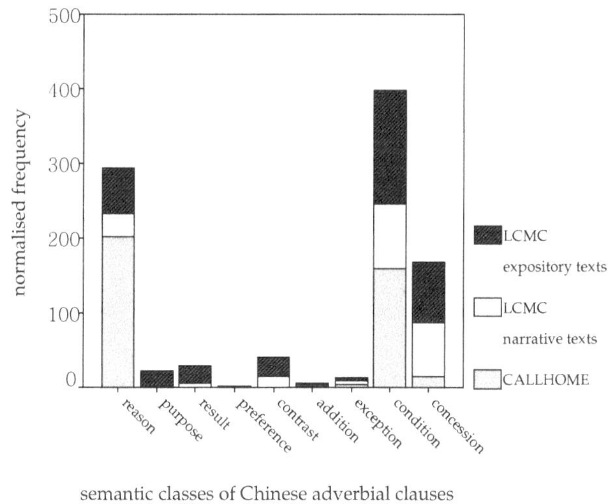

Figure 12: Contrasting CACs in LCMC and CALLHOME.

11 Clauses of condition occur as frequently in spoken Chinese (i.e. 159 frequencies per 100K tokens) as in expository texts (i.e. 153 frequencies per 100K tokens). See Table 49.

12 When comparing the frequencies of conditional clauses in both the CALLHOME corpus (i.e. 476 raw frequencies or 159 frequencies per 100K tokens) and the narrative texts of the LCMC corpus (i.e. 428 raw frequencies or 87 frequencies per 100K tokens), the LL score (82.14) is greater than the critical value for significance, 10.83, with 1 d.f. at $p<0.001$.

As mentioned earlier (see section 8.3.1), clauses of reason and condition are used significantly less frequently in narrative texts than in expository texts of written Chinese (see Table 47). In this respect, conversation does not resemble narrative texts by virtue of its disproportionate use of causal and conditional clauses. In stark contrast, clauses of purpose, result and contrast do not occur in the CALLHOME corpus, as shown in Table 49. This finding in part proves my hypothesis that conversation shows a similar distribution pattern of adverbial clauses to narrative texts in which these three adverbial clause types are markedly less frequent than other adverbial types. In the following section, I will discuss the distribution of non-overt subjects of Chinese adverbial clauses by comparison to the findings from the analysis undertaken on the basis of the LCMC corpus. I will then discuss the similarities and differences between spoken and written Chinese with regard to their choice of subject in adverbial clauses.

8.4 Distribution of non-overt subjects of CACs in CALLHOME

8.4.1 Type of control

Whilst non-overt subjects of Chinese adverbial clauses appear less frequently in CALLHOME than in the LCMC (see Table 50),[13] these non-overt subjects are typically controlled by (i.e. co-referential with) an NP in the context: contextual controllers account for 51% of the referential controllers that appear in the corpus (see Figure 13). In other words, control from previous context is the dominant type of control for PRO in adverbial clauses of spoken Chinese. As Ochs (1979: 62–64) and Tannen (1982a: 3) correctly observe, spoken discourse makes maximal use of context by which meaning is implied rather than stated,

13 The frequencies given in the table were standardised to a common base of 100,000 word tokens.

whereas written discourse makes background information explicit.[14] In written Chinese, on the other hand, the non-overt subjects of adverbial clauses typically co-refer to either a main clause subject (33%) or an NP in the context (31%) for their interpretation. They can also, however, co-refer freely (34%) i.e. their interpretation is arbitrary. Given that speakers rely on context more than writers do, it is hardly surprising that control of PRO from previous context is a prominent feature associated with adverbial clauses in spoken Chinese.

Chinese corpora	Main clause control		Control from outside main clause	No control i.e. arbitrary interpretation	No. of PROs
	Subject control	*Object control*			
LCMC	44 (*33%*)	3 (*2%*)	42 (*31%*)	45 (*34%*)	134 (*100%*)
CALLHOME	24 (*30%*)	2 (*3%*)	40 (*51%*)	13 (*16%*)	79 (*100%*)

Table 50: Types of control of PRO in LCMC and CALLHOME.

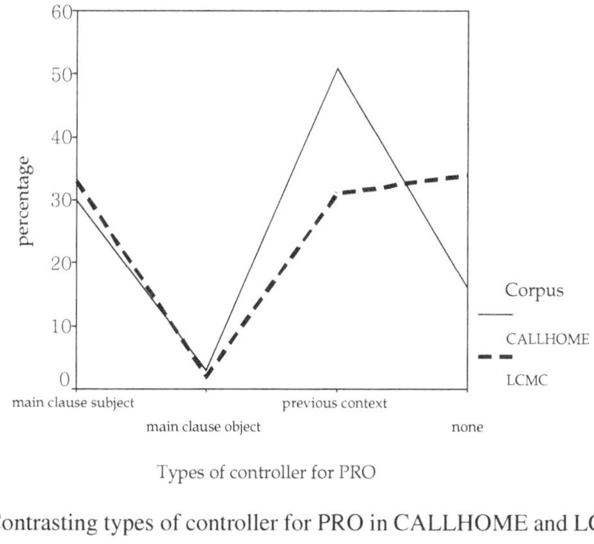

Figure 13: Contrasting types of controller for PRO in CALLHOME and LCMC.

14 Yet Rader (1982) reports that imaginative fiction relies heavily on context: it is maximally dependent on the contribution of background information on the part of the reader who works to make sense out of the story, using the same general principles by which s/he makes sense out of the everyday conversation. As written fiction's authors can count on readers to work to find out what is going on in the story, they do not have to spell everything out (cf. Widdowson, 1979: 174ff.).

8.4.2 Distribution of subjects across adverbial semantic classes

In Table 51, the LL scores indicate that the distribution of subjects varies significantly across adverbial semantic classes. As illustrated in examples (13) to (15) respectively, clauses of cause/reason, exception and condition take strikingly more overt subjects than non-overt ones in the CALLHOME corpus.[15] The relatively high frequencies of overt subjects in clauses of cause/reason and exception echo the findings obtained from the LCMC corpus in that these two types of adverbial clause favour non-overt subjects more strongly than other adverbials. This allows me to generalise a conclusion that overt subjects are commonly used in clauses of reason and exception in both spoken and written Chinese.

Semantic types of CACs	**Subject types of CACs**		**LL score**
	Overt NP	***PRO***	**(1 d.f., *p*<0.05)**
Clauses of time	0	0	0.00
Clauses of cause/reason	**551**	**55**	**471.29**
Clauses of purpose	0	0	0.00
Clauses of result	0	0	0.00
Clauses of preference	1	0	1.39
Clauses of contrast	0	0	0.00
Clauses of addition	1	1	0.00
Clauses of exception	**10**	**2**	**5.82**
Clauses of condition	**322**	**154**	**60.59**
Clauses of concession	19	23	0.38
Clauses of inference	0	0	0.00
Total:	904	235	419.39

Table 51: Distribution of subjects in CALLHOME across semantic classes of CACs.

15 The LL values for clauses of cause/reason, exception and condition are greater than 3.841, the critical value for significance with 1 d.f. at $p<0.05$.

Example (13)

588.64 594.86 A: <Fm2><Fa2>她们 因为 对 这个 粤 式 点心 很 感兴趣</Fa2> , 所以 就 她 也 建议 她 妈妈 在 家里 , 怕 她 妈妈 在家 , 退休 在家 没事儿 做 .</Fm2>

588.64 594.86 A: <Fm2><Fa2>*tamen* ***yinwei*** *dui* *zhege* *Yue*
they because as.for this Cantonese
shi *dianxin* *hen* *ganxingqu*</Fa2> , *suoyi* *jiu* *ta*
style dumplings very be.interested so then she
ye *jianyi* *ta* *mama* *zai* *jiali* , *pa* *ta* *mama*
also suggest her mother at home fear her mother
zaijia , *tuixiu* *zaijia* *meishier* *zuo* .</Fm2>
at.home retire at.home nothing do
"Because they are very interested in Cantonese cuisine, they suggest to their mother that she learn it at home for fear that she has nothing to do after she retires."

Example (14)

381.48 386.27 A: <Fm8>她 也 , 她 也 从 没有 明确 表示 过 , <Fa8>她 只是 说 ,

388.10 391.80 A: 她 只是 说 工作 重要 啦 , 她 只是 说 工作 还是 蛮 重要 的</Fa8> .</Fm8>

381.48 386.27 A: <Fm8>*ta* *ye* , *ta* *ye* *cong* *meiyou* *mingque*
she also she also ever have.not clearly
biaoshiguo , <Fa8>*ta* ***zhishi*** *shuo* ,
indicate she except.that say
"She was not quite explicit about it, except that [...]"

388.10 391.80 A: *ta* *zhishi* *shuo* *gongzuo* *zhongyao* *le* ,
she except.that say work important PART
ta *zhishi* *shuo* *gongzuo* *haishi* *man*
she except.that say job still quite
zhongyao *de*</Fa8> .</Fm8>
important PART
"[...] except that she said her job was important to her."

Example (15)

406.93 409.58 A: <Fm9><Fa9>他们 如果，他们 今年 回去 的话</Fa9>，他们 说 你 可以 跟 他们 一块儿 回来 .</Fm9>

406.93 409.58 A: <Fm9><Fa9>*tamen* **ruguo** , *tamen* *jinnian* *huiqu*
they if they this.year go.back
dehua</Fa9> , *tamen* *shuo* *ni* *keyi* *gen* *tamen*
so.to.speak they say you can with them
yikuaier *huilai* .</Fm9>
together return
"If they came back this year, they said you could go with them."

Spoken and written Chinese, however, do show some differences in the distribution of subjects in other adverbial semantic domains. Firstly, while the contrast between overt subject and PRO is marked in clauses of purpose and contrast in the LCMC, no evidence of such a marked contrast can be found in CALLHOME. As can be seen in Figure 14, the two kinds of adverbial clause are not used in spoken Chinese (cf. section 8.3.2), thereby precluding any comparison between overt and non-overt subjects in these adverbial clause types. Secondly, the two discourse modes of Chinese show a strikingly dissimilar distribution of subjects in clauses of concession; spoken Chinese does not exhibit a preponderance of overt subjects in concessive clauses as written Chinese does, as illustrated in Figure 15. The explanation of this unexpected result lies in the occurrences of the adverbial clauses of concession marked by the adverbial subordinator 不管 *buguan* "no matter" in CALLHOME. As can be seen from Table 52, those adverbial clauses marked by the subordinating conjunction *buguan* take more PROs than overt NP subjects as illustrated in example (16), whereas the reverse happens in the adverbial clauses introduced by other concessive subordinating conjunctions such as *suiran* and *jinguan*.

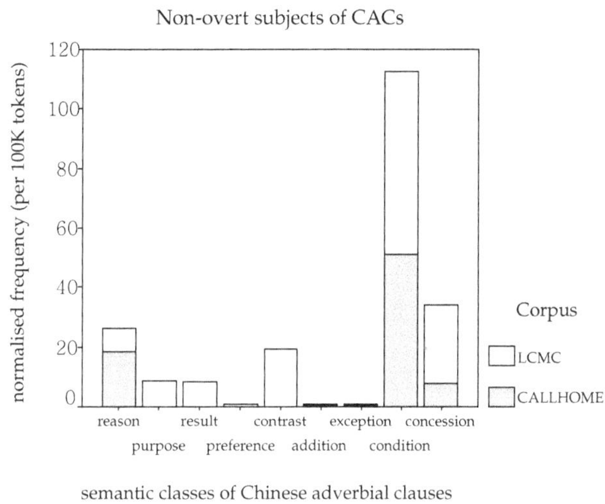

Figure 14: Contrasting non-overt subjects in CALLHOME and LCMC.

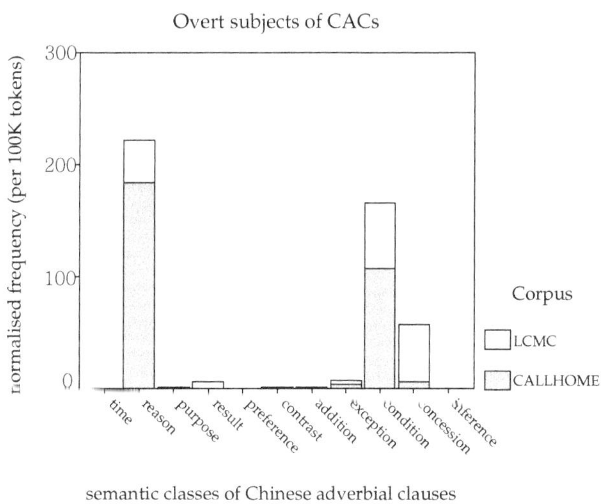

Figure 15: Contrasting overt subjects in CALLHOME and LCMC.

Adverbial subordinators of clauses of concession	**PRO**	**Overt NP subject**
纵 *zong*	0	0
纵使 *zongshi*	0	0
虽然 *suiran*	6	11
尽管 *jinguan*	0	2
虽 *sui*	0	0
虽说 *suishuo*	0	0
无论是 *wulunshi*	0	0
无论 *wulun*	1	0
不论是 *bulunshi*	0	0
不论 *bulun*	1	1
不管 ***buguan***	**16**	**4**
任 *ren*	0	0
甭管 *bengguan*	0	0

Table 52: Contrasting the distribution of subjects in clauses of concession.

Example (16)

664.06 666.13 B: 我 总 的 讲 来，我 觉得 父母 还是 引导 <Cc10>我们 </Cc10>,

666.08 668.54 B: {breath_noise} <Fm10><Fa10>不管 **PRO10** 怎么样 讲</Fa10>, 他们 买 了 很 多 书 给 我们 看 .</Fm10>

664.06 666.13 B: *wo* *zongdejianglai*, *wo* *juede* *fumu* *haishi*
I on.the.whole I think parents yet
yindao <Cc10>*women*</Cc10>,
give.guidance.to.sb. us
"On the whole, I thought our parents have endeavoured to give us guidance."

666.08 668.54 B: {breath_noise} <Fm10><Fa10>***buguan*** **PRO10**
whatever PRO
zenmeyang *jiang*</Fa10>, *tamen* *mai* *le* *hen*
how say they buy PERF very
duo *shu* *gei* *women* *kan* .</Fm10>
many books for us read
"They have bought a lot of books for us to read at any rate."

8.5 Chapter summary

I have proposed in this chapter that adverbial clauses in spoken Chinese should be classified into two subcategories i.e. adverbial subordinate clause and adverbial-main clause. An adverbial-main clause is the adverbial clause that is not associated with any main clause in the sentence; the main clause can, however, be inferred given the context. Adverbial subordinate clauses in spoken Chinese are characterised by two features commonly associated with spoken language as identified by Chafe (1982), namely fragmentation and involvement: (i) the adverbial clause and the main clause occur in separate turns of the same speaker rather than in a single turn i.e. they are broken down into several idea units and expressed in fragmented grammatical structures rather than in a complete sentence as occurs in written language, and (ii) the adverbial clause and the main clause are uttered by two different speakers i.e. interlocutors show their concern for or involvement in the interaction and progression of the conversation. Adverbial clauses in spoken Chinese exhibit yet another feature of speech in that the non-overt subject (PRO) of the adverbial clause is typically controlled by an NP in previous context rather than the main clause subject/object, confirming previous claims that speakers rely heavily on context for the interpretation of a missing element in an utterance. Chinese adverbial clauses, however, occur significantly more frequently in CALLHOME than in the LCMC. This finding is at variance with what was said in previous accounts of differences between speech and writing in that speakers tend to avoid complex syntactic structures such as subordination. The explanation for this lies in conversation's propensity for employing causal and conditional clauses for clarifying participants' actions, prompting the use of more adverbial clauses, especially adverbial clauses of reason and condition, in the spoken Chinese corpus.

In comparison with those findings obtained from the LCMC corpus, the adverbial clauses in the CALLHOME corpus were proved to resemble their counterparts in the LCMC corpus in two aspects. Firstly, there is a relatively low frequency of purpose, result and contrast clauses in both the CALLHOME corpus and the narrative texts of the LCMC corpus (i.e. categories K-R, A and G). Secondly, clauses of reason and exception use significantly more overt subjects than PROs in both the

CALLHOME and LCMC corpora. However, the adverbial clauses in spoken and written Chinese also differ in two respects. Firstly, clauses of purpose and contrast show no sign of taking PRO in favour of overt subject in the CALLHOME corpus as their counterparts do in the LCMC corpus. Secondly, in contrast to the findings taken from both the PFR and LCMC corpora i.e. that clauses of concession in written Chinese strongly favour overt NP subjects, there is not such a marked contrast between overt and non-overt subjects in the concessive clauses of spoken Chinese.

Chapter Nine
Conclusion

9.1 Summary of findings

In the introductory chapter of this book (section 1.2), I set out *seven* research objectives related to Chinese adverbial clauses. My research brought out the following results, presented in the following sub-subsections.

9.1.1 Identification of adverbial clauses

To identify adverbial clauses in my corpora, I carried out skeleton parsing on a sample text of approximately 100,000 word tokens (or about 2,500 sentences) taken from the PFR Chinese Corpus with a clearly defined parsing scheme of 17 constituent labels. The manually-parsed sample skeleton treebank is one of the very few extant Chinese treebanks (cf. Xue et al., 2000). While Chinese part-of-speech tagging (Liu et al., 1995; Zhang and Sheng, 1997) and word segmentation (Wong and Chan, 1996; Zhang and Sheng, 1996; Sun et al., 1998; Yuan and Kim, 1998; Sun et al., 2000) have been the subject of concerted research for many years, the syntactic annotation of Chinese corpora is a comparatively new field. Although much treebanking of English has occurred, relatively little of such work has been done on Asian languages, Chinese included (Han et al., 2002). As shown in my skeleton treebank, adverbial clauses in Chinese are typically overtly marked by a subordinating conjunction. Moreover, the difficulties that I encountered in the production of this treebank demonstrate some of the peculiarities of Chinese syntax. The particle 的 *de* is typically used to introduce a lengthy premodifier in a noun phrase. These long multi-word noun phrase premodifiers greatly complicate the structure of the noun phrase in which they occur and thus pose enormous problems in parsing a sentence in Chinese. Another noteworthy syntactic property is that some serial verb constructions tend to be used as if they were compound verbs. When these serial verb constructions occur, the two transitive verbs in series, unlike common transitive verbs, do not take an object separately within the construction. Rather, the serial construction as a whole is able to take the same direct object and the verbal suffix 了 *-le*. Thus they appear to be used as a compound verb functioning as a single unit.

9.1.2 Adverbial subordinators in Chinese

As no clear distinction has been made between coordinating conjunctions and subordinating conjunctions in Chinese grammars, I proposed in this book two working criteria for a given item to be regarded as an adverbial subordinator: first, it introduces a clause which must be linked to another clause in the same sentence; second, the relation of these two clauses is not of coordinate nature. There are in total 57 subordinators identified in the PFR corpus, most of which are correlative subordinators having either an adverb or a conjunction as their correlative. The correlatives are not obligatory and an adverbial subordinator can take more than one correlative.

9.1.3 Semantic classes of adverbial clauses

I adopted a problem-oriented tagging approach to identify adverbial clauses in my corpus and to analyse their semantic roles. This meant that only relevant parts of the corpus, not the entire corpus, were annotated to meet my specific research purposes: only the sentences in which the adverbial clause is overtly marked by a subordinating conjunction were annotated. I identified a total of 2,417 instances of adverbial clauses in the PFR corpus and subsumed them into eleven semantically based classes which include, in descending order of frequency, clauses of condition, clauses of concession, clauses of purpose, clauses of cause/reason, clauses of contrast, clauses of result, clauses of exception, clauses of addition, clauses of inference, clauses of preference and clauses of time. Some observations about these adverbial clauses were made. For instance, 而是 *ershi* "rather" interacts with negated verb forms and negative adverbs that occur in the main clause. In addition, the apparent overlap between purpose clauses and result clauses is marked by the use of the same adverbial subordinator 从而 *conger* to introduce these two kinds of adverbial clause. While time, inference and preference clauses occur relatively infrequently and are marked by no more than two adverbial subordinators, conditional and concessive clauses make up approximately half of the adverbial clauses studied and exhibit a vast diversity of subordinating conjunctions used to introduce them. Clauses of inference were considered as a distinct adverbial semantic class in this book as they can be distinguished from apparently functionally analogous conditional and concessive clauses.

9.1.4 A government and binding approach to the distribution of subjects of adverbial clauses

The non-overt subjects (PRO) in Chinese adverbial clauses (CACs) were proven to support the PRO theorem of Government and Binding (GB) Theory in that they occur only in ungoverned positions and are properly licensed. According to control theory, they can be referentially dependent on, or controlled by, another NP or an implicit argument (e.g. the agent of an action) in the main clause, or they are not controlled at all and have an arbitrary interpretation. As a feature specific to PRO in CACs, it can be controlled by an NP occurring in the context prior to the main clause. As this type of control cannot be explained by control theory, the Principle of the Separation of Reference and Role (PSRR) was used to account for it. Furthermore, it was shown that there is a high statistical significance for the hypothesis that preference for a particular kind of subject (either overt NP or PRO) depends on the interclausal semantic relations of adverbial clauses. I found that in the PFR corpus, overt NP subjects are preponderant in concessive clauses while null subjects mostly occur in conditional clauses. This distribution pattern is attributed to the fact that the subject of the adverbial clause may be different from that of the main clause, resulting in the occurrence of overt NP subject in favour of PRO, which is always co-referential with either the main clause subject/object or an NP in the context. The distribution of overt and non-overt subjects also differs significantly in clauses of purpose, contrast and result which favour the use of PRO and in causal clauses which favour overt NP subjects. Other types of adverbial clause, however, do not show a marked preference for either subject type such as clauses of exception, addition, inference, preference and time. An integrated approach which combines a theoretically-informed corpus-based approach with an information-structure-based approach was taken to explain the distribution of PROs across the semantic domains of adverbial clauses. An NP referential controller occurring in the main clause or previous context can be seen as given information and thus the subject of the adverbial clause which co-refers to it can be dropped as in clauses of condition, purpose, contrast and result. On the other hand, the subject of the main clause which is an NP with a brand-new referent and is different from that of the adverbial clause can be seen as new information. Thus the subject of the adverbial clause cannot be dropped as in clauses of concession and cause/reason.

9.1.5 Distribution of adverbial clauses across text types in written Chinese

The results obtained from the PFR corpus were compared with the results obtained from the Lancaster Corpus of Mandarin Chinese (LCMC), a balanced corpus with 500 samples of fifteen distinct text types, to explore the influence of text type on both the distribution of semantic classes of adverbial clauses and the distribution of subjects in the adverbial clause. While in both the PFR and LCMC corpora conditional and concessive clauses dominate all other semantic types of adverbial clause, a comparison of their occurrence in the journalistic texts of the LCMC corpus (i.e. press reportage, editorials and reviews) and that in the non-journalistic texts (i.e. other text categories remaining in the corpus) indicated that they are not a marked feature of journalistic writing. Rather, conditional and concessive clauses are most frequently used in category E (skills/trades/hobbies) and category N (adventure and martial arts fiction) of the corpus respectively. Other semantic classes of adverbial clauses also have interaction with different text types of the corpus. Reason and result clauses are closely related to category D (religion) and category J (scientific academic prose) in that they are most commonly used to describe the origin and development of a religion and to discuss methods and findings of a piece of research, whereas purpose clauses interact with category E (skills/trades/hobbies) and category F (popular lore) to give instructions for mastering a particular skill and hobby and to offer advice on issues related to local culture and everyday life such as fashion, diet, interpersonal relationship, family and careers.

9.1.6 Distribution of subjects of adverbial clauses across text types and semantic domains in written Chinese

It was shown that the distribution of subjects of adverbial clauses varies significantly across text types in the LCMC corpus. Yet this disguises the fact that the significant difference in the distribution of overt and non-overt subjects is merely appreciable in six out of fifteen text categories of the corpus. This does not, however, preclude text type from exerting an influence on the distribution of subjects in the adverbial clause. Results obtained from the LCMC corpus demonstrated that the distribution of subjects varies significantly across semantic domains of adverbial clauses as in the PFR corpus: while non-overt subjects are used overwhelmingly in clauses of contrast and purpose, overt subjects are mostly used in clauses of concession, reason and exception. In contrast to the results obtained from the PFR corpus, conditional clauses do not show a significant preponderance of non-overt subjects in the LCMC corpus. This unexpected finding gives some credence to the claim that text type influences the distribution of subjects in the adverbial clause. A closer examination of the distribution of subjects across text types in the five adverbial clause types giving statistically significant results on their choice of subject further confirms it: the contrast between the distribution of overt and non-overt subjects is marked in certain text categories only. Hence, the effect of the semantic domains of adverbial clauses on the distribution of PROs as shown in the PFR corpus indeed depends on text type. It was also shown that text type influences the choice of the type of control of PRO. Non-overt subjects with an arbitrary interpretation (PRO_{arb}) occur twice as frequently in the LCMC corpus as in the PFR corpus. They are most frequently used in text category E which is composed of articles on teaching particular skills and hobbies to general public. Since no specific referent is intended to be the reader in these articles, category E favours the use of PRO_{arb} more strongly than other text types.

9.1.7 Distribution of adverbial clauses and their subjects in spoken Chinese

In comparing spoken and written Chinese corpora, adverbial clauses in spoken Chinese typically demonstrate two features of speech i.e. fragmentation and involvement, as Chafe (1982) identified: (i) an adverbial clause occurring in several different turns from the associated main clause uttered both by the same speaker demonstrates a degree of fragmentation because both the adverbial clause and the main clause are expressed in several idea units or in fragmented grammatical structures; (ii) that the adverbial clause and the main clause are uttered separately by two different speakers who attempt to ensure communication is functioning well demonstrates a quality of involvement. A subcategory of adverbial clause, an adverbial-main clause, was proposed to address the peculiarity of spoken language in that the main clause to which an adverbial clause is subordinated is not always explicitly expressed and it can, however, be inferred from the context. A speaker's interpretation of a non-overt subject also relies heavily on context, as shown in the relatively higher frequency of controllers for PRO identified in the context (i.e. contextual controllers) than subject and object controllers in the main clause. In contrasting the distribution of adverbial clauses and their subjects in CALLHOME with that in the LCMC, I showed that (i) both conversation and narrative texts show a strikingly similar distribution pattern of adverbial clauses in that purpose, result and contrast clauses are relatively less frequent than other adverbial clause types; (ii) clauses of condition and cause/reason, however, have a disproportionately higher frequency of occurrence in conversation than in narrative texts; (iii) clauses of reason and exception take more overt subjects than PROs in both spoken and written Chinese; (iv) unlike their counterparts in written Chinese, clauses of concession in spoken Chinese do not show a marked preference for overt subjects, marking an important difference in the use of adverbial clauses between spoken and written Chinese.

9.2 Limitations of the present study

The spoken Chinese corpus used in this book contains just one type of spoken discourse i.e. telephone conversations. This is very limited in comparison with corpora such as the London-Lund Corpus of Spoken English (Svartvik and Quirk, 1980; Johansson, 1982), which represents six major speech situations: face-to-face conversations, public conversations including debates and interviews, telephone conversations, radio broadcasts, spontaneous speeches and prepared speeches. However, at the time of writing, there is no spoken Chinese corpus available which is a heterogeneous collection of varied kinds of spoken texts to match corpora such as London-Lund. Whilst I am aware that the findings based on a spoken corpus of conversation data cannot be easily transferred to some spoken discourse types, especially those which differ considerably in nature from conversation e.g. prepared public speeches, the CALLHOME corpus used in my work can at least throw some light on the primary differences between spoken and written Chinese.

9.3 Suggestions for future research

9.3.1 Annotation of functions of syntactic constituents

Further research can be conducted into the functional labelling of syntactic constituents in a treebank. That was not undertaken in this book. In my skeleton treebank, functional labels were put aside in order to give a consistent and accurate manual parsing. However, the annotation of syntactic functions may throw up interesting results regarding the range of functions that a phrasal category can take within a sentence; a phrasal category may assume a syntactic function that is not conventionally associated with it. Additionally, a functionally labelled treebank may provide a broader coverage of syntactic phenomena. Take, for example, the case of 把 *ba* constructions in Chinese as mentioned in my book (see Chapter Three, section 3.6.2.1). The annotation of traces for displaced constituents can better explain the peculiarity of those prepositional phrases headed by the preposition *ba*, in which the prepositional complement co-refers to the (displaced) null object of the following verb phrase. It is expected that more large-scale treebanks with expanded size and coverage will be built in the near future (cf. Han et al., 2002).

9.3.2 A contrastive study of adverbial clauses between English and Chinese

As mentioned earlier (see Chapter Two, section 2.2.1; Chapter Seven, section 7.1), the LCMC corpus is a Chinese match for the FLOB corpus (on written British English) in terms of sampling frame. The FLOB corpus has a matching American English corpus, the Freiburg-Brown Corpus of American English or Frown (Hundt et al., 1999). As the LCMC, FLOB and Frown corpora are comparable corpora, it is feasible to study Chinese in contrast with the two major varieties of English (McEnery et al., 2003; McEnery and Xiao, forthcoming). By examining the distribution of non-overt subjects of adverbial clauses in the fifteen text categories of the LCMC and FLOB/Frown corpora, the distribution patterns of non-overt subjects in Chinese and British/American English adverbial clauses could be compared.

9.4 Concluding remarks

This book is aimed at offering a theoretically informed, corpus-based, comprehensive analysis of adverbial clauses in spoken and written Chinese. Two advantages of the corpus-based approach are demonstrated in this book. Firstly, the exploitation of a representative corpus enables quantitative statements to be made on the distribution of linguistic forms across a language variety and avoids idiosyncratic bias present in studies based on a researcher's intuition (Collins, 1991; Fillmore, 1992). Secondly, in the study of a grammatical category, a sizeable corpus can provide researchers with a wealth of language data upon which to base their explanations (Meyers, 1991), and it allows these explanations to include information on authentic language use of the grammatical construction under consideration i.e. to be accountable to interpersonally-observable evidence (Sampson, 2001 and 2005).

References

Abeillé, A. (Ed.). 2003. *Treebanks: Building and Using Parsed Corpora (Text, Speech and Language Technology Volume 20)*. Dordrecht, Boston and London: Kluwer Academic Publishers.

Abraham, E. 1991. "Why 'because'? The management of given/new information as a constraint on the selection of causal alternatives". *Text* 11(3): 323–339.

Ackema, P. 2002. "A morphological approach to the absence of expletive PRO" in A. Neeleman and R. Vermeulen (Eds.) *UCLWPL 14 (2002)*. URL: <http://www.phon.ucl.ac.uk/home/PUB/WPL/uclwpl14.html> (accessed 15 May 2012).

Adams, E. 1970. "Subjunctive and indicative conditionals". *Foundations of Language* 6: 89–94.

Adams, M. 1987. "From Old French to the theory of pro-drop". *Natural Language and Linguistic Theory* 5(1): 1–32.

Aduriz, I., Arriola, J.M., Artola, X., Días de Ilarraza, A., Gojenola, K., & Maritxalar, M. 1997. "Morphosyntactic disambiguation for Basque based on the Constraint Grammar formalism" in *Proceedings of Recent Advances in NLP (RANLP'97)* (p. 282–288). Tzigov Chark, Bulgaria.

Åfarli, T., & Creider, C. 1987. "Nonsubject Pro-drop in Norwegian". *Linguistic Inquiry* 18(2): 339–345.

Agresti, A. 1992. "A survey of exact inference for contingency tables". *Statistical Science* 7(1): 131–177.

Akinnaso, F.N. 1982. "On the differences between spoken and written language". *Language and Speech* 25(2): 97–125.

Altenberg, B. 1984. "Causal linking in spoken and written English". *Studia Linguistica* 38(1): 20–69.

Altenberg, B., & Tapper, M. 1998. "The use of adverbial connectors in advanced Swedish learners' written English" in S. Granger (Ed.) *Learner English on Computer* (p. 80–93). London and New York: Longman.

Aoun, J. 1984. "A significant generalisation in Chinese" in W. de Geest and Y. Putseys (Eds.) *Sentential complementation: Proceedings of the International Conference Held at UFSAL, Brussels, June, 1983* (p. 11–21). Dordrecht, Holland: Foris.

Aoun, J., & Li, A. 1993. *Syntax of Scope*. Cambridge: MIT Press.

Archangeli, D., & Langendoen, T. (Eds.). 1997. *Optimality Theory: An Overview*. Oxford: Blackwell.

Aroonmanakun, W. 1997. "Referent resolution for zero pronouns in Thai" in A. Abramson (Ed.) *Southeast Asian Linguistic Studies in Honour of Vichin Panupong*. Bangkok: Chulalongkom University.

Artstein, R. 2003. Quantificational arguments in temporal adjunct clauses. Manuscript. Technion – Israel Institute of Technology. URL: <http://www.cs.technion.ac.il/~artstein/quant.pdf> (accessed 15 May 2012).

Aston, G., & Burnard, L. 1998. *The BNC Handbook: Exploring the British National Corpus with SARA*. Edinburgh, Scotland: Edinburgh University Press.

Ball, F. 2002. "Developing wordlists for BEC". *Research Notes* 8: 10–13.

Barnett, R., Calzolari, N., Flores, S., Hellwig, P., Kahrel, P., Leech, G., Melera, M., Montemagni, S., Odijk, J., Pirrelli, V., Sanfilippo, A., Teufel, S., Villegas, M., & Zaysser, L. 1996. *Preliminary Recommendations on Subcategorisation*. EAGLES Document EAG – CLWG – SYNLEX/P Version of Aug, 1996. URL: <http://www.ilc.cnr.it/EAGLES96/synlex/synlex.html> (accessed 15 May 2012).

Bar-Shalom, E., & Snyder, W. 1997. "Optional infinitives in Russian and their implications for the pro-drop debate" in M. Lindseth and S. Franks (Eds.) *Formal Approaches to Slavic Linguistics: The Indiana Meeting 1996* (p. 38–47). Ann Arbor: Michigan Slavic Publications.

Bateman, J., Forrest, J., & Willis, T. 1997. "The use of syntactic annotation tools: partial and full parsing" in R. Garside, G. Leech and A. McEnery (Eds.) *Corpus Annotation: Linguistics Information from Computer Text Corpora* (p. 166–178). London and New York: Longman.

Battistella, E. 1985. "On the distribution of PRO in Chinese". *Natural Language and Linguistic Theory* 3(3): 317–340.

Beal, J. 2000. Review of *Adverbial Clauses in Scots: A Semantic-Syntactic Study* by Martina Häcker. *English Language and Linguistics* 4(2): 324–328.

Beaman, K. 1984. "Coordination and subordination revisited: Syntactic complexity in spoken and written narrative discourse" in D. Tannen (Ed.) *Coherence in Spoken and Written Discourse* (p. 45–80). Norwood, New Jersey: Ablex.

Beijing Yuyan Xueyuan Yuyan Jiaoxue Yanjiusuo. 1986. *Xiandai Hanyu Pinlü Cidian* [Modern Chinese Word Frequency Dictionary]. Beijing: Beijing Yuyan Xueyuan Chubanshe [Beijing Institute of Language Press].

Belletti, A. 1982. "'Morphological' passive and PRO-drop: The impersonal construction in Italian". *Journal of Linguistic Research* 2(4): 1–34.

Bennis, H. 2002. Agreement, PRO and imperatives. Manuscript. Meertens Institute, Amsterdam.

Bhatt, R., & Pancheva, R. 2001. Conditionals. Manuscript. University of Texas, Austin and University of Southern California. URL: <http://www-bcf.usc.edu/~pancheva/bhatt-pancheva_syncom.pdf> (accessed 15 May 2012).

Biber, D. 1986a. "On the investigation of spoken/written differences". *Studia Linguistica* 40(1): 1–21.

Biber, D. 1986b. "Spoken and written textual dimensions in English: resolving the contradictory findings". *Language: Journal of the Linguistic Society of America* 62(2): 384–414.

Biber, D. 1988. *Variation Across Speech and Writing*. Cambridge: Cambridge University Press.

Biber, D. 1990. "Methodological issues regarding corpus-based analyses of linguistic variation". *Literary & Linguistic Computing* 5(4): 257–269.

Biber, D. 1992. "Using computer-based text corpora to analyse the referential strategies of spoken and written texts" in J. Svartvik (Ed.) *Directions in Corpus Linguistics:*

Proceedings of Nobel Symposium 82 Stockholm, 4–8 August 1991 (p. 213–252). Berlin and New York: Mouton de Gruyter.
Biber, D. 1993a. "Representativeness in corpus design". *Literary and Linguistic Computing* 8(4): 243–257.
Biber, D. 1993b. "Using register-diversified corpus for general language studies". *Computational Linguistics* 19(2): 219–241.
Biber, D., & Finegan, E. 1988. "Adverbial Stance Types in English". *Discourse Processes* 11(1): 1–34.
Biber, D., & Finegan, E. 1989. "Styles of stance in English: Lexical and grammatical marking of evidentiality affect". *Text* 9(1): 93–124.
Biber, D., & Finegan, E. 1991. "On the exploitation of computerized corpora in variation studies" in K. Aijmer and B. Altenberg (Eds.) *English Corpus Linguistics: Studies in Honour of Jan Svartvik* (p. 204–220). London and New York: Longman.
Biber, D., Conrad, S., & Reppen, R. 1998. *Corpus linguistics: investigating language structure and use*. Cambridge: Cambridge University Press.
Biber, D., Johansson, S., Leech, G., Conrad, S., & Finegan, E. 1999. *Longman Grammar of Spoken and Written English*. Harlow, Essex: Longman.
Bilgram, T., & Keson, B. 1998. The construction of a tagged Danish corpus. Paper presented at the 11th Nordic Conference on Computational Linguistics, January 28–30. Copenhagen, Denmark.
Bing, J. 1981. "The given/new distinction and the unmarked stress pattern" in V. Burke and J. Pustejovsky (Eds.) *Proceedings of the Eleventh Annual Meeting of the North Eastern Linguistic Society* (p. 13–21). Amherst, MA: Graduate Linguistic Student Association, University of Massachusetts.
Black, E., Eubank, S., Kashioka, H., Magerman, D., Garside, R., & Leech, G. 1996. "Beyond skeleton parsing: Producing a comprehensive large-scale general-English treebank with full grammatical analysis" in *Proceedings of the 16th International Conference on Computational Linguistics (COLING)* (p. 107–112). Copenhagen.
Blake, B. 1990. *Relational Grammar*. London: Routledge.
Bock, K. 1977. "The effect of a pragmatic presupposition on syntactic structure in question answering". *Journal of Verbal Learning and Verbal Behaviour* 16(6): 723–734.
Bodomo, A., & Luke, K.K. 2001. LFG and the Analysis of Chinese. Workshop for LFG 2001. The 6th International Conference on Lexical-Functional Grammar, June 25–27. Hong Kong, China.
Borer, H. 1980. "Empty subjects and constraints on thematic relations" in J.T. Jensen (Ed.) *Proceedings of the Tenth Annual Meeting of NELS (Cahiers linguistiques d'Ottawa,* Vol. 9). Toronto: Department of Linguistics, University of Toronto.
Borer, H. 1989. "Anaphoric AGR" in O. Jaeggli and K.J. Safir (Eds.) *The Null Subject Parameter* (p. 69–109). Dordrecht, Holland: Kluwer.
Borsley, R. 1999. *Syntactic Theory: A Unified Approach, Second Edition*. London and New York: Arnold.
Bresnan, J. (Ed.) 1982a. *The Mental Representation of Grammatical Relations*. Cambridge, MA.: MIT Press.

Bresnan, J. 1978. "A realistic transformational grammar" in M. Halle, J. Bresnan and G. Miller (Eds.) *Linguistic Theory and Psychological Reality* (p. 1–59). Cambridge, MA: MIT Press.

Bresnan, J. 1982b. "Control and complementation". *Linguistic Inquiry* 13(3): 343–434.

Bresnan, J. 1994. "Locative inversion and the architecture of universal grammar". *Language* 70(1): 72–131.

Bresnan, J. 2001. *Lexical-Functional Syntax*. Oxford: Blackwell.

Brown, P., & Levinson, S. 1987. *Politeness: Some Universals in Language Usage*. Cambridge: Cambridge University Press.

Burnard, L., & Todd, T. 2003. "Xara: an XML aware tool for corpus searching" in *Proceedings of Corpus Linguistics 2003* (p. 142–144).

Butler, C. 1985a. *Computers in Linguistics*. Oxford and New York: Basil Blackwell.

Butler, C. 1985b. *Statistics in Linguistics*. Oxford and New York: Basil Blackwell.

Cadenhead, R. 2001. *Sams Teach Yourself Java 2 in 24 Hours, Second Edition*. Indiana: Sams Publishing.

Chafe, W. 1976. "Givenness, contrastiveness, subjects, topics, and point of view." in C. Li (Ed.) *Subject and Topic* (p. 23–55). New York: Academic Press.

Chafe, W. 1979. "The flow of thought and the flow of language" in T. Givón (Ed.) *Discourse and Syntax* (p. 159–181). New York: Academic Press.

Chafe, W. 1980. "The deployment of consciousness in the production of a narrative" in W. Chafe (Ed.) *The Pear Stories: Cognitive, Cultural, and Linguistic Aspects of Narrative Production* (p. 9–50). Norwood, New Jersey: Ablex.

Chafe, W. 1982. "Integration and involvement in speaking, writing, and oral literature" in D. Tannen (Ed.) *Spoken and Written Language: Exploring Orality and Literacy* (p. 35–53). Norwood, New Jersey: Ablex.

Chafe, W. 1985. "Linguistic differences produced by differences between speaking and writing" in D. Olson, N. Torrance and A. Hildyard (Eds.) *Literacy, Language, and Learning: The Nature and Consequences of Reading and Writing* (p. 105–123). Cambridge: Cambridge University Press.

Chafe, W. 1986a. "Evidentiality in English conversations and academic writing" in W. Chafe and J. Nichols (Eds.) E*videntality: The Linguistic Coding of Epistemology* (p. 261–272). Norwood, New Jersey: Ablex.

Chafe, W. 1986b. "Writing in the Perspective of Speaking" in C. Cooper and S. Greenbaum (Eds.) *Studying Writing: Linguistic Approaches* (p. 12–39). Beverly Hills, London and New Delhi: Sage.

Chafe, W. 1987. "Cognitive constraints on information flow" in R. Tomlin (Ed.) *Coherence and Grounding in Discourse* (p. 21–51). Amsterdam and Philadelphia: John Benjamins Publishing Company.

Chafe, W. 1992. "The importance of corpus linguistics to understanding the nature of language" in J. Svartvik (Ed.) *Directions in Corpus Linguistics: Proceedings of Nobel Symposium 82 Stockholm, 4–8 August 1991* (p. 79–97). Berlin and New York: Mouton de Gruyter.

Chafe, W. 1994. *Discourse, Consciousness, and Time: The Flow and Displacement of Conscious Experience in Speaking and Writing*. Chicago: Chicago University Press.

Chafe, W., & Danielewicz, J. 1987. "Properties of spoken and written language" in R. Horowitz and S. Samuels (Eds.) *Comprehending Oral and Written Language* (p. 83–113). San Diego: Academic Press, INC.
Chafe, W., & Tannen, D. 1987. "The relation between written and spoken language". *Annual Review of Anthropology* 16(1987): 383–407.
Chanod, J.P., Tapanainen, P. 1995. "Tagging French – comparing a statistical and a constraint-based method" in *Proceedings of the Seventh Conference of the European Chapter of the Association for Computational Linguistics (EACL'95)* (p. 149–156). Association for Computational Linguistics, Dublin.
Chao, Y.R. 1968. *A Grammar of Spoken Chinese*. Berkeley and Los Angeles: University of California Press.
Chen, H.H. 1990. "A logic-based government-binding parser for Mandarin Chinese" in H. Karlgren (Ed.) *Proceedings of the 13th International Conference on Computational Linguistics (COLING'90)* (p. 48–53). Helsinki, Finland.
Chen, H.H., & Lee, J.C. 1996. "Identification and classification of proper nouns in Chinese texts" in *Proceedings of COLING – 96, Volume 1* (p. 222–229). Montreal, Canada.
Chen, P. 1986. Referent introducing and tracking in Chinese narrative. Unpublished Ph.D. thesis. University of California, Los Angeles.
Chen, P. 1990. The distribution and referential interpretation of empty categories in Chinese. Unpublished Ph.D. thesis. *Dissertation Abstracts International* 51(2): 492A.
Chevalier, J. 2004. "Heritage language literacy: Theory and practice". *Heritage Language Journal* 2(1): 1–19.
Chiou, F.D., Chiang, D., & Palmer, M. 2001. "Facilitating treebank annotation with a statistical parser" in *Proceedings of the Human Language Technology Conference (HLT 2001)*. San Diego, California.
Chiu, B. 1993. The inflectional structure of Mandarin Chinese. Unpublished Ph.D. thesis. University of Los Angeles.
Chomsky, N. 1957. *Syntactic Structures*. The Hague: Mouton.
Chomsky, N. 1965. *Aspects of the Theory of Syntax*. Cambridge, M.A.: MIT Press.
Chomsky, N. 1980. "On binding". *Linguistic Inquiry* 11: 1–46.
Chomsky, N. 1981a. *Lectures on Government and Binding*. Dordrecht, Holland: Foris.
Chomsky, N. 1981b. "On the representation of form and function". *The Linguistic Review* 1(1): 3–40.
Chomsky, N. 1981c. "Principles and parameters in syntactic theory" in N. Hornstein and D. Lightfoot (Eds.) *Explanation in Linguistics* (p. 123–146). London: Longman.
Chomsky, N. 1982. *Some Concepts and Consequences of the Theory of Government and Binding*. Cambridge, Massachusetts: MIT Press.
Chomsky, N. 1986a. *Barriers*. Cambridge, Massachusetts: MIT Press.
Chomsky, N. 1986b. *Knowledge of Language, its Nature, Origin, and Use*. New York: Praeger.
Chomsky, N. 1995a. "Bare phrase structure" in G. Webelhuth (Ed.) *Government and Binding Theory and the Minimalist Program* (p. 383–439). Cambridge and Oxford: Blackwell.
Chomsky, N. 1995b. *The Minimalist Program*. Cambridge, Massachusetts: MIT Press.

Chomsky, N., & Lasnik, H. 1993. "The theory of principles and parameters" in J. Jacobs, A. von Stechow, W. Sternefeld and T. Vennemann (Eds.) *Syntax: An International Handbook of Contemporary Research* (p. 506–569). Berlin: Walter de Gruyter.

Chu, C., & Chi, T.J. 1999. *A Cognitive-Functional Grammar of Mandarin Chinese*. Taiwan: Crane Publishing.

Cieri, C. 2000. Resources for robust analyses of natural language. Paper presented at the Conférence ROMAND 2000, October 19–20. Lausanne, Switzerland.

Cieri, C., & Liberman, M. 2000. "Issues in corpus creation and distribution: The evolution of the Linguistic Data Consortium" in *Proceedings of the Second International Language Resources and Evolution Conference*. Athens, Greece.

Cieri, C., Miller, D., & Walker, K. 2002. "Research methodologies, observations and outcomes in (conversational) speech data collection" in *Proceedings of the Human Language Technologies Conference*. San Diego, CA.

Claridge, C., & Walker, T. 2001. "Causal clauses in written and speech-related genres in Early Modern English". *ICAME Journal* 25: 31–64.

Coakes, S., & Steed, L. 2001. *SPSS: Analysis Without Anguish: Version 10.0 for Windows*. Brisbane, Australia: Wiley.

Cole, P., Hermon, G., & Sung, L.M. 1993. "Feature percolation". *Journal of East Asian Linguistics* 2(1): 91–118.

Comrie, B. 1986. "Conditionals: a typology" in E. Traugott, A. Ter-Meulen, J. Snitzer-Reilly, & C. Ferguson (Eds.) *On Conditionals* (p. 77–99). Cambridge: Cambridge University Press.

Conover, W.J. 1980. *Practical Nonparametric Statistics, Second Edition*. New York: John Wiley and Sons.

Cordin, P. 1980. "Una restrizione sulla coreferenza nelle frasi con PRO-drop". *Studi di Grammatica Italiana* 9: 339–357.

Couper-Kuhlen, E., & Thompson, S. 2000. "Concessive patterns in conversation" in E. Couper-Kuhlen and B. Kortmann (Eds.) *Cause, Condition, Concession, Contrast: Cognitive and Discourse perspectives* (p. 381–410). Berlin and New York: Mouton de Gruyter.

Crevels, M. 2000. "Concessives on different semantic levels: A typological perspective" in E. Couper-Kuhlen and B. Kortmann (Eds.) *Cause, Condition, Concession, Contrast: Cognitive and Discourse perspectives* (p. 313–339). Berlin and New York: Mouton de Gruyter.

Cristofaro, S. 2003. *Subordination*. Oxford: Oxford University Press.

Croft, W. 2001. *Radical Construction Grammar: Syntactic Theory in Typological Perspective*. Oxford: Oxford University Press.

Crystal, D. 1980. *A First Dictionary of Linguistics and Phonetics*. Boulder, CO: Westview.

Crystal, D. 1985. *A Dictionary of Linguistics and Phonetics, Second Edition*. New York: Basil Blackwell.

de Haan, P. 1991. "On the exploration of corpus data by means of problem-oriented tagging: Postmodifying clauses in the English noun phrase" in S. Johansson and A.-B. Stenström (Eds.) *English Computer Corpora: Selected Papers and Research Guide* (p. 52–65). Berlin: Mouton de Gruyter.

Deitel, H.M., & Deitel, P.J. 2002. *Java: How to Program, Fourth Edition*. London: Prentice Hall.
Di Eugenio, B. 1993. Understanding natural language instructions: A computational approach to purpose clauses. Unpublished Ph.D. thesis. University of Pennsylvania.
Diessel, H. 2001. "The ordering distribution of main and adverbial clauses: A typological study". *Language* 77(3): 433–455.
Dik, S. 1978. *Functional Grammar*. Amsterdam, New York and Oxford: North-Holland.
Dik, S. 1989. *The Theory of Functional Grammar, part 1*. Berlin: Mouton de Gruyter.
Dik, S. 1997. *The Theory of Functional Grammar, part 2*. Berlin: Mouton de Gruyter.
Ding, S.S., Lü, S.X., Li, R., Sun, D.X., Guan, X.C., Fu, J., Huang, C.Z., & Chen, Z.W. 1979. *Xiandai Hanyu Yufa Xianghua* [Lectures on Modern Chinese Grammar]. Beijing: Commercial Press.
Dorr, B., & Gaasterland, T. 2002. "Constraints on the generation of tense, aspect, and connecting words from temporal expressions". *Journal of Artificial Intelligence* Research 1(2002): 1–47.
Eckardt, R. 2003. "Manner adverbs and information structure: Evidence from the adverbial modification of verbs of creation" in E. Lang, C. Maienborn and C. Fabricius-Hansen (Eds.) *Modifying Adjuncts* (p. 261–305). Berlin and New York: Mouton de Gruyter.
Edwards, J. 1993. "Survey of Electronic Corpora and Related Resources for Language Researchers" in J. Edwards and M. Lampert (Eds.) *Talking data: Transcription and Coding in Discourse Research* (p. 263–310). London and Hillsdale, New Jersey: Erlbaum.
Eyes, E., & Leech, G. 1993. "Syntactic annotation: linguistic aspects of grammatical tagging and skeleton parsing" in E. Black, R. Garside and G. Leech (Eds.) *Statistically-driven Computer Grammars of English: The IBM/Lancaster Approach* (p. 36–61). Amsterdam: Rodopi.
Faraci, R. 1974. Aspects of the grammar of infinitives and *for* phrases. Unpublished Ph.D. thesis. MIT.
Farrell, J. 1999. *Java Programming: Comprehensive*. Cambridge, Massachusetts: Course Technology.
Feng, Z.W. 2002. "Evolution and present situation of corpus research in China". *Journal of Chinese Language and Computing* 11(2): 127–146.
Fillmore, C. 1992. "'Corpus linguistics' or 'Computer-aided armchair linguistics'" in J. Svartvik (Ed.) *Directions in Corpus Linguistics: Proceedings of Nobel Symposium 82 Stockholm, 4–8 August 1991* (p. 35–60). Berlin and New York: Mouton de Gruyter.
Finegan, E. 1982. "Form and function in testament language" in R. Di Pietro (Ed.) *Linguistics and the Professions: Proceedings of the Second Annual Delaware Symposium on Language Studies* (p. 113–120). Norwood, New Jersey: Ablex.
Flowerdew, J. 1993. "Variation across speech and writing in biology: A quantitative study". *Perspectives* 5(1): 75–87.
Foley, W., & van Valin, R. 1977. "On the viability of the notion of 'subject' in universal grammar". *BLS* 3: 293–320.

Foley, W., & van Valin, R. 1984. *Functional Syntax and Universal Grammar*. Cambridge: Cambridge University Press.

Ford, C. 1993. *Grammar in Interaction: Adverbial Clauses in American English Conversations*. Cambridge: Cambridge University Press.

Ford, C. 2000. "The treatment of contrasts in interaction" in E. Couper-Kuhlen and B. Kortmann (Eds.) *Cause, Condition, Concession, Contrast: Cognitive and Discourse perspectives* (p. 283–311). Berlin and New York: Mouton de Gruyter.

Ford, C. and Thompson, S. 1986. "Conditionals in discourse: a text-based study from English" in E. Traugott, A. Ter-Meulen, J. Snitzer-Reilly, & C. Ferguson (Eds.) *On Conditionals* (p. 353–372). Cambridge: Cambridge University Press.

Francis, W.N., & Kučera, H. 1964. *Manual of Information to Accompany 'A Standard Sample of Present-Day Edited American English, for Use with Digital Computers'*. Providence, RI: Department of Linguistics, Brown University.

Friedl, J. 1997. *Mastering Regular Expressions*. Sebastopol, California: O'Reilly & Associates, Inc.

Gao, Z.M. 1997. Automatic extraction of translation equivalents from a parallel Chinese-English corpus. Unpublished Ph.D. thesis. University of Manchester.

Gärdenfors, P. 1979. "Conditionals and changes of belief" in I. Niiniluoto and R. Tuomela (Eds.) *The Logic and Epistemology of Scientific Change*, Acta Philosophica Fennica 30 (1978), No. 2–4 (p. 381–404).

Garside, R. 1993. "The large-scale production of syntactically analysed corpora". *Literary and Linguistic Computing* 8(1): 39–46.

Garside, R., & McEnery, A. 1993. "Treebanking: The compilation of a corpus of skeleton-parsed sentences" in E. Black, R. Garside and G. Leech (Eds.) *Statistically-driven Computer Grammars of English: The IBM/Lancaster Approach* (p. 17–35). Amsterdam: Rodopi.

Gasde, H.-D. 1990. "Chinese relative clauses in the light of Chomsky's theory of government and binding". *Zeitschrift für Phonetik, Sprachwissenschaft und Kommunikationsforschung* 43(6): 785–790.

Gazdar, G., Klein, E., Pullum, G., & Sag, I. 1985. *Generalised Phrase Structure Grammar*. Oxford: Blackwell.

Givón, T. 1993. *English Grammar: A Function-Based Introduction, Volume II*. Amsterdam and Philadelphia: John Benjamins Publishing Company.

Givón, T. 2001. *Syntax: An Introduction, Volume II*. Amsterdam and Philadelphia: John Benjamins Publishing Company.

Graham, T. 2000. *Unicode: A Primer*. Foster City, Canada: M&T Books.

Green, G., & Morgan, J. 1981. "Writing ability as a function of the appreciation of differences between oral and written communication" in C. Frederiksen and J. Dominic (Eds.) *Writing: The Nature, Development, and Teaching of Written Communication* (p. 177–188). Hillsdale, New Jersey: Lawrence Erlbaum.

Greenbaum, S. 1973. "Adverbial *–ING* participle constructions in English" *Anglia* Band 91 Heft 1: 1–10.

Greenbaum, S., & Nelson, G. 1995. "Clause relationships in spoken and written English". *Functions of Language* 2(1): 1–21.

Greenbaum, S., & Nelson, G. 1996. "Positions of adverbial clauses in British English". *World Englishes* 15(1): 69–81.

Gumperz, J., Kaltman, H., & O'Connor, M. 1984. "Cohesion in spoken and written discourse: ethnic style and the transition to literacy" in D. Tannen (Ed.) *Coherence in Spoken and Written Discourse* (p. 3–19). Norwood, New Jersey: Ablex.

Guo, J. 1993. "PH: A Chinese Corpus". *Communications of COLIPS* 3(1): 45–48.

Häcker, M. 1999. *Adverbial Clauses in Scots: A Semantic-Syntactic Study*. Berlin and New York: Mouton de Gruyter.

Haegeman, L. 1984. "Parasitic gaps and adverbial clauses" *Journal of Linguistics* 20(2): 229–232.

Haegeman, L. 1994. *Introduction to Government and Binding Theory, Second Edition*. Oxford UK and Cambridge USA: Blackwell.

Haiman, J. 1978. "Conditionals are topics". *Language: Journal of the Linguistic Society of America* 54(3): 564–589.

Halliday, M.A.K. 1987. "Spoken and written modes of meaning" in R. Horowitz and S. Samuels (Eds.) *Comprehending Oral and Written Language* (p. 55–81). San Diego: Academic Press.

Halliday, M.A.K. 1989. *Spoken and Written Language*. Oxford: Oxford University Press.

Han, C.H., Han, N.R., Ko, E.S., & Palmer, M. 2002. "Development and evaluation of a Korean treebank and its application to NLP" in *Proceedings of the Third International Conference on Language Resources and Evaluation (LREC-2002)*. Las Palmas, Canary Islands, Spain.

Harbert, W. 1995. "Binding theory, control, and *pro*" in G. Webelhuth (Ed.) *Government and Binding Theory and the Minimalist Program* (p. 177–240). Cambridge and Oxford: Blackwell.

Haspelmath, M., & König, E. 1998. "Concessive conditionals in the languages of Europe" in J. Van der Auwera (Ed.) *Adverbial Constructions in the Languages of Europe* (p. 563–640). Berlin and New York: Mouton de Gruyter.

Hasselgård, H. 1992. "Sequences of spatial and temporal adverbials in spoken and written English" in G. Leitner (Ed.) *New Directions in English Language Corpora: Methodology, Results, Software Developments* (p. 319–328). Berlin: Mouton de Gruyter.

Hendrick, R. 1995. "Morphosyntax" in G. Webelhuth (Ed.) *Government and Binding Theory and the Minimalist Program* (p. 297–347). Cambridge and Oxford: Blackwell.

Hengeveld, K. 1998. "Adverbial clauses in the languages of Europe" in J. Van der Auwera (Ed.) *Adverbial Constructions in the Languages of Europe* (p. 335–419). Berlin and New York: Mouton de Gruyter.

Henry, A. 1990. Empty categories in Chinese. Unpublished Ph.D. thesis. University of Ulster.

Hinofotis, F. 1983. "The structure of oral communication in an educational environment: a comparison of factor-analytic rotational procedures" in J. Oller (Ed.) *Issues in Language Testing Research* (p. 170–187). Rowley: Newbury House.

Hoey, M. 1986. "Overlapping patterns of discourse organisation and their implications for clause relational analysis of problem-solution texts" in C. Cooper and S. Greenbaum (Eds.) *Studying Writing: Linguistic Approaches* (p. 187–214). Beverly Hills, CA: Sage.

Hoey, M., & Winter, E. 1986. "Clause relations and the writer's communicative task" in B. Couture (Ed.) *Functional Approaches to Writing: Research Perspectives* (p. 120–41). Norwood, New Jersey: Ablex.

Honal, M., & Schultz, T. 2003. "Correction of disfluencies in spontaneous speech using a noisy-channel approach" in *Proceedings of the 8th European Conference on Speech Communication and Technology (Eurospeech-2003)*. Genf, Switzerland.

Horová, E. 1976. "On position and function of English local and temporal adverbials". *Brno Studies in English* 12: 93–123.

Horrocks, G. 1987. *Generative Grammar*. London and New York: Longman.

Hou, X.C. 1998. *Xiandai Hanyu Xuci Cidian* [A Dictionary of Function Words in Modern Chinese]. Beijing: Peking University Press.

Howitt, D., & Cramer, D. 2001. A Guide to Computing Statistics with SPSS for Windows. Edinburgh: Prentice Hall.

Hu, J.H., Pan, H.H., & Xu, L.J. 2001. "Is there a finite vs. nonfinite distinction in Chinese?". *Linguistics* 39(6): 1117–1148.

Huang, J. 1984. "On the distribution and reference of empty pronouns". *Linguistic Inquiry* 15(4): 531–574.

Huang, J. 1987. "Remarks on empty categories in Chinese". *Linguistic Inquiry* 18(2): 321–337.

Huang, J. 1989. "Pro-drop in Chinese: A generalised control theory" in O. Jaeggli and K.J. Safir (Eds.) *The Null Subject Parameter* (p. 185–214). Dordrecht, Holland: Kluwer.

Huang, S.D., Bian, X.J., Wu, G., & McLemore, C. 1997. CALLHOME Mandarin Chinese lexicon. Technical report, Linguistic Data Consortium. URL: <http://www.ldc.upenn.edu/Catalog/LDC96L15.html> (accessed 15 May 2012).

Huang, Y. 1991. "A pragmatic analysis of control in Chinese" in J. Verschueren (Ed.) *Levels of Linguistic Adaptation: Selected Papers of the International Pragmatics Conference, Antwerp, August 17–22, 1987, II* (p. 113–145). Amsterdam: Benjamins.

Huang, Y. 1992. "Against Chomsky typology of empty categories". *Journal of Pragmatics* 17(1): 1–29.

Huang, Y. 1995. "On null subjects and null objects in generative grammar". *Linguistics* 33(6): 1081–1123.

Hundt, M., Sand, A., & Siemund, R. 1998. *Manual of Information to accompany the Freiburg-LOB Corpus of British English ('FLOB')*. URL: <http://khnt.hit.uib.no/icame/manuals/flob/INDEX.HTM> (accessed 15 May 2012).

Hundt, M., Sand, A., & Skandera, P. 1999. *Manual of Information to Accompany the Freiburg-Brown Corpus of American English ('Frown')*. URL: <http://khnt.hit.uib.no/icame/manuals/frown/INDEX.HTM> (accessed 15 May 2012).

Hyams, N. 1983. "The PRO-drop parameter in child grammars" in M. Barlow, D. Flickinger and M. Wescoat (Eds.) *Proceedings of the West Coast Conference on Formal Linguistics* (p. 126–139). Stanford: Stanford Linguistics Association. Department of Linguistics, Stanford University.

Ippolito, M. On the semantic composition of subjunctive conditionals. Manuscript. University of Tübingen. URL: <http://web.eecs.umich.edu/~rthomaso/lpw02/Ippolito.pdf> (accessed 15 May 2012).

Jackendoff, R. 1977. *X2-Syntax: A Study of Phrase Structure*. Cambridge, Massachusetts: MIT Press.

Jaeggli, O., & Safir, K.J. (Eds.). 1989. *The Null Subject Parameter*. Dordrecht, Holland: Kluwer.

Jang, Y.J., & Kim, S.Y. 2001. "Secondary predication and default case" in Nina Zhang (Ed.) *ZAS Papers in Linguistics (ZASPiL), Volume 26, Syntax of Predication*. URL: <http://www.zas.gwz-berlin.de/papers/zaspil/infos/index.htm> (accessed 15 May 2012).

Jin, W.Y., & Chen, L. 1995. "Identifying unknown words in Chinese corpora" in *Proceedings of Natural Language Processing Pacific Rim Symposium '95* (p. 234–239). Seoul, Republic of Korea.

Johannessen, J.B. 1998. *Coordination*. New York and Oxford: Oxford University Press.

Johansson, S. (Ed.). 1982. *Computer Corpora in English Language Research*. Bergen: Norwegian Computing Centre for the Humanities.

Johansson, S., Leech, G., & Goodluck, H. 1978. *Manual of Information to Accompany the Lancaster-Oslo-Bergen Corpus of British English, for Use with Digital Computers*. Oslo: Department of English, Oslo University.

Jones, C. 1985. Syntax and thematics of infinitival adjuncts. Unpublished Ph.D. thesis. University of Massachusetts.

Joseph, B. 1994. "On weak subjects and pro-drop in Greek" in I. Philippaki-Warburton, K. Nicolaidis and M. Sifianou (Eds.) *Themes in Greek Linguistics* (p. 21–32). Amsterdam: Benjamins.

Juffs, A. 1991. "Reciprocals in Chinese". *McGill Working Papers in Linguistics/Cahiers Linguistiques de McGill* 7(1): 26–40.

Jurafsky, D., & Martin, J. 2000. *Speech and Language Processing: An Introduction to Natural Language Processing, Computational Linguistics, and Speech Recognition*. Upper Saddle River, New Jersey: Prentice Hall.

Kahrel, P., Barnett, R., & Leech, G. 1997. "Towards cross-linguistic standards or guidelines for the annotation of corpora" in R. Garside, G. Leech and A. McEnery (Eds.) *Corpus Annotation: Linguistics Information from Computer Text Corpora* (p. 231–242). London and New York: Longman.

Kang, M.Y. 1988. Topics in Korean syntax. Unpublished Ph.D. thesis. MIT, Cambridge.

Kang, Y.S. 1986. Korean syntax and universal grammar. Unpublished Ph.D. thesis. Harvard University, Cambridge.

Kärkkäinen, E. 1996. "Preferred argument structure and subject role in American English conversational discourse". *Journal of Pragmatics* 25(1996): 265–701.

Karlsson, F. 1990. "Constraint grammar as a framework for parsing running text" in H. Karlgren (Ed.) *Proceedings of the 13th International Conference of Computational Linguistics, Volume 3* (p. 168–173). Helsinki, Finland.

Karlsson, F., Voutilainen, A., Heikkilä, J., & Antilla, A. 1995. *Constraint Grammar: A Language-Independent System for Parsing Unrestricted Text*. Berlin: Mouton de Gruyter.

Keenan, E. 1985. "Relative clauses" in T. Shopen (Ed.) *Language typology and syntactic description, Volume II (Complex constructions)* (p. 141–170). Cambridge: Cambridge University Press.

Kennedy, G. 1998. *An Introduction to Corpus Linguistics*. London and New York: Longman.
Keulen, F. 1986. "The Dutch computer corpus pilot project" in J. Aarts and W. Meijs (Eds.) *Corpus Linguistics II: New Studies in the Analysis and Exploitation of Computer Corpora* (p. 127–162). Amsterdam: Rodopi.
Kim, Y.B. 2002. "On concession". *Language and Information* 6(1): 1–18.
Kirk, J. 1994. "Taking a byte at corpus linguistics" in L. Flowerdew and A. Tong (Eds.) *Entering Text* (p. 18–49). Hong Kong: Language Centre, Hong Kong University of Science and Technology.
Kirkpatrick, A. 1993. "Information sequencing in Modern Standard Chinese in a genre of extended spoken discourse". *Text* 13(3): 423–453.
Kit, C.Y. 1992. "Parsing Chinese ba and bei constructions – an LFG approach" in *Proceedings of the 3rd International Conference on Chinese Information Processing* (p. 12–16). Beijing, China.
Kokvoá, E. 1992. "Anaphoric expressions across clause boundary in pro-drop languages". *Prague Bulletin of Mathematical Linguistics* 58: 39–63.
König, E. 1986. "Conditionals, concessive conditionals and concessives: Areas of contrast, overlap and neutralization" in E. Traugott, A. Ter-Meulen, J. Snitzer-Reilly, & C. Ferguson (Eds.) *On Conditionals* (p. 229–246). Cambridge: Cambridge University Press.
König, E., & Siemund, P. 2000. "Causal and concessive clauses: Formal and semantic relations" E. Couper-Kuhlen and B. Kortmann (Eds.) *Cause, Condition, Concession, Contrast: Cognitive and Discourse perspectives* (p. 341–360). Berlin and New York: Mouton de Gruyter.
Kortmann, B. 1995. "Adverbial participial clauses in English" in M. Haspelmath and E. König (Eds.) *Converbs in Cross-Linguistic Perspective: Structure and Meaning of Adverbial Verb Forms – Adverbial Particiiples, Gerunds –* (p. 189–237). Berlin and New York: Mouton de Gruyter.
Kortmann, B. 1997. *Adverbial Subordination: A Typological and History of Adverbial Subordinators Based on European Languages*. Berlin and New York: Mouton de Gruyter.
Kortmann, B. 1998. "Adverbial subordinators in the languages of Europe" in J. Van der Auwera (Ed.) *Adverbial Constructions in the Languages of Europe* (p. 457–561). Berlin: Mouton de Gruyter.
Koskenniemi, K. 1990. "Finite-state parsing and disambiguation" in H. Karlgren (Ed.) *Proceedings of the 13th International Conference of Computational Linguistics, Volume 3* (p. 229–232). Helsinki, Finland.
Koster, J. 1978. "Why subject sentences don't exist" in S.J. Keyser (Ed.) *Recent Transformational Studies in European Languages* (p. 53–64). Cambridge, Massachusetts: MIT Press.
Koster, J. 1984. "On binding and control". *Linguistic Inquiry* 15: 417–459.
Kouwenberg, S. 1990. "Complementiser pa, the finiteness of its complements, and some remarks on empty categories in Papiamento". *Journal of Pidgin and Creole Languages* 5(1): 39–51.
Kroll, B. 1977. "Combining ideas in written and spoken English: A look at subordination and co-ordination" in E.O. Keenan and T.L. Bennett (Eds.) *Southern California*

Occasional Papers in Linguistics 5: Discourse across Time and Space (p. 69–108). Los Angeles, California: Department of Linguistics, University of Southern California.

Kroll, B.M., & Vann, R.J. (Eds.). 1981. *Exploring Speaking-Writing Relationships: Connections and Contrasts*. Urbana, IL: National Council of Teachers of English.

Lakoff, R. 1971. "If's, and's, and but's about conjunctions" in C. Fillmore and T. Langendoen (Eds.) *Studies in Linguistic Semantics* (p. 114–149). New York: Holt, Rinehart, Winston.

Lakoff, R. 1982. "Some of my favourite writers are literate: the mingling of oral and literate strategies in written communication" in D. Tannen (Ed.) *Spoken and Written Language: Exploring Orality and Literacy* (p. 239–260). Norwood, New Jersey: Ablex.

Lambrecht, K. 1994. *Information Structure and Sentence Form: Topic, Focus, and the Mental Representations of Discourse Referents*. Cambridge: Cambridge University Press.

Lang, Y. 1989. A comparison of the grammatical characteristics of different text categories in the Lancaster-Leeds Treebank. Unpublished M.A. dissertation. Lancaster University.

LaPolla, R. 1993. "Arguments against 'subject' and 'direct object' as viable concepts in Chinese". *Bulletin of the Institute of History and philology* 63(4): 759–813.

Larson, R. 1985. "Bare-NP adverbs" *Linguistic Inquiry* 16(4): 595–621.

Lasnik, H., & Saito, M. 1984. "On the nature of proper government". *Linguistic Inquiry* 15: 235–289.

Lee, O. 1990. An investigation of given-new taxonomy in Korean discourse. Paper presented at the Annual Meeting of the International Conference on Pragmatics and Language Learning, April. 4th Urbana, IL.

Lee, T. 1986. Studies on quantification in Chinese. Unpublished Ph.D. thesis. University of California, Los Angeles.

Leech, G. 1992. "Corpora and theories of linguistic performance" in J. Svartvik (Ed.) *Directions in Corpus Linguistics: Proceedings of Nobel Symposium 82 Stockholm, 4–8 August 1991* (p. 105–125). Berlin and New York: Mouton de Gruyter.

Leech, G., & Eyes, E. 1997. "Syntactic annotation: treebanks" in R. Garside, G. Leech and A. McEnery (Eds.) *Corpus Annotation: Linguistics Information from Computer Text Corpora* (p. 34–52). London and New York: Longman.

Leech, G., & Garside, R. 1991. "Running a grammar factory. The production of syntacti cally analysed corpora or 'treebanks'" in S. Johansson and A.-B. Stenström (Eds.) *English Computer Corpora: Selected Papers and Research Guide* (p. 15–32). Berlin: Mouton de Gruyter.

Leech, G., Barnett, R., & Kahrel, P. 1996. *Recommendations for the Syntactic Annotation of Corpora*. EAGLES Document EAG-TCWG-SASG/1.8 Version of 11th March 1996. URL: <http://www.ilc.cnr.it/EAGLES96/segsasg1/segsasg1.html> (accessed 15 May 2012).

Lehmann, C. 1988. "Towards a typology of clause linkage" in J. Haiman and S. Thompson (Eds.) *Clause Combining in Grammar and Discourse* (p. 181–225). Amsterdam and Philadelphia: John Benjamins Publishing Company.

Levinson, S. 1983. *Pragmatics*. Cambridge: Cambridge University Press.
Li, A., 2001. The *ba* construction. Manuscript. University of Southern California. URL: <http://www.usc.edu/dept/LAS/ealc/chinling/audreyli.htm> (accessed 15 May 2012).
Li, C. 1985. Participant anaphora in Mandarin Chinese. Unpublished Ph.D. thesis. University of Florida.
Li, C., & Thompson, S. 1974. Chinese as a topic-prominent language. Paper presented at the 7th International Conference on Sino-Tibetan Languages and Linguistics, October 18–19. Atlantic, Georgia.
Li, C., & Thompson, S. 1976. "Subject and topic: A new typology of language" in C. Li (Ed.) *Subject and Topic* (p. 459–489). New York: Academic Press.
Li, C., & Thompson, S. 1989. *Mandarin Chinese: A Functional Reference Grammar*. Berkeley and Los Angeles: University of California Press.
Li, G. 1991. "[How far does the NP-movement apply in Mandarin Chinese]" (in Chinese). *Foreign Language Teaching and Research: A Quarterly of Foreign Languages and Cultures* 3(87): 17–24.
Li, J. 1997. "The *ba* construction in Mandarin Chinese: A serial verb analysis" in J. Black and V. Motapanyane (Eds.) *Clitics, Pronouns and Movement* (p. 175–216). Amsterdam and Philadelphia: John Benjamins Publishing Company.
Li, Shuqing, Zheng, Fang, Xu Mingxing, Song, Zhanjiang, & Fang Ditang. 1999. A Cantonese accent Chinese speech corpus. Paper presented at the 2nd International Workshop on East-Asian Language Resources & Evaluation (Oriental COCOSDA'99), May 13–14. Taipei, Taiwan.
Li, W., Pan, H.H., Zhou, M., Wong, K.F., & Lum, V. 1995. "Corpus-based maximal-length Chinese noun phrase extraction" in *Proceedings of Natural Language Processing Pacific Rim Symposium '95* (p. 246–251). Seoul, Republich of Korea.
Li, W.D. 2004. "Topic chains in Chinese discourse". *Discourse Processes* 37(1): 25–45.
Li, Y.F. 1990. "On V-V compounds in Chinese". *Natural Language and Linguistic Theory* 8(2): 177–207.
Li, Y.F. 1998. "Chinese resultative constructions and the uniformity of theta assignment hypothesis" in J. Packard (Ed.) *New Approaches to Chinese Word Formation: Morphology and the Lexicon in Modern and Ancient Chinese* (p. 285–310). Berlin and Germany: Mouton de Gruyter.
Liang, T., Lee, L.Y., & Yang, W.P. 1996. "Optimal weight assignment for a Chinese signature file". *Information Processing and Management* 32(2): 227–237.
Lin, H.C., & Soo, V.W. 1994. "Hypothesis scoring over theta grids information in parsing Chinese sentences with serial verb constructions" in *Proceedings of the 15th International Conference on Computational Linguistics (COLING'94)* (p. 942–948). Kyoto, Japan.
Lin, J.W. 2003. "Temporal reference in Mandarin Chinese". *Journal of East Asian Linguistics* 12(3): 259–311.
Liu, C.S. 1999. Anaphora in Mandarin Chinese and binding at the interface. Unpublished Ph.D. thesis. University of California, Irvine.
Liu, G. 1996. "On serial verbs in Chinese and their representation in HPSG" in *Proceedings of International Chinese Computing Conference (ICCC-96)* (p. 129–135). Singapore.

Liu, H.Y. 2003. *A Profile of the Mandarin NP: Possessive Phrases and Classifier Phrases in Spoken Discourse*. München, Germany: Lincom.
Liu, S.H., Chen, K.J., Chang, L.P., & Chin, Y.H. 1995. "A practical tagger for Chinese corpora" in *Proceedings of ROCLING, Volume 2* (p. 111–126).
Liu, Y.H., Pan, W.Y., & Gu, W. 1996. *Modern Chinese Grammar for Teachers of Chinese as a Second Language and Advanced Learners of Modern Chinese*. Taiwan: Shi Da Shu Yuan.
Ljung, M. 1997. "A Genre-based Study of English Subordinator-headed Non-finite and Verbless Adverbial Clauses" in T. Nevalainen and L. Kahlas-Tarkka (Eds.) *To Explain the Present: Studies in the Changing English Language in Honour of Matti Rissanen* (p. 375–394). Société Néophilologique: Helsinki.
Lo, W.K., Meng, H., & Ching, P.C. 2000. "Sub-syllabic acoustic modeling across Chinese dialects" in *Proceedings of the Second International Symposium on Chinese Speech Processing* (p. 97–100). Beijing, China.
Lo, W.K., Meng, H., & Ching, P.C. 2003. "Cross-language spoken document retrieval using HMM-based retrieval model with multi-scale fusion". *ACM Transactions on Asian Language Information Processing (TALIP)* 2(1): 1–26.
Lu, J. 1988. "Constraints on NP-movement in Mandarin Chinese". *Journal of Chinese Linguistics* 16(1): 1–30.
Lu, J.M., & Ma, Z. 1990. *Xuci* [Function Words]. Beijing: Renmin Jiaoyu Chubanshe.
Lü, S.X. 1999. *Xiandai Hanyu Babaici* [Eight Hundred Words in Modern Chinese]. Beijing: Commercial Press.
Luoma, S. 2003. *Assessing speaking*. Cambridge: Cambridge University Press.
Lyngfelt, B. 2000. OT semantics and control. Manuscript. University of Gothenburg. URL: <http://www.clt.gu.se/ot-semantics-and-control> (accessed 15 May 2012).
Mair, C. 1987. "*For/To*-Infinitival Clauses in Contemporary British English – A Study Based on the Material Collected in the Survey of English Usage, University College London". *English Studies* 68(6): 545–559.
Manzini, R. 1983. "On control and control theory". *Linguistic Inquiry* 14(3): 421–446.
Marantz, A. 1995. "The Minimalist Program" in G. Webelhuth (Ed.) *Government and Binding Theory and the Minimalist Program* (p. 349–382). Cambridge and Oxford: Blackwell.
Marcus, M., Kim, G., Marcinkiewicz, M., MacIntyre, R., Bies, M., Ferguson, M., Katz, K., & Schasberger, B. 1994. "The Penn Treebank: Annotating predicate argument structure" in *Proceedings of the Human Language Technology Workshop*. San Francisco: Morgan Kaufmann.
Marcus, M., Marcinkiewicz, M.A., Santorini, B. 1993. "Building a large annotated corpus of English: The Penn Treebank". *Computational Linguistics* 19(2): 313–330.
Martin, J. 1983. "Conjunction: The Logic of English Text" in J.S. Petofi and E. Sozer (Eds.) *Micro and Macro Connexity of Texts* (p. 1–72). Hamburg: Helmut Buske.
Martin, R. 1996. A minimalist theory of PRO and control. Unpublished PhD thesis. University of Connecticut, Storrs.
Martin, R. 1999. "Case, the extended projection principle, and minimalism" in S. D. Epstein and N. Hornstein (Eds.) *Working Minimalism* (p. 1–25). Cambridge, Massachusetts: MIT Press.

Martin, R. 2001. "Null case and the distribution of PRO". *Linguistic Inquiry* 32(1): 141–166.

Mason, O. 2000. *Programming for Corpus Linguistics: How to do Text Analysis with Java*. Edinburgh: Edinburgh University Press.

Master, P. 2002. "Information structure and English article pedagogy". *System* 30(2002): 331–348.

Matthiessen, C., & Thompson, S. 1988. "The structure of discourse and 'subordination'" in J. Haiman and S. Thompson (Eds.) *Clause Combining in Grammar and Discourse* (p. 275–329). Amsterdam and Philadelphia: John Benjamins Publishing Company.

McEnery, A., & Xiao, Z.H. 2002. "Domains, text types, aspect marking and English-Chinese translation". *Languages in Contrast* 2(2): 211–229.

McEnery, A., & Xiao, Z.H. 2004a. "Character encoding in corpus construction" in M. Wynne (Ed.) *Guide to Good Practice*. Oxford: Oxford University Press.

McEnery, A., & Xiao, Z.H. 2004b. "The Lancaster Corpus of Mandarin Chinese: A corpus for monolingual and contrastive language study" in M. Lino, M. Xavier, F. Ferreire and R. Silva (Eds.) *Proceedings of the Fourth International Conference of Language Resources and Evaluation (LREC) 2004* (p. 1175–1178). Lisbon, Portugal.

McEnery, A., & Xiao, Z.H. Forthcoming. "Parallel and comparable corpora: what are they up to?" in G. James (Ed.) *Corpus Linguistics and Translation Studies*. Clevedon: Multilingual Matters.

McEnery, A., Xiao, Z.H., & Mo, L.L. 2003. "Aspect marking in English and Chinese: Using the Lancaster Corpus of Mandarin Chinese for contrastive language study". *Literary and Linguistic Computing* 18(4): 361–378.

McEnery, A., Xiao, Z.H., & Tono, Y. 2005. *Corpus-based Language Studies: An Advanced Resource Book*. London: Routledge.

McEnery, T. 2003. "Corpus linguistics" in R. Mitkov (Ed.) *The Oxford Handbook of Computational Linguistics* (p. 448–463). Oxford: Oxford University Press.

McEnery, T., & Wilson, A. 2001. *Corpus linguistics: An Introduction, Second Edition*. Edinburgh: Edinburgh University Press.

McNeill, D., & Duncan, S. 2000. "Growth points in thinking-for-speaking" in D. McNeill (Ed.) *Language and Gesture* (p. 141–161). Cambridge: Cambridge University Press.

Meng, H., Chen, B., Khudanpur, S., Levow, G.-A., Lo, W.K., Oard, D., Schone, P., Tang, K., Wang, H.-M., & Wang, J.Q. 2004. Mandarin-English Information (MEI): Investigating translingual speech retrieval. *Computer, Speech and Language*.

Meyer, C. 2002. *English Corpus Linguistics: An Introduction*. Cambridge: Cambridge University Press.

Mizutani, S. 2000. "Rhetorical questions with conditional clauses: From meaning and logic to syntactics". *Mathematical Linguistics* 22(6): 252–256.

Modesto, M. 2000. "Null subjects without 'rich agreement'" in M.A. Kato and E.V. Negrão (Eds.) *Brazilian Portuguese and the Null Subject Parameter* (p. 147–174). Madrid, Spain: Iberoamericana; Frankfurt am Main, Germany: Vervuert.

Montolío, E. 2000. "On affirmative and negative complex conditional connectives" in E. Couper-Kuhlen and B. Kortmann (Eds.) *Cause, Condition, Concession, Contrast: Cognitive and Discourse perspectives* (p. 143–171). Berlin and New York: Mouton de Gruyter.

Newsome, V. 1958. "Because, since, as". *College English* 20(1): 298–303.
Nießen, S., & Ney, H. 2001. "Morpho-syntactic analysis for reordering in statistical machine translation" in *Proceedings of the Machine Translation Summit VIII* (p. 247–252). Santiago de Compostela, Galicia, Spain.
Nofsinger, R. 1991. *Everyday Conversation*. Newbury Park, London and New Delhi: Sage.
Noonan, M. 1985. "Complementation" in T. Shopen (Ed.) *Language typology and syntactic description, Volume II (Complex constructions)* (p. 42–140). Cambridge: Cambridge University Press.
Norman, J. 1988. *Chinese*. Cambridge and New York: Cambridge University Press.
O'Donnell, R.C. 1974. "Syntactic differences between speech and writing". *American Speech* 49(1–2): 102–110.
Oakes, M. 1998. *Statistics for Corpus Linguistics*. Edinburgh: Edinburgh University Press.
Oakes, M., & McEnery, T. 2000. "Bilingual text alignment – an overview" in S. Botley, A. McEnery and A. Wilson (Eds.) *Multilingual Corpora in Teaching and Research* (p. 1–37). Amsterdam: Rodopi.
Ochs, E. 1979. "Planned and unplanned discourse" in T. Givón (Ed.) *Syntax and Semantics, Volume 12: Discourse and Syntax* (p. 51–80). New York: Academic Press.
Ohso, M. 1976. A study of zero pronominalisation in Japanese. Unpublished Ph.D. thesis. Ohio State University.
Olson, D. 1980. "On language and literacy". *International Journal of Psycholinguistics* 7(1/2): 69–83.
Ong, W. 1982. *Orality and Literacy: The Technologising of the Word*. London: Methuen.
Oostdijk, N. 1991. *Corpus Linguistics and the Automatic Analysis of English*. Amsterdam: Rodopi.
Ouhalla, J. 1999. *Introducing Transformational Grammar: From Principles and Parameters to Minimalism, Second Edition*. London, Sydney and Auckland: Arnold.
Oviatt, S., & Cohen, P. 1989. "The effects of interaction on spoken discourse" in *Proceedings of the 27th Annual Meeting of the Association for Computational Linguistics* (p. 126–134). Vancouver, Canada: University of British Columbia.
Pan, S.W. 1989. "Chinese reflexive 'Ziji' and 'Pron-Ziji'". *CUNYForum: Papers in Linguistics* 14: 166–172.
Paul, W. 2005. "Adjectival modification in Mandarin Chinese and related issues". *Linguistics* 43(4): 757–793.
Pellegrino, M., & Scopesi, A. 1978. "Oral and written language in children: syntactical development of descriptive language". *International Journal of Psycholinguistics* 5(1): 5–19.
Perlmutter, D. 1980. "Relational grammar" in E. Moravcsik and J. Wirth (Eds.) *Current Approaches to Syntax (Syntax and Semantics 13)* (p. 195–229). New York: Academic Press.
Perlmutter, D. 1983. "Some proposed laws of basic clause structure" in D. Perlmutter (Ed.) *Studies in Relational Grammar 1* (p. 81–128). Chicago and London: University of Chicago Press.
Perlmutter, D., & Postal, P. 1977. "Towards a universal characterisation of passivisation". *BLS* 3: 394–417.

Philippaki-Warburton, I. 1987. "The theory of empty categories and the pro-drop parameter in Modern Greek". *Journal of Linguistics* 23(2): 289–318.
Piao, S. 2000. Sentence and word alignment between Chinese and English. Unpublished Ph.D. thesis. Lancaster University.
Piao, S. 2002. *User's Manual to the MLCT (Version 1)*. Lancaster: Department of Linguistics and Modern English Language, Lancaster University.
Piao, S., Wilson, A., & McEnery, T. 2002. A Multilingual corpus toolkit. Poster presented at the Fourth Annual Symposium on Corpus Linguistics and Language Teaching (AAACL 2002), November 2–4. Indianapolis, Indiana, USA.
Pollard, C., & Sag, I. 1987. *Information-based Syntax and Semantics*. Stanford: CSLI.
Pollard, C., & Sag, I. 1994. *Head-Driven Phrase Structure Grammar*. Chicago and London: University of Chicago Press.
Poole, M., & Field, T.W. 1976. "A comparison of oral and written code elaboration". *Language and Speech* 19: 305–311.
Postal, P.M. 1974. *On raising*. Cambridge, Massachusetts: MIT Press.
Prince, E. 1981. "Towards a taxonomy of given-new information" in P. Cole (Ed.) *Radical Pragmatics* (p. 223–255). New York: Academic.
Qin, A. 1998. Associative information network and applications to an intelligent search engine. Unpublished Ph.D. thesis. Chinese University of Hong Kong.
Quintero, M.J.P. 2002. *Adverbial Subordination in English: A Functional Approach*. Amsterdam: Rodopi.
Quirk, R., & Greenbaum, S. 1973. *A University Grammar of English*. London: Longman.
Quirk, R., Greenbaum, S., Leech, G., & Svartvik, J. 1985. *A Comprehensive Grammar of the English Language*. London: Longman.
Rader, M. 1982. "Context in written language: The case of imaginative fiction" in D. Tannen (Ed.) *Spoken and Written Language: Exploring Orality and Literacy* (p. 184–198). Norwood, New Jersey: Ablex.
Radford, A. 1988. *Transformational Grammar: A First Course*. Cambridge and New York: Cambridge University Press.
Radford, A. 1997. *Syntactic Theory and the Structure of English: A Minimalist Approach*. Cambridge and New York: Cambridge University Press.
Rai-Chu, S.C. 1982. *Chinese Grammar and English Grammar: A Comparative Study*. Taiwan: Commercial Press.
Ramsay, V. 1987. "The functional distribution of preposed and postposed 'if' and 'when' clauses in written discourse" in R. Tomlin (Ed.) *Coherence and Grounding in Discourse* (p. 383–408). Amsterdam and Philadelphia: John Benjamins Publishing Company.
Rayson, P., & Garside, R. 2000. "Comparing corpora using frequency profiling" in *Proceedings of the Workshop on Comparing Corpora held in conjunction with the 38th Annual Meeting of the Association for Computational Linguisitcs (ACL 2000)* (p. 1–6). Hong Kong, China.
Rayson, P., Berridge, D., & Francis, B. 2004. Extending the Cochran rule for the comparison of word frequencies between corpora. Paper presented at the 7th International Conference on the Statistical Analysis of Textual Data (JADT 2004), March 10–12. Louvain la Neuve, Belgium.

Redeker, G. 1984. "On differences between spoken and written language". *Discourse Processes* 7(1): 43–55.

Rissanen, M. 1989. "The conjunction *for* in Early Modern English". *Nowele* 14: 3–18.

Rissanen, M. 1998. "Towards an integrated view of the development of English: Notes on causal linking" in J. Fisiak and M. Krygier (Eds.) *Advances in English Historical Linguistics* (p. 389–406). Berlin and New York: Mouton de Gruyter.

Rissanen, M. 1999. "Syntax" in R. Lass (Ed.) *Cambridge History of the English Language, Vol. III: 1476–1776* (p. 187–331). Cambridge: Cambridge University Press.

Rizzi, L. 1982. "Negation, *wh*-movement and the null subject parameter" in *Issues in Italian Syntax* (p. 49–76). Dordrecht, Holland: Foris.

Rizzi, L. 1986. "Null objects in Italian and the theory of *pro*". *Linguistic Inquiry* 17: 501–558.

Rögnvaldsson, E. 1993. "Coordination, ATB-extractions, and the identification of *pro*" in H. Thráinsson, S. Epstein, and S. Kuno (Eds.) *Harvard Working Papers in Linguistics 3* (p. 153–180). Cambridge, Massachusetts: Harvard University Press.

Rothstein, S. 1992. "Case and NP licensing". *Natural Language and Linguistic Theory* 10: 119–139.

Rubin, A. 1980. "A theoretical taxonomy of the differences between oral and written language" in R.J. Spiro, B.C. Bruce and W.F. Brewer (Eds.) *Theoretical Issues in Reading Comprehension* (p. 411–438). Hillsdale, New Jersey: Lawrence Erlbaum.

Rudin, C. 1988. "On multiple questions and multiple wh fronting" Natural Language and *Linguistic Theory* 6: 445–501.

Russell, J. 2001. *Java Programming: For the Absolute Beginners*. Roseville, California: Prima Tech.

Sag, I., & Wasow, T. 1999. *Syntactic Theory*. Stanford: CSLI.

Saito, M. 1983. "Case and government in Japanese" in M. Barlow, D. Flickinger and M. Westcoat (Eds.) *Proceedings of the West Coast Conference in Formal Linguistics 2 (WCCFL 2)*. Stanford, California.

Saito, M. 1985. Some asymmetries in Japanese and their theoretical implications. Unpublished Ph.D. thesis. MIT, Cambridge.

Sampson, G. 1987. "The grammatical database and parsing scheme" in R. Garside, G. Leech and G. Sampson (Eds.) *The Computational Analysis of English: A Corpus-based Approach* (p. 82–96). London: Longman.

Sampson, G. 1995. *English for the Computer: The SUSANNE Corpus and Analytic Scheme*. Oxford: Clarendon Press.

Sampson, G. 2001. *Empirical Linguistics*. London and New York: Continuum.

Sampson, G. 2005. "Quantifying the shift towards empirical methods". *International Journal of Corpus Linguistics* 10(1): 15–36.

Schiffrin, D. 1985. "Multiple constraints on discourse options: A quantitative analysis of causal sequences". *Discourse Processes* 8(3): 281–303.

Scott, M. 2003. *Wordsmith Tools Manual*.

Scribner, S., & Cole, M. 1981. *The Psychology of Literacy*. Cambridge, MA: Harvard University Press.

Sells, P. 1985. *Lectures on Contemporary Syntactic Theories: An Introduction to Government-Binding Theory, Generalised Phrase Structure Grammar, and Lexical-Functional Grammar*. Stanford: Centre for the Study of Language and Information.

Shelly, G., Cashman, T., & Starks, J. 2001. *Java Programming: Introductory Concepts and Techniques*. Cambridge, Massachusetts: Course Technology.

Shu, H., Wooters, C., & Kimball, O. 2000. "The BBN BYBLOS 2000 conversational Mandarin LVCSR system" in *Proceedings of the 2000 Speech Transcription Workshop*. College Park, Maryland.

Siegel, S., & Castellan, N.J. 1988. *Nonparametric Statistics for the Behavioural Sciences, Second Edition*. New York: McGraw-Hill.

Singh, S., McEnery, T., & Baker, P. 2000. "Building a parallel corpus of English/Panjabi" in J. Véronis (Ed.) *Parallel Text Processing: Alignment and Use of Translation Corpora* (p. 335–346). Dordrecht, Boston and London: Kluwer.

Smith, C., & Erbaugh, M. 2001. "Temporal information in sentences of Mandarin" in L.J. Xu and J.M. Shao (Eds.) *New Views in Chinese Syntactic Research – International Symposium on Chinese Grammar for the New Millennium*. Hangzhou: Zhejing Jiaoyu Chubanshe.

Speas, M. 1997. "Optimality theory and syntax: null pronouns and control" in D. Archangeli and T. Langendoen (Eds.) *Optimality Theory: An Overview* (p. 171–199). Oxford: Blackwell.

Spelman-Miller, K. 2002. "Units of production in writing: Evidence of topic 'framing' in on-line writing research" in M. Georgiafentis and S. Varlokosta (Eds.) *Reading Working Papers in Linguistics 6* (p. 255–272). Reading: School of Linguistics and Applied Language Studies, University of Reading.

Sperberg-McQueen, C.M., & Burnard, Lou (Eds.). 2001. *Guidelines for Electronic Text Encoding and Interchange: XML-compatible Edition (TEI P4)*. Association for Computers and the Humanities/Association for Computational Linguistics/Association for Literary and Linguistic Computing. Chicago and Oxford. URL: <http://www.tei-c.org/release/doc/tei-p4-doc/html/index.html> (accessed 15 May 2012).

Stalnaker, R. 1975. "Indicative conditionals". *Philosophia* 5: 269–286.

Suen, C.Y. 1986. *Computational Studies of the Most Frequent Chinese Words and Sounds*. Singapore: World Scientific.

Sun, L., Xue, S., Qu, W.M., Wang, X.F., & Sun, Y.F. 2002. Constructing a large-scale Chinese-English parallel corpus. Paper presented at the 19th International Conference on Computational Linguistics (COLING 2002), August 24-September 1. Taipei, Taiwan.

Sun, M.S., Shen, D.Y., & Tsou, B. 1998. "Chinese word segmentation without using lexicon and hand-crafted training data" in *Proceedings of COLING-ACL '98, Volume 2* (p. 1265–1271). Montreal, Canada.

Sun, M.S., Sun, H.L., Huang, C.N., Zhang, P., Xing, H.B., & Zhou, Q. 2000. "Hua Yu: A word segmented and part-of-speech tagged Chinese corpus" in *Proceedings of the 2nd International Conference on Language Resources and Evaluation* (p. 1081–1085). Athens, Greece.

Svartvik, J., & Quirk, R. 1980. *A Corpus of English Conversation*. Lund: Lund University Press.

Szwedek, A. 1977. The thematic structure of the sentence in English and Polish. Paper presented at the Conference on Contrastive Analysis and Error Analysis. Stockholm, Sweden.

Tai, J. 1973. "A derivational constraint on adverbial placement in Mandarin Chinese". *Journal of Chinese Linguistics* 1(3): 397–413.

Tai, J. 1975. "On two functions of place adverbials in Mandarin Chinese". *Journal of Chinese Linguistics* 3(2/3): 154–179.

Tai, J. 1985. "Temporal sequence and Chinese word order" in J. Haiman (Ed.) *Iconicity in Syntax* (p. 49–72). Amsterdam and Philadelphia: John Benjamins Publishing Company.

Tang, J. 1989. "Chinese reflexives". *Natural Language and Linguistic Theory* 7(1): 93–121.

Tannen, D. 1982a. "Oral and literate strategies in spoken and written narratives". *Language: Journal of the Linguistic Society of America* 58(1): 1–21.

Tannen, D. 1982b. "The myth of orality and literacy" in W. Frawley (Ed.) *Linguistics and Literacy* (p. 36–50). New York and London: Plenum Press.

Tannen, D. 1982c. "The oral/literate continuum in discourse" in D. Tannen (Ed.) *Spoken and Written Language: Exploring Orality and Literacy* (p. 1–16). Norwood, New Jersey: Ablex.

Tannen, D. 1985. "Relative focus in involvement in oral and written discourse" in D. Olson, N. Torrance and A. Hildyard (Eds.) *Literacy, Language, and Learning: The Nature and consequences of Reading and Writing* (p. 124–147). Cambridge: Cambridge University Press.

Thompson, S. 1983. "Grammar and Discourse: The English Detached Participial Clause" in F. Klein-Andreu (Ed.) *Discourse Perspectives on Syntax* (p. 43–65). New York and London: Academic Press.

Thompson, S. 1984. "'Subordination' in formal and informal discourse" in D. Schiffrin (Ed.) *Meaning, Form and Use in Context: Linguistic Applications* (p. 85–94). Washington, DC: Georgetown University Press.

Thompson, S. 1985. "Grammar and written discourse: Initial vs. final purpose clauses in English". *Text* 5(1–2): 55–84.

Thompson, S. 1987. "'Subordination' and narrative event structure" in R. Tomlin (Ed.) *Coherence and Grounding in Discourse* (p. 435–454). Amsterdam and Philadelphia: John Benjamins Publishing Company.

Thompson, S., & Longacre, R. 1985. "Adverbial clauses" in T. Shopen (Ed.) *Language typology and syntactic description, Volume II (Complex constructions)* (p. 171–234). Cambridge: Cambridge University Press.

Toman, J. 1981. "Aspects of multiple Wh-movement" in R. May and J. Koster (Eds.) *Levels of Syntactic Representations* (p. 293–302). Dordrecht, Holland: Foris.

Tsao, F.F. 1979. *A Functional Study of Topic in Chinese: The First Step towards Discourse Analysis*. Taipei, Taiwan: Student Books.

Unicode Consortium. 2000. *The Unicode Standard Version 3.0*. Reading, Massachusetts: Addison-Wesley.

URL: <http://www.unicode.org/versions/components-3.0.1.html> (accessed 15 May 2012).

van Riemsdijk, H. 1978. "On the diagnosis of *wh*-movement" in S.J. Keyser (Ed.) *Recent Transformational Studies in European Languages* (p. 189–206). Cambridge, Massachusetts: MIT Press.
van Valin, R. 1993. "A synopsis of Role and Reference Grammar" in R. van Valin (Ed.) *Advances in Role and Reference Grammar* (p. 1–164). Amsterdam and Philadelphia, PA: John Benjamins.
van Valin, R. 2001. *An Introduction to Syntax*. Cambridge: Cambridge University Press.
van Valin, R., & LaPolla, R. 1997. *Syntax: Structure, Meaning & Function*. Cambridge: Cambridge University Press.
Virtanen, T. 1992. "Given and new information in adverbials: clause-initial adverbias of time and place". *Journal of Pragmatics: An Interdisciplinary Monthly of Language Studies* 17(2): 99–115.
von Fintel, K. 1999. "The presupposition of subjunctive conditionals" in U. Sauerland and O. Percus (Eds.) *The Interpretive Tract*, MIT Working Papers in Linguistics 25 (p. 29–44). Cambridge: MITWPL.
Voutilainen, A. 2001. Parsing Swedish. Paper presented at Nodalida'01, May 20–22. Uppsala, Sweden.
Wang, Y.F. 1995. "A corpus-based study of adverbial clauses in Mandarin Chinese conversations: A preliminary analysis" in Benjamin K T'sou and Tom B Y Lai (Eds.) *Language, Information and Computation: Proceedings of the 10th Pacific Asia Conference, 27–28 December 1995, Hong Kong* (p. 237–241). Hong Kong: Language Information Sciences Research Centre, City University of Hong Kong.
Wang, Y.F. 1998. "Conditionals in conversation: A corpus-based study from Chinese" in Hua Lin (Ed.) *Proceedings of the Ninth North American Conference on Chinese Linguistics, Volume II* (p. 279–296). Los Angeles: Graduate Student in Linguistics, University of Southern California.
Wang, Y.F. 1999. "The Information Sequences of Adverbial Clauses in Mandarin Chinese Conversation". *Journal of Chinese Linguistics* 27(2): 45–89.
Wang, Y.F. 2002. "The preferred information sequences of adverbial linking in Mandarin Chinese discourse". *Text* 22(1): 141–172.
Webelhuth, G. 1995. "X-bar theory and case theory" in G. Webelhuth (Ed.) *Government and Binding Theory and the Minimalist Program* (p. 17–95). Cambridge and Oxford: Blackwell.
Weiss, N. 2002a. *Elementary Statistics, Fifth Edition*. Boston, San Francisco and New York: Addison Wesley.
Weiss, N. 2002b. *Introductory Statistics, Sixth Edition*. Boston, San Francisco and New York: Addison Wesley.
Wheatley, B. 1996. *CALLHOME Mandarin Chinese Transcripts* LDC96T16. FTP FILE. Philadelphia, USA: Linguistic Data Consortium.
White, J. 1997. "Result clauses and the structure of degree phrases" in P. Backley and J. Harris (Eds.) *UCL Working Papers in Linguistics 9* (p. 315–333). London: University College London.
Widdowson, H.G. 1979. "The process and purpose of reading". *Explorations in Applied Linguistics* (p. 173–181). Oxford and London: Oxford University Press.

Wiebusch, T. 2005. Changes of categorisation in the Chinese numeral classifier system as revealed by a quantitative evaluation of historical corpora. Paper presented at the 5th International Conference on Practical Applications in Language and Computers (Palc 2005), April 7–9. Łódź, Poland.

Williams, E. 1980. "Predication". *Linguistic Inquiry* 11: 203–238.

Williams, E. 1992. "Adjunct control" in R. Larson, S. Iatridou, U. Lahiri and J. Higginbotham (Eds.) *Control and Grammar* (p. 297–322). Dordrecht, Boston and London: Kluwer.

Winter, E. 1982. *Towards a Contextual Grammar of English: The Clause and its Place in the Definition of Sentence*. London: George Allen & Unwin.

Wong, L.Y. 2002. The morphology, syntax, and semantics of adverbs in Cantonese. Unpublished M.Phil. thesis. University of Hong Kong.

Wong, P.K., & Chan, C. 1996. "Chinese word segmentation based on maximum matching and word binding force" in *Proceedings of COLING – 96 The 16th International Conference on Computational Linguistics, Volume 1* (p. 200–203). Montreal, Canada.

Woods, A., Fletcher, P., & Hughes, A. 1986. *Statistics in Language Studies*. Cambridge: Cambridge University Press.

Wright, P., & Hull, J. 1986. "Answering questions about negative conditionals". *Journal of Memory and Language* 25: 691–709.

Wu, J.M. 1982. *Chinese and English: A Comparative Study*. Beijing: Knowledge Press.

Wu, Z. 2000. Grammaticalisation and the development of functional categories in Chinese. Unpublished Ph.D. thesis. University of Southern California.

Wu, Z.M., & White, J.D. 1990. "Computer processing of Chinese characters: an overview of two decades research and development". *Information Processing and Management* 26(5): 681–692.

Xia, F., Palmer, M., Xue, N., Okurowski, M., Kovarik, J., Chiou, F.D., Huang, S.Z., Kroch, T., & Marcus, M. 2000. "Developing guidelines and ensuring consistency for Chinese text annotation" in *Proceedings of the Second International Conference on Language Resources and Evaluation (LREC-2000)*. Athens, Greece.

Xia, X.Y., & Wu, D.K. 1996. Parsing Chinese with an almost-context-free grammar. Paper presented at Conference on Empirical Methods in Natural Language Processing (EMNLP-96), May 17–18. University of Pennsylvania, Philadelphia

Xiao, Z.H. 2002. A corpus-based study of aspect in Mandarin Chinese. Ph.D. thesis. Lancaster University.

Xiao, Z.H., & McEnery, A. 2004. *Aspect in Mandarin Chinese: A Corpus-based Study*. Amsterdam: John Benjamins.

Xiao, Z.H., McEnery, A., Baker, P., & Hardie, A. 2004. "Developing Asian language corpora: standards and practice" in *Proceedings of the 4th Workshop on Asian Language Resources*. Sanya, China.

Xie, J.Y. 1997. Processing NP-trace and reflexives in Chinese. Unpublished Ph.D. thesis. City University of New York.

Xue, N.W., Chiou, F.D., & Palmer, M. 2002. "Building a large-scale annotated Chinese corpus" in *Proceedings of the 19th International Conference on Computational Linguistics (COLING 2002)*. Taipei, Taiwan.

Xue, N.W., Xia, F., Huang, S.Z., & Kroch, A. 2000. *The Bracketing Guidelines for the Penn Chinese Treebank (3.0).* URL: <http://www.cis.upenn.edu/~chinese/> (accessed 15 May 2012).

Yang, S.Y. 1992. "Dative alternation" in Chinese and English. Unpublished Ph.D. thesis. University of Connecticut.

Yeung, N.T. 1997. "Polite requests in English and Chinese business correspondence in Hong Kong". *Journal of Pragmatics* 27: 505–522.

Yu, S.W. 1999. *Xiandai Hanyu Yuliaoku Jiagong: Ciyu Qiefen Yu Cixing Biaozhu Guifen Yu Shouce* [Corpus annotation of Modern Chinese Corpora: Guidelines and Handbook on Word Segmentation and Part-of-Speech Tagging]. Beijing: Institute of Computational Linguistics, Peking University.

Yu, S.W., Zhu, X.F., Wang, H., & Zhang, Y.Y. 1998. *The Grammatical Knowledge-base of Contemporary Chinese – A Complete Specification.* Beijing: Tsinghua University Press.

Yu, W. 1988. "A-bound or not A-bound: An analysis of a topicalised antecedent of the anaphoric reflexive ziji in Chinese". *Linguistic Analysis* 18(3–4): 210–234.

Yuan, Y., & Kim, T.L. 1998. "Splitting-merging model of Chinese word tokenisation and segmentation" in B.K. Boguraev, R. Garigliano, and J. Tait (Eds.) *Natural Language Engineering, Volume 4, Part 4* (p. 309–324).

Zeng, R.F. 1998. *Bashisi nian changyongyuci diaocha baogaoshu* [A Survey of the Most Frequent Chinese Words for the Past 84 years]. Taipei: Commission on Chinese Language Promotion, Education Unit.

Zhan, P.M., Wegmann, S., & Lowe, S. 1998. "Dragon systems' 1997 Mandarin broadcast news system" in *Proceedings of the Broadcast News Transcription and Understanding Workshop* (p. 25–27). Lansdowne, VA.

Zhang, M., & Sheng, L. 1996. "An evaluation-based Chinese word segmentation system". *Journal of Information* 15(2): 40–52.

Zhang, M., & Sheng, L. 1997. "Tagging Chinese corpus using statistics techniques and rule techniques" in *Proceedings of 1997 International Conference on Computer Processing of Oriental Languages (ICCPOL'97)* (p. 503–506). Hong Kong, China.

Zhang, Y.J., & Yamamoto, K. 2001. "Analysis of spoken language for automatic paraphrasing" in *Proceedings of the 19th International Conference on Computer Processing of Oriental Languages (ICCPOL'2001)* (p. 290–293). Seoul, Korea.

Zhao, E.P. 1989. The categorical status of THAN and BI in English and Chinese comparative constructions. Unpublished Ph.D. thesis. University of Texas, Austin.

Zhou, X.P. 1991. Aspects of Chinese syntax: Ergativity and phrase structure. Unpublished Ph.D. thesis. University of Illinois, Urbana.

Zhu, D.X. 1982. *Yufa Xiangyi* [Lecture Notes on Chinese Grammar]. Beijing: Commercial Press.

Zhu, D.X. 2000. *Xiandai Hanyu Yufa Yanjiu* [A Grammatical Study of Modern Chinese]. Beijing: Commercial Press.

Zou, K. 1993. "The syntax of the Chinese *ba* construction". *Linguistics* 31(4): 715–736.

FSC
www.fsc.org
MIX
Papier | Fördert gute Waldnutzung
FSC® C083411

Kolibri 360 GmbH
Ferdinand-Jühlke-Straße 7
99095 Erfurt, Deutschland
produktsicherheit@kolibri360.de